THIRD EDITION

McDONALDIZATION
THE READER

GEORGE RITZER
University of Maryland

 PINE FORGE PRESS
An Imprint of SAGE Publications, Inc.
Los Angeles • London • New Delhi • Singapore • Washington DC

For information:

 Pine Forge Press
An Imprint of SAGE Publications, Inc.
2455 Teller Road
Thousand Oaks,
    California 91320
E-mail: order@sagepub.com

SAGE Publications Ltd.
1 Oliver's Yard
55 City Road
London EC1Y 1SP
United Kingdom

SAGE Publications India Pvt. Ltd.
B 1/I 1 Mohan Cooperative
    Industrial Area
Mathura Road,
    New Delhi 110 044
India

SAGE Publications Asia-Pacific
    Pte. Ltd.
33 Pekin Street #02-01
Far East Square
Singapore 048763

Printed in the United States of America

Library of Congress Cataloging-in-Publication Data

McDonaldization : the reader / edited by George Ritzer. —3rd ed.
    p. cm.
Includes bibliographical references and index.
ISBN 978-1-4129-7582-7 (pbk.)
    1. Civilization, Modern—1950- 2. Standardization—Social aspects—
United States. 3. United States—Social conditions—1980- I. Ritzer, George.

HN59.2.M423 2010
306.0973—dc22   2009031760

This book is printed on acid-free paper.

09   10   11   12   13   10   9   8   7   6   5   4   3   2   1

Acquisitions Editor:	David Repetto
Associate Editor:	Lindsay Dutro
Editorial Assistant:	Nancy Scrofano
Production Editor:	Astrid Virding
Typesetter:	C&M Digitals (P) Ltd.
Proofreader:	Dennis W. Webb
Indexer:	William Ragsdale
Cover Designer:	Gail Buschman
Marketing Manager:	Jennifer Reed Banando

Contents

PART II: THE McDONALDIZATION OF SOCIAL STRUCTURES AND INSTITUTIONS

Preface to the Third Edition

The second edition of this book underwent a major restructuring with the important addition of Part IV devoted to the relationship between McDonaldization and globalization. While this edition has not required such a major change, over a third of the book has been revised.

In several cases, new topics and essays have been added that demonstrate the reach of the McDonaldization thesis by extending it to bodies, ecology, tourism, architecture, and the latest developments on the Internet, including "eBayization." Chapter 12, Lee F. Monaghan's "McDonaldizing Men's Bodies: Slimming, Associated (Ir)Rationalities and Resistances," is not only new to this edition, but it fits nicely between the essay on the McDonaldization of the sex industries and before the one on the family. Chapter 18 is an essay by Carol Morris and Matt Reed which shows the applicability of the McDonaldization thesis to ecology. Other new topics and essays include "The McDonaldization Thesis and Cruise Tourism" by Adam Weaver (Chapter 22) and Kristine Peta Jerome's essay on the architecture of McDonald's restaurants and the ways in which their similarity around the world perpetuates globalization (Chapter 23). While the topic was dealt with in previous editions, the Internet gets a refreshing new treatment in Nathan Jurgenson's essay which, among other things, deals with the differences between Web 1.0 and 2.0 and the fact that the latter represents the *de*McDonaldization of the Internet (Chapter 15). Perhaps the most challenging new inclusion is Chapter 38 by Elif Izberk-Bilgin and Aaron Ahuvia which argues that McDonaldization may be in the process of being supplanted as a paradigmatic system by "eBayization."

A number of chapters cover topics dealt with in previous editions, but with new essays. These include Gary Wilkinson's piece on "McSchools for McWorld" (Chapter 14), Jos Gamble on "McJobs" in China (Chapter 16), an essay by Wayne Northcutt on the challenge posed by French activist José Bové to McDonald's in France, as well as to globalization more generally

(Chapter 28), and Hielke S. Van Der Meulen on the similar challenge posed by the Slow Food Movement based in Italy, but now increasingly global in scope and reach (Chapter 29).

Still other chapters have been updated by the authors. These include my "Introduction to McDonaldization" (Chapter 1) now derived from the latest, 5th edition of *The McDonaldization of Society* (2008). The other essays updated by their authors are those on the police, courts, and corrections (Chapter 10), Chapter 11 on the sex industries (dealing much more with the impact of Internet sex), and Chapter 13 on the family.

While this edition has been substantially revised and updated (there are 14 new chapters or revisions), the basic structure remains in place. However, coverage has been widened and deepened so that the book is now more suitable for use in an even wider range of courses, including introductory sociology and social problems.

What is especially interesting and gratifying is not only the continuing scholarly interest in McDonaldization, but also the increasingly wide range of topics to which the concept is being applied. We will certainly see further applications in the future, and it is hoped the student readers of this book will also be challenged to think about how their lives are being affected, positively and negatively, by McDonaldization, not only in the areas dealt with here, but in other areas of as well.

I would like to thank my assistant Jillet Sam for her immense help in putting this edition together. I am especially grateful to my once and future editor at Pine Forge Press, Jerry Westby, for his belief in my work in general, and this anthology in particular.

Reviewers

Thomas J. Burns, University of Oklahoma

Saul U. Cohn, Kansas State University

Janet Cosbey, Eastern Illinois University

Lee F. Hamilton, New Mexico State University

Eric G. Jorrey, Bowling Green State University

Salvador Jimenez Murguía, California State University San Bernardino

Linda A. Treiber, Kennesaw State University

Faye Linda Wachs, California State Polytechnic University-Pomona

PART I

McDonaldization

Basics, Studies, Applications, and Extensions

Part I opens with the Introduction from the The McDonaldization of Society, *5th edition (2008), in which the term "McDonaldization" is defined, and some of the indicators of the success of the model of this process, the McDonald's chain, are outlined. The effect of this process on many other businesses in the United States is discussed, as is the extension of this model to other businesses in many other parts of the world. In fact, the model has been adopted so widely elsewhere that McDonaldized firms overseas are exporting back to the United States, heightening the level of McDonaldization in the nation that lies at its source.*

Although much of the United States has experienced a high degree of McDonaldization and other parts of the world have been McDonaldized to some degree, it remains the case that many other sectors in the United States (see the discussion of rib joints below), and many more throughout the world, have experienced little or no McDonaldization. That being said, such sectors are likely to experience increasing McDonaldization in the coming years.

1

An Introduction to McDonaldization

George Ritzer

R ay Kroc (1902–1984), the genius behind the franchising of McDonald's restaurants, was a man with big ideas and grand ambitions. But even Kroc could not have anticipated the astounding impact of his creation. McDonald's is the basis of one of the most influential developments in contemporary society. Its reverberations extend far beyond its point of origin in the United States and in the fast-food business. It has influenced a wide range of undertakings, indeed the way of life, of a significant portion of the world. And having rebounded from some well-publicized economic difficulties, that impact is likely to expand at an accelerating rate in the early 21st century.

However, this is not a book about McDonald's, or even about the fast-food business, although both will be discussed frequently throughout these pages. I devote all this attention to McDonald's (as well as to the industry of which it is a part and that it played such a key role in spawning) because it

Editor's Note: From Ritzer, G., *McDonaldization of Society, Revised New Century Edition,* copyright © 2004, reprinted with permission of Sage Publications, Inc.

serves here as the major example of, and the paradigm for, a wide-ranging process I call *McDonaldization*—that is,

> the process by which the principles of the fast-food restaurant are coming to dominate more and more sectors of American society as well as of the rest of the world.

McDonaldization has shown every sign of being an inexorable process, sweeping through seemingly impervious institutions (e.g., religion) and regions (European nations such as France) of the world.

The success of McDonald's itself is apparent: In 2006, its revenues were $21.6 billion, with operating income of $4.4 billion. McDonald's, which first began operations in 1955, had 31,667 restaurants throughout the world at the beginning of 2007. Martin Plimmer, a British commentator, archly notes:

> There are McDonald's everywhere. There's one near you, and there's one being built right now even nearer to you. Soon, if McDonald's goes on expanding at its present rate, there might even be one in your house. You could find Ronald McDonald's boots under your bed. And maybe his red wig, too.

McDonald's and McDonaldization have had their most obvious influence on the restaurant industry and, more generally, on franchises of all types:

1. According to the International Franchise Association, there were 767,483 small franchised businesses in the United States in late 2006, and they did about $1.5 trillion in annual sales. They employed more than 18 million people. Franchises are growing rapidly; over 57% of McDonald's restaurants are franchises. McDonald's invested in a Denver chain, Chipotle, in 1998 and became its biggest investor in 2001. At the time, Chipotle had 15 stores. By the time McDonald's divested itself of its interest in the company on October 13, 2006, there were over 500 Chipotle restaurants. (Starbucks, the current star of the fast-food industry, interestingly refuses to franchise its operations.)

2. In the restaurant industry, the McDonald's model has been adopted not only by other budget-minded hamburger franchises, such as Burger King and Wendy's, but also by a wide array of other low-priced fast-food businesses. As of the beginning of 2007, Yum! Brands, Inc. operated 34,277 restaurants in over 100 countries under the Pizza Hut, Kentucky Fried Chicken, Taco Bell, A&W Root Beer, and Long John Silver's franchises. Yum! Brands has more outlets than McDonald's, although its total sales ($9.5 billion in 2006) is not nearly as high. Subway (with over 27,000 outlets

in 85 countries) is one of the fastest-growing fast-food businesses and claims to be—and may actually be—the largest restaurant chain in the United States. The Cleveland, Ohio, market, to take one example, is so saturated with Subway restaurants (over 100 of them) that one opened recently *inside* the Jewish Community Center.

3. The McDonald's model has been extended to casual dining—that is, more upscale, higher-priced chain restaurants with fuller menus (for example, Outback Steakhouse, Chili's, Olive Garden, Cheesecake Factory, and Red Lobster). Morton's is an even more upscale, high-priced chain of steakhouses that has overtly modeled itself after McDonald's: "Despite the fawning service and the huge wine list, a meal at Morton's conforms to the same dictates of uniformity, cost control and portion regulation that have enabled American fast-food chains to rule the world." In fact, the chief executive of Morton's was an owner of a number of Wendy's outlets and admits: "My experience with Wendy's has helped in Morton's venues." To achieve uniformity, employees go "by the book": "an ingredient-by-ingredient illustrated binder describing the exact specifications of 500 Morton's kitchen items, sauces and garnishes. A row of color pictures in every Morton's kitchen displays the presentation for each dish."

4. Other types of business are increasingly adapting the principles of the fast-food industry to their needs. Said the vice chairman of Toys "R" Us, "We want to be thought of as a sort of McDonald's of toys." (Interestingly, Toys "R" Us is now in decline because of its inability to compete with the even more McDonaldized Wal-Mart and its toy business.) The founder of Kidsports Fun and Fitness Club echoed this desire: "I want to be the McDonald's of the kids' fun and fitness business." Other chains with similar ambitions include Gap, Jiffy Lube, AAMCO Transmissions, Midas Muffler & Brake Shops, Great Clips, H&R Block, Pearle Vision, Bally's, Kampgrounds of America (KOA), KinderCare (dubbed "Kentucky Fried Children"), Jenny Craig, Home Depot, Barnes & Noble, and PETsMART. Curves, the world's largest chain of women's fitness centers, was founded in 1995, and by 2007 there were an astounding 10,000 of them in 44 countries.

5. As we will see throughout this book, it is possible to view a wide range of the most contemporary phenomena as being affected directly or indirectly by the McDonald's model (and McDonaldization). Among them are text messaging, multitasking, mobile cell phone use and entertainment (e.g., Mobizzo), iPods, MySpace, YouTube, online dating (e.g., match.com), Viagra, virtual vacations, and extreme sports.

6. McDonald's has been a resounding success in the international arena. Over half of McDonald's restaurants are outside the United States (in the mid-1980s, only 25% of McDonald's were outside the United States). The majority (233) of the 280 new restaurants opened in 2006 were overseas (in the United States, the number of restaurants increased by only 47). Well over half of the revenue for McDonald's comes from its overseas operations. McDonald's restaurants are now found in 118 nations around the world, serving 50 million customers a day. The leader by far, as of the beginning of 2007, is Japan with 3,828 restaurants, followed by Canada with over 1,375 and Germany with over 1,200. There are currently 780 McDonald's restaurants in China (but Yum! Brands operates over 2,000 KFCs—the Chinese greatly prefer chicken to beef—and 300 Pizza Huts in China). McDonald's has added 100 new restaurants a year in China and had a goal of 1,000 restaurants by the opening of the 2008 Beijing Olympics (but KFC added 400 a year!). As of 2006, there were 155 McDonald's in Russia, and the company plans to open many more restaurants in the former Soviet Union and in the vast new territory in Eastern Europe that has been laid bare to the invasion of fast-food restaurants. Although there have been recent setbacks for McDonald's in Great Britain, that nation remains the "fast-food capital of Europe," and Israel is described as "McDonaldized," with its shopping malls populated by "Ace Hardware, Toys "R" Us, Office Depot, and TCBY."

7. Many highly McDonaldized firms outside the fast-food industry have also had success globally. Although most of Blockbuster's 9,000-plus sites are in the United States, about 2,000 of them are found in 24 other countries. Wal-Mart is the world's largest retailer with 1.8 million employees and over $312 billion in sales. There are almost 4,000 of its stores in the United States (as of 2006). It opened its first international store (in Mexico) in 1991; it now has more than 2,700 units in Puerto Rico, Canada, Mexico, Argentina, Costa Rica, El Salvador, Guatemala, Honduras, Nicaragua, Brazil, China, Korea, Japan, Germany, and the United Kingdom. In any given week, more than 175 million customers visit Wal-Mart stores worldwide.

8. Other nations have developed their own variants on the McDonald's chain. Canada has a chain of coffee shops called Tim Hortons (merged with Wendy's in 1995), with 2,711 outlets (336 in the United States). It is Canada's largest food service provider with nearly twice as many outlets as McDonald's in that country. The chain has 62% of the coffee business (Starbucks is a distant second with just 7% of that business). Paris, a city whose love for fine cuisine might lead you to think it would prove immune to fast food, has a large number of fast-food croissanteries; the revered French bread has also been McDonaldized. India has a chain of fast-food

restaurants, Nirula's, that sells mutton burgers (about 80% of Indians are Hindus, who eat no beef) as well as local Indian cuisine. Mos Burger is a Japanese chain with over 1,600 restaurants that, in addition to the usual fare, sell Teriyaki chicken burgers, rice burgers, and "Oshiruko with brown rice cake." Perhaps the most unlikely spot for an indigenous fast-food restaurant, war-ravaged Beirut of 1984, witnessed the opening of Juicy Burger, with a rainbow instead of golden arches and J. B. the Clown standing in for Ronald McDonald. Its owners hoped it would become the "McDonald's of the Arab world." In the immediate wake of the 2003 invasion of Iraq, clones of McDonald's (sporting names like "MaDonal" and "Matbax") opened in that country complete with hamburgers, french fries, and even golden arches.

9. And now McDonaldization is coming full circle. Other countries with their own McDonaldized institutions have begun to export them to the United States. The Body Shop, an ecologically sensitive British cosmetics chain, had, as of 2006, over 2,100 shops in 55 nations, 300 of them in the United States. American firms have followed the lead and opened copies of this British chain, such as Bath & Body Works. Pret A Manger, a chain of sandwich shops that also originated in Great Britain (interestingly, McDonald's purchased a 33% minority share of the company in 2001), has over 150 company-owned and -run restaurants, mostly in the United Kingdom but now also in New York, Hong Kong, and Tokyo. Pollo Campero was founded in Guatemala in 1971 and by mid-2006 had more than 200 restaurants in Latin America and the United States. In the latter, 23 restaurants were in several major cities, and the company planned to open 10 more in such cities by the end of 2006. (Jollibee, a Philippine chain, has 10 U.S. outlets.) Though Pollo Campero is a smaller presence in the United States than the American-owned Pollo Tropical chain (which has 80 U.S. outlets), Pollo Campero is more significant because it involves the invasion of the United States, the home of fast food, by a foreign chain.

10. IKEA (more on this important chain later), a Swedish-based (but Dutch-owned) home furnishings company, did about 17.6 billion euros of business in 2006, derived from the over 410 million people visiting their 251 stores in 34 countries. Purchases were also made from the 160 million copies of their catalog printed in over 44 languages. In fact, that catalog is reputed to print annually the second largest number of copies in the world, just after the Bible. IKEA's Web site features over 12,000 products and reported over 125 million "hits" in 2006. Another international chain to watch in the coming years is H&M clothing, founded in 1947 and now operating 1,345 stores in 24 countries with plans to open another 170 stores

by the end of 2007. It currently employs over 60,000 people and sells more than 500 million items a year. Based in Spain, Inditex Group, whose flagship store is Zara, overtook H&M in March 2006 to become Europe's largest fashion retailer with more than 3,100 stores in 64 countries.

11. Much of the above emphasizes the spatial expansion of McDonald's and other McDonaldized businesses, but in addition they have all expanded temporally. McDonald's is shifting its focus from adding locations to adding hours to existing locales, therefore squeezing greater profits from each of them. For example, McDonald's did not at first offer breakfast, but now that meal has become the most important part of the day, and McDonald's dominates the fast-food breakfast market (although Starbucks is seeking to challenge its preeminence). There is also a trend toward remaining open on a 24/7 basis. While less than 1% of McDonald's restaurants operated nonstop in 2002, almost 40% were operating that way by late 2006. Time, like space, is no barrier to the spread of McDonald's and McDonaldization.

McDonald's as a Global Icon

McDonald's has come to occupy a central place in American popular culture, not just the business world. The opening of a new McDonald's in a small town can be an important social event. Said one Maryland high school student at such an opening, "Nothing this exciting ever happens in Dale City." Even big-city and national newspapers avidly cover developments in the fast-food business.

Fast-food restaurants also play symbolic roles on television programs and in the movies. A skit on the legendary television show *Saturday Night Live* satirized specialty chains by detailing the hardships of a franchise that sells nothing but Scotch tape. In the movie *Coming to America* (1988), Eddie Murphy plays an African prince whose introduction to America includes a job at "McDowell's," a thinly disguised McDonald's. In *Falling Down* (1993), Michael Douglas vents his rage against the modern world in a fast-food restaurant dominated by mindless rules designed to frustrate customers. *Moscow on the Hudson* (1984) has Robin Williams, newly arrived from Russia, obtain a job at McDonald's. H. G. Wells, a central character in the movie *Time After Time* (1979), finds himself transported to the modern world of a McDonald's, where he tries to order the tea he was accustomed to drinking in Victorian England. In *Sleeper* (1973), Woody Allen awakens in the future only to encounter a McDonald's. *Tin Men* (1987) ends with the early 1960s heroes driving off into a future represented by a huge golden arch looming in the distance. *Scotland, PA* (2001) brings *Macbeth* to the Pennsylvania of the 1970s. The famous murder scene from the Shakespeare play involves, in this case, plunging a doughnut king's head into the boiling oil of a deep fat fryer. The McBeths then use their ill-gotten gains to transform the king's greasy spoon café into a fast-food restaurant featuring McBeth burgers. The focus of the movie *Fast Food Nation* (2006) is a fictional fast-food chain ("Mickey's"), featuring its hit hamburger ("The Big One"), the beef processor that supplies the meat, and the plight of the illegal Mexican immigrants who work there.

Further proof that McDonald's has become a symbol of American culture is to be found in what happened when plans were made to raze Ray Kroc's first McDonald's restaurant. Hundreds of letters poured into McDonald's headquarters, including the following:

> Please don't tear it down! . . . Your company's name is a household word, not only in the United States of America, but all over the world. To destroy this major artifact of contemporary culture would, indeed, destroy part of the faith the people of the world have in your company.

In the end, the restaurant was rebuilt according to the original blueprints and turned into a museum. A McDonald's executive explained the move: "McDonald's . . . is really a part of Americana."

Americans aren't the only ones who feel this way. At the opening of the McDonald's in Moscow, one journalist described the franchise as the "ultimate icon of Americana." When Pizza Hut opened in Moscow in 1990, a Russian student said, "It's a piece of America." Reflecting on the growth of fast-food restaurants in Brazil, an executive associated with Pizza Hut of Brazil said that his nation "is experiencing a passion for things American." On the popularity of Kentucky Fried Chicken in Malaysia, the local owner said, "Anything Western, especially American, people here love. . . . They want to be associated with America."

One could go further and argue that in at least some ways McDonald's has become more important than the United States itself. Take the following story about a former U.S. ambassador to Israel officiating at the opening of the first McDonald's in Jerusalem wearing a baseball hat with the McDonald's golden arches logo:

> An Israeli teen-ager walked up to him, carrying his own McDonald's hat, which he handed to Ambassador Indyk with a pen and asked: "Are you the Ambassador? Can I have your autograph?" Somewhat sheepishly, Ambassador Indyk replied: "Sure. I've never been asked for my autograph before."

As the Ambassador prepared to sign his name, the Israeli teen-ager said to him, "Wow, what's it like to be the ambassador from McDonald's, going around the world opening McDonald's restaurants everywhere?"

Ambassador Indyk looked at the Israeli youth and said, "No, no. I'm the American ambassador—not the ambassador from McDonald's!" Ambassador Indyk described what happened next: "I said to him, 'Does this mean you don't want my autograph?' And the kid said, 'No, I don't want your autograph,' and he took his hat back and walked away."

Two other indices of the significance of McDonald's (and, implicitly, McDonaldization) are worth mentioning. The first is the annual "Big Mac Index" (part of "burgernomics"), published, tongue-in-cheek, by a prestigious magazine, the *Economist*. It indicates the purchasing power of various currencies around the world based on the local price (in dollars) of the Big Mac. The Big Mac is used because it is a uniform commodity sold in many different nations. In the 2007 survey, a Big Mac in the United States cost an average of $3.22; in China it was $1.41; in Switzerland it cost $5.50; the costliest was $7.44 in Iceland. This measure indicates, at least roughly, where the cost of living is high or low, as well as which currencies are undervalued (China) and which are overvalued (Switzerland). Although the *Economist* is calculating the Big Mac Index only half-seriously, the index represents the ubiquity and importance of McDonald's around the world.

The second indicator of the global significance of McDonald's is the idea developed by Thomas Friedman that "no two countries that both have a McDonald's have ever fought a war since they each got McDonald's." Friedman calls this the "Golden Arches Theory of Conflict Prevention." Another tongue-in-cheek idea, it implies that the path to world peace lies through the continued international expansion of McDonald's. Unfortunately, it was proved wrong by the NATO bombing of Yugoslavia in 1999, which had McDonald's at the time (as of 2007, there are sixteen McDonald's there).

To many people throughout the world, McDonald's has become a sacred institution. At that opening of the McDonald's in Moscow, a worker spoke of it "as if it were the Cathedral in Chartres, . . . a place to experience 'celestial joy.'" Kowinski argues that indoor shopping malls, which almost always encompass fast-food restaurants, are the modern "cathedrals of consumption" to which people go to practice their "consumer religion." Similarly, a visit to another central element of McDonaldized society, Walt Disney World, has been described as "the middle-class hajj, the compulsory visit to the sunbaked holy city."

McDonald's has achieved its exalted position because virtually all Americans, and many others, have passed through its golden arches (or by its drive-through windows) on innumerable occasions. Furthermore, most of us have been bombarded by commercials extolling the virtues of McDonald's, commercials tailored to a variety of audiences and that change as the chain introduces new foods, new contests, and new product tie-ins. These ever-present commercials, combined with the fact that people cannot drive very far without having a McDonald's pop into view, have embedded McDonald's deeply in popular consciousness. A poll of school-age children showed that 96% of them could identify Ronald McDonald, second only to Santa Claus in name recognition.

Over the years, McDonald's has appealed to people in many ways. The restaurants themselves are depicted as spick-and-span, the food is said to be fresh and nutritious, the employees are shown to be young and eager, the managers appear gentle and caring, and the dining experience itself seems fun-filled. Through their purchases, people contribute, at least indirectly, to charities such as the Ronald McDonald Houses for sick children.

The Long Arm of McDonaldization

McDonald's strives continually to extend its reach within American society and beyond. As the company's chairman said, "Our goal: to totally dominate the quick service restaurant industry worldwide. . . . I want McDonald's to be more than a leader. I want McDonald's to dominate."

McDonald's began as a phenomenon of suburbs and medium-sized towns, but later it moved into smaller towns that supposedly could not support such a restaurant and into many big cities that were supposedly too sophisticated. Today, you can find fast-food outlets in New York's Times Square as well as on the Champs-Elysées in Paris. Soon after it opened in 1992, the McDonald's in Moscow's Pushkin Square sold almost 30,000 hamburgers a day and employed a staff of 1,200 young people working two to a cash register. In early 1992, Beijing witnessed the opening of what still may be the world's largest McDonald's, with 700 seats, 29 cash registers, and nearly 1,000 employees. On its first day of business, it set a new one-day record for McDonald's by serving about 40,000 customers. McDonald's can even be found on Guantanamo Bay Naval Base in Cuba and in the Pentagon.

Small, satellite, express, or remote outlets, opened in areas that could not support full-scale fast-food restaurants, are also expanding rapidly. They are found in small storefronts in large cities and in nontraditional settings such as museums, department stores, service stations, and even schools. These satellites typically offer only limited menus and may rely on larger outlets for food storage and preparation. A flap occurred over the placement of a

McDonald's in the new federal courthouse in Boston. Among the more striking sites for a McDonald's restaurant are at the Grand Canyon, in the world's tallest building (Petronas Towers in Malaysia), as a ski-through on a slope in Sweden, and in a structure in Shrewsbury, England, that dates back to the 13th century.

No longer content to dominate the strips that surround many college campuses, fast-food restaurants have moved right onto many of those campuses. The first campus fast-food restaurant opened at the University of Cincinnati in 1973. Today, college cafeterias often look like shopping-mall food courts (and it's no wonder, given that campus food service is a multi-billion-dollar-a-year business). In conjunction with a variety of "branded partners" (for example, Pizza Hut and Subway), Marriott now supplies food to many colleges and universities. The apparent approval of college administrations puts fast-food restaurants in a position to further influence the younger generation.

We no longer need to leave many highways to obtain fast food quickly and easily. Fast food is now available at many, and in some cases all, convenient rest stops along the road. After "refueling," we can proceed with our trip, which is likely to end in another community with about the same density and mix of fast-food restaurants as the locale we left behind. Fast food is also increasingly available in hotels, railway stations, and airports.

In other sectors of society, the influence of fast-food restaurants has been subtler but no less profound. Food produced by McDonald's and other fast-food restaurants has begun to appear in high schools and trade schools; over 50% of school cafeterias offer popular brand-name fast foods such as McDonald's, Pizza Hut, or Taco Bell at least once a week. Said the director of nutrition for the American School Food Service Association, "Kids today live in a world where fast food has become a way of life. For us to get kids to eat, period, we have to provide some familiar items." Few lower-grade schools as yet have in-house fast-food restaurants; however, many have had to alter school cafeteria menus and procedures to make fast food readily available. Apples, yogurt, and milk may go straight into the trash can, but hamburgers, fries, and shakes are devoured. Fast-food restaurants also tend to cluster within walking distances of schools. The attempt to hook school-age children on fast food reached something of a peak in Illinois, where McDonald's operated a program called "A for Cheeseburger." Students who received As on their report cards received a free cheeseburger, thereby linking success in school with McDonald's. In Australia, toy versions of food featured by McDonald's are being marketed to children as young as three. The toys include "fake McDonald's fries, a self-assembling Big Mac, milkshake, Chicken McNuggets, baked apple pie and mini cookies." Many fear that playing with such toy food will increase children's interest in eating the real thing.

The military has also been pressed to offer fast food on both bases and ships. Despite criticisms by physicians and nutritionists, fast-food outlets have turned up inside over 30 U.S. general hospitals and in about 30% of children's hospitals. Although no private homes yet have a McDonald's of their own, meals at home often resemble those available in fast-food restaurants. Frozen, microwavable, and prepared foods, which bear a striking resemblance to meals available at fast-food restaurants, often find their way to the dinner table. There are even cookbooks—for example, *Secret Fast Food Recipes: The Fast Food Cookbook*—that allow one to prepare "genuine" fast food at home. Then there is also home delivery of fast foods, especially pizza, as revolutionized by Domino's.

Another type of expansion involves what could be termed "vertical McDonaldization"; that is, the demands of the fast-food industry, as is well documented in Eric Schlosser's *Fast Food Nation*, have forced industries that service it to McDonaldize in order to satisfy its insatiable demands. Potato growing and processing, cattle ranching, chicken raising, and meat slaughtering and processing have all had to McDonaldize their operations, leading to dramatic increases in production. That growth has not come without costs, however. Meat and poultry are more likely to be disease-ridden, small (often non-McDonaldized) producers and ranchers have been driven out of business, and millions of people have been forced to work in low-paying, demeaning, demanding, and sometimes outright dangerous jobs. For example, in the meatpacking industry, relatively safe, unionized, secure, manageable, and relatively high-paying jobs in firms with once-household names like Swift and Armour have been replaced with unsafe, nonunionized, insecure, unmanageable, and relatively low-paying positions with largely anonymous corporations. While some (largely owners, managers, and stockholders) have profited enormously from vertical McDonaldization, far more have been forced into a marginal economic existence.

McDonald's is such a powerful model that many businesses have acquired nicknames beginning with Mc. Examples include "McDentists" and "McDoctors," meaning drive-in clinics designed to deal quickly and efficiently with minor dental and medical problems; "McChild" care centers, meaning child-care centers such as KinderCare; "McStables," designating the nationwide race horse–training operation of Wayne Lucas; and "McPaper," describing the newspaper *USA TODAY*.

McDonald's is not always enamored of this proliferation. Take the case of We Be Sushi, a San Francisco chain with a half-dozen outlets. A note appears on the back of the menu explaining why the chain was not named "McSushi":

> The original name was McSushi. Our sign was up and we were ready to go. But before we could open our doors we received a very formal letter from the lawyers of, you guessed it, McDonald's. It seems that McDonald's has cornered the market on every McFood name possible from McBagle [sic] to McTaco. They explained that the use of the name McSushi would dilute the image of McDonald's.

So powerful is McDonaldization that the derivatives of McDonald's, in turn, exert their own powerful influence. For example, the success of *USA TODAY* has led many newspapers across the nation to adopt shorter stories and colorful weather maps. As one *USA TODAY* editor said, "The same newspaper editors who call us McPaper have been stealing our McNuggets." Even serious journalistic enterprises such as *The New York Times* and *The Washington Post* have undergone changes (for example, the use of color) as a result of the success of *USA TODAY*. The influence of *USA TODAY* is blatantly manifested in the *Boca Raton News,* which has been described as "a sort of smorgasbord of snippets, a newspaper that slices and dices the news into even smaller portions than does *USA TODAY*, spicing it with color graphics and fun facts and cute features like 'Today's Hero' and 'Critter Watch.'" As in *USA TODAY,* stories in the *Boca Raton News* usually start and finish on the same page. Many important details, much of a story's context, and much of what the principals have to say are cut back severely or omitted entirely. With its emphasis on light news and color graphics, the main function of the newspaper seems to be entertainment.

Curves is a derivative of McDonald's in the women's fitness area. Its phenomenal growth led to Cuts Fitness for Men, which began operations in 2003. Its founder said, "I wanted to be the men's version of Curves, loud and clear." By 2006 there were over 100 Cuts franchises, with 200 more sold. The franchise has become international, and the first Cuts for women opened in late 2005.

Like virtually every other sector of society, sex has undergone McDonaldization. In the movie *Sleeper,* Woody Allen not only created a futuristic world in which McDonald's was an important and highly visible element, but he also envisioned a society in which people could enter a machine called an "orgasmatron" to experience an orgasm without going through the muss and fuss of sexual intercourse.

Similarly, real-life "dial-a-porn" allows people to have intimate, sexually explicit, even obscene conversations with people they have never met and probably never will meet. There is great specialization here: Dialing numbers such as 555-FOXX will lead to a very different phone message than dialing 555-SEXY. Those who answer the phones mindlessly and repetitively follow "scripts" such as, "Sorry, tiger, but your Dream Girl has to go. . . . Call right back and ask for me." Less scripted are phone sex systems (or Internet chat rooms) that permit erotic conversations between total strangers. The Internet, the webcam, and various Web sites (e.g., audreylive.com, Jen 'n Dave) now permit people even to see (though still not touch) the person with whom they are having virtual sex. As Woody Allen anticipated with his orgasmatron, "Participants can experience an orgasm without ever meeting or touching one another."

> In a world where convenience is king, disembodied sex has its allure. You don't have to stir from your comfortable home. You pick up the phone, or log onto the computer and, if you're plugged in, a world of unheard of sexual splendor rolls out before your eyes.

In New York City, an official called a three-story pornographic center "the McDonald's of sex" because of its "cookie-cutter cleanliness and compliance with the law." These examples suggest that no aspect of people's lives is immune to McDonaldization.

Various pharmaceuticals can be seen as McDonaldizing sex. Viagra (and similar drugs such as Cialis) do this by, for example, making the ability to have sex more predictable. Such drugs also claim to work fast and to last for a long time. MDMA (ecstasy) breaks down social inhibitions for perhaps four hours and tends to increase social (including sexual) connectedness.

The preceding merely represents the tip of the iceberg as far as the long arm of McDonaldization is concerned. A number of scholars have analyzed the McDonaldization of the following:

- Mountain climbing (e.g., reliance on guidebooks to climbing routes)
- Criminal justice system (police profiling, "three strikes and you're out")
- Family (quick fixes to family problems in books, TV shows)
- Drug addiction (a simple linear view of the problem and solution)
- Internet (Web browsers homogenizing use and experience)
- Farming (reliance on chemicals and biotechnology)
- Education (standardized curricula, lesson plans)
- Religion (megachurches and their "franchises")
- Politics ("drive-through democracy")

The Dimensions of McDonaldization

Why has the McDonald's model proven so irresistible? Eating fast food at McDonald's has certainly become a "sign" that, among other things, one is in tune with the contemporary lifestyle. There is also a kind of magic or enchantment associated with such food and its settings. The focus here, however, is on the four alluring dimensions that lie at the heart of the success of this model and, more generally, of McDonaldization. In short, McDonald's has succeeded because it offers consumers, workers, and managers efficiency, calculability, predictability, and control. . . .

Efficiency

One important element of the success of McDonald's is *efficiency*, or the optimum method for getting from one point to another. For consumers, McDonald's (its drive-through is a good example) offers the best available way to get from being hungry to being full. The fast-food model offers, or at least appears to offer, an efficient method for satisfying many other needs, as well. Woody Allen's orgasmatron offered an efficient method for getting people from quiescence to sexual gratification. Other institutions fashioned on the McDonald's model offer similar efficiency in exercising, losing weight, lubricating cars, getting new glasses or contacts, or completing income tax forms. Like their customers, workers in McDonaldized systems function efficiently by following the steps in a pre-designed process.

Calculability

Calculability emphasizes the quantitative aspects of products sold (portion size, cost) and services offered (the time it takes to get the product). In McDonaldized systems, quantity has become equivalent to quality; a lot of something, or the quick delivery of it, means it must be good. As two observers of contemporary American culture put it, "As a culture, we tend to believe deeply that in general 'bigger is better.'" People can quantify things and feel that they are getting a lot of food for what appears to be a nominal sum of money (best exemplified by McDonald's current "Dollar Menu," which played a key role in recent years in leading McDonald's out of its doldrums and to steadily increasing sales). In a recent Denny's ad, a man says, "I'm going to eat too much, but I'm never going to pay too much." This calculation does not take into account an important point, however: The high profit margin of fast-food chains indicates that the owners, not the consumers, get the best deal.

People also calculate how much time it will take to drive to McDonald's, be served the food, eat it, and return home; they then compare that interval to the time required to prepare food at home. They often conclude, rightly or wrongly, that a trip to the fast-food restaurant will take less time than eating at home. This sort of calculation particularly supports home delivery franchises such as Domino's, as well as other chains that emphasize saving time. A notable example of time savings in another sort of chain is LensCrafters, which promises people "Glasses fast, glasses in one hour." H&M is known for its "fast fashion."

Some McDonaldized institutions combine the emphases on time and money. Domino's promises pizza delivery in half an hour, or the pizza is free. Pizza Hut will serve a personal pan pizza in 5 minutes, or it, too, will be free.

Workers in McDonaldized systems also emphasize the quantitative rather than the qualitative aspects of their work. Since the quality of the work is allowed to vary little, workers focus on things such as how quickly tasks can be accomplished. In a situation analogous to that of the customer, workers are expected to do a lot of work, very quickly, for low pay.

Predictability

McDonald's also offers *predictability,* the assurance that products and services will be the same over time and in all locales. The Egg McMuffin in New York will be, for all intents and purposes, identical to those in Chicago and Los Angeles. Also, those eaten next week or next year will be identical to those eaten today. Customers take great comfort in knowing that McDonald's offers no surprises. People know that the next Egg McMuffin they eat will not be awful, although it will not be exceptionally delicious, either. The success of the McDonald's model suggests that many people have come to prefer a world in which there are few surprises. "This is strange," notes a British observer, "considering [McDonald's is] the product of a culture which honours individualism above all."

The workers in McDonaldized systems also behave in predictable ways. They follow corporate rules as well as the dictates of their managers. In many cases, what they do, and even what they say, is highly predictable.

Control

The fourth element in the success of McDonald's, *control,* is exerted over the people who enter the world of McDonald's. Lines, limited menus, few options, and uncomfortable seats all lead diners to do what management wishes them to do—eat quickly and leave. Furthermore, the drive-through (in some cases, walk-through) window invites diners to leave before they eat. In the Domino's model, customers never enter in the first place.

The people who work in McDonaldized organizations are also controlled to a high degree, usually more blatantly and directly than customers. They are trained to do a limited number of things in precisely the way they are told to do them. This control is reinforced by the technologies used and the way the organization is set up to bolster this control. Managers and inspectors make sure that workers toe the line.

A Critique of McDonaldization: The Irrationality of Rationality

McDonaldization offers powerful advantages. In fact, efficiency, predictability, calculability, and control through nonhuman technology (that is, technology that controls people rather than being controlled by them) can be thought of as not only the basic components of a rational system but also as powerful advantages of such a system. However, rational systems inevitably spawn irrationalities. The downside of McDonaldization will be dealt with most systematically under the heading of the irrationality of rationality; in fact, paradoxically, the irrationality of rationality can be thought of as the fifth dimension of McDonaldization.

Criticism, in fact, can be applied to all facets of the McDonaldizing world. As just one example, at the opening of Euro Disney, a French politician said that it will "bombard France with uprooted creations that are to culture what fast food is to gastronomy." Although McDonaldization offers many advantages (explained later in this chapter), the book focus is on the great costs and enormous risks of McDonaldization. McDonald's and other purveyors of the fast-food model spend billions of dollars each year detailing the benefits of their system. Critics of the system, however, have few outlets for their ideas. For example, no one sponsors commercials between Saturday-morning cartoons warning children of the dangers associated with fast-food restaurants.

Nonetheless, a legitimate question may be raised about this critique of McDonaldization: Is it animated by a romanticization of the past, an impossible desire to return to a world that no longer exists? Some critics do base their critiques on nostalgia for a time when life was slower and offered more surprises, when at least some people (those who were better off economically) were freer, and when one was more likely to deal with a human being than a robot or a computer. Although they have a point, these critics have undoubtedly exaggerated the positive aspects of a world without McDonald's, and they have certainly tended to forget the liabilities associated with earlier eras. As an example of the latter, take the following anecdote about a visit to a pizzeria in Havana, Cuba, which in some respects is decades behind the United States:

> The pizza's not much to rave about—they scrimp on tomato sauce, and the dough is mushy.
>
> It was about 7:30 P.M., and as usual the place was standing-room-only, with people two deep jostling for a stool to come open and a waiting line spilling out onto the sidewalk.
>
> The menu is similarly Spartan. . . . To drink, there is tap water. That's it— no toppings, no soda, no beer, no coffee, no salt, no pepper. And no special orders.
>
> A very few people are eating. Most are waiting. . . . Fingers are drumming, flies are buzzing, the clock is ticking. The waiter wears a watch around his belt loop, but he hardly needs it; time is evidently not his chief concern. After a while, tempers begin to fray.
>
> But right now, it's 8:45 P.M. at the pizzeria, I've been waiting an hour and a quarter for two small pies.

Few would prefer such a restaurant to the fast, friendly, diverse offerings of, say, Pizza Hut. More important, however, critics who revere the past do not seem to realize that we are not returning to such a world. In fact, fast-food restaurants have begun to appear even in Havana (and many more are likely after the death of Fidel Castro). The increase in the number of people crowding the planet, the acceleration of technological change, the increasing pace of life—all this and more make it impossible to go back to the world, if it ever existed, of home-cooked meals, traditional restaurant dinners, high-quality foods, meals loaded with surprises, and restaurants run by chefs free to express their creativity.

It is more valid to critique McDonaldization from the perspective of a conceivable future. Unfettered by the constraints of McDonaldized systems, but using the technological advances made possible by them, people could have the potential to be far more thoughtful, skillful, creative, and well-rounded than they are now. In short, if the world was less McDonaldized, people would be better able to live up to their human potential.

We must look at McDonaldization as both "enabling" and "constraining." McDonaldized systems enable us to do many things we were not able to do in the past; however, these systems also keep us from doing things we otherwise would do. McDonaldization is a "double-edged" phenomenon. We must not lose sight of that fact, even though this book will focus on the constraints associated with McDonaldization—its "dark side."

Illustrating the Dimensions of McDonaldization: The Case of IKEA

An interesting example of McDonaldization, especially since it has its roots in Sweden rather than the United States, is IKEA. Its popularity stems from the fact that it offers at very low prices trendy furniture based on well-known Swedish designs. It has a large and devoted clientele throughout the world. What is interesting about IKEA from the point of view of this book is how well it fits the dimensions of McDonaldization. The similarities go beyond that, however. For example, just as with the opening of a new McDonald's, there is great anticipation over the opening of the first IKEA in a particular location. Just the rumor that one was to open in Dayton, Ohio, led to the following statement: "We here in Dayton are peeing our collective pants waiting for the IKEA announcement." IKEA is also a global phenomenon—it is now in 34 countries (including China and Japan) and sells in those countries both its signature products as well as those more adapted to local tastes and interests.

In terms of *efficiency,* IKEA offers one-stop furniture shopping with an extraordinary range of furniture. In general, there is no waiting for one's purchases, since a huge warehouse is attached to each store (one often enters through the warehouse), with large numbers of virtually everything in stock.

Much of the efficiency at IKEA stems from the fact that customers are expected to do a lot of the work:

- Unlike McDonald's, there are relatively few IKEAs in any given area; thus, customers most often spend many hours driving great distances to get to a store. This is known as the "IKEA road trip."

- On entry, customers are expected to take a map to guide themselves through the huge and purposely maze-like store (IKEA hopes, like Las Vegas casinos, that customers will get "lost" in the maze and wander for hours, spending money as they go). There are no employees to guide anyone, but there are arrows painted on the floor that customers can follow on their own.

- Also upon entry, customers are expected to grab a pencil and an order form and to write down the shelf and bin numbers for the larger items they wish to purchase; a yellow shopping bag is to be picked up on entry for smaller items. There are few employees and little in the way of help available as customers wander through the stores. Customers can switch from a shopping bag to a shopping cart after leaving the showroom and entering the marketplace, where they can pick up other smaller items.

- If customers eat in the cafeteria, they are expected to clean their tables after eating. There is even this helpful sign: "Why should I clean my own table? At IKEA, cleaning your own table at the end of your meal is one of the reasons you paid less at the start."

- Most of the furniture sold is unassembled in flat packages, and customers are expected to load most of the items (except the largest) into their cars themselves. After they get home, they must break down (and dispose) of the packaging and then put their furniture together; the only tool supposedly required is an Allen wrench.

- If the furniture does not fit into your car, you can rent a truck on site to transport it home or have it delivered, although the cost tends to be high, especially relative to the price paid for the furniture.

- To get a catalog, customers often sign up online.

Calculability is at the heart of IKEA, especially the idea that what is offered is at a very low price. Like a McDonald's "Dollar Menu," one can get a lot of furniture—a roomful, even a houseful—at bargain prices. As with value meals, customers feel they are getting value for their money. (There is even a large cafeteria offering low-priced food, including the chain's signature Swedish meatballs and 99-cent breakfasts.) However, as is always the case in McDonaldized settings, low price generally means that the quality is inferior, and it is often the case that IKEA products fall apart in relatively short order. IKEA also emphasizes the huge size of its stores, which often approach 300,000 square feet or about four to five football fields. This mammoth size leads the consumer to believe that there will be a lot of furniture offered (and there is) and that, given the store's reputation, most of it will be highly affordable.

Of course, there is great *predictability* about any given IKEA—large parking lots, a supervised children's play area (where IKEA provides personnel, but only because supervised children give parents more time and peace of mind to shop and spend), the masses of inexpensive, Swedish-design furniture, exit through the warehouse and the checkout counters, boxes to take home with furniture requiring assembly, and so on.

An IKEA is a highly *controlled* environment, mainly in the sense that the maze-like structure of the store virtually forces the consumer to traverse the entire place and to see virtually everything it has to offer. If one tries to take a path other than that set by IKEA, one is likely to become lost and disoriented. There seems to be no way out that does not lead to the checkout counter, where you pay for your purchases.

There are a variety of *irrationalities* associated with the rationality of IKEA, most notably the poor quality of most of its products. Although the furniture is purportedly easy to assemble, many are more likely to think of it as "impossible-to-assemble." Then there are the often long hours required to get to an IKEA, to wander through it, to drive back home, and then to assemble the purchases.

The Advantages of McDonaldization

This discussion of the fundamental characteristics of McDonaldization makes it clear that, despite irrationalities, McDonald's (and other McDonaldized systems such as IKEA) has succeeded so phenomenally for good, solid reasons. Many knowledgeable people, such as the economic columnist Robert Samuelson, strongly support the McDonald's business model. Samuelson confesses to "openly worship[ing] McDonald's," and he thinks of it as "the greatest restaurant chain in history." In addition, McDonald's offers many praiseworthy programs that benefit society, such as its Ronald McDonald Houses, which permit parents to stay with children undergoing treatment for serious medical problems; job-training programs for teenagers; programs to help keep its employees in school; efforts to hire and train the handicapped; the McMasters program, aimed at hiring senior citizens; an enviable record of hiring and promoting minorities; and a social responsibility program with goals of improving the environment and animal welfare.

The process of McDonaldization also moved ahead dramatically undoubtedly because it has led to positive changes. Here are a few specific examples of such changes:

- A wider range of goods and services is available to a much larger portion of the population than ever before.

- Availability of goods and services depends far less than before on time or geographic location; people can now do things, such as text message, e-mail, arrange dates online, and participate in MySpace, in the middle of the night, activities that were impossible before.

- People are able to acquire what they want or need almost instantaneously and get it far more conveniently.

- Goods and services are of a far more uniform quality; at least some people even get better-quality goods and services than before McDonaldization.

- Far more economical alternatives to high-priced, customized goods and services are widely available; therefore, people can afford things (e.g., virtual vacations via the Internet rather than actual vacations) they could not previously afford.

- Fast, efficient goods and services are available to a population that is working longer hours and has fewer hours to spare.

- In a rapidly changing, unfamiliar, and seemingly hostile world, the comparatively stable, familiar, and safe environment of a McDonaldized system offers comfort.

- Because of quantification, consumers can more easily compare competing products.

- Certain products (for example, exercise and diet programs) are safer in a carefully regulated and controlled system.

- People are more likely to be treated similarly, no matter what their race, sex, sexual orientation, or social class.

- Organizational and technological innovations are more quickly and easily diffused through networks of identical operators.

- The most popular products of one culture are more easily disseminated to others.

What Isn't McDonaldized?

This chapter should give you a sense of McDonaldization and of the range of phenomena to be discussed throughout this book. In fact, such a wide range of phenomena can be linked to McDonaldization that you may begin to wonder what isn't McDonaldized. Is McDonaldization the equivalent of modernity? Is everything contemporary McDonaldized?

Although much of the world has been McDonaldized, at least three aspects of contemporary society have largely escaped the process:

- Those aspects traceable to an earlier, "premodern" age. A good example is the mom-and-pop grocery store.

- New businesses that have sprung up or expanded, at least in part, as a reaction against McDonaldization. For instance, people fed up with McDonaldized motel rooms in Holiday Inns or Motel 6s can stay instead in a bed-and-breakfast, which offers a room in a private home with personalized attention and a homemade breakfast from the proprietor.

• Those aspects suggesting a move toward a new, "postmodern" age. For example, in a postmodern society, "modern" high-rise housing projects would make way for smaller, more livable communities.

Thus, although McDonaldization is ubiquitous, there is more to the contemporary world than McDonaldization. It is a very important social process, but it is far from the only process transforming contemporary society.

Furthermore, *McDonaldization is not an all-or-nothing process*. There are degrees of McDonaldization. Fast-food restaurants, for example, have been heavily McDonaldized, universities moderately McDonaldized, and mom-and-pop grocers only slightly McDonaldized. It is difficult to think of social phenomena that have escaped McDonaldization totally, but some local enterprise in Cuba or Fiji may yet be untouched by this process.

Thinking Critically

1. Is there really any such thing as McDonaldization?

2. Is McDonald's the best example of McDonaldization? In light of its problems, and the rise of Starbucks, would the latter now be a better example? Should we relabel the process "Starbuckization"?

3. Is the fast food-restaurant really as important as is suggested here?

4. Can you think of any other dimensions of McDonaldization?

5. Can rationality ever really be irrational?

This chapter, from The McDonaldization of Society, *deals with the precursors to the fast-food restaurant and the concept of McDonaldization. The key figure in this history is the German social theorist Max Weber (1864–1920), who pioneered the contemporary sociological conception of the bureaucracy and created the best-known theory of rationalization. The bureaucracy was the paradigm for the rationalization process in Weber's day. That process is described here using the same dimensions as were used in Chapter 1 to define the essence of McDonaldization. This should not be surprising because my theory of McDonaldization is based on, and closely related to, Weber's theory of rationalization. One key difference, however, is that whereas Weber focused largely on production, the focus of McDonaldization is consumption, which has come to rival, even exceed, the importance of production, especially in highly developed nations like the United States. It is this that leads to the conclusion that the fast-food restaurant, whose home is obviously in the realm of consumption, is a better paradigm today for the rationalization or McDonaldization of society than the bureaucracy.*

I also explore Weber's famous idea that rationalization (now McDonaldization) creates an "iron cage" from which it is increasingly difficult for us to escape. Although this continues to be a useful image, I reexamine it in Chapter 3, which offers another way of thinking about the structure of McDonaldization.

2

Precursors

Bureaucracy and Max Weber's Theory of Rationality, Irrationality, and the Iron Cage

George Ritzer

McDonaldization did not emerge in a vacuum; it was preceded by a series of social and economic developments that not only anticipated it but also gave it many of the basic characteristics touched on in Chapter 1. In this chapter, I will look briefly at the notion of bureaucracy and Max Weber's theories about it and the larger process of rationalization.

Bureaucratization: Making Life More Rational

A *bureaucracy* is a large-scale organization composed of a hierarchy of offices. In these offices, people have certain responsibilities and must act in

Editor's Note: From Ritzer, G., *McDonaldization of Society, Revised New Century Edition,* copyright © 2004, reprinted with permission of Sage Publications, Inc.

accord with rules, written regulations, and means of compulsion exercised by those who occupy higher-level positions.

The bureaucracy is largely a creation of the modern Western world. Although earlier societies had organizational structures, they were not nearly as effective as the bureaucracy. For example, in traditional societies, officials performed their tasks because of a personal loyalty to their leader. These officials were subject to personal whim rather than impersonal rules. Their officers lacked clearly defined spheres of competence, there was no clear hierarchy of positions, and officials did not have to obtain technical training to gain a position.

Ultimately, the bureaucracy differs from earlier methods of organizing work because of its formal structure, which, among other things, allows for greater efficiency. Institutionalized rules and regulations lead, even force, those employed in the bureaucracy to choose the best means to arrive at their ends. A given task is broken down into components, with each office responsible for a distinct portion of the larger task. Incumbents of each office handle their part of the task, usually following preset rules and regulations, and often in a predetermined sequence. When each of the incumbents has, in order, handled the required part, the task is completed. In handling the task in this way, the bureaucracy has used what its past history has shown to be the optimum means to the desired end.

Weber's Theory of Rationality

The roots of modern thinking on bureaucracy lie in the work of the turn-of-the-century German sociologist Max Weber. His ideas on bureaucracy are embedded in his broader theory of the *rationalization* process. In the latter, Weber described how the modern Western world managed to become increasingly rational—that is, dominated by efficiency, predictability, calculability, and nonhuman technologies that control people. He also examined why the rest of the world largely failed to rationalize.

As you can see, McDonaldization is an amplification and extension of Weber's theory of rationalization. For Weber, the model of rationalization was the bureaucracy; for me, the fast-food restaurant is the paradigm of McDonaldization.

Weber demonstrated in his research that the modern Western world had produced a distinctive kind of rationality. Various types of rationality had existed in all societies at one time or another, but none had produced the type that Weber called *formal rationality*. This is the sort of rationality I refer to when I discuss McDonaldization or the rationalization process in general.

What is formal rationality? According to Weber, *formal rationality* means that the search by people for the optimum means to a given end is shaped by rules, regulations, and larger social structures. Individuals are not left to their own devices in searching for the best means of attaining a given objective. Weber identified this type of rationality as a major development in the history of the world: Previously, people had been left to discover such mechanisms on their own or with vague and general guidance from larger value systems (religion, for example). After the development of formal rationality, they could use institutionalized rules that help them decide—or even dictate to them—what to do. An important aspect of formal rationality, then, is that it allows individuals little choice of means to ends. In a formally rational system, virtually everyone can (or must) make the same, optimal choice.

Weber praised the bureaucracy, his paradigm of formal rationality, for its many advantages over other mechanisms that help people discover and implement optimum means to ends. The most important advantages are the four basic dimensions of rationalization (and of McDonaldization).

First, Weber viewed the bureaucracy as the most efficient structure for handling large numbers of tasks requiring a great deal of paperwork. As an example, Weber might have used the Internal Revenue Service, for no other structure could handle millions of tax returns so well.

Second, bureaucracies emphasize the quantification of as many things as possible. Reducing performance to a series of quantifiable tasks helps people gauge success. For example, an IRS agent is expected to process a certain number of tax returns each day. Handling less than the required number of cases is unsatisfactory performance; handling more is excellence.

The quantitative approach presents a problem, however, little or no concern for the actual quality of work. Employees are expected to finish a task with little attention paid to how well it is handled. For instance, IRS agents who receive positive evaluations from their superiors for managing large numbers of cases may actually handle the cases poorly, costing the government thousands or even millions of dollars in uncollected revenue. Or the agents may handle cases so aggressively that taxpayers become angered.

Third, because of their well-entrenched rules and regulations, bureaucracies also operate in a highly predictable manner. Incumbents of a given office know with great assurance how the incumbents of other offices will behave. They know what they will be provided with and when they will receive it. Outsiders who receive the services that bureaucracies dispense know with a high degree of confidence what they will receive and when they will receive it. Again, to use an example Weber might have used, the millions of recipients of checks from the Social Security Administration know precisely when they will receive their checks and exactly how much money they will receive.

Finally, bureaucracies emphasize control over people through the replacement of human judgment with the dictates of rules, regulations, and structures. Employees are controlled by the division of labor, which allocates to each office a limited number of well-defined tasks. Incumbents must do those tasks, and no others, in the manner prescribed by the organization. They may not, in most cases, devise idiosyncratic ways of doing those tasks. Furthermore, by making few, if any, judgments, people begin to resemble human robots or computers. Having reduced people to this status, leaders of bureaucracies can think about actually replacing human beings with machines. This replacement has already occurred to some extent: In many settings, computers have taken over bureaucratic tasks once performed by humans. Similarly, the bureaucracy's clients are also controlled. They may receive only certain services and not others from the organization. For example, the Internal Revenue Service can offer people advice on their tax returns but not on their marriages. People may also receive appropriate services in certain ways and not others. For example, people can receive welfare payments by check, not in cash.

Irrationality and the "Iron Cage"

Despite the advantages it offers, bureaucracy suffers from the *irrationality of rationality*. Like a fast-food restaurant, a bureaucracy can be a dehumanizing place in which to work and by which to be serviced. Ronald Takaki characterizes rationalized settings as places in which the "self was placed in confinement, its emotions controlled, and its spirit subdued." In other words, they are settings in which people cannot always behave as human beings—where people are dehumanized.

In addition to dehumanization, bureaucracies have other irrationalities. Instead of remaining efficient, bureaucracies can become increasingly inefficient because of tangles of red tape and other pathologies. The emphasis on quantification often leads to large amounts of poor-quality work. Bureaucracies often become unpredictable as employees grow unclear about what they are supposed to do and clients do not get the services they expect. Because of these and other inadequacies, bureaucracies begin to lose control over those who work within and are served by them. Anger at the nonhuman technologies that replace them often leads employees to undercut or sabotage the operation of these technologies. All in all, what were designed as highly rational operations often end up quite irrational.

Although Weber was concerned about the irrationalities of formally rationalized systems, he was even more animated by what he called the "iron cage" of rationality. In Weber's view, bureaucracies are cages in the sense that people are trapped in them, their basic humanity denied. Weber feared most that bureaucracies would grow more and more rational and that rational principles would come to dominate an accelerating number of sectors of society. He anticipated a society of people locked into a series of rational structures, who could move only from one rational system to another— from rationalized educational institutions to rationalized workplaces, from rationalized recreational settings to rationalized homes. Society would eventually become nothing more than a seamless web of rationalized structures; there would be no escape.

A good example of what Weber feared is found in the contemporary rationalization of recreational activities. Recreation can be thought of as a way to escape the rationalization of daily routines. However, over the years, these escape routes have themselves become rationalized, embodying the same principles as bureaucracies and fast-food restaurants. Among the many examples of the rationalization of recreation are Club Med, chains of campgrounds, and package tours. Take, for example, a thirty-day tour of Europe. Buses hurtle through only the major cities in Europe, allowing tourists to glimpse the maximum number of sites in the time allowed. At particularly interesting or important sights, the bus may slow down or even stop to permit some picture taking. At the most important locales, a brief stopover is planned so visitors can hurry through the site, take a few pictures, buy a souvenir, then hop back on the bus to head to the next attraction. With the rationalization of even their recreational activities, people do live to a large extent in the iron cage of rationality.

Thinking Critically

1. Is the bureaucracy as important today as it was in Weber's day (circa 1900)?

2. Was the bureaucracy in Weber's day a good example of what he called rationalization?

3. In what ways is today's bureaucracy different from what it was when Weber wrote?

4. Is today's bureaucracy a good example of rationalization?

5. Can a bureaucracy ever truly be an iron cage?

One way to think about the "iron cage" is that it represents a vision of the social geography of McDonaldization. That is, our social landscape is so dominated by McDonaldized settings of all types that we are imprisoned in them; there is no escape from them. However, when one thinks about this geographically (and in many other ways), it is clear that as ubiquitous as these settings are, there is certainly ample room for escape. Thus, this chapter posits an image of contemporary society as being characterized by "islands" of McDonaldization in a "sea" (the rest of society) that is either less or non-McDonaldized. This image seems to fit today's reality better than the iron cage because we are able to move easily from McDonaldized islands (e.g., a fast-food restaurant) to the less- or non-McDonaldized settings that surround them (e.g., the family, although it, too, is becoming McDonaldized; see Chapter 13) and are still predominant (although perhaps not for much longer).

These islands are described, following the film maker George Romero and his cult classic, Dawn of the Dead, as housing the "dead." That is, people may be viewed as being dead in these settings in various senses, especially because they are expected to conform to what is expected of them and not to act creatively. Although this is certainly true, it is also the case that much life is found in these McDonaldized settings (think of Disneyland, or better yet, Las Vegas). Combining the ideas of death and life with islands, the image of the social geography of McDonaldization that is communicated here is "islands of the living dead." To some degree how alive or dead these islands are, and even how dominant they become, is up to us as consumers, workers, managers, owners, and so on. After all, we can either accept the death they offer us, or we can choose to enliven them. Of course, we can also reject them completely leading to a less-, or even a non-, McDonaldized society.

3

Islands of the Living Dead

The Social Geography of McDonaldization

George Ritzer

I focus in . . . this article on the social geography . . . of the McDonaldization of society. This, of course, is based on Max Weber's famous work on rationalization and his vision of the social world as being increasingly encased in an "iron cage" of rationalization. This metaphor can be interpreted in various ways, but one that has not been explored systematically is from the perspective of social geography.

On the surface, when examined from this geographic point of view, the image of an iron cage seems to convey the sense of an entire society, or even world, enclosed by an overarching system of rationalization. Although this is one geographic image, the fact is that Weber famously lacked a sense of society (let alone the world) as a whole but instead focused on specific structures, institutions, and domains. Thus, it could be argued that it would be

---

Editor's Note: From Ritzer, G., "Islands of the Living Dead: The Social Geography of McDonaldization" in *American Behavioral Scientist,* 42(2), October 2003, reprinted with permission from Sage Publications, Inc.

more accurate to say that Weber envisioned a series of iron cages rather than a single, overarching cage. He did see such cages growing more numerous with more and more sectors of society coming to be rationalized. In addition, he believed that the bars on these cages were growing stronger, thicker, and harder. However, this does not yield a view of a society as a whole (or the world) growing increasingly rationalized. . . .

Whatever the real possibilities of . . . a seamless system of McDonaldized sites arising in the future, the fact remains that today it is more accurate to think of those sites as islands of McDonaldization.

In fact, Weber's actual image of the social geography of rationalization comes closer to another social geography—Foucault's sense of a "carceral archipelago"—to which it is often contrasted. On the surface, the image of an iron cage communicates a totally enclosed system, whereas that of a "carceral archipelago" conveys a sense of relatively individual, even isolated, rationalized systems with great gaps—the relatively free and open "seas"—between them. However, as we have already seen, Weber, like Foucault, envisions just such a series of "islands" of rationalization, and the iron cage imagery is clearly in line, at least on each of the islands, with Foucault's carceral vision of what those islands are like. For his part, Foucault, especially in his thoughts on "discipline," has a rationalized view of the world—or at least of the islands in the archipelago—not unlike that of Weber.

However, when we turn to the contemporary rationalized world—one that I have described in terms of McDonaldization—the issue arises as to whether either of these images—iron cage (at least in the totalistic sense in which it is usually interpreted) or carceral archipelago—is an adequate description of it. In fact, it is clear almost immediately that both are inadequate. In no way can we think of society as a whole as an iron cage of rationality. Although we can certainly think in terms of islands of McDonaldization, those islands lack bars; they are not carceral in any sense of the term; people are *not* locked into these islands. Thus, I would like to use this article as an occasion to develop a vision of the social geography of McDonaldization that, although it is related to Weber's "iron cage" and Foucault's "carceral archipelago," differs from both in significant ways. . . .

The appropriate phantasmagoric social geographic image, with a bow to Hollywood and its "B" movies, is islands of the living dead. Notable sources for this view are George Romero's movies *The Night of the Living Dead* (1968) and especially its sequel *Dawn of the Dead* (1979). The latter, in fact, takes place in . . . one of the most important of these islands: a shopping mall.

Islands

Foucault's vision of an archipelago is far closer to the metaphor being developed here than the image conveyed by those who interpret Weber as offering a sense of an overarching iron cage. It is clear that there is no way that we can think of society today in terms of an iron cage and, furthermore, it is almost impossible to envision a scenario—especially one involving the increasing prevalence and preeminence of consumption settings—in which the result is such an all-embracing phenomenon in the future. The abysmal failure of the Soviet Union to create such a system would seem to make it clear that its successful development and implementation is, to put it mildly, unlikely. Developments in capitalist societies indicate that McDonaldized systems are likely to grow more numerous, and the "bars" that surround them are likely to grow thicker and stronger, but they are likely to remain enclaves of rationalization in a larger society that is less—or even not—rationalized.

It is far more accurate to think in terms of islands of rationalization or McDonaldization:

- Factories are increasingly rare in the United States and those comparatively few that continue to exist are likely to be surrounded by decaying and destroyed remnants of the far greater number of factories that used to dot the American landscape;
- in the city, any given block might have a fast-food restaurant or a Gap store, but in between we are still likely to find traditional, individually owned and operated, small shops and businesses and even abandoned shops or empty lots;
- the suburbs are likely to be dotted with highly rationalized shopping malls composed almost exclusively of McDonaldized shops and businesses;
- small towns are likely to see their downtown business areas decimated by fast-food restaurants and a Wal-Mart, all built on the road out of town or on its periphery;
- every 20 miles or so on the main highway from Washington, D.C., to New York City (and many other highways) one finds rest stops now exclusively offering food from one of the many fast-food franchise systems that are so increasingly prevalent;
- even on the Las Vegas Strip with its famous, and highly McDonaldized, casino-hotels, there are numerous non-McDonaldized small businesses remaining in the spaces between them;
- on a cruise ship, the tourist may be trapped on a McDonaldized "island," and may visit the areas of "real" islands along the way that are almost as McDonaldized, but just beyond the ship's railing, as well as the borders of the island enclaves that are visited, are far less rationalized, even non- or irrational, worlds; and

- Disney World is clearly a McDonaldized island and innumerable other such islands have grown up around it in Orlando, Florida (as well as around the other Disney theme parks in California, Japan, and France [and now Hong Kong]), but there remain areas in the environs that have not yet been McDonaldized.

One could extend such examples but it is obvious that in none of these locales do we find an iron cage of McDonaldization but rather many islands defined by their high degree of rationalization. Although it is true that there are an increasing number of such islands, and that number is likely to increase even further in the future, this allows us to see that there remain non-McDonaldized areas, often quite vast in scope, in the interstices that exist between the islands. These interstices can be undeveloped land; non-McDonaldized settings; nonrational or irrational domains; areas that once were, but are no longer, McDonaldized; as well as areas that have not-yet-been, but likely soon-will-be, McDonaldized. Thus, it is not only possible but remains quite easy, at least from a social geographic point of view, for those who so wish to avoid the McDonaldized islands and seek out and find non-McDonaldized alternatives.

Of course, that leads, almost immediately, to the issue of why so many people are increasingly drawn to the McDonaldized islands and, conversely, are so unwilling to venture off into the non-McDonaldized spaces that offer alternatives to them. There is clearly a kind of magnetism associated with McDonaldized settings and consumers are increasingly drawn to them. That magnetism comes, of course, from the clever, attractive, and aggressive marketing and advertising campaigns undertaken by the firms that own McDonaldized settings. Thus, the magnetism is not intrinsic to the systems but manufactured by them, especially their public relations, marketing, and advertising arms or firms hired by them. The non-McDonaldized alternatives—for example, independently owned businesses—lack the resources to make themselves similarly magnetic. Thus, although the "sea" of settings continues to be overwhelmingly populated by non-McDonaldized systems, many consumers are drawn to the islands of rationalization and routinely bypass the numerous nonrationalized or less-rationalized alternatives along the way. Why people do this is also linked to the next section of this analysis: the "living" that takes place on these islands.

Living

There is a great deal of living taking place on the McDonaldized islands being analyzed here; there is much that is lively, full of life, associated with them. This is often lost sight of in the focus on the critiques of rationalization and McDonaldization, especially the irrationalities of rationality intimately associated with them. We must attend to the fact that large numbers of people are drawn to these islands and seem to derive a great deal of pleasure from their visits. For example, people seem to enjoy the food at fast-food chains such as McDonald's, Burger King, Taco Bell, Pizza Hut, and Starbucks. Egg McMuffins, burgers, tacos, pizzas, and double espressos are downed with great gusto and in huge quantities. Furthermore, in many senses, it is more the fun associated with fast-food restaurants than the food consumed in them that attracts consumers. This is most obvious in the case of children drawn by the toy and movie promotions and the carnival-like atmosphere of at least some fast-food restaurants. Adults seem to enjoy watching their children having fun and, in addition, derive their own gratifications from visiting fast-food restaurants. Similarly, the shoppers at the Gap, Old Navy, and Banana Republic arrive in droves and joyously grab clothing from the racks, try on various garments, and bring them home in great numbers. Whatever scholars may say of a critical character about such settings—how they manipulate customers, the mediocre quality of what they have to offer—we cannot ignore the fact that so many people seem to be having such a terrific time in them and in consuming what they have to offer.

This is even more true of the large and famous islands in the archipelago of McDonaldized consumption. The Mall of America, Disney World, the Las Vegas Strip, and the Destiny cruise ship are among the most desired destinations for not only American consumers, travelers, and tourists but those from much of the rest of the world as well. Disney World's self-designation as "the happiest place on earth" also could be employed by these other settings, and the behavior of visitors to these settings does little to belie such claims. At the Mall of America, people seem to be having a great time shopping and shuttling between the mall and the amusement park found under the same roof. For children, and their parents, a visit to Disney World seems like the culmination of a lifelong ambition. Joyous faces abound on the rides, in the attractions, and in the various hotels, shops, and restaurants. Gamblers in Las Vegas are in the world mecca of gambling, and they act like it (at least until they have to tote up the inevitable losses), and the transformation of the town into more of a family tourist attraction makes even the nongamblers happy as they can visit indoor malls attached to casino-hotels, see circus acts at Circus Circus, watch a sea battle at Treasure Island, view the water show at Bellagio, and take a gondola ride at the Venetian.

Thus, a great deal of living takes place on these McDonaldized islands; there is a lot of life to them. The critical orientation to be discussed in the following section should not cause us to lose sight of this fact. There is certainly a paradox here; a paradoxical relationship between the life of these islands and the "death" we are about to discuss, a paradox we will deal with in the conclusion to this article.

Death

In what senses can we think of McDonaldized islands as "dead," as being associated with "death"? Of interest, Jean Baudrillard focuses on the cemetery, which in terms of this article can be considered a means of consuming death and the dead. Indeed, at least some cemeteries (the famous Forest Lawn Cemetery in Los Angeles) have, similar to other cathedrals of consumption, sought to become spectacular to attract a larger "clientele." However, the key point is that modern cemeteries represent the separation of death from life, whereas in earlier societies the two were intimately related. Cemeteries were (and are) "ghettos" for the dead and, in a sense, the McDonaldized islands being discussed here are similar ghettos separated from life. According to Baudrillard, death is controlled "in anticipation of the future confinement of life in its entirety." We can think of McDonaldized islands as settings in which large portions of life have come to be confined— in which some of life has clearly come to be separated from the rest of life. Furthermore, Baudrillard is making it clear here (as we have above) that the confinement of life in its entirety—Weber's iron cage—is not yet a reality. Baudrillard seems to believe unequivocally that such a fully carceral system is an inevitability, but at this point, such a reality only looms in the distance. Regardless of whether Baudrillard is right about the future, his vision of the present is consistent with the island metaphor being employed here.

People are, as we have seen, living on these islands, but it is a life that, by definition, is clearly separated from the rest of existence (the "sea" surrounding the islands). Separation implies alienation, and it could be argued that life in those settings is alienated from the rest of life. Instead of life flowing naturally into and out of these islands, the living that takes place on them tends rather to take place in largely autonomous settings; it is a relatively segregated form of living that takes place in these settings. Furthermore, the life on one island is different and separated from the living that is to be found on other islands. Thus, one is virtually forced to leave one's everyday life to participate in the living found on the Vegas Strip, Disney World, or Mall of America. This is even true of more local and everyday islands such as the nearby mall, superstore, or even franchise restaurant. Furthermore, one must leave the life experienced in one setting to experience the form of living to be found on another island. All of this is certainly living, but it is a ghettoized form of living taking place in a similarly ghettoized context. It is living, but a form of living separated from the rest of life.

Although there is life on McDonaldized islands, it is arguably at least a different form of life, if not less of a form of life, than that found in at least some of the non-McDonaldized interstices between the islands. One way of looking at what is different about life on McDonaldized islands is Weber's conception of life in the rationalized world and its cold skeletal hands. Clearly, Weber associates death with rationalization in general and, more specifically, with the death of the life-affirming character of sex. However, we need not go back to Weber for a theoretical resource on this—Baudrillard offers a similar view in his discussion of the segregated world of death and cemeteries as "a meticulously regulated universe." Thus, McDonaldized islands fit Baudrillard's view that life "is no longer anything but a doleful, defensive bookkeeping, locking every risk into its sarcophagus." Thus, in contrast to Ulrich Beck's view that we live in a risk society and the fact that risk undoubtedly remains a reality in the interstices between the islands, life on McDonaldized islands is virtually risk free. Although in some senses this is highly desirable, in many other senses it is undesirable, especially in leading to a dull, boring, routine form of existence. This is at least one of the senses in which we can say that those who "live" on these islands are "dead." This is clearly the case for the workers who do nothing but dull, boring, and routine work. Furthermore, the workers spend a considerable part of their day on the islands. However, it is also true for customers, although they spend far less time there. For example, the food that they eat, and what they are required to do to get the food, are well described as being dull, boring, and routine.

Following Baudrillard, death characterizes life on these islands in another way. McDonaldized settings seek to optimize rationalization; according to Baudrillard, they seek "perfection." That is, they seek to be all positivity, to eliminate all negativity. However, such an approach renders a world in which everything resembles "the smile of a corpse in a funeral home." A more lively setting would permit positivity and negativity to coexist. To put it in other Baudrillardian terms, McDonaldized systems are dead because they lack "evil" (as well as "seduction" and "symbolic exchange"). Therefore, what they need is an injection of such evil. That is, they need more of the things associated with life—instability, seduction, ambivalence, "the natural disorder of the world."

McDonaldized systems are also, again in Baudrillard's terms, "ecstatic" systems. That is, they are hypertelic, expanding in a seemingly limitless manner (see Stephenson's association of franchises with viruses). Expansion seems out of control with the result that the system as a whole "shines forth in its pure and empty form." One of Baudrillard's major examples of ecstasy is cancer, and thus, the association of McDonaldization with this process clearly also links it to death. The ecstatic expansion of the growth of McDonaldization not only means more islands of McDonaldization but also more empty, dead, or dying settings.

Furthermore, in Baudrillard's view, the dead are transformed into a "stuffed simulacrum of life." One is tempted to describe the diners who have finished their massive "value meals" in fast-food restaurants in similar terms, but the idea of simulacra has broader applicability to the islands of McDonaldization. That is, these islands are characterized, even dominated, by simulations. Examples are legion, including the various casino-hotels in Las Vegas (Paris, Mandalay Bay), all of the "worlds" in Disneyland, "eatertainment" sites such as Rainforest Cafe, and so on. Is real life going on there, or is the living that we find there merely a faint copy of what life should be all about? If we answer yes to the second question then this is a second sense in which we can associate what transpires on the islands as being associated with death. That is, it is nothing more than a simulation of life, not life itself. Furthermore, living, at least for a time, in these simulated worlds, can people do anything but live a life dominated by simulation?

The most direct association between the geographic settings of concern here and death is Kowinski's work on the shopping mall and what he calls the "Zombie Effect." That is, the structure of malls induces consumers to wander about them for hours in a near-endless pursuit of goods and services. Of course, the idea of zombies brings us back to the living dead, specifically the movies of George Romero. In *Dawn of the Dead* (1979), Romero's zombie-consumers are set loose in a Cleveland shopping mall. This image can be extended to all consumers in all McDonaldized settings who are simultaneously alive and dead: the living dead—zombies.

Conclusion

This article has made the case not only for a social geography of the McDonaldized world but a specific social geographic image—"islands of the living dead." This is seen as a more accurate image, at least for the time being, of the state of McDonaldization in society. It may be that at some point in the future, Foucault's vision of a "carceral" archipelago or even the view . . . associated with Weber of an all-encompassing "iron cage" might be more accurate, but that remains to be seen. The strength of the image presented here is that it accurately conveys a sense of still-isolated "islands" of McDonaldization; it makes it clear that there is much that is positive about these islands (the "living" that takes place on them); and it offers a critical orientation toward them, their "dead" structures, and their tendency to deaden the life that transpires within their confines.

Thinking Critically

1. Do you feel like you live in a carceral archipelago?

2. Do you feel like you live in an iron cage?

3. Do you feel like your life is spent moving from one island of the living dead to the next?

4. In what ways are you alive on these islands?

5. In what ways are you dead on these islands?

Chapter 4 reports on an empirical study to determine whether the entire restaurant business in the United States has been McDonaldized, specifically whether it has come to be dominated by chains. The author distinguishes between fast-food and full-service restaurants and finds that while, as expected, fast-food restaurants are dominated by chains, the latter have made only minimal inroads into the full-service sector. The implication is that full-service restaurants have not been highly McDonaldized. Of course, being part of a chain is related to, but far from a perfect indicator of, a high degree of McDonaldization. That is, it is possible that full-service restaurants have grown increasingly McDonaldized even though they are not part of chains.

4

On Mass Distribution

A Case Study of Chain Stores in the Restaurant Industry

Joel I. Nelson

M y argument in this chapter is straightforward: The presence of chains or systems of mass distribution is neither total nor fully explained. Considerable literature argues that mass production is not a monolithic development, and I argue the same case with respect to retail trade. I focus on one segment of the retail industry—restaurants. Restaurants have been singled out as the quintessential instance of chain store organization (Ritzer), and eating outside the home represents a burgeoning segment of consumer expenditures. If mass distribution follows mass consumption, then chains ought to develop throughout the industry. Using the idea that innovations occur oppositionally in proximate or adjacent fields, I suggest that there is good reason to believe that substantial segments of the industry are composed of single, independent establishments, and this in spite of the growing

Editor's Note: From Nelson, J., "On Mass Distribution: A Case Study of Chain Stores in the Restaurant Industry," in *Journal of Consumer Culture, 1*(1), 141–160, copyright © 2001, reprinted with permission of Sage Publications, Ltd.

and substantial size of the market. My research draws on the distinction between full-service and fast-food restaurants and shows that mass distribution develops in a bipolar fashion—in a manner at odds with the popular conception of a world of restaurants awash in chain store development. . . .

Chains in Fast-Food and Full-Service Restaurants

Industry Background

Figure 4.1 provides the historical backdrop for examining the distribution of chains in the restaurant industry. The figure graphically juxtaposes two indicators across the 30-year period covered by this research: the comparative distribution of fast-food and full-service restaurants and changing expenditures for eating out. As to the first of these issues, the bar columns indicate the distribution of restaurant types; the respective number in each type is shown along the axis on the left. The figure indicates the dramatic

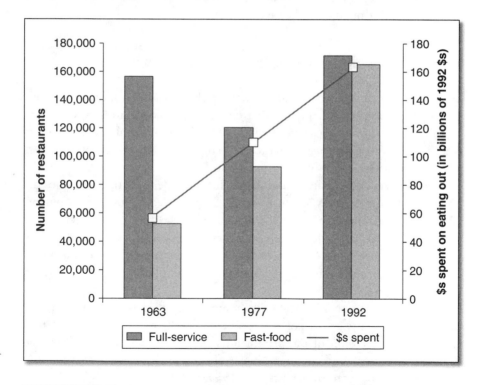

Figure 4.1   Full-Service and Fast-Food Restaurant Establishments and Dollars Spent on Eating Out, 1963–1992 (in 1992 dollars)

rise of fast-food restaurants over this nearly 30-year time period . . . [but] there is no indication that full-service restaurants are increasingly peripheral. While full-service restaurants do not grow at the same rate as fast-food restaurants, their numbers over the 30-year period have hardly diminished and in fact have increased by about 9%.

. . . Growth in all of these restaurants reflects (and indeed may partially have caused) rising consumer expenditures in eating outside of the home. Changes in expenditures are displayed by the trendline and the axis on the right-hand side of the figure indicating the actual dollars spent on eating out.

The juxtaposition of the trendline for expenditures and the changing proportions of restaurants suggests that the full-service sector remains a forceful competitor for consumer spending. While full-service restaurants increasingly garner smaller proportions of the market than in the past, the dollar sums involved are substantial and rose over the three time periods— $47 billion in 1963, $64 billion in 1977, and $85 billion in 1992 (all in 1992 dollars). If chains as mass distribution systems are a function of mass consumer markets, then chains ought to proliferate across various types of restaurants. But my data indicate that they do not. . . .

Conclusions and Discussion

In the context of the widespread growth of chains throughout the fast-food sector, it is somewhat surprising that chains in a related industry would be as minimal as they are, particularly in light of the substantial size of the market. To explain this apparent paradox, I suggested that proximate markets grow oppositionally and further that the full-service sector—with extensive menus, service, and on-site preparation—has provided few opportunities for the high-profit margins of interest to large-scale capital development. Data . . . documented that growth in chains in the full-service sector was indeed minimal and additionally outlined the possible ways full-service chains might cope with restraints on profits by generating high-volume sales. In this review, restaurants overall are not as commonly chained as Ritzer, for example, suggested.

Equally important are the findings suggesting that restaurants are not marginalized by the growth of fast-food chains. The data in Figure 4.1 indicate continual erosion of the proportions of the market controlled by the full-service sector, but not at a level reflective of increasing marginality. Furthermore, this pattern persists into 1997 as well. . . .

The conclusions here are straightforward: Different profit environments generate different market structures and different strategies for survival.

Thinking Critically

1. Are full-service restaurants themselves becoming increasingly McDonaldized?

2. What do you think of McDonaldized, full-service chains of restaurants like Olive Garden, Red Lobster, and Outback?

3. What is the future of the gourmet restaurant?

4. What is the relationship of social class and economic standing to the growth of both full-service and fast-food restaurants?

5. Given the range of options, where would you rather eat most of the time? Why? Given the spread of McDonaldization, will you still have much of a choice in the future?

Chapter 5 on "rib joints" describes another aspect of the restaurant business that has not been McDonaldized to any great degree. As the authors put it, "There is no fast food in a rib joint. The food arrives as dictated by the desire of the proprietor or by the dictates of cooking the ribs, which 'takes as long as it takes.'" The authors see the rib joint as a kind of deviant setting in which behavior that rebels against modern society in general, and McDonaldized society in particular, is encouraged. Similarly, the shady characters who run rib joints are very unlike the straight businesspeople who operate McDonald's franchises.

My distinction among three types of people—those who see McDonaldization as creating a "velvet," an "iron," or a "rubber" cage—is used to distinguish among rib joint patrons. Those who see McDonaldization as a velvet cage love such enterprises and are unlikely to ever make their way into a rib joint. Those who view it as rubber cage will venture out of their McDonaldized world on occasion for a change of pace but quickly return to it. Those who view the McDonaldized world as an iron cage are the real hope for non-McDonaldized settings such as rib joints because they are likely to become loyal patrons of such settings. That is, if they see themselves in an iron cage, and such a position offends them, they are likely to try to escape to places such as rib joints.

While the rib joint can be seen as an alternative to McDonaldization, such joints could come to be McDonaldized, but that would mean their demise as a genuine alternative to the increasingly ubiquitous McDonaldized meal.

5

A Sociology of Rib Joints

P. D. Holley and D. E. Wright, Jr.

O nly barbeque restaurants that feature ribs may be classified as "rib joints." . . . This ideal type includes the following deviant aspects.

1. A location that is usually difficult to find. . . . This joint seldom advertises; patrons learn about it by "word of mouth" and by the occasional "lifestyles" section of some metropolitan newspaper or magazine written by a reporter looking for an "offbeat" story, or by an annual exercise of rating local restaurants. The best rib joints must be searched out . . . utilizing referrals from locals, such as service station attendants.

2. The location may seem "shady," "suspicious," or "questionable," even to a typical patron. The normal reaction to such locations would be uncertainty, if not fear, as to whether one should be in this part of town or in this neck of the woods. . . .

3. A building or facility itself may be of dubious nature, with a run-down exterior, messy woodpile, smokers, and parts scattered around. The interior should represent a mixture of plain and gaudy . . . This is to be opposed to

the brightly lit, spic-and-span atmosphere of the mainstream eatery. The restroom may only minimally meet health department standards and may even have a Portapotty out back. . . . The furnishings are "odd," perhaps reminiscent of the 1950s era. Soot from the smoker may be visible on the ceiling, fan blades, and other places routinely inaccessible to cleaning. Thus, patrons are left to wonder about health department regulations.

4. The staff of a rib joint, and especially the proprietor, may seem of a dubious, shady, deviant nature. Such staff may treat patrons, especially first-time patrons, with what appears as indifference.

5. "Regulars" of the rib joint are disdainful of newcomers, especially if these newcomers seem ill at ease or if the novices are "dressed up."

The Rib Joint Experience

Eating ribs is a greasy and messy enterprise. . . .

The attraction of barbeque . . . may well incorporate a unique style of preparation, dependent on the experience, ability, and passion of the pit-boss. Even with a desire for consistency in outcome, unpredictability from one time to the next may reign supreme. Further, there are elements of mystery in that ingredients of the sauces are matters of extreme secrecy. The recipes for everyday eating fail the patron of a rib joint, especially the novice . . . who must abandon the old recipes for eating out and create or learn a new one. In this, one can expect the novice to be uncomfortable and probably not to enjoy the first experience in a rib joint—there is often no menu to be leisurely examined and reviewed. The sometimes impatient server recites a jargon-filled menu that must typically be explained and repeated so that one simply can be sure of what one is hearing. The novice either blindly selects something or is assured by a regular ribber or server to "trust me" on a particular order. In other joints, the menu is posted on the wall, with little in the way of item description or explanation.

Absent are menu items for children; unless they eat ribs, they are out of place. The ideal rib joint is not prepared to serve children and serves them regular meals, allows children to eat off their parents' plates, or improvises on the spot. Rib eating is for "adults."

There is no fast food in a rib joint. The food arrives as dictated by the desire of the proprietor or by the dictates of cooking the ribs, which "takes as long as it takes." Furthermore, when the ribs run out, nothing else can substitute, since there are no other entrée items on the menu.

Dining with others is a social occasion . . . in which to create and demonstrate invidious comparisons among people in terms of respectability. . . . Alternatively, especially in fast-food eateries, dining becomes a safe and routinized activity with no special meaning beyond merely providing sustenance.

None of this is true in ribbing. First, the basics of fire-cooked meat brings to mind something of a dangerous experience. . . . Second, a rib meal is anything but routinized and fast. . . . Further, in its very essence, a rib meal is antisnob, antiyuppie, antihierarchical. Traditionally, a meal wholly or primarily of meat is a sign of egalitarianism among the select few who together partake of the meal. Such a meal meant a time of celebration, a special occasion. The rib meal, consisting of the basics of fire-cooked meat, is interpreted by many ribbers as a return to "primal," basically a return to times before status hierarchies became institutionalized and the practice of eating became cluttered with "manners" and a seemingly endless variety of equipment.

Ribbing is an "earthy" experience. It is difficult if not impossible to pretend to be better than others with food in one's hand, with grease and sauce on one's mouth and hands, and wearing a bib and/or a napkin stuck in the neck of one's shirt.

The rib joint's fare itself is messy. And, even with the improvements in pork quality, it is in opposition to the current "health food" craze which emphasizes small and infrequent helpings of low-fat, well-cooked meat.

It is difficult to have what most etiquette books would consider to be "bad table manners" in a rib joint. One is expected to have a "dirty-fingers, greasy mouth, crunchy-bone experience." In a rib joint, one eats with one's hands; puts one's elbows on the table; wears a bib or even places a napkin in one's shirt or uses many paper towels as napkins (from a paper towel roll prominently displayed on the table); gets one's face smeared; passes food from one person to another and/or from one plate to another; smacks one's lips; exclaims loudly about how good the food is; licks one's fingers and lips so as not to miss a drop of meat, juice, and sauce; and freely and openly uses toothpicks. As one eats, one begins to stack the gnawed-bare bones in a pile on the table, clearly as a trophy of one's accomplishments. In short, one must unlearn "good table manners." Neither Julia Child nor Emily Post—both of whom would heartily disdain rib table manners—is likely to show up for a meal at a rib joint. . . .

Part of the meaning of ribbing is counter to modern society; it is a rebellious act. Further, it is an act imbued with a "we against the world" attitude, or at least a "we against the 'straights,'" that is to say against those who do not "do ribs." In doing ribs, one is, among other things, thumbing one's nose at mainstream society. Ribbers see themselves as independent from mainstream customs, free from the need to be well thought of. Last, there develops among ribbers an ethnocentrism, an aloofness toward the outside world, toward those who put on airs, and toward those who eschew ribs. Ribbers are smug in their knowledge that they understand what truly fine food and good eating are. Simultaneously, ribbers pity and ridicule those not initiated to ribs.

The Rib Joint Proprietor

There are few true "individualists" any longer, but the rib joint proprietor may qualify. Typically, the proprietor is male and something of a reprobate, someone who has chosen to avoid or leave the mainstream of typical employment and working for someone else, having chosen to enter one of the most failure prone of businesses, the food-services business. Further, the proprietor is in a business little known and little appreciated by the society at large, as evidenced by the small number of rib joints in the United States. . . . To open a rib joint would seem like "risky business" indeed. However, success in the common sense seems not to be the major motivating force. While not opposed to financial success, most rib joint proprietors appear to be motivated more by a desire to get out of the mainstream and by the desire to provide a good meal for their patrons. . . . Many . . . refuse to do what would be necessary for fame and fortune, choosing instead to serve friends and to enjoy themselves. In this, most rib joint proprietors have a demeanor that seems to say "take me as I am—I am not changing; if I cannot make it as I am, I will do something else." . . .

At best a marginal person, the proprietor has the ability to interact with and serve those of varying socioeconomic and ethnic backgrounds, and to make the dining experience an enjoyable one, to which many return. Usually serving as owner, manager, cashier, server, and cook (or pit-boss), the proprietor presents himself to the customer in active, multiple, and unique ways. . . .

One rule intimately known by ribbers is "call first." Rib joints are notorious for opening and closing at odd hours. In many joints, the proprietor prepares a certain number of slabs of ribs per day—when those are sold, the doors are closed. Often, the owner will close the joint for a month or so while on vacation, fully expecting the clientele to return when he is ready to get back to work.

The rib joint proprietor possesses a passion, a vision, a method, and a secret. The passion is for ribs—real barbeque. His vision is to serve up the best ribs there are, and on a regular basis. The method he has perfected over time, combining particular woods, a certain type of smoker, the application of a marinade, a rub and/or sauce, particular cuts of meat, involves slow cooking with periods of doing nothing interspersed with the attention and care of a perfectionist. Sauces, sometimes invented by the pit-boss, and at other times inherited from family members or friends, represent a crowning achievement. Unique sauces . . . have certain ingredients as carefully guarded secrets. Unique dry rubs . . . maintain ingredients as mysterious.

When the rib joint proprietor dies (or for some reason closes the operation), the continuation of the joint is not at all certain. Sauce secrets may be taken to the grave. Children or other employees may have neither the skill, experience, or passion possessed by the proprietor. Food quality may not be consistent with that of the founder. Or, there may be conflict among spouses, children, other relatives, and others over ownership, control, and management of the joint, as in the case of the Wild Horse Bar-B-Que. These factors seem to explain the tenuous life of the rib joint.

Rib Joint Patrons

Ritzer delineates three types of people based on their attitudes and behavior toward "McDonaldization." The first type refers to those who view the consequences of rationalization as constituting a "velvet cage" connoting that these patrons like McDonald's and welcome it. The second views the consequences as a "rubber cage" with both advantages and disadvantages from which they occasionally and temporarily seek escape. The third group shares with Weber the belief that the disadvantages are more numerous and are similar to an ever-expanding "iron cage" from which ultimately there may be no escape. The velvet cagers always eat at the McDonald's of the modern world, the rubber cagers eat there during the work week and when pressed for time, and the iron cagers never eat there and are fearful that McDonald's will soon be the only type of eatery available.

The velvet cagers would of their volition never select a rib joint. Such persons, when found in rib joints, arrive reluctantly, in the company of others who persuaded them against their "better judgment," and are unlikely to return again. These people are not likely to order ribs, unless there is nothing else on the menu; if they have ribs, they may attempt to cut the meat from the bone and consume the meat with a fork. These patrons are noticeably uncomfortable and consider rib joints as barbaric and archaic. They are people who do not want eating and dining to be an adventure.

Patrons who are in the rubber cage category are like "weekend warriors" who are looking for an alternative to the ho-hum routine of the week and not content with certain features of the fast-food eateries. They are willing to risk some uncertainty in finding alternatives—on occasion. While frequenting "barbeque restaurants," these patrons may also wander into a rib joint by accident but are adventurous enough to brave the deviant (or is it, in their eyes, "cute"?) aspects of the joint to stay and try the main dish. Such patrons will even follow the local custom of throwing good table manners to the winds and dine in appropriate rib fashion; in short, they enjoy themselves. Such rubber cagers may return on more than one occasion and bring others with them. However, these people view ribbing as a sometime thing to do when one has time and as only one of numerous alternatives to fast-food eateries. Last, rib joint patrons of this second type do not qualify as the ideal type patron in that they remain attached to the highly rationalized fast-food eateries and do not internalize an image of themselves as being first and foremost rib connoisseurs.

It should be noted that the rubber cagers are both boon and bane to the rib joint proprietor. On the one hand, they constitute a healthy portion of the joint's clientele, help to popularize particular joints, and introduce first-timers who may eventually become aficionados. On the other hand, these patrons tend truly not to understand the culture and significance of rib joints and from time to time contaminate the joint with culture from the outside world; examples would be for these patrons, who have dined in the joint on occasion, to believe that the proprietor is indebted to them, to expect that they can make special requests, or to be in a hurry. Further, by popularizing the joint, the rubber cagers may serve, unintentionally, to destroy the joint by making it too successful.

The third type of patron is those who view the McDonald's of the world as anathema—pure disaster. As patrons of rib joints, these people do so by choice—indeed, the rib joint is the first thought when eating out occurs. These regulars view themselves as "ribbers" or "rib addicts" and thoroughly delight in the ambiance, decor, food, and manners (or lack thereof) of the joint. These people also differ from the previous type in that for the true rib joint patron, eating here is not a sometime affair to be done when one happens to think about it or when one has enough time. The true patron *always* thinks first of ribs and makes time for them. These patrons are like "sojourners" who "pine for the old days" and view themselves as out of touch with the modern, as alienated from modern food culture. They do not necessarily romanticize the past, but they prefer it when it comes to dining. Further, these patrons view the velvet cagers with disdain and the rubber cagers with wariness. True patrons may even attempt to discourage the first-timers or velvet cagers from staying or returning. The wariness toward the rubber cagers is because of the possibility that they may over-popularize the joint, or make it so successful that the joint and proprietor become upscale.

The Future of the Rib Joint

In sum, the rib joint and a rib meal are anachronisms. The very nature of the rib joint makes it unlikely that ribbing will catch on as has Mexican and Italian dining. Franchises, drive-up windows, faster service, and so on may all find their way into fringes of the rib culture. Barbeque establishments may be located in malls. However, the uniqueness of the food, the proprietor, and the patrons guarantees restricted popularity and limited expansion. . . .

The steady pace of modernization with its emphasis on speed, efficiency, impersonalization, and processing is another source of concern for the rib joint subculture. The very success of some rib joints has caused some proprietors and some businesspeople (ever attentive to making a buck) from outside the subculture to attempt "rationalizing" the rib meal and to make of it the next "McDonald's." Were the rib joint given too much attention, were it to be mass marketed and mainstreamed, the rib joint as described here would die. . . .

But, it is our prediction that the rib joint will persist. We further predict that the rib joint will remain outside the mainstream food culture. . . .

A major factor in the perpetuation of the rib joint is the modernization process and its tendency to "McDonaldize" everything it touches. Rib joints are out-of-step anachronisms, throwbacks to other times, like the "mom and pop" corner stores with their more personalized and less mechanized, less standardized services. To the extent there is a backlash to the modern, whether this backlash is for only the weekend experiment or as a way of life, rib joints will find a niche in the effort to correct for the alienating effects of modernity. To the extent that poor, yet entrepreneurial men and women are produced in this culture, the rib joint will persist. . . .

Long live the rib joint!

Thinking Critically

1. What is the future of the "rib joint" in the age of McDonaldization?

2. What is it about rib joints that might lead people to eat in them?

3. What is it about rib joints that might lead people to pass them up and eat in fast-food restaurants?

4. In what ways is the rib joint an anachronism?

5. In what ways is the critique of McDonaldization animated by a romanticization of places like rib joints?

In this chapter, Bryman applies his four elements of Disneyization to McDonald's and finds that the latter is, to a large degree, Disneyized. (In other works, he has shown how Disney is McDonaldized in various ways.) The following are the basic dimensions of Disneyization that characterize McDonald's.

Theming. This is the "story," really "stories," that McDonald's tells about itself and communicates aggressively to everyone it comes into contact with—suppliers, workers, and especially consumers. There actually are many different stories (for children, parents, teenagers, grandparents, etc.), but one overall theme is that this is a "happy" place for all. This happiness is found in the smile of counter people and of Ronald McDonald, as well as in the "Happy Meal."

Merchandising. McDonald's sells all sorts of stuff beyond the food on offer at the restaurants. Most notable are various toy promotions as well as the merchandise for sale on its Web site.

Dedifferentiation of Consumption. This involves the interpenetration of various forms of consumption, for example, when McDonald's promotes Disney movies and McDonald's restaurants are found in Disney theme parks. Another is the existence of McDonald's restaurants in shopping malls where many other things are for sale.

Emotional Labor. McDonald's employees are expected not only to smile, but to be friendly and happy.

6

McDonald's as a Disneyized Institution

Alan Bryman

McDonaldization is a trend that George Ritzer has argued is enveloping more and more spheres of contemporary society, but it is by no means the only way of conceptualizing change. Ritzer himself remarks at one point that for him it "is simply one important trend, one important way of thinking about contemporary developments." This comment provides an admission ticket for a number of different narratives of change. Such further ways of conceptualizing change should not be seen as contestants in a struggle for our attention but as additional ways of getting to grips with what is happening around us. They are not alternatives: They provide leverage on those areas that notions such as McDonaldization do not fully allow us to encapsulate.

One such additional way of thinking about change that I have suggested in earlier work is the idea of Disneyization. This notion was deliberately set up as a parallel set of changes to those associated with McDonaldization. Ritzer argued that McDonald's provided a paradigm whose underlying principles were spreading their tentacles around more and more sectors of

Editor's Note: From Bryman, A., "McDonald's as a Disneyized Institution," in *American Behavioral Scientist*, 47(2), October 2002, reprinted with permission of Sage Publications, Inc.

society, even though the principles themselves preexisted the first McDonald's restaurant. In a similar vein, I developed the idea of Disneyization as "the process by which *the principles* of the Disney theme parks are coming to dominate more and more sectors of American society as well as the rest of the world." In other words, I substituted the phrase "Disney theme parks" for "the fast-food restaurant" in Ritzer's definition of McDonaldization in coming up with a definition of Disneyization.

An interesting twist on this issue is provided by several suggestions in Ritzer's work that theme parks, and the Disney ones in particular, exemplify McDonaldization. Although I have expressed some doubts about whether the Disney theme parks fit the McDonaldization picture in terms of calculability, in other words, whether the parks emphasize quantity at the expense of quality, it fits well in terms of the other three dimensions. The Disney theme parks and all theme parks modeled on them provide predictable tourist entertainment, exert considerable control over their guests (including control through the use of nonhuman technologies), and are highly efficient in their processing of guests.

However, as with other spheres in which McDonaldization has wrought its impact, to describe the Disney theme parks as McDonaldized does not capture entirely their significance or impact. And, indeed, the quotation from Ritzer's work cited above leads us to think that he is unlikely to subscribe to such a view either. The notion of Disneyization was born out of this kind of reflection: What do the Disney theme parks express that is significant and that is having a growing impact on modern society? In formulating Disneyization, I came up with four dimensions or aspects:

1. *Theming:* the use of a narrative that is consciously imposed on a particular sphere and which envelops consumers,

2. *Dedifferentiation of consumption:* denotes simply the general trend whereby the forms of consumption associated with different institutional spheres become interlocked with each other and increasingly difficult to distinguish,

3. *Merchandising:* a term I use simply to refer to the promotion of goods in the form of, or bearing, copyright images and logos, including such products made under license, and

4. *Emotional labor:* entails control over the employee so that socially desired emotions are exhibited during service transactions.

Walt Disney and the Disney company did not invent any of these principles any more than the McDonald brothers and Ray Kroc invented the principles of McDonaldization. Instead, the Disney theme parks exemplify these principles. The high-profile nature and huge success of the Disney theme parks may have played an important role in promoting the spread of the principles but the parks should not be seen as their wellspring.

It was previously noted that Ritzer depicted the Disney theme parks as McDonaldized. But could we turn the picture around and ask whether McDonald's is a Disneyized institution? The fit may not be a perfect one but the four principles that underpin Disneyization have come to the fore in more recent times than those associated with McDonaldization. The latter can be traced back, as Ritzer frequently observes, to F. W. Taylor and Henry Ford, but the principles of Disneyization are much more closely connected with the rise of consumerism. If we take the view that, if nothing else, consumerism refers to people's purchase of goods and services they do not need and the sustained efforts of a host of organizations to supply consumers with these unnecessary goods and services, this is a collection of features that has become especially prominent in more recent times.

Can a case be made, then, that McDonald's is a Disneyized organizational form? We should not be overly surprised if this were the case because there are numerous ways in which the two are connected. They were both built up by visionary entrepreneurs, they both have strong corporate cultures, they both have universities, they both emphasize the advantages of automation, they both emphasize the family, and so on. It is even the case that when Ray Kroc joined the Red Cross at the end of World War I, he says in his biography that there was another young man who had lied about his age to get in. Kroc writes, "He was regarded as a strange duck, because whenever we had time off and went out on the town to catch girls, he stayed in camp drawing pictures." So, by a strange quirk of fate, the two men who nurtured two of the most prominent brands and companies of the last 100 years spent time together in a Red Cross company.

McDonald's as a Disneyized Institution

I will turn now to the question of how far McDonald's corresponds to the four dimensions of Disneyization that have been outlined.

Theming

McDonald's can be viewed as themed in different ways and at different levels. As Gottdiener has observed, franchised chains of restaurants such as McDonald's essentially provide a theme that is themselves. This theme is

expressed in the corporate decoration, modes of service delivery, staff clothing, and various architectural cues that are pervasive features of these establishments. Beardsworth and Bryman have referred to such theming as
reflexive theming, whereby the theme, the brand, and its expression become
coterminous. With reflexive theming, the organization does not draw on
external devices for its narratives; instead, the thematic elements are internally generated and then continuously reproduced. "Each themed setting
refers reflexively to itself and to the population of clones which reflect it and
are reflected by it."

Such theming, then, is essentially self-referential and refers to those relatively rare instances in which a brand provides its own organizational narrative, a feature that also can be seen in the Disney theme parks and other realms
of the Disney empire. McDonald's as a company is acutely aware of its
self-referential theming. It portrays its eating environments as experiences.
Benjamin Barber quotes Jim Cantalupo, then president of international operations, who explains how McDonald's "is more than just price. It's the whole
experience which our customers have come to expect from McDonald's. It's
the drive-thrus . . . it's the Playlands . . . it's the smile at the front
counter . . . it's all those things . . . the experience." When Ray Kroc once
observed, "when you are in this business you are in show business," he was
drawing attention to the way in which the development of a brand has to do
with turning the perception of it into an experience by which it becomes
instantly recognizable. Certainly, both Shelton and Manning and Callum-
Swan have drawn attention to the way in which there are theatrical or dramatic connotations to a McDonald's visit. Thus, when it is suggested by the
latter writers that "McDonald's is a brilliantly conceived dramatic production," it is the brand as a unique eating experience that is crucial. Similarly, in
an interview for *Foreign Policy* in 2001, chief executive officer Jack Greenberg
was quoted as saying, "When you enter the restaurant, you enter the brand.
And so the challenge for all of our local franchisees and local management
around the world is to ensure a minimum level of consistency." The opening
in 2001 of the Golden Arch hotel in Zurich, where the headboards on the beds
are in the shape of a golden arch, is an interesting illustration of the use of a
brand as mechanism for theming. Such extensions of the McDonald's theme
reflect the faith in brands such as McDonald's that have come to connote consistency of quality. As Twitchell has observed, with branding, "what is being
bought is place, prestige, comfort, security, confidence, purpose, meaning."
Thus, McDonald's as a company is acutely aware of the significance of its
brand as a provider of meaning and organizer of experiences.

But theming in McDonald's does not rest solely at the level of reflexive
theming. There are other ways in which theming reveals itself. One is that
there is a constant overlay of a narrative of family in the advertising and

images associated with the company. It is routinely depicted (or perhaps it would be more accurate to say that it routinely depicts itself) as a clean, safe haven for families to refuel at relatively low cost. As Law points out, this appeal to families is emphasized through a tendency to personalize its advertising and through the suggestion that in this fun place the family will be reinforced. Kincheloe observes that family values are frequently deployed in McDonald's advertising as part of a nostalgic reference to an idealized past.

This familial discourse is a powerful one in that the company is well aware of its appeal to children and indeed engages in many tactics to enhance that appeal. The image of the family at McDonald's renders parents more amenable to children's pester power and the association with low- risk eating in a safe environment provides a reassuring setting for families. Watson also has noted the intensive use of family imagery in McDonald's advertising in East Asia.

However, there is also evidence of McDonald's becoming increasingly attracted to the use of external narratives in its restaurants. Chicago's own rock 'n' roll McDonald's serves as an illustration of the use of this kind of development. In 2001, an article in the *New York Times* announced that a huge McDonald's was planned for Times Square that would have the ambience of a Broadway theatre. Schlosser wrote that when he visited the McDonald's near Dachau concentration camp, it had a Wild West theme. Yan describes a themed McDonald's in Beijing in which the restaurant was decorated like a ship and crew members wore sailor uniforms rather than conventional McDonald's garb. The narrative was one of Uncle McDonald's Adventure, which is meant to entail a round-the-world trip with Uncle McDonald. Also, the company has announced that it is going to refurbish some of its outlets as traditional diners, thereby drawing on a motif that is an extremely popular thematic focus for American restaurant chains. Bone reported in the *Times* that not only was Denny's remodeling some of its restaurants "to give the nostalgic feel of traditional diners" but McDonald's was doing the same and had just opened its "first diner-style outlet in Kokomo, Indiana, and customers are lining up to eat such old-fashioned American fare as turkey steak and mashed potato." A second has since opened in another town in Indiana. It remains to be seen whether these McDonald's diners will be rolled out more widely but the fact that they are experimenting with such theming is very telling about the directions that the company is considering.

A further sign of theming is the use of ethnic theming. In the United Kingdom, for example, the company often features lines that are themed in terms of Indian or Italian cooking (both of which are very popular among the British). Gordon and Meunier report that in spring 2000, McDonald's launched a raft of locally themed meals. In one month, the enthusiast could buy a burger with a different French cheese on each day of the week. The following month, "gourmet" meals were available in the south of France. Gourmet was signified by being able to eat burgers topped with ratatouille or by ice cream with a black currant sauce topping.

Therefore, in several ways, McDonald's restaurants can be viewed as themed. The growing use of theming that goes beyond reflexive theming and theming in terms of family may be due to a belief that although the company does provide a certain kind of experience, as Cantalupo suggests, it increasingly needs to do more in this regard. Pine and Gilmore have suggested that with regard to what they call the *experience economy,* companies increasingly need to raise consumers' experiences to new levels that will be highly memorable. Although it is unlikely that McDonald's would want to turn itself into a chain of themed restaurants that become destinations in their own right, especially in view of the financial difficulties experienced by such chains in the past few years, the slow move in some of its outlets to a more distinctive kind of theming may prove an interesting long-term development in terms of Disneyization.

Merchandising

There is evidence of merchandising in McDonald's as well as theming. It can be seen in the availability of a wide range of merchandise bearing its logos or characters. The McDonald's Web site has a very large amount of merchandise for sale at a variety of prices. These include clothing items such as baseball caps and t-shirts to nostalgia items such as cookie jars. The McDonald's in the Disney Marketplace in Orlando had a particularly wide range of merchandise when I visited the area in 2000. Merchandising has to a certain extent been extended by the McKids range of children's clothing. Referring to this range in his *Foreign Policy* interview, Greenberg said, "It happens to be licensed to Wal-Mart, but it's our brand and we get a royalty for it." Although merchandising in McDonald's is by no means as extensive as in Disney theme parks, there is evidence that the restaurant chain has incorporated this element of Disneyization.

Dedifferentiation of Consumption

There are two main ways in which dedifferentiation of consumption can be seen in relation to McDonald's. One is through the way its tie-ins with companies such as Disney become the context for the distribution of toys or when it latches onto new toy crazes such as the Beanie Babies. These toys have attracted enthusiasts who collect them; there is a Web site for sharing of information about them and an annual convention for collectors. Most new Disney films are involved in cross-promotional tie-ins with McDonald's so that as Pecora and Meehan report in the context of their U.S. component of the Global Disney Audiences Project, "Given Disney's promotional agreement with McDonald's, the McDonald's in the mall had been decorated with *Hunchback* streamers and promotional displays. It offered special *Hunchback* meals with *Hunchback* place mats, napkins, paper cups, etc." But it is the distribution of free toys that is the key feature for us in terms of dedifferentiation of consumption. Wolf points out that the exclusive McDonald's/Disney alliance produced a 23% increase in Happy Meals in the United States. In 1997, this made for a 7% increase in sales. In the process, McDonald's became the largest distributor of toys in the world. It is not surprising, therefore, that the participant researchers in the Global Disney Audiences Project noted that their interviewees in several countries frequently noted the prominence of tie-ins with Disney films. However, it is not just Disney films that are tied in to McDonald's—films such as *Space Jam* also have been involved in this way. Although writers, for example, Wolf, claim that such tie-ins can result in very significant improvements in food sales for McDonald's, the movie tie-in with food is by no means a recipe for success, as Taco Bell found with its cross-promotion with *Godzilla*. The significance of such tie-ins for the present discussion is simply that the distribution of free toys as a lure for children can be viewed as evidence of the dedifferentiation of consumption because it involves elements of the sale of both food and toys. It also should be noted that this form of the dedifferentiation of consumption is often a focus for criticism because it is seen as evidence of the manipulation of consumers and of children in particular. The Archbishop of Canterbury has criticized such tie-ins and singled out Disney for particular disapproval, saying, "The Disney empire has developed this to an unprecedented pitch of professionalism."

The second main way in which we find dedifferentiation of consumption in relation to McDonald's is the way in which it is frequently implicated in settings that bring together a variety of forms of consumption. Examples are the obvious ones, such as the presence of McDonald's in malls, but there are others too, such as its location in theme parks. Ritzer has observed that McDonald's is often found in the modern ballpark. He and Stillman depict the growth of food courts featuring McDonald's and other chains as one of the ways in which the modern ballpark seeks to make the overall experience of spectatorship "more spectacular and enchanted." Certainly, the company's plans in terms of this feature of Disneyization are ambitious. In the Afterword to Kroc's autobiography, Kroc's coauthor Robert Anderson mentions the appearance of McDonald's in a hospital, tollway services plazas, military bases, shopping malls, and amusement parks. He quoted from the 1985 annual report, "Maybe—someday—McDonald's will be found on aircraft carriers and commercial airliners. In sports stadiums and fine department stores." As a strategy, this is not always successful, as the company found when it was forced because of poor levels of patronage to close many of its outlets that were located in Wal-Mart stores.

Emotional Labor

Emotional labor is a key feature of McDonald's restaurants. It is a component of the Quality Service and Value ethos from Ray Kroc's days that remains a central tenet of the faith. Its importance is drilled into franchisees and managers at the Hamburger Universities. Crew members at the customer interface are widely expected to engage with diners in a friendly way to enhance the pleasurable nature of the dining experience and to increase the likelihood of more items being purchased. Royle, for example, on the basis of his European research on McDonald's, has written that the company's employees "are expected to control themselves *internally* by being pleasant, cheerful, smiling and courteous to customers, even when customers are rude and offensive." It is very much part of the show business atmosphere that Kroc felt was such an important component of the success of the restaurants. It can be seen in the previously quoted remark by Jim Cantalupo, then president of international operations, when he refers to the significance of "the smile at the front counter." As Fantasia points out in connection with the reception of McDonald's in France, the American ambience is a very important aspect of its success there among youth, and it is the deployment of emotional labor that plays an important role in creating that ambience. It is striking that when Kincheloe interviewed a woman originally from Hong Kong, she explained how as a girl her enthusiasm for McDonald's was such that she used to play role-playing games in which she would "churn up a big smile, and say, 'How can I help you today? May I please have your order?'"

Emotional labor is not without its problems for crew members. As Leidner has shown, the scripted nature of interactions with clients and the need to act in a way that can be inconsistent with how one actually feels—especially in the face of difficult customers—can be a deeply alienating experience. However, the main point in relation to the current discussion is that McDonald's exhibits this dimension of Disneyization.

However, there is a further dimension to emotional labor at McDonald's, and it is one that was neglected in the original exposition of Disneyization. It is not just crew workers who are involved in exhibiting emotional labor; managers are also involved in a form of emotional labor in that they are trained and encouraged to become subservient to the McDonald's corporate ethos and culture. Leidner writes that the company seeks to produce managers with "ketchup in their veins." The Hamburger University plays a significant role in inculcating this corporate spirit. In part, the training is conducted to instruct managers in the correct operational procedures to maximize the kind of uniformity of process and product for which the company is famous. But also, as Leidner observes, managers' zeal is worked on to ensure they understand as fully as possible the reasons for adherence to protocol so that they are more likely to ensure that there is no transgression. The training is concerned, therefore, with "building commitment and motivation" as much as instruction in McDonald's ways of doing things. The kind of company loyalty that is required and engendered is a form of emotional labor on the part of those who are required to exhibit it. Much like Disney's University, the managers also are introduced to the company's history and to the words of its founder to enhance the emotional appeal of the corporate culture.

Reflection

There does, then, seem to be evidence to support my contention that McDonald's is a Disneyized institution. Once again, I am not suggesting that McDonald's has copied the Disney theme parks, although that may sometimes have occurred. In particular, it may be worth drawing a distinction between *structural* and *transferred* Disneyization. The former "reflects a complex of underlying changes of which the Disney theme parks are exemplars." Transferred Disneyization is where the principles of the Disney theme parks are transferred into another sphere. A similar kind of distinction also could be made in relation to McDonaldization, although in practice it is difficult to distinguish between concrete cases of Disneyization or McDonaldization in terms of which process has taken place. However, the point is that McDonald's exhibits tendencies that are *exemplified* by the Disney theme parks. There may be an element of imitation in many cases (as with transferred Disneyization), but this is by no means necessarily the case.

Thinking Critically

1. Is the world growing more Disneyized than McDonaldized?

2. What are the similarities/differences between Disneyization and McDonaldization?

3. Does the theory of Disneyization accord too much importance to an amusement park? To Disney?

4. In what ways does the string of Disney Worlds around the world form an iron cage? A carceral archipelago? Islands of the living dead?

5. In what ways are both Disneyization and McDonaldization expressions of American culture?

As we have already seen, and will see to an increasing degree as this book proceeds, McDonaldization has spread far beyond the fast-food industry. Among the many things that would seem to be impervious to McDonaldization are daredevil acts such as mountain climbing. Yet as Ian Heywood shows in Chapter 7 even mountain climbing has been McDonaldized to some degree. He sees climbing as a "recreational escape attempt," and clearly one of the things that people attracted to such an activity are escaping is the McDonaldization of society. Yet because it attracts a number of people, climbing comes under pressure to rationalize from social, political, and especially commercial sources.

Heywood focuses on adventure climbing, a distinctive British tradition that is perceived as something close to pure sport. It involves things such as physical skill, technical ability, moral qualities, and character. There is a great deal of unpredictability and risk associated with it. The joy comes from the climbing itself and not necessarily the end of reaching the top. Adventure climbing represents genuine escape to those who practice it. However, Heywood identifies three things that make this form of climbing less adventurous and more rationalized. First, there are now guidebooks that greatly reduce the unpredictability of climbing. Second, there now exists an enormous amount of scientifically tested and technologically sophisticated equipment created by commercial interests to generate profits. All of this equipment makes previously difficult routes easier and safer. Third, training for mountain climbing has also been McDonaldized so that climbers have greater control over potential risks. As a result of all this, adventure climbing has become "more predictable and controllable." Those who want risky and unpredictable climbs can still find them, but the majority, especially those who are new to the sport and have been raised in the McDonaldized society, will gravitate toward more McDonaldized ways of climbing mountains.

7

Urgent Dreams

Climbing, Rationalization, and Ambivalence

Ian Heywood

Climbing as Escape?

The efforts of a sport like climbing to evade societal rationalization invariably become deeply paradoxical under contemporary conditions. Climbing, like other escape attempts, shows every indication of coming under rationalization pressure. There are "external" pressures, deriving from commercial sources (markets, competition, etc.) but also from social or political circumstance—for example, the need . . . for climbing to present itself to the rest of society, or at least to the media, as a legitimate recreation or sport able to make reasonable claims, sometimes against the arguments of competing groups, for access to increasingly scarce natural resources.

There are also less obvious but in some ways more interesting internal pressures, which I will outline by discussing the contrast, much debated

Editor's Note: From "Urgent Dreams: Climbing, Rationalization, and Ambivalence" by Ian Heywood, 1994, *Leisure Studies, 13,* 179–194. Used with permission.

recently within the climbing world, between "sport climbing" and "adventure climbing."

The term "adventure climbing" is an attempt to describe a distinctive British climbing tradition and to contrast this tradition with a new approach, initially developed in Europe: "sport climbing." In adventure climbing, the climbing team (usually of two or three) starts from the ground, without much in the way of preliminary inspection, and ascends to the top relying on a brief guidebook description, direct observation and experience, and protecting themselves with ropes and leader-placed, removable devices which do not damage the rock surface. In high standard sport climbing, generally short (one pitch) routes are "worked," perhaps over days or weeks, with the climber repeatedly resting or falling onto the frequent bolts or pitons which provide security; in most sport climbs, the climber is very unlikely to suffer serious injury however many times he or she falls, jumps, or rests on the protection. The same could not be said for many adventure climbs.

Adventure climbing, its adherents argue, is inherently and uniquely challenging and satisfying; it is a pure or authentic form of the sport. For many, it . . . stands out against the rationalizing tide engulfing so many other areas of social life. For its critics, sport climbing reduces a complex activity involving the whole person to technique and strength, to what is determined by genetic inheritance or acquired by intensive training. "Real" climbing is seen to demand, from time to time, not just physical performance, not just *technical* qualities, but *moral* qualities and qualities of *character* as well.

Treated as a cultural phenomenon, adventure climbing represents for many participants a genuine escape attempt, a small but important challenge to the encroachments of rationalization. This is not of course to say that the practice of adventure climbing is routinely disorganized, impulsive, conducted in a kind of romantic stupor; on the contrary, it demands an approach which is ordered, deliberate, clear-headed, and circumspect.

This said, there is about the notion of adventure climbing something fundamentally at odds with the outlook and values belonging to the process of rationalization as it has been understood and described by writers from Weber onward. Rationalization demands the objectification of the phenomena it confronts; it must make them into its "materials," more or less discrete entities related to one another in relatively simple, potentially intelligible and manipulable ways. It is interested in predictability, simplicity, and effective control. The powerful rhetoric associated with rationalization restricts self-reflection to operational considerations. It is typically thought of as value-neutral, focused on devising and implementing effective means, so that the primary satisfactions available to rationalizers derive from the results of the process, not the process itself.

Adventure climbing, on the other hand, does not treat rock as a material to be subjugated and mastered technically. The rock surface is not to be modified to provide better holds or protection; it must be encountered as it is, "phenomenologically," in all its rich complexity of texture, form, and angle. The climber does not really know from one moment to another whether the next move will be possible or not, the process is unpredictable and the outcome uncertain. The satisfactions of climbing are intrinsic rather than extrinsic; neither "getting to the top" nor even "surviving" is really intelligible as a satisfactory end unless it is thought of as part of the process of climbing itself. Finally, authentic climbing is always accompanied by risk, the possibility of injury or even death. This is profoundly alien to rationalization, in which risk is to be minimized and death constitutes a limit condition; it must be avoided for as long as possible.

Yet might we not want to question just how "adventurous" a lot of adventure climbing is? I shall consider three ways in which it is perhaps a bit less "raw," a little more "processed," than its protagonists might like to admit. First, for most climbers a current guidebook is almost as important as a rope. Guidebooks are an invaluable source of information not just about where the route goes but about its grade of difficulty, its degree of danger, its atmosphere, the amount of "exposure" (big drops which are difficult to ignore), whether it is likely to be enjoyable in the wet, whether an escape onto an easier route nearby can be engineered if things get unpleasant, and so on. For middle grade and harder routes, a modern guidebook will provide an overall grade for the climb, which incorporates a view of technical difficulty, whether or not the difficulties are sustained, and how "serious" (difficult to protect, dangerous) the climb is. Individual pitches are given the technical grade of the hardest move; this is meant to indicate the objective physical difficulty of a move irrespective of its dangers or situation. Experienced climbers can often read between the lines of a route description to extract additional information in the form of inferences, significant omissions, the first ascent date, and so forth. Thus guidebooks contain enormous amounts of information, much of it in a codified, convention-governed form; with these descriptions the competent interpreter approaches the climb with a considerable amount of reliable, intersubjectively verified knowledge. Unpredictability is significantly reduced, while the climber's ability to objectify and control the climbing environment increases. Objectification, predictability, and control are, of course, hallmarks of rationalization.

Second, I want to consider climbing gear: footwear, clothes, protection devices. A vast amount could be written on this topic. Briefly however, each of these categories of equipment has been, and continues to be, the subject of scientific and technological research. Rock climbing footwear has improved steadily over the postwar period; light boots or slippers now fit closely, enable the climber to feel the texture and shape of the rock, and are shod with high-friction "sticky" rubber originally developed for aircraft tires. Rock climbers, and more particularly mountaineers, can now buy (if they can afford them!) well-designed garments which are, to some extent, water-resistant, breathable, and windproof. Protection equipment, including ropes, harnesses, belay plates, wire alloy "nuts," and advanced camming devices have all improved the safety of the climber beyond anything that those of us who stared climbing in the 1960s could have imagined possible. Literally thousands of high-quality routes, for years considered too dangerous for all but an elite of "hardmen," can now be enjoyed by a much wider constituency of ordinary mortals. For the experienced climber placing protection devices properly and using knowledge of the route derived from the guidebook, the activity is usually, under controlled circumstances, controlled, predictable, and relatively safe. Or perhaps it would be more accurate to say that uncertainty and danger can be, if the climber so chooses, controlled.

Third, I turn to the importance of training. Prior to the 1970s, few climbers trained seriously. Some had strenuous manual jobs, which helped with strength and stamina, but usually people got "climbing fit" by climbing. During the 1970s, elite climbers began to realize the advantages of specialized, systematic work with weights on climbing walls and boulders. Dieting, flexibility exercises, and even mental training to produce a relaxed but focused attitude all became commonplace. These ideas have spread in recent years so that now most climbers who consider themselves at all serious about their sport train: running, watching their diets, using weights and walls, stretching, and so on. Many develop rigorous "scientific" or systematic routines based on up-to-date sport research and training practice. All this can give the climber more control, it can render the activity more predictable, and it can make it less likely that, at a given grade, the climber will be confronted by physical or even mental demands that exceed available resources.

To summarize, I have argued that recent developments in so-called adventure climbing, in particular the information quality of contemporary guidebooks, the effectiveness of new equipment, and the evolution of training methods, have progressively rendered the activity more predictable and controllable. Now the danger, the unpredictability, the risk, the irrationality of climbing are substantially matters of *choice*; climbers can have their activity raw, medium, or well-done according to how they feel or what they want from the sport. . . . Adventure climbing has itself already gone a considerable way toward its rational transformation.

Thinking Critically

1. Can mountain climbing, especially of something like Mt. Everest, ever be McDonaldized to a high degree?

2. Would you want to climb mountains in a non-McDonaldized way?

3. Would you want to climb mountains in a McDonaldized way?

4. Would McDonaldized mountain climbing still represent an escape?

5. Aren't the gains in safety from McDonaldizing mountain climbing worth the disadvantages associated with it?

Eric Schlosser is the author of the international bestseller, Fast Food Nation. *In the following interview, Schlosser discusses, and expresses surprise over, the wide-reaching influence of the fast-food industry. Although he sees positive effects, Schlosser focuses on the costs associated with this industry such as increasing uniformity and conformity, the obesity epidemic, deskilled labor, and the horrendous working conditions in the slaughterhouses that supply the fast-food industry with its meat products. Schlosser goes beyond describing these problems to suggest reforms such as a prohibition on advertising unhealthy food to children, better pay and working conditions, and a stronger federal food safety program. Concerned about these and other problems, Schlosser has sworn off fast food, at least until the industry mends its ways and seeks to deal with its worst abuses.*

8

A Conversation With Eric Schlosser, Author of *Fast Food Nation*

Q: *Whether the product is furniture, books, clothes, or food, chains are taking over independent businesses across the country and the world. What prompted you to focus on fast food?*

A: The fast-food industry is enormous—and enormously influential. The fast-food chains demonstrated that you could create identical retail environments and sell the same products at thousands of different locations. The huge success of McDonald's spawned countless imitators. The founders of the Gap later said they'd been inspired by McDonald's and Kentucky Fried Chicken. The key to all these businesses is uniformity and conformity. So by looking at fast food I'm trying to explain how communities throughout the United States have lost a lot of their individuality over the past 20 years and have started to look exactly the same.

Editor's Note: From "A Conversation with Eric Schlosser, author of *Fast Food Nation*," published by Houghton Mifflin.

http://www.houghtonmifflinbooks.com/booksellers/press_release/schlosser/. Reprinted with permission of The Houghton Mifflin Company.

Q: Fast Food Nation begins with a look at Cheyenne Mountain and the Colorado Springs area. Why did you focus on this part of the country?

A: Well, I could have chosen just about any suburban community and told much the same story. But Colorado Springs appealed to me because its growth has neatly paralleled the growth of the fast-food industry. The city feels like a place on the cutting edge—like Los Angeles in the 1950s—a glimpse, maybe, of America's future. The high-tech economy there, and the kind of thinking that goes with it, seems linked to the fast-food industry's worship of new gadgets and technology. And I wanted to set the book somewhere in the American West, the part of the country that embodies our whole spirit of freedom and independence and self-reliance. Those are the very qualities that the fast-food industry is now helping to eliminate.

Q: Why has the fast-food industry grown so quickly around the world?

A: Here in the States, I think, fast food is popular because it's convenient, it's cheap, and it tastes good. But the real cost of eating fast food never appears on the menu. By that I mean the cost of the obesity epidemic fast food has helped to unleash, the social costs of having such a low-wage workforce, and the health costs of the new industrialized agriculture that supplies the big restaurant chains.

Overseas, much of fast food's appeal stems from its Americanness. Like Hollywood movies, MTV, and blue jeans, fast food has become one of our major cultural exports.

Q: How do fast-food restaurants benefit from "de-skilled" jobs and from high turnover among their employees?

A: A reliance on cheap labor has been crucial to the fast-food industry's success. It's no accident that the industry's highest rate of growth occurred during a period when the real value of the U.S. minimum wage declined by about 40 percent. The chains have worked hard to "de-skill" the jobs in their kitchens by imposing strict rules on how everything must be done, selling highly processed food that enters the restaurant already frozen or freeze-dried and easy to reheat, and relying on complex kitchen machinery to do as much of the work as possible. Instead of employing skilled short-order cooks, the chains try to employ unskilled workers who will do exactly as they're told. The chains are willing to put up with turnover rates of 300 to 400 percent in order to keep their labor costs low. It doesn't really matter to them who comes or goes, since this system treats all workers as though they're interchangeable.

Q: *When you were doing your research for the book, what surprised you the most?*

A: I guess it was the far-reaching influence of this food that surprised me most. Because it's something you never really think about. Fast food is everywhere, it seems so mundane, taken for granted. But it has changed what we eat, how we work, what our towns look like, and what we look like in the mirror. I also was amazed to learn that much of fast-food's taste is manufactured at a series of chemical plants off the New Jersey Turnpike.

Q: *Do you feel that the fast-food industry has made any positive impressions on our culture?*

A: In the early days, I think the industry embodied some of the best things about this country. It was started by high school drop-outs who had little training, by entrepreneurs who made it big by working hard. Guys like the McDonald brothers didn't rely on focus groups, marketing surveys, or management consultants with MBAs. They just set up their grills and started cooking. It's ironic that what they created turned into such a symbol of faceless, ruthless corporate power. It's a very American story, both good and bad. . . .

Q: *One of the book's most arresting passages describes your visit to a slaughterhouse in which the working conditions are atrocious. How have slaughterhouses gotten away with such poor management and treatment of employees for so long? Do you foresee any changes in this industry in the near future?*

A: The meatpacking industry now employs some of the poorest, most vulnerable workers in the United States. Most are recent immigrants. Many of them are illiterate and don't speak English. Many are illegals. A generation ago, meatpacking workers belonged to strong unions that could fight for better pay and working conditions. But today's workers often feel that they can't speak out, rightly afraid they will be fired or deported. It's amazing to me how well hidden these abuses remain. I think the media's lack of interest in the plight of meatpacking workers has to do with their skin color. If blond-haired, blue-eyed workers were being mistreated this way, there'd be a huge uproar.

I think the working conditions in the nation's meatpacking plants could improve very quickly—almost overnight. The fast-food chains have the power to say to their suppliers: treat your workers better or we won't buy meat from you anymore. McDonald's is the world's largest purchaser of beef. It recently issued strict guidelines to its suppliers on the humane treatment and slaughter of animals. I think McDonald's should now show the same kind of compassion for human beings.

Q: What changes would you like to see instituted within the fast-food industry and the government agencies regulating it?

A: I'd like the fast food industry to start assuming some of the real costs it now imposes on the rest of society. And I don't think the chains are going to pay those costs willingly. The right legislation will have to do the job. I'd like to see a total ban on the advertising of unhealthy food to children. If a grown man or woman wants to buy a bacon-double-cheeseburger with large fries, well, great, it's a free country. But the fast-food chains should not be allowed to spend millions advertising fatty, unsafe food for children. Obesity is now the second leading cause of death in the United States, after smoking. In the interest of public health, we've banned cigarette ads directed at adults. We should do at least as much to protect children. Such a ban, among other things, would encourage McDonald's to sell Happy Meals that aren't so laden with fat.

I'd like to see a rise in the minimum wage, tougher enforcement of overtime laws, and new OSHA regulations designed to protect employees who work at restaurants late at night. All of these things will help improve the lives of fast food workers—the biggest group of minimum wage earners in the United States.

And I'd like to see a complete overhaul of the federal food safety system, which at the moment is spread across a dozen separate agencies. We should have a single food safety agency, completely separate from the Department of Agriculture, that has power over the fast food industry and its suppliers. We should be able to demand recalls of tainted food, and we should be able to impose fines on companies that deliberately sell bad meat. Right now millions of Americans are needlessly being sickened by what they eat.

Q: Are you a vegetarian? Do you eat fast food?

A: I have a lot of respect for people who are vegetarian for religious or ethical reasons. Despite all my research, however, I'm still a carnivore. My favorite meal, by far, is a cheeseburger with fries. But I don't eat ground beef anymore. I've seen firsthand what goes into it, and I'm angry about the careless greed of the meatpacking industry. I still eat beef, though I always try to buy meat that's been produced by ranchers who care about their animals and the land. And no, I won't eat fast food anymore. Not until the industry changes its ways.

Thinking Critically

1. Have communities lost their individuality because of the spread of the fast-food restaurant and McDonaldization?

2. How would you feel about working in a de-skilled job?

3. Is the fast-food industry "a symbol of faceless, ruthless corporate power"?

4. Do you think the federal government should get involved in legislating the fast-food industry so that, for example, it is prevented from advertising unhealthy food to children?

5. Could vegetarianism be McDonaldized?

The McDonaldization thesis is not without its critics. In this chapter, one of today's leading social thinkers outlines some of the major criticisms. The first is that in looking at McDonald's around the globe, it is clear that it adapts to, and is modified by, local cultures. Thus, McDonald's is not nearly as uniform as suggested by the McDonaldization thesis (this issue will be addressed in much more detail in Part IV of this volume). Second, the perspective is accused of giving insufficient attention to the opposition to it (some of this is dealt with in Part III). Finally, there is the issue of whether McDonaldization adds anything new to earlier theories, especially Weber's theory of rationalization. Overall, Turner concludes that none of these, or other, criticisms constitute a fundamental challenge to the validity and utility of the McDonaldization thesis.

9

McDonaldization

The Major Criticisms

Bryan S. Turner

T he McDonaldization thesis has been an important and influential debate in contemporary sociology because it illustrates an issue that has been central to the sociological account of modernity. *The McDonaldization of Society* was explicitly a study in Weberian sociology insofar as it described the rationalization of contemporary society. It also can be seen correctly as a contribution to the study of global consumption. The book was revised partly in response to critics and has produced a variety of valuable research projects in modern sociology . . .

The major lines of criticism and comment on the McDonaldization thesis have been fairly well developed. First, there has been an issue about the extent and uniformity of McDonald's as an illustration of cultural standardization

Author's Note: For advice and information on McDonald's in developing this analysis, I would like to thank the following people: Ayca Alemdaroglu (University of Cambridge), Mona Abaza (American University of Cairo), Greg Burton and Sue Kenny (Deakin University, Australia), and Bill Thornton (National Cheng University, Taiwan).

Editor's Note: From Turner, B., "McDonaldization: The Major Criticisms," in *American Behavioral Scientist,* 47(2), October 2003, reprinted with permission of Sage Publications, Inc.

where critics have argued that around the world, McDonald's products and packaging are adjusted to and modified by local cultures. In Asia, ethnographic studies, for example, in James Watson's *Golden Arches East,* have demonstrated that McDonaldization is not a uniform process. . . . Second, in the original study, Ritzer failed to provide an account of how McDonaldization as an iron cage could be resisted. In his subsequent work and in the debate, the avenues of resistance have been given considerable attention. The rise of the antiglobalization movement has been a vivid, and occasionally violent, testimony to global political responses to McDonald's as a symbol of Americanization. The negative social, health, and economic consequences of McDonald's have been fully explored in both serious political economy and popular critique, for example, in Eric Schlosser's *Fast Food Nation* or John Vidal's *McLibel.* Finally, there are various contributions to sociological theory that broadly address the question as to whether the debate has contributed anything new to the rationalization thesis that we have inherited from Weber and critical theory. Perhaps the best answer to that criticism comes from Barry Smart, who has observed that the real value of Ritzer's study has been to force us to attempt a general sociological understanding of the central feature of modern society, thereby "provoking a theoretical and practical debate concerning key novel and defining features of our contemporary world and forcing us to define our response to crucial aspects of our everyday world." We can take this statement as a broad translation of Weber's injunction that our duty as sociologists is to understand the characteristic uniqueness of the times in which we live.

Much of the critical debate with Ritzer's analysis is not, however, a fundamental challenge to his account of McDonald's because the criticisms often amount merely to extensions, corrections, or additions to the thesis. For example, the ethnographic illustrations about localization or glocalization have primarily brought an empirical richness to the abstract theorization of rationalized production and consumption. We need to develop these ethnographic observations to another level as a genuine theoretical step beyond the Weberian model of rationalism. To engage in a debate over McDonaldization, we need to see the McDonald's case study as a contribution to Weberian economic sociology in the sense that Ritzer has shown us how the rationalization of distribution and popular consumption is a historical elaboration of Weber's analysis of the rationalization of production. To address Ritzer's thesis more directly, we might ask what social or economic transformations of the McDonaldization process would result in the falsification of the rationalization theory?

Thinking Critically

1. Does the fact that McDonald's adapts to local cultures around the world undermine the McDonaldization thesis?

2. In what ways have you resisted McDonaldization?

3. In what ways have others resisted McDonaldization?

4. Should McDonaldization be resisted?

5. In what ways could we falsify the McDonaldization thesis; that is, find data that question, if not undermine, it?

PART I

Pedagogical Questions

1. Define the "McDonaldization of society." What are the four dimensions of McDonaldization?

2. What are the structural and administrative transformations that industries go through as they McDonaldize? Discuss the effects of McDonaldization on the national and global labor force.

3. What does "irrationality of rationality" mean? Cite examples of it beyond those discussed in this part of the book.

4. What key characteristics distinguish the bureaucratic system from the prebureaucratic system? Compare these two systems in terms of efficiency, calculability, predictability, and control through nonhuman technology.

5. How does Weber define formal rationality? Why does formal rationality limit substantive rationality?

6. Bureaucratic organization expands in modern societies to perform many complex tasks efficiently. However, it also generates dysfunctions that lead to alienation and inefficiency. Identify some of the rationalities and irrationalities of the bureaucracy in the daily rounds of life.

7. What is Disneyization? What are the common characteristics of Disneyization and McDonaldization? How does Disneyization operate in McDonaldized spaces?

8. How does the college education system adapt to McDonaldization? Are classes and their requirements McDonaldized?

9. How does McDonaldization transform personal space and the presentation of the self? Does it leave room for individuality?

10. How have cultural standardization and the trend toward globalization affected you, your family, and your community? List both the pros and cons. Have the benefits outweighed the drawbacks?

11. Spend a few hours walking or driving around your local community. Do types of chain stores differ according to the residential patterns? Does each neighbourhood have the same stores? Are there economic, social, and ethnic patterns in the neighbourhoods that have the same types of chain stores?

12. Could the organic food movement be a challenge to the intensity of McDonaldization in agriculture and food industry? Is the spread of organic chain stores a demonstration of McDonaldization?

13. McDonaldization theory suggests that the organizational principles that underlie McDonald's are increasingly dominating the entire society. If you have computer access, visit the website of your college and look at the application procedures. How is academic success measured? Examine the importance of nationally standardized tests as indicators of a student's qualifications.

14. Find a copy of the book *1984*, George Orwell's satire of a totalitarian bureaucracy. How do the rationally enacted rules and regulations operate in the depicted monumental state bureaucracy? How does bureaucracy invade privacy in the book? Draw parallels to our contemporary society. How do data mining, electronic records of credit card purchases, surveillance cameras, and new information technologies threaten privacy?

PART II

The McDonaldization of Social Structures and Institutions

Part II begins with Chapter 10, which offers an overview of the McDonaldization of America's police, courts, and corrections. Matthew Robinson describes how the four dimensions of McDonaldization fit all these elements of the legal system. Efficiency is manifest in the police force in the shift from two- to one-person patrol cars, in the courts with the increasing frequency of plea bargaining, and in corrections with the current efforts to expedite executions. In terms of calculability, there is within the police an emphasis on available funds and number of officers on the street; in the courts we find longer sentences and offenders serving a larger proportion of their sentences; and in prisons there is a focus on more prisons, more prisoners, and more executions. Greater predictability is exemplified by police profiling, "going rates," and "three strikes and you're out" in the courtroom, as well as risk classification in the prisons. Finally, increasing control is best exemplified by the new "supermax" prisons. Most distinctive about this essay is its discussion of the irrationality of this seemingly rational process—especially that, in spite of, or perhaps because of, McDonaldization, Americans are less sure of receiving justice from the justice system than they have been in the past.

10

McDonaldization of America's Police, Courts, and Corrections

Matthew B. Robinson

There is no aspect of people's lives that is immune to McDonaldization. This includes crime and criminal justice. To date, there is only one published examination of how crime and criminal justice are McDonaldized.

David Shichor's article, "Three Strikes as a Public Policy: The Convergence of the New Penology and the McDonaldization of Punishment" (1997), demonstrates how the metaphors of getting "tough on crime" and fighting a "war on drugs" have led to penal policies based exclusively on deterrence and incapacitation. These policies have resulted in longer prison sentences, a rapid growth in prison populations, and prison overcrowding. Three-strikes state laws, now in place in more than half of the United States, were meant to increase the *efficiency* of the criminal justice process, were to be based on scientific *prediction* of dangerousness, and were to protect citizens in a *cost-efficient* manner. In fact, the opposite of what was expected has occurred, at least in the state of California, where its three-strikes law is the most widely used among all the states. Billions of dollars have been spent in the application of the state's three-strikes law on relatively minor offenders, courts are

---

Editor's Note: This chapter was revised for this volume from the first and second editions of *McDonaldization: The Reader* (2002, 2006).

backlogged with additional trials, and correctional facilities are overpopulated. Although crime fell, it fell everywhere across the country, in states with three-strikes laws and without. California counties that used the laws more had smaller declines in crime than those counties that used the laws less. Similar to the fast-food industry, "rationalized" methods of delivering products have produced irrational results. California citizens are getting the opposite of what they were promised.

This chapter builds on Shichor's preliminary analysis by linking the trend of McDonaldization to increasingly efficient, scientific, costly, and control-oriented systems of police, courts, and corrections in the United States. Using its basic elements, I illustrate how the McDonaldization of U.S. criminal justice has resulted in irrational criminal justice policy.

Criminal Justice in the United States

The "criminal justice system" is a term that represents the three interdependent components of police, courts, and corrections. There are actually 51 criminal justice systems in the United States, one for each state and one for the federal government. Police agencies are responsible for investigating alleged criminal offenses, apprehending suspected criminal offenders, assisting the prosecution with obtaining criminal convictions at trial, keeping the peace in the community, preventing crime, providing social services, and upholding Constitutional protections. Courts are responsible for determining guilt or innocence of suspected offenders at trial (adjudication), sentencing the legally guilty to some form(s) of punishment, interpreting laws made by legislative bodies, setting legal precedents, and upholding Constitutional protections. Finally, corrections agencies are responsible for carrying out the sentences of the courts by administering punishment and providing care and custody for accused and convicted criminals in line with Constitutional protections.

Although each of these agencies of criminal justice has its own goals, they also share the goals of the larger criminal justice system, which include reducing crime and doing justice. The meaning of reducing crime is clear; doing justice implies both catching, convicting, and punishing criminals *and* assuring that innocent people do not fall victim to wrongful punishment by assuring that individual Constitutional rights are protected.

Our nation's justice systems face a continual balancing act attempting to achieve both forms of justice. The pendulum shifts back and forth between an emphasis on catching, convicting, and punishing criminals and an emphasis on assuring that Constitutional rights of suspected offenders are protected. This chapter demonstrates that the U.S. criminal justice system has become McDonaldized; the result is that U.S. police, courts, and corrections favor the former conception of justice (crime control) at the expense of the latter (due process).

Efficiency and Criminal Justice

The importance of efficiency in America's criminal justice system has always been stressed, but perhaps never in our nation's history as in the past three decades. When systems of criminal justice are more focused on catching, convicting, and punishing criminals than assuring fairness and impartiality, efficiency of the systems becomes the most important value; informal processes are used in place of formal processes to expedite criminal justice operations and to hold a larger proportion of criminals accountable for their criminal acts.

To the degree that cases move through the criminal justice system like an "assembly line," criminal justice practice is much like a fast-food production line. Modern criminal justice practice aims to be efficient, even at the cost of due process rights of defendants. Adherence to efficiency can be seen within each of the components of the justice system, including police, courts, and corrections.

Policing

The increased use of directed and aggressive patrol techniques (aimed at high crime areas), as part of a problem-oriented policing strategy, provides evidence for the emphasis on efficiency in policing. Police occupy certain areas of the city more than others to most efficiently use their resources. The zero-tolerance policing in our nation's largest cities, aimed at eliminating social and physical incivilities (untended people and places) is further evidence of an allegiance to efficiency. These efforts are aimed at doing away with signs of disorder (such as homeless citizens and grafitti) before they lead to major crimes. The fact that directed and aggressive patrol is disproportionately used against the nation's poor (who are disproportionately minorities) and that zero-tolerance policing produces unnecessary use of police force and hostility between inner-city residents and police seems to be irrelevant to most police agencies because the goal of efficient crime control takes precedence.

The shift from two- to one-officer police cars, based on the realization that one-officer cars are just as effective as those occupied by two officers, provides further evidence for the importance of efficiency in policing. Then, there is the growth of technology in policing, from crime analysis and crime mapping, to fingerprinting and computers in squad cars, suggesting that policing is much more focused on proactive strategies than it has been historically. Changes such as these to police practice in the United States are aimed at making policing more efficient at detecting and even preventing crime. For sure, police are discovering more crime, and the use of additional evidence makes it easier to convict alleged criminals. The effect on the other conception of justice, however, is rarely considered by police.

Courts

The popularity of plea bargaining provides strong evidence for the significance of efficiency in U.S. courts. The ideal of U.S. justice is an "adversarial" process, whereby prosecutors and defense attorneys fight for the truth and justice in a contest at trial. Yet, an administrative system is in effect, as evidenced by the substantial use of plea bargaining in courts; these cases are handled informally in hallways and offices rather than in courtrooms. Instead of criminal trials where prosecutors and defense attorneys clash in an effort to determine the truth and do justice for all concerned parties, prosecutors, defense attorneys, and sometimes judges "shop" for "supermarket" justice through plea bargaining. Amazingly, more than 95% of all accused felons plead guilty and waive their right to trial in exchange for lesser sentences.

Criminal trials are now the exception to the rule of plea bargaining. Plea bargaining is an informal process whereby defendants plead guilty to lesser charges in exchange for not taking up the court's valuable time and spending the state's money on trials. In this process, individuals give up their Constitutional rights to cross-examine witnesses, to present a defense, to not incriminate themselves, to testify on their own behalf, and to appeal their convictions, all in exchange for a dismissal or reduction in charges, and/or a lesser sentence. This is an irrational process driven by efficiency as a value, especially given the evidence that some innocent people plead guilty to crimes they did not commit in the face of overwhelming coercion to plead guilty.

The original approval of plea bargaining by the Supreme Court in 1971 was based more on the pragmatic concern that the criminal justice system could not assure every accused criminal his or her Constitutional rights rather than a concern for justice. In other words, plea bargaining achieves only one thing—a more efficient court. Most criminologists and criminal justice scholars view plea bargaining as an unjust process driven by large numbers of caseloads, understaffed courts, and the renewed emphasis on using law enforcement to solve drug use and public order offenses. That is, it does not protect the right of citizens to a criminal trial, nor does it give the guilty what they deserve.

Corrections

A renewed emphasis on efficiency can be found in the increased use of incarceration to achieve incapacitation and deterrence of large numbers of inmates. The United States has shifted its focus away from the treatment of individuals to the handling of aggregates, creating the illusion of a more efficient system of justice. The net of criminal justice is now cast much wider than in previous decades. Increased use of imprisonment is discussed in the following section on calculability. Here, it simply should be noted that a greater use of imprisonment implies to consumers that the criminal justice system will be more efficient in preventing crime because it will prevent criminality by those currently locked up (hence serving the function of incapacitation) and instill fear in those considering committing crimes (hence serving the function of deterrence). In fact, prisons offer little protection from crime, especially in the long run; approximately 90% of inmates will be released. Criminals typically enter prisons uneducated, unskilled, and unemployable. They typically exit the same way, but also angry, bigger physically, stigmatized, and to a large degree, dependent on the government.

Other evidence of increased efficiency in corrections includes legislative efforts to expedite executions by limiting appeals and the elimination of gain time and parole by states and the federal government. In terms of the former issue, speeding up the application of the death penalty is an effort to increase the deterrent effect of the punishment. Convicted murderers on death row will now spend an average of more than 10 years on death row. This has led states to push for expediting the process. Federal law now allows death row inmates only one federal appeal unless new evidence proves clearly and convincingly that the person is innocent. Ironically, the nation's capital punishment machinery is actually less efficient than ever. Whereas more than 100 people nationally are sentenced to death every year, less than 50 are now executed. This is one reason why there are now more than 3,000 people awaiting executions in American prisons. The elimination of gain time and parole (early release from prison) is a major factor contributing to prison overcrowding, which is another irrational result of the supposedly rational criminal justice system. More than a dozen times, federal courts have ordered state correctional facilities to reduce overcrowding or face major fines and withdrawal of federal funding.

Calculability and Criminal Justice

A greater emphasis has been placed on calculability in criminal justice during the past three decades—policymakers seem much more satisfied with *more* criminal justice (quantity) than with *better* criminal justice (quality). Victimless crimes have at virtually all times in our nation's history been criminalized, and we have fought numerous wars on drugs; yet, the most recent such war under Presidents Ronald Reagan, George H. Bush, Bill Clinton, and George W. Bush has stressed much more criminal justice intervention than at any time in our nation's history. As a nation, we have spent hundreds of billions on the war on drugs since 1980; the cost of the drug war increased from more than $1 billion in 1981 to more than $20 billion in 2003. The federal agency responsible for the nation's drug war—the Office of National Drug Control Policy (ONDCP)—changed its budgeting approach in 2003, removing dollars spent on law enforcement and imprisonment for the war on drugs from the budget (even though state governments and the federal government are still spending that money). This miraculously shrunk the size of the drug war budget to "only" $12 billion. Yet, in 2005, there were 250,000 people incarcerated in prisons for drug offenses. At roughly $25,000 per year per inmate, that's more than $6 billion for imprisonment costs caused by the drug war. These costs are no longer part of the budget! Also not included in the drug war budget are dollars spent arresting those in possession of drugs. There were 1.4 million people arrested for drug law violations in 2006; 13% of all arrestes for that year. More than 80% were arrested for mere possession of drugs. The largest portion of drug war funding is intended for domestic law enforcement (policing in the United States) as opposed to treatment and prevention; domestic social programs (such as welfare) have also been cut dramatically to pay for the war on drugs. The largest spending increases between the end of the Clinton presidency and the latest year of the George W. Bush presidency (1996 and 2008) were for international spending and interdiction, whereas prevention and treatment increased less. Research shows that the most effective means of curbing drug abuse is through prevention and treatment; yet, the justice system operates on the dubious premise that if we just do more of what has already proven ineffective, eventually it will work.

Policing

Politicians in the 1990s promised to place "100,000 *more* cops on the street." In September 1994, President Clinton signed the Violent Crime Control and Law Enforcement Act; the stated purpose of which was "to prevent crime, punish criminals, and restore a sense of safety and security to the American people." This law allowed for the hiring of 100,000 new police, the construction of thousands of new prison cells, and the expansion of the death penalty to dozens of additional types of murders. Assuming that we ever achieve the goal of 100,000 more police, there will never actually be anything close to 100,000 more police on the streets *at one time*. It takes at least five additional officers to provide one additional officer on the street around the clock because of varied shifts, vacations, illnesses, and so forth. An additional 100,000 new police officers would only account for 20,000 additional officers around the clock. An additional 100,000 police on the street would increase the ratio of police officers to citizens from 2.7 per 1,000 citizens to 3.1 per 1,000 citizens. This largely symbolic promise was aimed at little more than appealing to Americans' allegiance to calculability, a value promoted by the fast-food industry. In other words, citizens will not actually be safer, even though they may intuitively be satisfied with the government for trying.

We also see calculability in asset forfeitures in the nation's drug war. The reward for police is being allowed to confiscate and keep some drug-related assets. To some degree, law enforcement officials have come to rely on drug assets to purchase equipment and conduct training so that police can exterminate drug use. The majority of law enforcement agencies in the United States have asset forfeiture programs in place. Federal agencies seize hundreds of millions in cash and property annually. The irony of police using drug assets to fight drug use is lost on taxpayers, who are the primary criminal justice consumers.

Courts

Longer sentences have been put in place for virtually all crimes, which is indicative of calculability because citizens have been sold on the idea that more punishment is better. It is also evident in laws that require offenders to serve greater portions of their sentences—the so-called "truth in sentencing" laws. A truth in sentencing law was first enacted in 1984, the same year that parole eligibility and good-time credits were restricted or eliminated. Approximately 30 states and the District of Columbia met the Federal Truth-in-Sentencing Incentive Grants program eligibility criteria. Eleven states adopted truth in sentencing laws in 1995, one year after funding was established by Congress. Incentive grants were awarded by the federal government to 27 states and the District of Columbia, and another 13 states adopted a truth in sentencing law requiring some offenders (usually violent offenders) to serve a specific percentage of their sentence.

Corrections

Calculability means building *more* prisons, sending *more* people to prison, and sending *more* people to their deaths through capital punishment. The imprisonment rate in the United States has historically been relatively constant. It has fluctuated over the years, but never until the 1970s did it consistently and dramatically increase. In fact, scholars had written about the "stability of punishment" because there was so little fluctuation in the nation's incarceration rate for so long. Beginning in 1973, the United States began an imprisonment boom unprecdented in our nation's history.

Since the early 1970s, there has been approximately a 6% increase each year in imprisonment, although this has slowed in the 21st century. In the 1990s, the growth in imprisonment was between 3% and 9% every year; this fell to 2% each year between 2000 and 2005. Approximately half of the increases have occurred because of violent criminal incarceration, and much of the remainder is because of drug incarcerations; from 1980 to 1993, the percentage of prisoners in state prisons serving sentences for drug offenses more than tripled and in federal prisons more than doubled. By 2005, 20% of all incarcerated people were locked up for drug crimes. The United States now has more than twice the rate of prisoners per 100,000 citizens as any other democracy, and more than 5 times the rate of democracies such as Canada, England, Germany, and France. Even though the United States has only 5% of the world's population, it boasts nearly 25% of the world's prisoners.

The ironic fact remains, however, that drug use trends have largely been unaffected since 1988, and drug abuse levels have actually increased. Crime rates have fallen, but 75% of the declines have been due to factors outside of criminal justice, such as an aging population, economic improvements, legalized abortions, and so forth. An increased commitment to calculability— more criminal justice—has not resulted in substantial reductions in crime rates or drug use and abuse.

Predictability and Criminal Justice

If one were to assess fairly the performance of our nation's criminal justice system in terms of crime control over the past century, one could conclude that there is little likelihood of being subjected to it; that is, the most predictable thing about it has been its futility. Even today, the chance of being apprehended, convicted, and sentenced to imprisonment is highly unlikely for all crimes other than murder.

The criminal justice system operates on the assumption that catching, convicting, and punishing criminals serves as a deterrent to crime (it causes fear in people, and thus they do not commit crimes). The most important factor in the effectiveness of deterrence is the certainty of punishment, that is, the likelihood of being punished. Research on deterrence has consistently found that the severity of a sentence has less of a deterrent effect than sentence certainty. United States criminal justice performs poorly in providing certain, swift punishments that outweigh the potential benefits of committing crimes. For every 100 serious street crimes (as measured in the National Crime Victimization Survey), about 40%, or 40, are known to the police (as measured in the Uniform Crime Reports). Of these 40, only one-fourth (approximately 10) will lead to an arrest. Of these 10, some will not be prosecuted, and others will not be convicted. Only about 3% of the original 100 serious street crimes will lead to an incarceration.

Putting more cops on the street and increasing the use of prison sentences are efforts to make criminal justice outcomes more predictable. Yet, these efforts do not result in crime prevention. The criminal justice system will never know about most crime unless we put a police officer on every street corner in the United States and give police greater freedom to investigate alleged crimes. As long as Americans desire freedom from an overzealous government and value their Constitutional protections, the criminal justice system will largely be a failure.

Policing

Police officers now attempt to apprehend suspects by using offender profiling methods, which allow them to develop a picture of the offender based on elements of his or her crime. The scientific method has always been a part of modem policing, at least since the 1830s under Sir Robert Peel in England. Only in the past two decades, however, has offender profiling been used by police. The aims of this are to increase the accuracy of predictions about who committed crimes based on the characteristics of the crime scenes left behind by offenders.

Police also try to accurately predict who is likely to get into trouble with the law before they commit criminal acts. They focus on particular types of people because of their own personal experience or that of their institution and profession, which suggests that certain people are more likely to violate the law. This practice, known as "police profiling," results in startling disparities in police behavior based on class and race. Police use "extralegal" factors such as race, ethnicity, gender, and so forth, as a proxy for risk. This is supported by courts as legitimate when extralegal factors are used in conjunction with some legal factor. For example, courts have stated that as long as the totality of the circumstances warrants the conclusion of the officer that the subject was acting suspiciously, race can be part of the circumstances considered by the officer. So, an African American male driving the speed limit on a major highway would be suspicious, not just because of the man's skin color, but because no one drives the speed limit on a major highway. In this scenario, police officers may suspect the man of transporting drugs. These elements of predictability in policing lead to difficulties in police–minority interactions, disproportionate use of force against people of color, and disrespect for the law generally. Studies in dozens of states as well as national data collected by the Bureau of Justice Statistics now show police profiling to be a reality.

Courts

Courts in the United States are highly predictable in much of what they do. The main actors in this process within the criminal courts—the prosecutor, the defense attorney, and the judge—enter the courtroom daily knowing essentially what will happen each day. The courtroom workgroup is made up of this collective of individuals who interact, share goals, follow court norms, and develop interpersonal relationships. This concept is important because it helps us understand why their overriding concern is speeding up the process and finishing cases as efficiently as possible, often to the detriment of doing justice. It also helps us understand how legal issues can be predictably resolved. Ideally, members of the courtroom workgroup play their own roles and have their own goals; in reality, each member's main job is not to rock the boat in the daily operations of U.S. courts.

Because of the strong interpersonal relationships among workgroup members, *going rates* are established in bail and sentencing. The process of plea bargaining, discussed earlier, serves as an excellent example. In studies of plea bargaining, cases are disposed of with great regularity and predictability meaning that the resulting sentence is reliably predicted based on the nature of the charges and the defendant's prior record. A going rate is established for particular types of crimes committed by particular types of people, one which becomes established over time and which is learned by each member of the courtroom workgroup. Plea bargains typically closely parallel this going rate, and defendants charged with particular crimes can easily learn what sentence they are likely to face if they plead guilty.

At the sentencing phase in the courts, criminal penalties are highly predictable. Generally, the most important factors include the seriousness of the offense and the offender's prior record, so that the more serious the offense and the longer the prior record, the more severe the sentence will be. Mandatory sentences now establish a minimum sanction that must be served on a conviction for a criminal offense. Thus, everyone who is convicted for a crime that calls for a mandatory sentence will serve that amount of time. Indeterminate sentences that allowed parole and determinate prison sentences that could be reduced by good-time or earned-time credits have been replaced by mandatory sentences across the country. Furthermore, sentencing guidelines have been established to make sentences more predictable and scientifically based on a set of criteria including prior record, offense seriousness, and previous interactions with the justice system. Sentencing grids reduce the discretion of judges and thus shift power to government prosecutors. The sentencing guidelines that produce such predictable sentences at the federal level were recently struck down the United States Supreme Court. So far, nothing has been created to replace them, meaning sentencing at the federal level may become more disparate based on factors such as race, class, and gender of offender.

The best example of mandatory sentences are the three-strikes laws, discussed earlier, which are in effect in more than half of our states. The logic of three-strikes laws is to increase penalties of second offenses and to require life imprisonment without possibility of parole for third offenses. These laws usually do not allow sentencing courts to consider particular circumstances of a crime, the duration of time that has elapsed between crimes, and mitigating factors in the background of offenders. The offender's potential for rehabilitation, ties to community, employment status, and obligations to children are also not taken into account. In other words, sentencing laws aimed at increasing predictability end up also producing illogical sentencing practices. A large share of people sentenced under three-strikes laws are actually very minor offenders who have created little harm to society; yet, each will be incarcerated in a prison at a cost of approximately $30,000 per inmate per year.

Corrections

Risk classification in corrections entails a great degree of prediction, as well. Individuals convicted of crimes can be put on probation, incarcerated in jail or prison, or subjected to some intermediate sanction; one's punishment is determined largely by offense seriousness, prior record, and behavior during previous criminal justice interventions. Each form of punishment entails more or less supervision, fewer or greater rules to follow (e.g., probation versus intensive supervision probation), and/or greater restrictions on movement and activities (e.g., minimum versus maximum security). The most violent and/or unmanageable inmates are now placed in isolation or incarcerated for 23 hours of the day in super-maximum security (supermax) prisons. These issues are discussed in the section on control that follows.

Control and Criminal Justice

In the past three decades, the United States has witnessed a rapid expansion of criminal justice, an expansion that is driven not by facts about crime or increasing crime rates but instead by politics, fear, and an increasingly punitive attitude about crime and toward criminals. This expansion is literally unparalleled in history; yet corresponding decreases in crime have not been achieved. Indeed, street crime decreased throughout the 1990s, but only about one-quarter of this decrease is attributable to imprisonment.

Policing

Under the guise of the war on crime and the war on drugs (and now the war on terrorism), U.S. police have been freed to gather and use much more evidence against suspects to obtain criminal convictions in court. For example, police are empowered to stop, detain, and question people who fit the "profile" of drug couriers in airports, even without probable cause. They are permitted to use dogs to search travelers' luggage without probable cause. Police are entitled to stop motorists without probable cause and to conduct searches of automobiles without a warrant. They are permitted to obtain warrants based on informants' tips. Police enjoy the "good-faith exception" that allows courts to use evidence obtained in error by the police as long as police erred in good faith. Police also can claim exigent circumstances to justify gathering and using unlawful evidence, including evidence that was in their plain view or within reach.

Also, police can seize a person's property through asset forfeiture programs based on suspicion of drug activity. The burden of proof falls on the accused to prove that he or she is not involved in the drug trade; even when this is accomplished, the government can keep up to 30% of the property for administrative purposes. All of this is inconsistent with the presumption of innocence and due process, as well as at least one conception of justice defined earlier. More importantly, these changes in the law enlarge the net of control cast on citizens of the United States.

The USA PATRIOT Act, passed by Congress in the wake of the terrorist attacks of September 11th, 2001, allows police the right to access medical, financial, library, educational, and other personal records of any people as long as a significant purpose is for the gathering of foreign intelligence and to forbid librarians and business owners and employees from informing people that their records have been requested or seized. Government agents can request warrants from the top secret Foreign

Intelligence Surveillance Court in New York City to collect evidence even in the case of non-terrorism criminal matters, without probable cause of criminal activity, as long as the government swears it is collecting vital foreign intelligence information as part of the investigation. According to a report by the United States Justice Department, the USA PATRIOT Act has been used across the nation for normal criminal matters totally unrelated to terrorism. The USA PATRIOT Act also allows government agents to tap any and all phones of citizens and monitor their Internet use, tracking every phone call made and received and every web site visited. Under orders from the Justice Department, police can also enter people's homes and seize their property without even informing them a search has taken place (through "sneak and peak warrants"). Further, law enforcement agencies are empowered to spy on religious and political organizations and individuals without any evidence of criminal activity.

Courts

As noted earlier, these changes in policing abilities are largely because of court decisions. The federal judiciary and the Supreme Court in particular have become more firmly entrenched in crime control values rather than due process values. That is, judges nominated by conservative presidents and appointed by conservative senators have, during the past three decades, eroded many of the gains for U.S. civil liberties won during the Warren Supreme Court of the 1960s. They have done so, at least in theory, to make it easier for the criminal justice system to exert control over criminals.

The Rehnquist Court was the least likely Court in the past four decades to decide cases in favor of individual defendants and most likely to decide cases in favor of state governments, respectively. The Rehnquist Court was associated, at least in part, with the strongly conservative nature of the Chief Justice himself. For example, Rehnquist's successful efforts to limit federal habeas corpus appeals stemmed from his disgust over what he saw as abuses of such appeals by criminal defendants during his career as a lawyer and judge.

Since the 1980s and especially in the 1990s, the federal government has exerted more and more influence over state and local governments when it comes to crime control efforts. As a result, federal courts are empowered to restrict the rights of criminal defendants and to broaden the power of crime control agencies, thereby increasing the power of the government and the amount of control it has over the lives of citizens. And this is exactly what they have done, especially in matters related to law enforcement powers in the wars on crime and drugs.

Corrections

In the 1970s, 1980s, and 1990s, state spending for correctional budgets dramatically increased but fell for non-Medicare welfare, highways, and higher education. These figures are evidence of increased control efforts by the criminal justice system. They are also criticized for being a disinvestment in the nation's future. Funding in the first decade of the 21st century continued to grow, even as states faced the promise of long-term budget deficits due to the economic downturn in the United States.

The clearest control issue in criminal justice revolves around corrections. Correctional facilities are now state of the art in terms of their use of technology to manage inmates. Increased use of other technologies include electronic monitoring of offenders under house arrest.

The so-called supermax prisons are the epitome of control. Offenders in supermax prisons have restricted contact with other inmates and with correctional personnel. Many inmates are locked in their cells for most of the day. The stark cells have white walls and bright lights on at all hours of the day and night. Front doors are completely closed, and there are no windows. Examples of supermax facilities include Marion (Illinois) and Pelican Bay (California). In such prisons, prisoners are confined to their cells for 23 hours per day and can only take showers 2 to 3 times per week. When inmates are transferred, they are shackled in hand cuffs and sometimes leg irons. Temperatures inside these facilities consistently register in the 80s and 90s.

The supermax facility gives us another interesting parallel between criminal justice and the fast-food industry. Technically, nothing can be *more* maximum than "maximum" custody, yet now we have supermax custody. In fast food, french fries used to come in small, medium, and large. Now they come in medium, large, and extra large: The extra-large sizes are "supersized," "biggie sized," and even "super supersized" and "great biggie sized." French fries provide the fast-food industry top profit margins. The McDonaldized fast-food industry tricks consumers into paying very high prices for a very small portion of potato using deceptive terms such as those just mentioned to convince consumers they are getting a good deal; the McDonaldized criminal justice system creates the illusion through the term "supermax custody" that these institutions keep Americans safe. In fact, most supermax inmates will one day be released into society, having to readjust to living with other people. And the costs to taxpayers just to build such facilities can be more than $130,000 per inmate.

Despite a rallying cry against big government, the nation's federal government controls states by mandating certain criminal justice activities for funding. It assures control over state efforts to reduce crime by promising billions of dollars to states that follow its lead. Two examples include allocating prison funds to states that require offenders to serve at least 85% of their sentences and encouraging states to try juveniles as adults. States agree to engage in such criminal justice practices so that they will not lose resources from the federal government. Hence, criminal justice policy at the state level flows less from its potential efficacy than from the state's financial concerns. The politicization of crime at the national level has created this paradox, another irrationality of U.S. criminal justice.

Control in criminal justice affects not only those subjected to policing and criminal penalties, but also has great effects on those who work within the nation's criminal justice system, including police, members of the courtroom workgroup, probation and parole officers, and personnel inside our nation's correctional facilities. Much like workers in the fast-food industry, workers in criminal justice agencies are trained *not* to think and question but to simply operate in a preordained way. Police officers act in ways consistent with the values of their subculture, members of the courtroom workgroup act in ways consistent with the norms of the court, and courtroom personnel, correctional officers, and parole and probation officers are constrained by large numbers of caseloads. This is McDonaldization at its finest. In the fast-food industry, workers have been de-skilled to the point of absurdity in an effort to produce a consistent, predictable product and to minimize the likelihood of employee error. Many of the jobs in criminal justice are also requiring fewer and fewer critical-thinking skills.

Conclusion

This chapter specified some of the relationships between McDonaldization and the U.S. systems of police, courts, and corrections. From the analysis presented, it is clear that our criminal justice system has fallen victim to McDonaldization and its basic dimensions. Given the frequency of exposure to our nation's fast-food establishments, Americans have probably come to expect these qualities from many institutions and services other than fast-food restaurants. Americans now expect easy solutions to complex problems such as crime. This makes it easier for politicians to tout and sell fast and easy solutions to the nation's crime problem.

Unfortunately, as U.S. police, courts, and corrections have become McDonaldized, irrational policies have resulted. That is the major point of this chapter: The criminal justice system, much like the fast-food industry, has rationalized, but in the process has delivered something entirely different;

because of its increased devotion to the values of McDonaldization—efficiency, calculability, predictability, and control—irrational policies have developed out of a rationalized system of criminal justice. Americans are now less sure of receiving justice from their justice systems. This is true even though we have created *more* criminal justice today, even though we have made criminal justice practice *more* predictable, and even though Americans may now believe they are safer because of *more* control over criminals exerted by the government.

Thinking Critically

1. What are the advantages of McDonaldizing the police, courts, and corrections?

2. What are the disadvantages of McDonaldizing the police, courts, and corrections?

3. If you could choose one of these to McDonaldize, which one would it be? Why?

4. If you could choose one of these that it would be a bad idea to McDonaldize, which one would it be? Why?

5. Is U.S. criminal justice better or worse off because of McDonaldization?

The reading (Chapter 11) "McDonaldization of the Sex Industries?" by Kathryn Hausbeck and Barbara Brents does an excellent job of taking all the dimensions of McDonaldization and applying them in a very systematic manner to the sex industry. One of the distinctive characteristics of this essay is the discussion of resistance to each of these dimensions by sex workers, customers, owners, and the sex industry itself. However, there is far greater acquiescence than resistance in this realm and most other areas of the social world.

Like many other commodities, sex has been McDonaldized. There is something unique and particularly disturbing, however, about the infiltration of this process into this area of our lives. While the McDonaldization of public aspects of our lives is disturbing enough, when it affects this most private, mysterious, and intimate of realms, it seems particularly troubling. Nevertheless, we have witnessed the rationalization and bureaucratization of sex even though it seems particularly intrusive and injects sterility into something that is supposed to be anything but sterile. The authors close this essay by relating their argument to that of Weber: "It also threatens to entrap us in Weber's fearsome iron cage: coldly colonizing our imaginations and brushing up against our skins." This image of McDonaldized systems touching us physically, and even entering and controlling our consciousness, brings concerns over McDonaldization to a whole new level.

11

McDonaldization of the Sex Industries?

The Business of Sex

Kathryn Hausbeck and Barbara G. Brents

Taken together the topless or nude dance clubs, adult bookstores, adult movies, digital content for cell phones and other mobile devices, online sex in all its forms, sex toys, adult magazines, adult comics, erotic trading cards, adult pay per view TV, dungeons, phone sex services, escort services, street prostitution, and legalized brothel prostitution constitute a huge and burgeoning sex industry in the United States. . . .

Does this expansion of the sex industry reflect the same pattern of rationalization and McDonaldization that characterizes other rapidly growing segments of the service economy?

Dimensions of McDonaldization: Putting the Sex Industry to the Test

We will explain each of the four dimensions of McDonaldization, consider the ways in which various parts of the sex industry are acquiescing to

Editor's Note: Excerpts (revised) from Hausbeck, K., & Brents, B., *McDonaldization of the Sex Industries? The Business of Sex,* copyright © 2002, McGraw Hill. Reproduced with permission of The McGraw Hill Companies.

rationalization; discuss how this process affects owners, workers, and customers; and then examine the ways in which other parts of the adult industry continue to resist these trends.

Efficiency: Rule #1 for Fast-Food Sex

. . . In the sex industry, consumer desire for easy access and fast choices requires sexual relations to be compartmentalized into efficient units of consumption. This way of being sexual results in commodified and often superficial interactions. Further, where sex is defined as simply experiencing an orgasm, it is reduced to a mechanistic act in which the most efficient means to achieve the desired goal of climax is the most rational. This is the Taylorization of sex. Sexual efficiency becomes commercially defined human sexuality, disconnected from human spirituality or long-term emotional connection between participants. It is this version of sexuality that is marketed and sold in McDonaldized aspects of the adult industry.

Acquiescence: Owners

The legal brothels in Nevada are organized so that, for men, obtaining sex is much more efficient than typical ways of meeting and negotiating sex with potential female partners. A customer entering most Nevada brothels will generally ring a doorbell, and by the time the customer gets inside and is greeted by the manager, the working women are lined up and waiting for the customer to choose among them. This "line-up" demands that women stand in a prescribed manner (no special posing, no gestures, no sales pitches allowed!) while each makes a brief introduction. In some brothels, the manager usually encourages the customer to make a choice quickly, so as not to waste anyone's time. Most brothels and workers have hand-designed or printed menus (designed to look like restaurant menus) listing available services, though the customer will have to go to the prostitute's room to actually negotiate prices and services. Typically, a deal is struck between the brothel worker and client that specifies the acts, the amount of time allocated for completion, and the cost of the transaction. The customer pays prior to service, the brothel worker takes payment to the manager who then sets a timer to keep track of the length of the exchange. When the time that was paid for is up, a manager will knock on the prostitute's door and advise her to end the transaction, or "renegotiate" for more money and more time. Efficiency dominates in this world of timed intimacy; both owner and prostitute benefit from this rationalized model of sexual exchange.

Acquiescence: Workers

For the workers, on the one hand, efficiency can mean streamlining inter-actions with clients while maximizing earnings and tips. On the other hand, efficiency can result in de-skilling and rationalizing workers in a manner that alienates them from their own labors and that may result in lower earnings and tips.

A good example of the former trend has emerged in the erotic dance business. In the typical gentlemen's club, dancers performances are timed to the length of a song, usually three minutes. Each dancer does a two-song set on a central stage for tips. They then work the floor to entice customers to pur-chase lap dances. Lap dances provide individual customers more intimate, erotic performances bounded by the length of a song for a set fee. In clubs that accept customer requests, dancers complain about customers who will request a lengthy song, in the hopes of making their dancing dollar stretch.

On the other hand, workplaces that are organized around efficiency can de-skill workers and result in alienation. A good example is the phone sex industry. Here, many companies have "scripts" or guides that direct the phone sex worker to say certain things in particular ways in order to gener-ate the highest fees from the customer. While this is an efficient business move, it curtails the creativity of employees and reduces the interaction between phone sex workers and clients to formulaic and scripted encounters.

Acquiescence: Customers

The sex industry has grown the most where it breaks sexual pleasures down to their most basic, easily packaged, mass-produced components, allowing maximum profitability while offering the customer easy access to goods and services, quick and convenient choices, and hassle-free exit from the encounter. This trend is seen regardless of whether we are talking about a client in a brothel, a customer in a strip club, or a shopper in an adult store.

Technology has been absolutely critical in the growth of the sex industry. The implications of technology can be seen in all four areas of McDonaldization. Technology has developed in ways that has met con-sumers' demands for efficiency at the same time as owner demands for prof-its. Consumers' calls to escort services are routed from a centralized telephone operator to workers via cell phones. This allows the escort or dancer to get to the customer as quickly as possible. This also allows own-ers to advertise speedy delivery of the dancer, sometimes claiming that she will be at your door in less than 30 minutes—quicker than take-out Thai food! The advent of home video technology in the 1980s produced porn "to go." For consumers, public adult movie theaters of the 1970s were replaced by the easy and cheap availability of a wide variety of adult films on video, to be viewed in the privacy and convenience of their own homes. Now a wide array of adult digital content is beamed to handheld mobile devices as well as to home computers.

Perhaps the most efficiently organized arena of the sex industry has come through the growth of Internet. The range of sexual content and variety of means of distribution seems bounded only by the imagination. Digital content can be directed immediately wherever a consumer wants it, a home computer, a cell phone, an iPod—efficiency in accessibility, affordability, and anonymity. It began with the efficiency of being able to meet, screen, date, and have virtual sex with individuals in online chat rooms without leaving their home. Now customers can pay for real-time individual performers to appear on their computer screen and respond immediately to their sexual requests. Consumers can download almost any adult movie they want and can even select and pay for only the scenes they want. Digital content is highly efficient to distribute for business owners. From large web portals that simply amass access to pre-existing content to individuals who produce porn from web cams in their homes, setting up a business can be considerably cheaper and more efficient than a brick and mortar building. This is why efficiency is the dominant operating principle in much of the sex industry: It creates a market of consumers for the products and offers services for sale that are quick, safe, convenient, and increasingly profitable.

Resistance

The sex industry is a service industry that involves, even more than other aspects of the service industry, emotional labor. Emotional labor has an interesting and contradictory relation to McDonaldization. At the same time as the industry moves to rationalize, package, make efficient, quantify, and control the emotions surrounding sex and sexuality, the very nature of emotions breeds a resistance to McDonaldization. Both customers and service providers have resisted the reduction of sexual pleasure to a Taylorized assembly line. They avoid sexual fantasy and desire that is so efficient that it becomes sterile, unexciting, and cold. A German visitor to Atlanta's gentlemen's clubs commented, "For Europeans . . . it has the sex appeal of a dishwasher." Similarly, many American consumers want more from their sex industry purchase than simply a quick and convenient exchange. It is common for sex workers to report that customers want at least the appearance of intimacy, or the simulation of closeness and affection during the exchange, and many customers are willing to pay more to get it. Customers, on the one hand, seek ease in attaining this intimacy. But customers also value seemingly authentic listening, flirting, complimenting, and feigning pleasure as important parts of the fantasy world of the sex industry. While these affective and emotive interactions are commodified for sale, they simultaneously resist easy reduction to purely efficient profit-driven exchange.

To make the sex industry fully efficient means dissolving the veil of fantasy that is a critical component of the adult industry. For example, it would be much cheaper for adult magazines to do what the advertising industry is increasingly doing and replace expensive models with flawless computer-generated men and women. However, this would obliterate the fantasy of seeing a real person with a "real" story to tell, thus making the possibility for "really" having sex with her or him impossible. This would not sell subscriptions. Indeed, a growing component of the adult film and magazine industry is content that presents "real" people, having "really spontaneous" sex. Indeed, Tristan Taoramino's film, *Chemistry*, was awarded the Adult Video Network's Best Gonzo Release. The film was about a group of porn stars living together for 36 hours having spontaneous and seemingly authentic sex.

It is the legal business of selling intercourse itself that has most strongly resisted the trend toward efficiency. In Nevada's legal brothels, too much formalized interaction (i.e., being assigned a number and a prostitute, having predesignated packages of services with fixed prices that set strict limits on the physical contact and interaction, etc.) and the resulting efficiency is unlikely to either generate new customers or encourage repeat business. While a "line-up" allows for fast and efficient choice of sexual partners, most brothels will allow men to bypass the line-up and have a drink at the bar. Some customers make a choice from the women who mingle with him at the bar. But a person can also simply have a drink and leave. Indeed, many brothels are moving toward creating an even less rationalized singles bar, party atmosphere in the bar area to draw higher paying customers. Prices and services are still individually negotiated between customer and prostitute. None of these options is very efficient from the perspective of owners. Probably the most significant resistance to efficiency in the brothel is the fact that there are no standardized ways of performing sexual acts. While some women claim to know efficient ways to bring a man to climax in a set period of time, these procedures have not been standardized or systematized. There is still no assembly-line approach to the provision of sex; all the "tricks of the trade" that prostitutes report using to encourage an efficient sexual encounter still require customization to the particular needs, desires, and physiological capacities of each client.

Resistance to efficiency also comes in the organization of the sex industry. The fastest growth within the sex industry is coming from an expansion of the larger, more rationally organized, corporate businesses, and in these we see the best examples of McDonaldization. The exotic-dancing industry is probably the best example of this trend. Chain-like businesses are increasingly visible in gentlemen's clubs. But the industry still remains very fragmented. . . . The largest number of strip clubs, as is the case in other segments of the sex industry, are small, independently owned, and run as they have always been run by entrepreneurs who dared to oppose society's sexual norms. As a result, these businesses are not highly rationalized; there are no standard wages, skills, training, or workplace rules. Only the largest adult businesses have developed enough staff, capital investment, legal security, or customers to maximize efficiency through a fully rationalized organization. So, while the fastest growing sectors of the adult industry may appear to be acquiescing to efficiency—customers getting more convenient ways to purchase sexual products and services, and workers experiencing more standardization—the bulk of the industry resists the trend toward corporate efficiency.

Ironically, too much efficiency threatens to become inefficient in the adult industry: For customers, efficiency emphasizes outcomes over process, which can be alienating; for workers, efficiency can limit employee autonomy and alienate employees from their own embodied labors; and for owners, too much efficiency either in the rationalization of workers or in the rationalization of services to clients can easily result in the destruction of the very desires that sustain their profitability. There is a fine line between too little and too much efficiency when it comes to rationalizing sexual exchanges.

Predictability: Standardizing Sexuality and Desiring the Familiar

. . . The complexities of sexual desire are reduced to marketable commodities in the commercial arena of public life. There is an implied predictability inasmuch as only sexual desires that are recognizable and able to be reproduced are available for mass production. For business owners, mass production makes replication possible, desirable, and profitable. For consumers, there is safety and comfort in knowing what to expect around every corner: each burger tasting like the last, each hotel room looking like the last, each experience feeling like the last.

Acquiescence: Owners

Owners of adult businesses benefit from predictability in their industry in two ways. First, cultivating a desire for predictable interactions in their clientele allows owners to mass-produce sexual goods and services using a formulaic approach to commercializing sexuality, significantly increasing profits. Diversity, unpredictability, unique sexual products and services are more expensive, resource-intensive, and difficult to generate and sell. This is why in much of the industry the sexuality that is for sale is heterosexual sexuality dominated by traditional gender roles and hegemonic notions of beauty. Second, to the extent that predictability requires conformity and standardization, owners may use formal models for the production of their services by routinizing their employees, their business practices, and, to the extent the market will allow, their interactions with clients. As we have shown, owners have difficulty reducing all interactions to assembly-line efficiency, but many at times do conform to a predictable set of repertoires. This reinforces corporate efficiency and streamlines business through its simplified predictability.

Owners can capitalize on this predictability as well in the organization of business. While not a trend that has hit all parts of the sex industry, the more chain-like gentlemen's clubs have begun to share some management functions, manager training, and legal advice. The advantage is in making some of the unpredictabilities of the market disappear.

Acquiescence: Workers

The requirement of predictability offers guidelines for the behavior and appearance of sex workers, which can be liberating to the extent that formalized scripts require less personal innovation and investment; but it also can stifle creativity, individual choice, and style among laborers in the adult industry. For example, in adult film, there is a language of pleasure and desire scripted into the plot line (however simplistic it may be), encoded in the camera angles, and reinforced by the soundtracks. Certain facial expressions, close-up shots, and noises are blended to give the viewing audience a sense of the intensity of the sexual encounter, as well as a sense of what is "really" desirable, exciting, and clear evidence of pleasure. While this formula may reveal itself to savvy viewers as simplistic, even a caricature, the repetitious nature of American pornography attests to the application of a tested and marketable model of sexual intimacy that is produced with only slight variations for consumption by the mass viewing public.

So, too, with strip clubs: While the decor, the clientele, the bodies and attire of the dancers, and the norms of the establishment may differ, the basic formula for the interaction between dancer and client is predictable. Sexuality in strip clubs is constructed through a subtle but repetitive series of moves, gestures, interactions, and props. Sexy clothing that is removed to the rhythm of loud music, gyrating hips, seductive flirtations with customers which reveal enough flesh to entice, but not enough to satisfy without the client offering more money, are all part of the commercial construction and sale of sexual fantasy in dimly lit strip clubs throughout the sex industry.

The more we, as a society, become accustomed to affordable, mass-produced products, the more consumers desire the predictable. As pornographic magazines, adult videos, and the Internet mass-produce images, a model's physical appearance becomes predictable. Women and men working as dancers, models, or actors must conform to cultural norms of stereotypical beauty. They must be of a particular size, within a range of predictable hair colors, makeup, and body dimensions. Reconstructive surgery increases the uniformity and predictability of body types, and what the actual body may lack in uniformity, computer enhancement can add.

Acquiescence: Customers

The sex industry has grown where it has provided consumers the comfort of predictability in an industry that is often associated with the exotic and unexpected. "Adult superstores" seek mainstream customers by mimicking the predictable look of a Blockbuster or Kmart. The Hustler Hollywood chain sells sex toys, DVDs, and magazines in brightly lit storefronts that resemble mainstream clothing or book stores. Upscale gentlemen's clubs—dark, smoky rooms with neon or strobe lights, loud throbbing music, small tables, and couches with bars around the perimeter—also design their spaces to be predictable. The chain-like gentlemen's clubs are opening with uniform slogans, similar or at least recognizable names, the result being that a customer can go to a Deja Vu strip club in Atlanta and trust it will be as familiar as the one in Nashville or Las Vegas. The comfort of a friendly woman taking money at the door and large male bouncers roaming the crowd exudes an aura of predictable safety from any uncontrollable libidinal urges or jealous tempers.

Nevada's legal brothel industry, while in many ways resisting total predictability, has grown to the extent that it can provide consumers with legal sexual services that in important ways are the same from house to house and relatively unchanging over time. Women working in brothels are required by Nevada state law to be disease-free before beginning a shift at the brothel. They are checked for gonorrhea and chlamydia once a week and for HIV and syphilis once a month. Condoms are always required. The "guarantee" that a brothel will provide clean, disease-free women has been important in the continued existence of the legal brothel industry in Nevada. The resulting predictability has opened the brothel industry to a wide range of customers who might otherwise be frightened away from purchasing sex because of the potential for contracting sexually transmitted diseases.

Resistance

Again, the majority of adult businesses are small independent businesses, and they resist predictability just as much as they resist efficiency. Even in upscale gentlemen's strip clubs there are no uniforms, no scripts for dancers, and the rules of the house vary greatly. Regulations and zoning ordinances that have a huge impact on the development of the sex industries vary from one locale to the other, so it is difficult to ensure predictability of location or legal parameters governing adult industry interactions between geographic regions. And again, because both customers and services resist rationalizing all aspects of human interaction, there is wide variability in what dancers, prostitutes, and performers will do to fulfill sexual fantasies. There is a market value for at least the illusion of unpredictable and "special" sexual encounters.

The bottom line is that a certain amount of predictability in the presentation and purchase of sexual goods and services seems to be necessary to increase consumer comfort and participation in the adult industry, at the same time too much predictability diminishes the unique and private expression of sexuality. Moreover, perfect predictability seems to take away the very things that customers crave so much—personal attention, some element of surprise, exotic settings, and personally erotic situations.

Control: Robotic Sexuality?

Acquiescence: Owners

As we described above, little has done more to facilitate the growth of the sex industry than technology. Technology has been developed not only to increase efficiency for consumers but also to increase owners' control over the work environment in a way that increases profits. Technology has been harnessed to help frame, monitor, and limit both the work environment and the provision of sexual services. Automatic screens in peep shows strictly control how much a customer gets to see. Security systems watch and record everything in gentlemen's clubs. Even the simplest technology of a kitchen timer regulates the customer's time with prostitutes in brothels, ensuring both safety and profitability.

Reliance on technology allows business owners to control the sexual exchange in ways that are increasingly reducing the need for physical human interaction. From phone sex businesses, to virtual sex in video chat rooms, to mobile online pornography, business owners can provide a wide range of sexual services to customers without their ever leaving their homes or touching another human body. Digital technology means owners can record and replay workers, thus reducing the need for actual live temperamental bodies or workers. Distributing sexual services digitally means more exchanges can be sold using less labor. Surveillance equipment allows owners to monitor workers more closely, thus ensuring their compliance with work rules as well as adherence to legal regulations. Violation of local regulations can be very dangerous and expensive for owners who legally have to defend themselves to protect their business interests.

Acquiescence: Workers

Medical technology, especially reconstructive surgery, has allowed workers to extend control over the body itself. Diversity in women's bodies can be reigned in—fat cut off here, implants added there, scars removed, makeup permanently added. Women's performing bodies literally become cyborg-like machines, carefully crafted for a particular look, with interchangeable parts. Success for dancers in the gentlemen's clubs, on the Internet, or in pornographic videos demands rigid control over the appearance of bodies, as well as over workers' labors.

Technological control in the sex industry reaches beyond the cyborgian reconstruction of bodies to simulate mass-produced images of beauty into the control of workers' time, movements, and interactions. Strip club dancers are surveilled by remote camera as they interact with clients. They are surveilled as they interact with one another in dressing rooms. Brothel prostitutes are timed as they are providing services to their customers. Phone sex workers' conversations are taped and timed. Sex workers experience technological control both as a means to offer a safer workplace and as a means to regulate and control all of their movements, labors, and dealings with customers. While this control primarily means more profits for owners, it also means more safety for workers. Control over interactions means control over potentially unruly customers. A prostitute who is with a client after the kitchen timer sounds is usually immediately checked both to help her negotiate for more money and to make sure she is safe. Surveillance protects against customers who demand too much.

Acquiescence: Customers

For customers in the sex industry, technological control is often an insignificant part of McDonaldization. That is, consumers are so accustomed to being surveilled, timed, and rationally structured in their commercial dealings that this experience is not significantly different in the adult industry.

Resistance

However, here, too, there is resistance. In some ways the industry is less restrictive of workers than in the past. Most workers in the sex industry are independent contractors, which means that employers have much less control over working hours and shifts. The development of satellite technology in the phone industry has transformed the way in which labor is organized in the phone sex industry. The business of phone sex has in some cases evolved from being provided from a central location where women sit in large rooms with headsets and can be easily monitored by supervisors to being provided by women who work out of their homes. The pressures to provide the cheapest labor possible combined with changes in technology allow a business to seek out women wherever they are cheapest and least regulated by governments. Increasingly, a customer may be speaking to a phone sex worker anywhere in the world without even knowing it. This brings a whole new level of simulation to the fantasy of the girl next door!

Technology has allowed sex workers to themselves run their own businesses, interacting directly with clients. Many strippers, adult film stars, and brothel workers have their own websites. The low capital investment often required to get a website running means that workers in many parts of the industry can use this form of technology to interact directly with customers themselves.

As we have indicated, much of what is produced and sold in the sex industry involves emotional labor and at least feigned intimate interactions. Just as customers and workers resist efficiency and predictability, so too they resist complete control. Phone sex workers do have scripts, but workers report that it is their ability to act, impersonate, and respond to particular desires and needs that brings customers back. There is little use of computerized recordings. Although simulated dancers are well within the Internet's technological capability, customers still prefer live dancers who can interact, via computer, in real time. In sum, technology has been the handmaiden to the emergence of, and explosive growth within, the sex industry, and yet technology has not yet been fully deployed in the control of workers or in the Taylorization of sex.

Calculability: Bigger, More, Faster, Cheaper, Better

Acquiescence: Owners

In rationalized systems, quantification and calculability supersede quality in rank importance. "Good, better, best" corresponds to "big, bigger, biggest";

"Large fries only $.99" or "Now, 50% more . . . FREE!" are examples of calculability at work. One web portal offers over 150,000 hours of adult movies for 8 cents a minute. Calculability ensures the greatest and most efficient profit possible for business owners, and it allows consumers to know what to expect of their transactions.

Acquiescence: Workers

Quantification is not just apparent in the time it takes to purchase particular interactions, it also becomes a part of the measure of quality of service provided by workers. The "quality" of the goods—usually bodies—is measured in inches. For most body measurements, "more" is typically equated with "better." Many pornographic magazines advertise "more" of whatever is being sold. It is common in ads to boast more pictures, more sex acts, bigger penises, larger breasts, better bodies. The slogan of one gentlemen's club chain is "1000s of beautiful girls and three ugly ones." In a society where the breast has become fetishized, the bigger is praised as better. *Exotic Dancer* magazine contains stories of dancers whose income increased dramatically as they were surgically transformed from a 38D to a 42EEE bra size.

Acquiescence: Customers

As we discussed above, the process of McDonaldization in the sex industry has broken sexual interactions into component parts and sold them back to us. Moreover, these parts have been quantified in ways that can be easily measured. As we have shown, in brothels, phone sex, and live exotic dancing, interactions are typically negotiated and sold by the minute. Pleasure becomes measured in minutes; the purchase of sex is based on an agreed-upon act (or set of acts) in a fixed amount of time, for an agreed-upon price. Phone sex is measured and paid for by the minute, gentlemen's club dances are measured and paid for in the time it takes for a song. Basically, in a McDonaldized sex industry, the standard unit of sexual pleasure is the minute.

Resistance

The most resistance to McDonaldization comes in the small and fragmented businesses, where calculability and economies of scale are not common routes to economic success. At a businesswide level, most sex industries are strictly regulated and regulations vary from locale to locale.

This means that it becomes difficult, if not impossible, for most businesses to rationalize costs in a predictable way. While the few chain-like gentlemen's clubs are centralizing tasks like management training and legal advice, their licensing fees, taxes, legal costs, and so on still vary greatly from location to location. The small businesses, because of a variety of legal and liability issues, hire dancers, escort workers, and prostitutes as independent contractors, and most of the pay for support staff comes from tips by the dancers. It becomes difficult to quantify and predict their input and output in calculating costs of business. Owners of brothels, for example, still do not calculate in any precise way their customer demographics. Financial figures are nearly impossible to locate, as large sections of the industry are still cash-based, which makes it even more difficult to tally, count, and keep track of profits.

The internet has also allowed an enormous amont of user-generated content to become available for free. Consumers can create their own videos, their own erotic photos and upload them to sites like EroShare, YouPorn, and PornoTube. The amount of adult videos and images that are freely available to online viewers has increased tremendously in recent years. Indeed, commercial producers have an increasingly difficult time marketing content for pay. Online piracy has cut into the profits of adult movie producers.

And finally, the reliance on emotional labor means that it is hard to quantify and calculate all services provided. Desires and fantasies of customers are widely variable, difficult to measure or quantify, and hard to sell with a slogan like "Large fries, $.99." Calculability is difficult when an important part of the product or service being sold is amorphous: attitude, emotions, intimacy.

Acquiescence or Resistance?

In sum, McDonaldization is based upon efficiency, predictability, control, and calculability. In the sex industry, there is a complex pattern of both acquiescence and resistance to these trends. A good example comes from a recent article about the Nevada brothels in a local tourist magazine. Advertising the Chicken Ranch, the author boasts, " . . . [T]he cat-house has been the greatest Western institution. Today, it is bigger, better, glossier than ever and it is operated more efficiently than ever. . . . [T]he girls often display a genuine concern for the male patrons beyond 'satisfying their needs, and often their dreams.'" However, given that efficiency, predictability, control, and calculability are, perhaps, the most common and sought-after conditions of consumer life as we move through the 21st century, continued

McDonaldization is a likely path in the ongoing expansion and normalization of the adult industry in the United States.

McDonaldizing Sex?
Fast Food vs. Flesh and Fantasy

Why focus on the McDonaldization of sex? In doing so, are we asserting that there is something about sex that is different from fast food, that is special, even sacred? After all, in many ways the business of selling sex/sexuality is just like commodifying other products and selling them for profit. In modern, capitalist society most of us take for granted that almost anything can be packaged, marketed, and sold. Regardless of whether or not we are critical of this process of commodification—and as sociologists, a healthy skepticism of this trend is well warranted—the empirical reality is that shopping and nearly constant consumption had become hallmarks of our American lifestyle at the end of the 20th century. The use of sex to sell other nonsexual products and the sale of sexuality itself are part of the trend in a service-industry-based consumer society. To sell sex, in any one of its many forms, is to sell a product within a licensed, regulated, business environment for the purpose of generating profit. Structurally, then, this is no different than commercialization of other social interactions or services in order to sell products and generate profit.

On one hand, if this is convincing, then a paper investigating trends toward the McDonaldization of the sex industry would be somewhat passé; after all, Ritzer explains the general historical, sociocultural, and economic trend toward McDonaldization quite well. On the other hand, there *is* something different when the commodity being sold is sex. The question is *why*, sociologically, does it seem that the commercialization of sexuality warrants special consideration?

Even when the context of the exchange of sexual products or services occurs in an efficient, rational, calculable environment that feels comfortable, clean, and safe, this McDonaldization of sex is still distinctive compared to the McDonaldization of other aspects of our lives. Perhaps this should not be surprising, given that sex is typically seen as most appropriately located deep within the private sphere, and human sexuality is often thought of as a highly individual alchemy of desire. This is the crux of the question of how rationalized sex in a McDonaldized adult industry differs from other rationalized, McDonaldized business endeavors. First, sex is typically associated with the private realm of everyday life where the imperatives of the government, the marketplace, and public life do not tread; to sell sex as a commercial venture is to intrude on the sanctity of private life. Second, sexuality is not simply private, it is an expression of our innermost desires. Most of us rarely discuss the intimacies and precise details of our sex lives with others. Third, there is often an aura of uncertainty and mystery that shrouds the reality of desiring bodies, the physicality of sexual contact, the specific enactments of intimacy that characterize our sex lives. Taken together, sex(uality), being located in the private sphere and being thought of as uniquely personal and shrouded in mystery, distinguishes its rationalization from the rationalization of other commercial services. When sex is sold, there is often a fascination with its introduction into public life; uncloseting certain variations of sexual desires by codifying them in commercial enterprises makes visible that which is typically unseen and offers a public glimpse at the ways in which "others" experience parts of their sexuality.

The McDonaldization of sex is a pragmatic business endeavor in the context of an increasingly rationalized public sphere, where standardization allows the service industry to commodify social exchanges for profit. At the same time, however, the McDonaldization of sex marks the encroachment of the iron cage into the depths of the private sphere, into one of the most personal and apparently uniquely individual areas of human interaction: sexuality. Its commodification intrigues us by suggesting that desires and sexual interactions might be patterned, knowable recipes that lend themselves easily to packaging and standardization. For example, where a person may not feel fully secure with the secrets of great sex or the intricate intimacies of what others experience as "normal" sexuality or desires, it is fascinating—sometimes positive and interesting and sometimes alienating or worse—to see how corporate enterprises have apparently identified these secrets and developed formulaic sexual exchanges that are marketable and enticing to a large consuming public while remaining intimate enough to be fulfilling. This is the enigmatic nature of the rationalization of sex; it is a microcosm of the contradictory nature of American discourses and attitudes toward sex and sexuality in general.

Our society celebrates Viagra and restricts access to birth control. We fuel a rapidly growing adult industry, even as most American children do not receive any substantive, formal sex education. We collectively fixate on descriptions of various politician's sex lives, even as we alternately condemn them and dismiss it all as unimportant nonsense. Given this, it is not surprising that rationalized commercial sex is apparently a trend that many Americans crave (evidenced by growth of the sex industry in its McDonaldized forms), even as so many of us decry the commodification and McDonaldization of our bodies, our desires, and our private, intimate lives.

The Bottom Line: Erotic Bureaucracy and Sex in a McDonaldized World

... McDonaldization *is* "bureaucratic seduction." At first glance, this might seem to be a contradictory term. After all, where is the sensuality in red tape? Where is the mystery and eroticized anticipation in scripted, staged, and hurried commercial interactions? Upon further examination, however, it is clear that McDonaldized industries offer a plethora of products, full of consumer choices that are safe, colorful, relatively inexpensive, apparently convenient, reliable, and familiar; this is potentially very profitable for workers and owners. In short, then, McDonaldization *is* seductive; at the same time, however, the bureaucratic regimentation of rationalized economies of desire and standardized commercial sex are a sterile intrusion of the public sphere into the private, of the social into the personal, which makes any uncritical endorsement of McDonaldization seductively and deceptively simple. Beneath the aura of ease, opportunity, and freedom in a rationalized adult industry is a cold, alienating bureaucratic formation that employs bodies and desires in the profit-making enterprise of global capitalism.

This, then, is the sublime irony of McDonaldized sex. It is the bureaucratically ordered structure that makes certain kinds of consumer pleasures possible and that creates a larger range of consumers for the growing adult industry, even as this process leads to greater dehumanization, less diversity of desires, and more stratification. A McDonaldized sex industry is convenient for some consumers, safer and more lucrative for some workers, and profitable for owners, but it also threatens to entrap us in Weber's fearsome iron cage: coldly colonizing our imaginations and brushing up against our skin.

Thinking Critically

1. In what ways is sex impervious to McDonaldization?

2. What aspects of sex would be benefited by McDonaldization? How?

3. What aspects of sex would be adversely affected by McDonaldization? How?

4. How have new technologies, especially those associated with the Internet, affected the McDonaldization of sex?

5. In what ways is your own sex life McDonaldized?

6. In what ways do we (you) resist the McDonaldization of sex?

Lee Monaghan has done a two-pronged study of participants in weight-loss classes in England and the idea that what is produced by such regimens is the McDonaldization of bodies, or "McBodies." On the one hand, he is critical of the McDonaldization thesis for focusing on structures (e.g. the McDonaldized structure of fast food restaurants as well as of such weight loss classes) and what they do to people. In this, he argues that the thesis seems to blame the structures (e.g. of the fast food industry) for causing obesity rather than looking at individuals (and their bodies) and the role that they play in their own obesity. In other words, the McDonaldization thesis tends to focus on "structure" rather the "agency" of the people involved. Furthermore, he sees the McDonaldization thesis, as it is applied to this issue, leading to a negative view of fatness as a "discredited bodily state" and to a view of people as being passive in the McDonaldized structures of, for example, fast food restaurants and being unable to resist their pressures. On the other hand, he examines these weight-loss classes from the perspective of McDonaldization and its basic dimensions. He finds that these settings are McDonaldized, although they had elements that contradict or complicate a simplistic conclusion about them. However, he wants to make it clear that no matter how McDonaldized the structures, people are not passive in them, but are "complicit" in the process of McDonaldization. In addition, they also have the capacity to resist the McDonaldization of these settings and of their bodies (by, for example, using various quantifiable data—on the relationship between weight, blood pressure, and illness and morbidity—to argue that being overweight is not necessarily related to ill health and premature death).

12

McDonaldizing Men's Bodies?

Slimming, Associated (Ir)Rationalities and Resistances

Lee F. Monaghan

Introduction: A Counterintuitive Argument

Using Ritzer's *McDonaldization of Society* thesis as a reference point, and data from a qualitative study of men and weight-related issues, this article contributes sociologically to burgeoning critical obesity studies . . .

Ritzer takes the fast-food restaurant as an exemplar of a rationalized organization, though he only briefly mentions obesity. And his critical attention focuses on an industry that allegedly causes much obesity, much in line with 'common-sense' thinking, i.e. 'the attitude of everyday life' which, in Anglophone culture, is largely fatphobic or sizist comprising prejudice and discrimination towards people who are seen as fat in everyday life. In short,

Editor's Note: From Monaghan, L. F. (2007). McDonaldizing Men's Bodies? Slimming, Associated (Ir)Rationalities and Resistances. *Body & Society 13*(2), 67–93. Reprinted with permission from Sage Publications, Ltd.

Ritzer does not critique the social construction of so-called obesity as a massive problem that must ultimately be corrected at the level of the individual body. Writing about the irrationalities, or unintended consequences, of an efficient organization like McDonald's, Ritzer states: '[t]here is much talk these days of an obesity epidemic (including children) and many observers place a lot of the blame on the fast-food industry, its foods, and its emphasis on "super-sizing" everything.' With this type of account, abstracted, homogenized and objectified 'fat bodies' are passive McDonaldized bodies, the irrational consequence of Western rationalization. That, of course, is a simplified and stigmatizing narrative. It retrospectively denies human agency while reproducing the idea that fatness is a discredited bodily state that should be fixed.

There may be good reasons to be critical of the fast-food industry. However, this article does not draw from Ritzer's reiteration of common-sense thinking about obesity causation. To do so would itself mean reproducing a simplified, bite-sized and efficient account about health and its determinants alongside sizist stereotypes of fatness and consumption. Nonetheless, Ritzer will be used as a reference point when empirically exploring the manufacturing of fatness as a correctable problem. That is, when exploring the idea that fatness is an unwanted bodily state that should be remedied. Ritzer will also be used when considering whether men's bodies, primarily in the context of a slimming club, were actually rationalized in practice, plus possible irrationalities and meaningful resistances to these processes. In so doing, this article presents a counterintuitive argument, where industries that allegedly cause much obesity, such as McDonald's, are formally compared to organizations in the front line in the war on obesity . . .

Focusing largely on a mixed-sex commercial slimming organization, this article maintains that the rationalizing principles of the fast-food industry are, somewhat ironically, more or less observable in the contemporary fight against fat. Constructing fatness as a correctable problem entails calculability, efficiency, predictability and technological control. Because obesity is officially classed as a disease, such rationalizing processes are wrapped in velvet and may be *more or less* acceptable in everyday life. This is because they are intended to 'help' people (risky bodies, bodies at risk) pursue their supposed best interests. Here promissory bodywork may seduce, rather than simply trap, people who want to be seen to be socially responsible and self-caring. Approaching Ritzer from the perspective of embodied sociology— that is, where bodies are the source, location and medium of society—the following is predicated on the idea that much of what is done to bodies often depends on what bodies do to themselves. That means people who are

striving to lose or manage weight may be more or less complicit in rationalization: lived bodies are not only amenable to McDonaldized production
but also self-reproduction. Through diet and other means, people seek self-
improvement, happiness and healthiness, though there may also be irrationalities and meaningful resistances to these multi-directional processes in
everyday life . . .

The author and a research associate generated data during nine months
ethnography at four mixed-sex weight-loss classes in north-east England
(neither of us sought to lose weight). Classes were organized by a commercial slimming club, Sunshine, and run by three consultants: Danny, Sandy
and Judy. Names of research sites and contacts are pseudonyms. Research
also included 37 in-depth interviews with men, 18 of whom were current or
former slimming club members. The interviewees' mean age was 43, and
most men were of white ethnicity and presenting as heterosexual. A range of
occupations is represented, though men from the slimming club were mainly
from a working-class background . . .

Calculability

According to Ritzer, Western societies are increasingly quantifiable and
calculable. This means emphasizing numerical standards, with quantity
becoming a surrogate for quality. As discussed below, calculability, which
works in tandem with other aspects of rationalization, is a recurrent theme
in the socially organized fight against fat. Far from being a scientifically neutral undertaking, calculability is a socially embedded process that was also
more or less acceptable and resistible among men contacted during this
research, even when taking arms in the war on fat . . .

Calculability was recurrent. All members started their weekly session by
getting weighed. This preceded the group 'image therapy' session, where
members congregated and, under the guidance of the consultant, discussed
their quantifiable weight-loss efforts and goals. During these sessions,
Sandy mentioned successful slimmers from her classes, and classes from
around the country, who had lost a specified amount of weight to the exact
half pound. Consultants also reiterated to their classes the importance of
calculating their dietary intake when, for example, members lost weight
(with weight serving as an efficient and inexpensive proxy for fat).
Referring to a new member, who lost 10 pounds within two weeks of joining, Judy told her class: 'If you want results like Jack then you should weigh
and measure!'

All slimmers were advised to adopt a calculative orientation to diet or
at least 'keep an eye on the little things that add up.' This is because diet

was assumed to manifest itself in the McDonaldized body; that is, a body controlled by calculability which may otherwise signify an 'inappropriate' relationship with food (the obese, fast-food indulging and 'out-of-control' body in common-sense McDonaldized accounts). The slimming club handbook, which all members received and were advised to read when first joining, listed numeric values for specified quantities of food and drink as calculated by a dietician. These values were also continually updated and revised, allegedly in response to the changing content and availability of foods on the market. This quantitative information was posted on the organization's website and communicated to members in class.

In recognizing that there are degrees of McDonaldization, it is worth flagging that Sunshine's dietary approach to weight-loss was not only about numbers but also macro-nutritional content. Permitted items were basically divided according to protein or carbohydrate content (colour coded respectively as red and green), with slimmers focusing on one or another particular food group on any particular day. This so-called 'healthy-eating' or 'food optimizing plan' was intended to replace a sustained focus on calories or 'points,' as was the case with a rival weight-loss organization, Fat Fighters. Hence, Sunshine's system comprised calculability, but it was wrapped in velvet and presented as more simple and efficient than another (more economically successful) weight-loss programme. Tim said this informed his decision to join Sunshine rather than Fat Fighters: 'My wife's been on Fat Fighter things and it's a point system. It didn't really appeal to me, that counting every morsel I put in me mouth' (Interview 26).

Even so, calculative rationality ran through Sunshine's 'plan' like words through a stick of rock. Members did not count 'points' but they were advised to count 'syns,' which were allocated to energy-dense items. Again, these numbers were listed in the club handbook. Experienced members had little difficulty citing and calculating 'syn' values from memory. As can be seen with Richie, this was related to feasibility talk, which was intended to minimize feelings of deprivation:

A guy has up to 15 syns a day. So does a woman but women tend to stick to 10 syns. What syns are: they're simply foods with fat in them, saturated or whatever. So if you ate too much of them it would prevent you from losing weight because it's basically the unhealthy part so to speak. That's what I class it as. But it means for myself, for example—I'm a chocoholic—I can have a two-fingered Kit Kat and a packet of Quaver crisps every day of the week and that's less than my 15 syns. That would be about 13½ to 14 syns. Now I have 15 syns a day. So if I was a drinker at the end of the [working] week I have 75 syns. I can go to the pub and have 75 syns' worth of drink; 70 syns is a bottle of vodka. (Interview 29)

Following Judy's previous comment on Jack's 10-pound weight-loss, consultants also advised members to weigh and measure foodstuffs. This advice ostensibly had variable significance for members, depending on their dieting careers and weight-loss success. Consultants often explicitly directed their recommendations to new members and established members encountering difficulties. However, this was inclusive: it was common for those regularly attending classes to either gain weight or not lose as much weight as anticipated, representing a continual source of personal disappointment and frustration (also discussed below). Faced with this, Sandy publicly advised her congregation: 'If your weight-loss is a bit dodgy you may have to get the kitchen measuring scales and jug out and do a sheet listing what you've eaten.' These utensils were also offered as prizes during a weekly raffle, alongside digital pedometers, thereby furthering calculable efforts to rationalize the fleshy body and bodywork.

Calculability was unavoidable but consultants conceded: 'Nobody sticks to the plan 100 percent.' This public admission from Judy was obviously framed by organizational imperatives and the continual search for profits. Referring to continuously weighing food, rather than counting syns, and in rejecting the idea that theirs was a temporary 'fad' diet, Judy advised her group: 'This is a lifelong commitment and it just wouldn't be normal to weigh your food all the time.' Thus, flexibility, or a more 'relaxed' approach, was 'allowed' and even encouraged by consultants who also had direct personal experience of the vicissitudes of slimming. Similar to their shared orientation to the BMI, this could be typified as a 'rubber' or 'velvet cage' rather than an 'iron cage,' with the intention of 'ameliorating some of the problems associated with McDonaldization.' However, bars were still present and even Sunshine's velvet-covered 'syn' system was impractical and restrictive in contexts of everyday life . . .

Finally, calculability informed various challenges to McDonaldization—the rationalization of resistance. Thus, some men resisted the attribution of health risks and problems to their 'excess' weight. They 'denied injury' by citing quantifiable biomedical criteria while still seeking to lose weight, given their expressed wish to 'fit in' socially. That included Dom, a slimmer, who lost about 7 stone then suffered a heart attack. Still weighing over 20 stone, Dom publicly agreed with Sandy in class that if he had not already lost a significant amount of weight then he would probably be dead. However, Dom told me a week later outside the club that he did not think his weight caused his heart problems, adding that his friend died of a heart attack yet weighed just 10½ stone. Dom added that, after his mother died of heart failure, all of his family underwent medical tests and he had the lowest cholesterol despite being the heaviest. Furthermore, he said his blood pressure increased after he lost several stone, which he found perplexing. Dom thought his hypertension was related to the stresses of moving to his current place of residence, where his young children were bullied on account of his weight and where teenage boys smeared excrement on his car-door handles. I visited Dom at his home. At least a third of the houses on this council estate were boarded up and awaiting demolition. While I could not confirm Dom's reported metabolic health (calculations such as blood pressure) I would not treat his account simply as a 'sad tale.' To do so would be to give consent, through silence, to larger iniquitous structures which work on and through socially located bodies. Aphramor, in reviewing scientific literature in relation to what is known about physiological responses to stress and its relation to social inequality, casts a highly politicized light on Dom's words. It is also worth adding that Dom smoked 'at least 20 plus a day' for the past 30 years, and there is evidence that smoking is much more hazardous to health than obesity. Smoking is also related to experiences of social inequality, yet such experiences are often ignored within the personally and politically disappointing war on fat.

Efficiency

Using a large collaged British roadmap as a prop, and citing Bernard as an example of somebody on the 'fast track' to weight-loss, Sandy told her group it's possible to 'eat your way slim' by following the plan 100 percent. However, they could also take a 'scenic route' and lose weight more slowly. She added that the club 'gives' members the tools to take whatever route they preferred. Sandy added, in a light-hearted tone, that if they take the scenic route they may also go for a swim in the sea, meaning their weight-loss journey could be as relaxed as they wanted it to be. Stan quipped to those who were sat nearby, 'I've been deep sea-diving.' Another man joked, 'I've been on a detour to the Caribbean!' (LM's field diary)

Efficiency entails searching for the optimum means to a given end. For fast-food industries, efficiency comprises streamlined work operations, simplified products and putting customers to work. As indicated above and discussed further below, efficiencies were more or less identifiable within and around Sunshine alongside resistances and irrationalities.

Ritzer briefly describes the seductive efficiencies of the 'diet industry,' referring to low-calorie food that is often pre-prepared, freeze-dried and microwaveable. These mass-produced items are often sold in supermarkets, with some leading slimming organizations producing these branded items. However, Sunshine did not manufacture these. In constructing a sense of superiority in a highly competitive market, female consultants told me such items offered little satiety, were nutritionally suspect, and were expensive. In short, these women talked up the irrationalities of efficient rationality in order to distance Sunshine from these foods. Danny adopted a different stance. He favoured ready meals, produced by Fat Fighters. He often told his group about various frozen foods that were on special offer at local supermarkets, along with scripted commentary on their syn value. This was a no-fuss or McDonaldized approach to food preparation, though other men did talk about taking time to prepare food for themselves and their families and their chef-like abilities.

Ritzer also mentions bestseller diet books that promise efficiencies in time and effort. Bernard purchased cookery books from Sunshine. However, although Bernard was an efficient slimmer, he stressed the importance of variety not efficiency with regard to food. It should also be noted that these books were not presented as 'dieting' aides given the organizational rhetoric about food optimizing, with 'quick fix' diets defined as unsustainable and counter-productive. This view, often shared within and outside slimming clubs, and given forceful expression within critical obesity literature, is a further example of the irrationality of rationality. Interestingly, this was anticipated, countered, and turned to productive ends by consultants. In short, awareness of this irrationality meant that consultants underscored the need for ongoing commitment to the slimming club.

Even so, efficiency talk, if not actual efficient, was recurrent. Sandy enthusiastically told members about the possibility of speedy weight-loss. During interviewing, male slimmers also mentioned 'speed foods' that reportedly accelerated weight-loss (e.g. pulses, strawberries and mushrooms). Promised efficiency was also crystallized in Sunshine's literature. After describing the plan as 'a lifestyle, not a life sentence,' Sandy shown me promotional pamphlets with glossy pictures of appetizing meals and said: 'That's our Success Express plan. It's the fastest way to lose weight.' Thus, even though Sunshine customers were offered the 'option' of taking the 'scenic route,' the commonly expressed goal was to lose weight quickly. Efficiency was the ideal and was publicly commended and rewarded, with the 'slimmer of the week' receiving a basket of fruit, which other members, not the slimming club, supplied at the consultant's request.

Of course, material bodies are not infinitely malleable and may be highly intransigent . . . However, slimming is typically a long and frustrating process. Even with commitment and regular attendance, the common discrepancy between effort and reward at Sunshine provided the conditions of possibility for moments of ironic comedic laughter among members. Correspondingly, the idea of efficiency was a narrative resource, especially among consultants, for 'talking up' the possibility of successfully losing weight, promoting hope and 'selling' the plan. This sometimes included talk about the physicality of men's typically larger bodies, as voiced by Danny. He explained to my slim research associate that men usually lose weight more quickly than women because men are physically larger. Such talk, sustained in the face of contrary evidence, was obviously homogenizing and treated men as an undifferentiated mass.

McDonaldized efficiency, or speedy results, may have been the ideal. Nonetheless, some male slimmers warned others about rapid weight-loss, which could occur with Sunshine's plan (especially during the first few weeks). According to their cautionary tales, which implicitly rendered inefficient slimming more acceptable to those struggling to lose weight, increased efficiency equalled increased risk. Stinson notes that such talk helps to make irrational situations understandable, while critical obesity literature makes the point that these bodily practices are physiologically risky.

Several men were chatting among themselves. Following news about Dom's recent heart attack, Ernie said that Dom did not 'feel well' after losing weight. Ernie then talked about what he considered the massive and worrying dangers of dramatic weight-loss and 'crash' diets: 'It's dangerous, I don't agree with it. In fact I was reading a book on it, and you need to lose it gradually. Your heart and kidneys lose fat and they need to stabilise, along with your muscles. And it takes time. Now, Dom, he lost 22 pounds in his first week here.' Al, who was listening to this, openly agreed. (LM's field diary)

Efficiency also manifested itself in other ways: namely, the organization of classes. At Danny's club, members wishing to bypass the usual queue for the scales and then quickly leave, were efficiently processed through 'express checking.' However, most slimmers queued to get weighed. Sunshine deliberately manufactured the queue. Paul, a team manager and member of Sandy's class, told me that Sunshine's success depended on mutual support among members. The queue was planned because it provided an opportunity for members to congregate and share weight-loss ideas. That, of course, served to streamline the organization's work operations, with members acting as co-consultants. In addition, it is worth observing that, in order to get weighed, members slowly proceeded past a series of staffed desks (mainly staffed voluntarily by members) displaying weight-loss merchandise that members could, and often did, buy. This also relates to Bryman's (1999) ideas on 'Disneyization' and the 'dedifferentiation of consumption,' i.e. visitors to one sphere must go through another, which helps to increase profits. This obviously provides fuel for a larger machine that constructs fatness as a correctable problem.

Other features of the slimming class complicated the idea of McDonaldized efficiency. Unlike the McDonald's drive-thru, the group therapy session held after the weigh-in was not intended to be time efficient. Many members welcomed this. At £4.25 per session, they wanted 'to get the most' for their money. Yet, as with McDonald's burgers, value for money was illusory. The ingredients constituting this commoditized experience cost very little for slimming clubs. This experience included a sense of 'collective effervescence,' or ritually derived energy, which emerged during bodily co-presence in morally significant space. However, this experience was not palatable for all. Some members, whom I observed tapering their last few visits to Judy's class by leaving immediately after being weighed, said the sessions were too long. Doug, who had recently stopped attending, along with his wife, said: 'I find that particular slimming club goes on far too long. You shouldn't have to sit there for an hour. I mean, I've been getting home late. And we've both said that's enough. You know? It's, it's barmy' (Interview 17).

Slimming classes, and the slimming experience more generally, were nonetheless organized in a way that was efficient for the organization. This relates to bodily labour or 'putting customers to work,' which was intended to streamline fleshy bodies but which was actually about streamlining work operations for a money-making business. This is an important aspect of McDonaldization and is the last theme discussed here in relation to efficiency.

Putting customers to work enables the fast-food industry to achieve efficiencies and this process was unashamedly put in motion at the slimming club. Just as McDonald's customers have to undertake much of the work that is done by employees in a traditional restaurant (e.g. placing a food order, taking it to the table, disposing of the waste), the slimming clubs sought to put bodies to work albeit under a collective ethos that stressed mutual 'support.' Thus, 'big losers,' at the invitation of their consultant, played a leading role in manufacturing fatness as a correctable problem. Sandy would sometimes get regular members, like Bernard and Al, to head the image therapy as part of an interactive question-and-answer session. For them, this unpaid labour was a source of satisfaction. It was defined as an opportunity to 'help' others and 'give something back' to an organization that was 'helping them' to lose a significant amount of weight. Other slimmers, forming the so-called 'social team' (Sandy had 38 members on this team), also provided free labour. This work not only included staffing stalls, which Al did most weeks, but also backstage administrative support and greeting new prospective members. This labour was necessary in Sandy's classes, which sometimes attracted up to 80 people per session. Similar to McDonald's customers, loyalty was as much emotional as rational.

In sum, rather than an all-or-nothing process, efficiency or talk of efficiency was more or less observable but also resistible at this mixed-sex slimming club. Instances ranged from promoting fast-track weight-loss to the very organization of the class, wherein fatness was reproduced as a problem to be corrected by members through bodywork. Efficiency was also intertwined in complex and contradictory ways with other aspects of McDonaldization, such as predictability.

Predictability

Predictability 'involves an emphasis on, for example, discipline, systematization, and routines so that things are the same from one time or place to another.' Predictability is part of the socially organized fight against fat . . .

Aspects of predictability were centrally organized and observed in the delivery of the class. Danny said about his training as a consultant: 'the training is exactly the same so whenever you walk into any slimming class it should always be the same' (Interview 18). According to Ritzer (2004: 102–4), McDonaldization is often attractive because things become reassuringly the same. He states that fast-food restaurants, similar to the predictable shopping mall, *aim* to offer safe, pleasant environments devoid of nasty surprises. The same could be said about slimming classes, though the overt aim of predictable pleasantness had a covert dark side.

In all the classes researched, there was a standardized focus on the positive. This was the common organizational response to members' often-fraught and frustrating efforts consistently and efficiently to lose weight. As well as the usual motivational talk from consultants, and what one man called 'happy clappy' rituals (i.e. receiving a round of applause when losing weight), there were awards (e.g. shiny stickers) and catchphrases that were more often intended for women (e.g. 'little pickers have big knickers'). Here fatphobia and sizism, which could also be highly infantilizing, worked in tandem with sexism and the predictable yet covertly oppressive message that some bodies are less acceptable than others. Of course, all of this was coated with artificial sweetener or, to use Ritzer's metaphor, the iron cage of rationality was wrapped in velvet. This was also evidenced in the classes' decorative style. All had posters on their walls. These featured 'success' stories (members who had lost a lot of weight, but not necessarily maintained this, as reported in local newspapers), graphs showing some members' weight-loss over time, and other motivational paraphernalia that conveyed the message that the system was infallible.

According to Sunshine's centralized, corporately produced, script those following the plan could expect predictable weight-loss. This was intended to be reassuring and rational. In a fatphobic society, fee-paying slimmers wanted to know they would lose weight. During the induction session at Judy's class, she assured new arrivals that if they followed the plan 'properly' during their first week: 'I guarantee you'll lose weight. If you don't, you'll get your money back. [As an aside] You'll be the first in 36 years to get your money back though.' This was a standard sales pitch. Danny reiterated this to new members in his class. While new members often lost 'big numbers' during their first week, there were exceptions. Also, as with Ernie and plenty of other members, the expected loss of one to two pounds per week thereafter did not always materialize. Weight gain was also common. A predictable consequence was that there was a high rate of attrition. Defaulting members also seldom responded to Sunshine's standard 'support letter,' which, in Sandy's larger class, was handled by her admin social support team . . .

Technological Control

Technology is intertwined with the social construction of fatness as a correctable problem. This element of rationalization, according to Ritzer (2004: 15), entails exerting control over people as a counterfoil to human unpredictability. Here McDonaldized bodies become cyborg bodies.

For some men, nonhuman technology *facilitated* rather than *replaced* their efforts to lose weight. For example, Information Technologies (IT)—that is, online facilities—were noted above in relation to calculability and predictability. People using Sunshine's IT facilities, such as Bernard, still continuously worked on their bodies as part of a reflexive project of the self. Hence, human control was not relinquished to technology. Yet, while consultants often recommended the club's online resources, this aspect of technological rationalization was not necessarily time efficient. During image therapy, those in Danny's class discussed in detail a cumbersome way of calculating online the syn value of Fat Fighter's foods. Even so, when slimmers debated this esoteric resource they presented themselves as being *seen* to be doing something. That may have been personally and transiently therapeutic for individuals, but it also reproduced the unacceptability of fatness and continued fatphobia. Such is the irrationality of slimming, where people who in all likelihood would not reach and sustain their target weight, exercised and complied with fat hatred.

There were other slimming club technologies, besides IT or the actual dietary plan itself. The central piece of rationalizing hardware, saturated with ambivalence, was the digital weighing scales. Sunshine's scales were capable of weighing the heaviest of members. That was important for Dom, who weighed about 33 stone when he first joined. According to Ruppel Shell, early 20th-century diet books described the weighing scales as a '"materialized conscience" that weighed not only bodies, but worthiness.' This measurement of worthiness continues with feelings of embarrassment and shame being a corollary for some men. Dom told me that when he first learned his weight at Sunshine, 'the floor could've opened up and swallowed me up. I was in two minds whether to go back or not' (Interview 21).

Dom was not an isolated case. Other men also reported a problematic relationship with the weighing scales. Paul talked about his experiences using his home scales. To provide additional context, Paul peaked at 21 stone before regularly attending Sandy's club with his wife, Liz. Paul had since lost 8 stone, but maintaining most of this loss was a daily struggle that was not helped by 'compulsively' going on the scales. After giving the scales to Sandy, Paul said he followed the club's recommendation of only being weighed once a week at the club. Surrendering the scales had symbolic as well as emotional significance. It reasserted the centrality of the organization in weighing unpredictable bodies, on the premise that members may feel 'down' about their daily weight fluctuation and regain weight through 'comfort eating':

> I am what's known as a compulsive scale hopper. Because I am terrified of getting to the stage I was before, and it's a real, real fear. I do not want to get that big again. So unbeknown to me, what I've been doing is [I've] been very, very compulsively getting on the scales two and three times a day. So much [so that] . . . it was hindering me at maintaining. And I started to gain, because I was so intent on keeping these scales happy. I was falling back into my old habits of being depressed. So I was eating. So yesterday we wrapped our scales up and gave them to Sandy. We haven't got a set of scales now. And that was a big milestone. (Interview 23)

Such talk gives empirical expression to critical theoretical commentary on McDonaldization. Following Ritzer, but also Heidegger on technology as destiny and Simmel on the tyrannizing effects of objective culture, Weinstein and Weinstein discuss how people may feel 'oppressed' and 'humiliated' by technology but also 'appeal to technology for salvation.'

Biomedical technology, which again is obviously not a concern specific to the slimming club ethnography, should also be mentioned. Biomedicine promises individualized technological 'fixes' for the 'problem' of obesity. The biomedical conception of human bodies, drawing from a mechanical metaphor, provides fertile ground for the colonization and control of humans by nonhuman technology. Of course, medicine also has iatrogenic consequences, that is, medicine may do more harm than good. The remainder of this section briefly notes the promises and problems of bariatric surgery: a technology which, according to recent research, is much riskier than originally thought, especially for men and older patients.

Bariatric surgery is typically performed on people who, according to the WHO's criteria, are categorized as 'obese class III' (BMI ≥ 40 kg/m^2). The International Diabetes Institute identifies surgery as a possibility for those with a BMI ≥ 30 kg/m^2, who are defined as 'severely obese,' while Oliver states that some bariatric surgeons will operate on people with a BMI of 32: for example, somebody who is 5 ft 10 inches and weighs just under 16 stone (223 pounds). Bariatric surgery is a McDonaldized intervention, since the goal is to permanently control somebody's appetite, behaviour and digestion so that weight-loss becomes much more likely and sustainable. If human unpredictability is the major obstacle to certain, predictable and efficient weight-loss, then surgery is a rationalized response that is intended to control the recipient's ability to eat what and when they desire . . .

Nobody interviewed for this research had received bariatric surgery. However, Jason's sister-in-law underwent this and experienced problems. Jason did not elaborate, but he felt other people's faith in biomedicine was not well founded:

'People see surgical teams and health interventions as the Holy Grail, the saving' (Interview 32). Roy had faith and he was awaiting bariatric surgery on the NHS. This former slimming club member had previously lost 11 stone but regained it and weighed about 28 stone when I interviewed him (he had previously received an abdominoplasty on the NHS, which entails removing loose skin from the stomach after dramatic weight-loss). Roy considered himself 'fit for the size of us' but, in line with anticipatory medicine (predicted health problems) and pragmatic considerations, he hoped to gain longevity and mobility by losing weight and keeping it off. Roy's concern to 'do the right thing' corresponded with recent fatherhood and his demonstration of social fitness, a situationally appropriate display of gendered selfhood. Importantly, Roy had to demonstrate to clinicians his worthiness for bariatric surgery by losing weight over six consecutive months with the help of a dietician. Replacing human with nonhuman technology, at least for some bodies processed by Britain's publicly funded NHS, is dependent upon the ability to exert self-control.

Roy's decision was situationally rational for him relative to what he described as a low-risk operation: a position mediated through his interactions with clinicians at a time when clinical certainty about low risk was not medically justified. However, there were resistances and, to employ rationalized criteria, these seem reasonable given Flum et al.'s research. This study among 16,155 patients reported that men had a 7.5 percent mortality rate within the first year of surgery with this figure rising to 11.1 percent for those aged 65 years or older. That said, even before Flum et al.'s research, concerns about weight-loss surgery emerged from 'below,' from fat activists. Although fat activists are often very large and conceivably have the most to gain from surgery, they have offered eloquent and convincing arguments online when warning others about iatrogenesis (resisting technological rationalization through IT). Contrary to Ritzer's depiction of the Internet as dehumanizing, which has been critiqued by others, virtual communities may actually help forge alternative and more positive definitions that resist the dehumanizing anti-fat campaign.

Resisting surgery is not only an organized political response from activists. Andy, who weighed about 18 stone and recently rejoined Sunshine after a previous failed attempt, dismissed surgical weight-loss interventions. His words captured the mood of most respondents, though other men also emphasized the importance of the work ethic, that is, of personally achieving weight-loss in line with the religious underpinnings of the rationalized health movement:

> I don't think any man alive would go through that. No. I tell a lie. There's some that have it really bad that are stuck, that are 40 stone, that type. But the average person, average man, overweight man in Britain, would not go to the extent of having that done. (Interview 25)

That included male slimmers who would be medically classed as morbidly obese but who, like Roy, nonetheless endorsed cosmetic surgery to remove loose skin associated with substantial yet personally achieved weight-loss. Endorsing human over nonhuman technological control over diet, rather than rejecting surgery per se, fitted with the meanings, practices and interests promoted in slimming clubs. After all, these organizations profit from a behavioural 'solution' to 'the obesity problem.' Rejecting bariatric surgery also fitted well with the current position of successful slimmers and others who were risk averse. Before becoming a slimmer and weighing 26 stone, Bernard toyed with the idea of surgery after seeing 'something on the tele about a guy who'd had his stomach stapled' but he subsequently rejected this technology after losing a significant amount of weight through diet. Presenting himself as a sage adviser for imagined others, Bernard emphasized the importance of a healthy lifestyle, then remarked: 'I don't think these things [surgery and pharmaceuticals] should be for anybody' (Interview 22). For Dom, procedures surrounding the operation were considered dangerous, alongside other 'after effects' that were explained to him when he enquired at the hospital. After talking about a 10 percent mortality risk from anaesthesia,

Dom reflected on the possibility of post-operative infections, then laughed 'Oh, we'll give that a miss then' (Interview 21).

Other larger men, like Joe who was not from the slimming club, also resisted weight-loss surgery. Joe was not averse to the idea of slimming given the hopes and expectations of significant others: he had previously tried losing weight after his mother 'bullied' him to try the drug Orlistat, which, as ironically discussed by Oliver, could be considered more of a cosmetic intervention and is 'no different than eyeliner except for the flatulence.' Joe learnt this first hand, experiencing faecal incontinence in public. He quickly stopped taking this other technological 'fix' saying 'It was the worst thing I ever done.' With regard to weight-loss surgery, he stated the following with reference to people who are made to feel unacceptable because of the social meanings encircling their weight. Here Joe not only resisted technology by invoking the 'natural,' he also rejected McDonaldized efficiency while adding that reduced meal sizes equalled reduced quality of life for people who cannot be assumed to be unhealthy because of their size:

> This is where they staple your stomach. Nah. Like I said to the doctor, 'If I want to do it, I'm going to do it.' The natural way. The way it should be done. Not all this quick fix thing. Because, at the end of the day, if it's a quick fix it's going to have a reverse effect, I think. I mean this thing where they put a band on your stomach to reduce your stomach. I mean, it's a case of, what's your quality of life like after you've had it? You know what I mean? And it's, it's, nah. . . . I seen one on MTV, *I Want a New Life* or something like that. And it was some girl that they done. And yeah, the results, fantastic. But you think to yourself that she's now got to go through the rest of her life eating minute little things. And she's not going to enjoy herself. She was one of these people who [says] 'I'm not happy because I'm overweight. I'm depressed.' She's one of these people who were walking around with her head down. But, I mean, you've got to accept yourself for what you are. Some people are big, some people are small. Some people have got ginger hair. You know what I mean? You are what you are. And you've got to accept yourself for what you are. And I mean, yeah, in some situations it is very unhealthy for people. But I'm sure that's not the case for everybody. (Interview 5)

In sum, while technology plays a recurrent and at times irrational role in McDonaldizing fatness as a fixable problem, its meanings were also subject to reinterpretation and resistance. While, for many male slimmers, rationalization was pursued through self-directed and less physically invasive technology—namely, the slimming plan, the effects of which were routinely measured through the weighing scales—for other big men, such as Roy who had abandoned slimming, bariatric surgery was seductive in a context of anticipatory medicine. Yet resistance was still strong among men outside slimming clubs, as evidenced by Joe, who, like Roy, was one of my biggest contacts and would be medically labelled morbidly obese.

Conclusion: Resisting McDonaldized Accounts and Processes

Medicalized fatness is often considered the irrational consequence of Western rationalization. The common narrative is that developed nations are awash with convenience foods that are making everyone 'fat.' Despite the critical edge to his work, Ritzer draws from this picture when discussing the irrationality of rationality. Such reasoning is itself McDonaldized because it is simplified, efficient and seductive. It is also sociologically unfulfilling and questionable. This type of account reproduces the pejorative (stigmatizing) status of 'obesity' while retrospectively denying human agency. Rather than reiterating such thinking, this article critically explored the process of manufacturing fatness as a correctable problem and what that might mean among men in everyday life. Calculability, efficiency, predictability and technological control are the central organizing principles of the fast-food industry, and the above explored the degree to which these work around, on and through men's bodies as part of the current war on fat.

Using the slimming club ethnography as the main point of reference leads me to the following conclusion: there are many observable, but not universally accepted and effective, efforts to McDonaldize men's bodies. Certainly, rationalization was a recurrent theme. Whether referring to the weighing and measuring of bodies and foodstuffs or biomedical technologies proposing an efficient means of bypassing human unpredictability, rationalizing principles were observable. It may seem counter-intuitive to draw a formal sociological comparison between an industry that allegedly causes much obesity and those seeking to ameliorate it, but, in using qualitative data and the idea of McDonaldization as a reference point, this comparison is justified. McDonaldizing processes are perhaps unsurprising in commercial slimming clubs that promise efficient, rationalized solutions to a public and private problem. Counting 'syns,' using online computer facilities and promoting 'fast-track' weight-loss, in turn, all reproduce the pejorative status of fatness as well as the ideology of individual responsibility. However, the slimming club was a critical case for considering the degree to which men's bodies were McDonaldized in practice. Such a consideration is necessary because objectified bodies are also embodied subjects, capable of resistances and forging alternative definitions of the situation. Interestingly, it was found that even in the slimming club, attempts to uniformly rationalize men's bodies and bodily practices were confounded. Even in this engine of anti-fat sentiment and sensibility, people were not passive McDonaldized dopes, just as their bodies could not be standardized like the Big Mac.

Amidst observable and generalized rationalization, there were subtle variations, complexities and resistances. Rationalization and resistance were multidimensional and uneven processes, even within a specific fat-fighting organization like Sunshine. To be sure, many slimmers embraced rationalization; weight-loss can be a panacea of sorts in a world where 'the obese' are stigmatized as irrational and out of control. The slimming club could be considered a potentially revitalizing cult, promising salvation and rebirth within the broader secular religion of health. However, some observations, which render McDonaldizing processes contestable and (un)intentionally resistible, included: the common rejection of the BMI; dismissing 'quick fix' or 'crash' diets (while nonetheless following a modified diet that sometimes resulted in massive and quick weight-loss); limited success in losing weight, or maintaining weight-loss, despite proclaimed intentions and sanctions; eschewing streamlined slimming products, such as ready meals; and rejecting biomedical technologies that promise to make weight-loss much easier. Of course, even resistances like these, which, somewhat paradoxically, may have made aspects of rationalization more palatable, were often shaped and constrained by the organizational imperatives of an industry rationally seeking profits. For example, slimming consultants were unlikely to promote bariatric surgery when the economics and ideology of their organization revolved around behavioural change. Slimming clubs also risked alienating and discouraging men if they followed or rigidly imposed the BMI, hardly a wise business move!

This article not only explored rationalizing processes and resistances, or attempts to ameliorate some of the worst features of McDonaldization. Reference was also made to irrationalities, the unintended consequences of rationalization. The focus on irrationalities tallies with critical obesity studies and also fits with the concerns of sociology, which has a tradition of interrogating the cold, dark side of Western rationalization. Irrationalities associated with efforts to McDonaldize men's bodies ranged from turning commensality into a guilt-laden obstacle to the reduced quality of life that some men attributed to bariatric surgery. Other irrationalities included: viewing foodstuffs in numerical terms rather than as a source of nutrition or pleasure; the compatibility of a 'healthyeating plan' and slimming with practices that would otherwise be considered risky (e.g. in relation to alcohol); perpetuating an oversimplified or misleading picture of what determines health; feeling ill when rapidly losing weight; gaining weight despite investments in time, energy and money in becoming slimmer; and so on.

Given the above, it is hardly surprising that there was a high rate of attrition among slimmers, who experienced frustration and disappointment when struggling weekly to lose weight and keep it off. Within the larger society it is often acknowledged that 'diets do not work' and, even when weight-loss diets are wrapped in velvet and repackaged under a different name, achieved slimness often remains a Holy Grail. Even so, it is a highly valued goal that literally millions of women and men repeatedly strive to achieve, regardless of the resources needed to do that and possible risks to the physical and social body. This sacrificial action, although critically viewed here as an irrationality of rationality, makes sense for individuals seeking to avoid social censure for their fatness. However, an argument running through this study is that the institutionalized war on obesity is highly questionable . . .

Thinking Critically

1. What are Monaghan's criticisms of the application of the McDonaldization thesis to weight loss and fatness?

2. Given those criticisms, why then does he proceed to use the principles of McDonaldization to analyze weight loss classes?

3. In what ways are those classes McDonaldized? In what ways are they not McDonaldized?

4. In what ways are people complicit in their problems with weight?

5. Aren't there structures to be blamed for the epidemic in obesity? Aren't fast food restaurants to blame because of the high fat, high calorie food they sell, including to children?

Sara Raley examines contradictory developments and changes in the family from the perspective of McDonaldization. On the one hand, the structure of the family seems to be de-McDonaldizing. That is, the once highly predictable nuclear family (mom, dad, and 2.2 children) is in decline, and a whole range of different and highly unpredictable family forms are on the rise (never-married single parents; unmarried cohabiting heterosexual couples who may never marry; gay and lesbian couples who, with few exceptions, cannot marry; blended families with children from various marriages; married couples that are childless by design; grandparents tending to grandchildren; and so on). This change from a highly McDonaldized form to one far less McDonaldized is traceable to many factors including the fact that although the early form was efficient (as well as having many of the other characteristics of McDonaldization), many found it (like the fast-food restaurant) unsatisfying, even oppressive, perhaps even an "iron cage." The emphasis now is more on the quality of the relationship (e.g., romance, a good marriage) and on the lives of the children that result rather than such quantitative factors as number of years in a perhaps unfulfilling marriage or the number of children reared.

On the other hand, when one looks at everyday family life one finds a considerable trend in the direction of McDonaldization. This is seen, for example, in the impatience of married (or cohabiting) partners to move into a relationship and to see quick results, their reliance on the quick fixes offered by popular books and TV shows, their dependence on a variety of nonhuman technologies, their utilization of a wide range of McDonaldized settings for family activities, and so on. In spite of these and other changes, Raley hypothesizes that the family may be uniquely suited to retard the spread of McDonaldization.

13

McDonaldization and the Family

Sara Raley

Any discussion about "the family" invariably must begin with a description of what is meant by the term "family." At midcentury, the conceptualization of what constituted a family was narrow. The ideal typical family (and also the most prevalent) was white, middle class, and nuclear with a husband sole-earner, a stay-at-home wife, and children. However, this conceptualization as the ideal has come under fire during the past few decades, as the "cookie cutter" nuclear family has been replaced by a widely diverse set of family types, including the never-married single parent, unmarried cohabiting heterosexual couples who eschew marriage, same-sex unions who cannot marry even if they desire it, blended families made up of couples with children from their previous marriages, married couples who choose to remain child free, and grandparents residing with their grandchildren. The trend toward greater family diversity (and greater recognition of diversity than existed even at midcentury) reflects a process of de-McDonaldization as families place more emphasis on the quality of bonds between family members than the predictability offered by the heterosexist, gender-specialized arrangement of the 1950s.

Editor's Note: This chapter was originally written for the second edition of this volume.

In stark contrast to what is happening with the shifts in family structure, however, are the day-to-day realities of family life. The daily activities of families seem to have undergone a process of McDonaldization as people look for instant gratification in their relationships, and family time is governed more and more by technology such as television, cell phones, video game systems, and computers. Thus, shifting family structures pose a challenge to the process of McDonaldization, and aspects of the McDonaldized world continue to seep into family life.

The De-McDonaldization of the Family Structure

Perhaps the most obvious indication that family structure has undergone a process of de-McDonaldization is the wide variety of paths to forming a family. In the 1950s, this was fairly straightforward and easily predicted: A man meets a woman, they marry, and if all goes well with his job, he becomes the breadwinner, and she stays at home to raise children. Although this did not characterize all families at midcentury, it fit the majority (even among racial minority and low-income families). Today, however, even the expectation that a man will partner up with a woman is uncertain. Gay and lesbian couples are a small, but increasingly visible type of family that calls the notion that a family begins with the union of a man and woman into question.

Although marriage is not as inevitable as it once was, it is still very common. Most people who can legally marry, do. But just as the pathway to marriage has shifted, so too has the structure of marriage itself. The slow erosion of rigid gender roles in addition to declines in male wages and expanded opportunities for women in the workplace have made dual-earning the modal arrangement among married couples, including those with children. In most dual-earning couples, the male is still the primary earner, but a growing number of couples include cobreadwinners and wives who outearn their husbands. Families with stay-at-home fathers are still a very small group, but even employed married fathers have stepped up their participation in child-rearing and pick up more of the housework slack. Therefore, families are exercising a wider range of earning and care-taking arrangements that do not always fall along the predictable gender-specialized lines.

Not only are breadwinning and caregiving arrangements more fluid in contemporary marriages, but it is also no longer a given that the marriage will be a lifetime partnership. The slow rise in divorce rates over time and high rates of remarriage imply that marriage is not a once-in-a-lifetime experience; it may happen two, three, or even four times (especially if you are a celebrity). This makes familial relationships incredibly complex and highly unpredictable. For example, a woman may experience several immediate family relationships over the course of her life: her parents (who may or may not be married, may or may not be living together, and may or may not be heterosexual), siblings, step-siblings, half-siblings, a first husband, a same-sex cohabiting partner, step-children, half-children, and nonresident biological children.

In addition to marriage, most people have children at some point in their lives. Yet, even this dimension of family life has become less certain over time. A small but growing minority of couples, not limited by infertility, is opting for a childfree lifestyle. Rather than seeking fulfillment through having children, these couples take pleasure in fulfilling careers and maybe a pet or two. For those who do become parents, it is no longer a social prerequisite that mothers and fathers be married, or even that there *is* a mother and father. It is more common now than in previous decades for childbearing to take place outside of marriage, particularly among low-income men and women.

These trends raise the question: why did family structure shift? Particularly given how stable the conventional nuclear family was, and that U.S. society has placed a higher value on efficiency, rationality, and predictability as time goes on, it seems odd that so many Americans would choose to reject this model. This rejection seems to come at the hands of many who found the arrangement oppressive. Despite all of the McDonaldized advantages it had to offer, it did not offer fulfillment to people who did not wish to have children, to women who found housework depressing, to men who found breadwinning to be stressful, to homosexuals who did not wish to partner up with someone of the opposite sex, or to couples who were trapped in unsatisfying marriages. So underlying the changes in family structure was a movement toward building rewarding relationships and having satisfying family relationships (e.g., remaining married out of want rather than out of obligation or having children because you want them, not because you are "supposed" to have them).

Today, there is an intense focus on the quality of family life, particularly on raising high-quality children and forming high-quality marital relationships. Demographers argue that families have transitioned from wanting a high "quantity" of children to desiring high "quality" children. This emphasis on "quality" children is evidenced by the cultural shift toward "intensive mothering" and "involved fathering," two terms that have received a great deal of popular press in the past decade.

Among middle- and upper-class parents, these parental investments in children start as early as the pregnancy. Expectant parents (both women *and* men) immerse themselves in books about pregnancy and parenting, enroll in Lamaze and prebirthing classes, put earphones of classical music against their pregnant bellies, settle on names long before the fetus reaches full term, and carry around sonogram pictures as if the child were already born. Once babies are born, the nurturing continues and accelerates. Children are enrolled in preschool classes to enhance their cognitive development, even in families with nonemployed mothers. The very best preschools can have waiting lists several years long, so that children need to be put on the list before they are even born. Then parents race to sign their children up for various extracurricular activities such as art classes, sports teams, and music lessons. Although poor parents do not necessarily have the means or desire to enroll their children in countless activities to enhance their development, this group of parents often has some of the highest educational and occupational aspirations for their children. Parental involvement in poor families is more likely to be characterized by protecting children's physical safety in urban areas and providing their children's material needs (perhaps by forgoing some of their own material needs).

The trend toward high parental investment might seem counterintuitive given that as time goes on, children are less economically useful to their parents. Children no longer offer the benefit of unpaid labor on the farm, neither do they offer much help in the form of paid labor given child labor laws in the United States. Further, the establishment of the federal Social Security system and Medicare as well as the availability of nursing centers, means children are not as essential for parents' old age security (although the Social Security system is facing a bit of a crisis in recent years, it was growing strong at the time of declining fertility).

Not only do children not offer much economic utility, they are expensive. For many middle- and upper-class families, it is even normative for children to expect their parents will pay for their college tuition, and sometimes their postgraduate educations. Indeed, young adults are attending college at record rates, many on their parents' dime. Children also reside in their parents' homes longer, often through young adulthood (and often rent-free). This has many parenting experts wondering why Americans have any children at all, particularly low-income men and women, who have less disposable income to devote to childrearing. Children now cost much more money than they give in return, and yet parents seem to be investing in their children more than ever.

Obviously, children offer something other than economic value to their parents, and this is probably why people have them. Today, emotional bonds more aptly characterize the parent-child relationship than economic ones. Parents get joy from their children's accomplishments rather than their financial return. This is not to say that parents did not get joy or have love for their children in years past, only that there was an economic component of the relationship that does not seem to be as strong today.

In addition to high-quality children, people also aspire to enter high-quality romantic partnerships. The importance of romantic love in contemporary relationships is a relatively recent phenomenon, given that historically marriage has been conceptualized as a committed economic partnership.

In the past, economic gains to marriage were clearer: Men gained unpaid labor and women gained economic security. Now that gendered roles are changing (albeit slowly), and marital stability has decreased, the gains to marriage are ambiguous and less tangible. Women can earn a living outside the home, and so they do not necessarily need men for economic security (although gender discrimination and the gendered wage gap persist, so women are still disadvantaged in the labor market). Women may also be less willing to do the unpaid labor in the home. Hence, when men and women do cohabitate or marry, their marriages may be of higher quality because there may be a greater focus on companionship and romantic love than on economic exchange. Women have expanded opportunities to work outside the home if they so desire, may be more empowered to voice their opinions pertaining to family matters, and enjoy greater agency to leave unfulfilling marriages. Men may have lost a bit of power inside the home, but they might feel less pressure to be the sole breadwinner (a job loss might not be as devastating to the family) and find relationships with their children more rewarding.

Expectations about what partners should get from relationships, and marriages in particular, still have some economic basis, but added to it is the expectation that a partner should also be a lover and a friend. This is evidenced by the fact that a woman's standard of living generally declines after a divorce, and yet women remain much more likely to initiate a divorce than men. Therefore, women are obviously seeking more than just economic support when they marry.

Among some groups, the aspirations for a good marriage are so high that people will delay marriage until midlife or indefinitely. For example, some scholars argue that low-income men and women have disproportionately lower marriage rates than middle- and high-income couples because they do not feel they have achieved the necessary prerequisites for a good marriage, such as economic stability and a long-standing romance. For many men and women, being "happily married" seems more important than just being married.

In sum, shifts in family structure offer some of the more striking examples of trends toward de-McDonaldization. Families, or perhaps more appropriately, individuals within families, have successfully challenged the dominant arrangement of the white, middle-class, nuclear family with the breadwinner father and stay-at-home mother. This arrangement, which seemed to offer the most predictability for organizing family life, has been replaced by a wide variety of family structures. These additional arrangements may not offer as much stability as the 1950s ideal, but they may create satisfying (i.e., better quality) relationships for people. Although there are movements to reinstate the traditional nuclear family of yesteryear as the ideal, the increasing tolerance for family structures that deviate from this family type gives people more choices to construct relationships in unique ways that fit their wants and needs.

McDonaldization of Everyday Family Life

Although it might seem that people are more interested in forming emotionally fulfilling partnerships than those in previous generations, it also seems as if many people are falling short of this goal. It is difficult to ignore the rise in marital instability as well as the high level of volatility of cohabiting relationships—many cohabiting relationships dissolve because they turn into marriages, but not all. Part of this may have to do with expanded life spans—as people live longer, they have to live together longer, and the prospect of spending the next 60 to 70 years together may seem more daunting than just spending the next 30 or 40. At the same time, it seems as if some degree of calculation might be going on in marital relationships. Just as people expect instantaneous results when they dine in fast-food restaurants, people may expect instant gratification from their romantic partnerships. The impatience to "see results" may be part of the reason a high percentage of marriages that end in divorce do so within a few years and why so many cohabiting relationships are short-lived. When couples run into obstacles or disagreement, they may be more likely to exit the relationship than stay the course. The extreme examples of this are the widely publicized celebrity marriages, such as that of Britney Spears, which last only hours or a few days.

When spouses do not get the immediate results they expect from the relationship, they might turn to prepackaged advice in the form of self-help books rather than seeking in-depth, personalized marriage counseling. These self-help books are written by people who may or may not be professionals and who are completely removed from the unique circumstances of any individual marriage. Although these books might offer some small insights to a couple, they are unlikely to single-handedly save a relationship. Yet, the appeal of quick and easy fixes to conflict is reflected in the near universal familiarity with John Gray's *Men Are From Mars, Women Are From Venus,* which argues men and women must learn to accept the "natural" differences between the sexes to establish healthy communication and develop deep connections. Essentially, the book offers advice for couples who accept and follow gendered stereotypes.

The popularity of quick fixes to family issues is further evidenced by one of the most popular daytime television talk shows, *Dr. Phil.* Dr. Phil, a television personality, offers succinct solutions to a variety of complex family issues in less than an hour. His straight talk one-liners make navigating family relationships sound easy. In fact, Dr. Phil's advice is so revered that he even wrote a best-selling dieting book despite being a bit overweight himself. (It is also worth noting that the "relationship expert" Dr. John Gray lost little credibility after divorcing his first wife.)

One caveat to these relationship books is that they still underscore the trend toward high-quality relationships. This is because the interest alone in these types of self-help books and television shows indicates that people are looking for more out of their relationships than just financial gain. There may not have been a market for these kinds of books or shows in previous decades, because the concerns over having a happy marriage and/or maximizing a child's cognitive development were not nearly as intense as they are today. The idea of seeking marriage counseling or needing to read to their child every night would have seemed foreign to a young couple in the 1950s. Yet today, some couples seek counseling, or listen to John Gray's *Men Are From Mars, Women Are From Venus* book on tape, before they are even married.

In addition to the impatience to make a marriage work, there may be impatience to see the marital relationship come to fruition. This may seem like an odd perspective given that young people are more likely to delay marriage than in the past. How could people be impatient to marry or partner up if they are increasingly putting off this decision? First, it does not seem as if marriage is delayed because people are spending more time hunting around for Mr. or Ms. Right. A more common, and probable, explanation of delayed marriage is that people are investing more time in educational and leisure pursuits. Their sole focus as young adults is not on finding a good mate, but rather finding a good job. It was often joked that when women went to college in the 1970s, they were seeking their "Mrs." degree, whereas now that argument does not seem to carry much weight for recent cohorts of women who are actually graduating from college at higher rates than their male counterparts. In fact, *because* young people are focusing so intensely on their studies or burgeoning careers, they may arrive at their late 20s in a state of panic, realizing they have not yet connected with a mate.

Popular reality television shows such as *The Bachelor* and *Who Wants to Marry My Dad?* are prime examples of the impatience with which some segments of the American population are approaching marriage. Even though these programs are made for television, they are reflective of what is going on in some segments of the viewing public. For example, "speed dating" has become quite popular in major cities. Potential dating partners gather together in a group, have a one-on-one conversation with each individual in the group for a few minutes, and then make a list of the people they find worthy of further dates. Internet matchmaking, another example of this, has virtually exploded over the past decade. People select dating partners by scanning online McDonaldized profiles, which include short snippets of a person's occupation, interests, and hobbies that generally offer no credible insight into a person's depth or originality. People may still form high-quality relationships as a result (or perhaps in spite of) this process, but the process itself is certainly McDonaldized.

Perhaps the most striking evidence of how the family has McDonaldized is the extent to which families have embraced nonhuman technology. Families are allowing the technology to seep into their homes and pervade their most intimate relationships. In fact, new technologies are increasingly targeted toward families, particularly parents and children. Verizon's "Family Share Plan" for cellular phones is a prime example, where cell phone communication between family members is "free" (after you pay for phones for each family member, activation fees, and the flat monthly fee). This encourages families to hook up all of their members to cell phones, controlling the means of their communication. Cell phones in hand, families no longer have to be together to stay in touch. Although this may mean that families are more closely connected than ever before, it can also mean spotty cell phone calls ("Can you hear me now?") replace quality face-to-face dinner conversations. The implications of this technology for family life are unclear.

What is clearer is that family time may increasingly involve convening around the television rather than the dinner table given that families (1) spend large amounts of time watching television and (2) are less likely to have one member of the family devoting time solely to household work such as preparing home-cooked dinners. Ready-made dinners might be picked up from grocery stores or take-out restaurants on the way home, or perhaps frozen dinners are zapped in the microwave. Parents may contend with "vanishing children" who come home from school and immerse themselves in technology—heading straight to the television to watch their favorite programs or to the computer to play video games, surf the Internet, download music, or "instant message" their friends. Although not all families can afford to own a computer or to be hooked up to the Internet, families are more likely than other types of households to both own a computer and have the Internet streaming into their households. Hence, the technology is increasingly affecting how families spend their time.

Family time is also increasingly structured and scripted. Families may even incorporate time management strategies they learn at the workplace into their family life so that they "make the most" of family time. Examples include creating a family calendar where family dinners or talks and spousal "date nights" are squeezed between sports practices, music lessons, birthday parties, sleepovers, and parental work schedules. When families want to get away together, they travel to McDonaldized amusement parks such as Six Flags or every child's media-generated fantasy, Disneyland. Almost every experience is preplanned in these parks, so parents do not have to come up with creative ways to entertain and interact with their children—Disney has done all the work. Families only need to decide which ride to go on first and what time to stop and eat at the McDonaldized restaurants to refuel. In addition to amusement parks, shopping malls are another hot spot for families to spend time together. Malls are popular because there is something for everyone: toy stores for young children, music and apparel stores for teenagers, and electronic, home, and department stores for parents. Eating is simplified by the food court, where everyone can select their favorite fast food and dine together in the centralized seating area.

Finally, family celebrations such as birthdays, anniversaries, and graduations may also be homogenized, taking place at the nearest chain restaurant, complete with singing waiters and a brownie sundae for dessert. In sum, virtually every aspect of the day-to-day lives of families has been McDonaldized in one way or another.

The Family as an Institution: Can It Retard the McDonaldization of U.S. Society?

Although family life has been highly influenced by the process of McDonaldization, it is also an institution uniquely suited to hinder and challenge the principles of McDonaldization governing U.S. society. Perhaps the most distinctive characteristic of contemporary U.S. families is that they are (presumably) made up of people who care for each other and perhaps even have love or altruistic feelings toward one another. Unlike other social institutions, such as corporations or governments, families are not motivated strictly by profit. At least for the parent-child relationship, an emotional connection is a major, if not the primary, dimension of the bond. Although financial gain or efficiency may be a component of the familial relationship, families seem to be less focused on economic gain than in years past.

Within families, people have the freedom to construct their own family norms and create unique traditions together (or at least the adults in the family can). As employees and consumers, however, people are subject to the McDonaldized norms and stipulations dictated by corporations and the government. In fact as the workplace and the consumption landscape become increasingly rationalized, homogenized and impersonal, people can, and probably do, seek refuge in their family life. The "nothingness" of the outside world may be part of the reason why families are investing so heavily in their children and raising the standards for their marital relationships. Although not wholly free of restraint, family life may be a space where they can choose to value authenticity and creativity. It may also be one of the few areas people can get a reprieve from the focus on efficiency, calculability, predictability, and control that they experience at work and in consuming.

Additionally, families have the power to hijack elements of the McDonaldized world, such as the nonhuman technologies that control people's lives, and use them to humanize relationships and create authenticity. This is in direct conflict with the way such technology has traditionally created distance between people and depersonalized nonfamily interactions. Rather than allowing the technology to govern their lives, which is all but inescapable in corporate America, families have the opportunity to use technology to bring family members closer. Returning to the cell phone example used earlier, such technology can actually be used to strengthen family bonds. Verizon's mission is not to bring families closer, but to maximize its profits by hooking as many people as possible up to its cell phones. It wants everyone to be talking on cell phones as often as possible, racking up those minutes. Families, however, can subvert these goals by making careful decisions about how they use the technology in their family life. So, rather than allowing cell phone conversations to replace face-to-face interactions or keeping people connected to bosses when they are supposed to be spending time together as a family, the technology could be used by employees on business trips as a means to have more contact with their family members. Further, extended family bonds, which may grow distant over time as people move and are geographically separated, may be rekindled with the magic of cell phone technology. Adult siblings and parents with adult children living on separate coasts who may not otherwise be able to afford the costly plane travel or high landline telephone bills, may remain in close contact via low-cost cell phone programs and free e-mail, which they may access at work or the public library if they do not have a home computer.

Conclusion

Even though the process of McDonaldization continues, structural changes in the family pose a threat to the trend. People seem to want deep, authentic connections in their family relationships, and they seem willing to sacrifice some level of predictability to achieve these goals (hence the movement away from the white, middle-class nuclear ideal). However, what the McDonaldized world has to offer them in the way of "enchanting" technologies such as television shows, cell phones, and Web surfing may be difficult for families to reject, even when such technologies are likely to control and erode quality family time. Families have the power to use these technologies for their own non-McDonaldized purposes (using e-mail to keep in close and meaningful contact with distant relatives rather than sending meaningless forwards to acquaintances), but only if they make conscious efforts to do so.

Thinking Critically

1. Is the de-McDonaldization of the family structure more of a good or a bad thing? Why?

2. Is the McDonaldization of everyday family life more of a good or a bad thing? Why?

3. Think about the relationship between the McDonaldization of family structure and everyday family life.

4. Would you rather raise your family in a McDonaldized or a de-McDonaldized fashion? Explain your choice.

5. Would you expect the greatest resistance to McDonaldization to come from within the family?

Gary Wilkinson looks at the McDonaldization of the state educational system in England. Education (and much else) in England is far more McDonaldized than it is in the U.S. because, among other things, of more centralized control by the state. Among the issues discussed by Wilkinson is the obsession with quantifiable indicators such as student test scores and comparative rankings of schools (through "league tables"). In focusing on such quantifiable variables, the "Government has come to believe . . . you do indeed fatten a pig by weighing it." Schools are constantly audited on a variety of numerical measures giving rise to what has come to be known as the "audit society." Great predictability is demanded of schools as a result of the introduction in 1988 of a nation-wide educational curriculum. Further, much of what takes place in the schools is tightly scripted and this is accomplished at the cost of diversity and distinctive identity in the schools. Control is exercised over the schools both by an elaborate bureaucratic system, as well as by nonhuman technologies such as measurement and checking instruments, as well as scripts. There are lots of these controlling mechanisms, but none of the agencies involved in exercising this control is a professional organization of educators. All of this has led to the creation of "McSchools." Wilkinson ends by invoking some of my other ideas on this issue such as "reenchanting" the schools by, for example, making that which is "unspectacular" in education "spectacular." That is, the need to focus on the everyday activities of education making them not only the center of concern but where the true spectacle of education—excellent teachers finding new and exciting ways to educate students—is to be found.

14

McSchools for McWorld?

Mediating Global Pressures With a McDonaldizing Education Policy Response

Gary Wilkinson

The McDonaldization of the English State Education System

Efficiency and Calculability

Efficiency and calculability, two key features of all McDonaldized systems, can be perceived both as motivations driving education policies or outcomes of their implementation. Efficiency masquerades as a seemingly value-free term with a deceptive appearance of scientific neutrality and, as an abstract principle, is, as Neave notes, 'unassailable.' But difficulties arise when it is applied to public sector activity where we find that the superficial unassailability of the efficiency principle is rather more contestable.

Editor's Note: Excerpts from "McSchools for McWorld? Mediating Global Pressures with a McDonaldizing Education Policy Response" by Gary Wilkinson, *Cambridge Journal of Education, 36,* 81–98, March 2006. Used with permission.

Chambers English dictionary defines efficiency as 'power to produce the result intended' and it is this invocation of goal-directed purpose which immediately suggests two areas of ideological and practical disputation when applied to education: first, in a state school system, the 'result intended' is defined at a state level and therefore has a political flavour, spiced with ideological notions of education's purposes and possibilities; second, one of the main tenets of managerialist efficiency is a stress on outcomes or outputs, rather than inputs or process. At a national level, this emphasis promotes a utilitarian philosophy which implies that engagement in education is only beneficial insofar as it produces 'outputs' and, further, where these outputs are defined in relation to potential economic productivity, implies that education is a matter for wealth acquisition rather than a public good. Two corollaries follow. First, if education is about personal gain in the marketplace, then arguments such as university students paying for their own education become more persuasive. Second, knowledge economies require workers competent in only appropriate knowledge so we have seen a shift in English schools to a focus on so-called 'transferable skills' and away from the arts and humanities. Primary schools, for example, now have only three 'core' subjects: mathematics, English and science. Charles Clarke's description of education for its own sake as 'a bit dodgy' and contempt for classics and history supports an interpretation of the introduction of national strategies for numeracy and literacy (skills rather than subjects) as an attempt to subtly change perceptions of school mathematics and English such that the utilitarian skills they develop are valued over and above any study of them as an academic exercise—they are valued only insofar as they are servants of McWorld.

The quest for efficiency in state school system, has translated into education policy which appears obsessed with measurable indicators. So, improved efficiency has come to be equated with better 'results intended' where results equate to academic attainment measured through public examinations understood here as the examination of a syllabus where both the curriculum and assessment methods are set above the level of the individual school and the performance of individual schools is published. These include not only GCSE's, GNVQs or A levels at secondary and post-secondary level, but also Standard Assessment Tasks (SATs) at secondary Year 9 and primary Years 2 and 6. Efficiency in English state schools, then, appears to have one principal measure, academic attainment, and at primary level, even this relates only to mathematics, English and science. At national level, education policy had necessitated and directed the development of measuring technologies and the establishment of agencies or specialist arms of Government departments charged with policing these to such an extent that one might be convinced that the Government has come to believe that you do indeed fatten a pig by weighing it. The effect, has Hargreaves notes, is that 'schools and teachers have been squeezed into the tunnel vision of test scores achievement targets and leagues tables of accountability.'

Within Ritzer's framework, the obsession with measurement tools to demonstrate efficiency can be seen as a preoccupation with calculability which refers to 'an emphasis on the quantitative aspects of products sold.' It reduces services and the qualitative experiences of those delivering and using them to numbers echoing again Taylorist ideas of scientific management and measurement at work. Rose too notes this post-war evolution of quantification in modern states:

> The invention of programmes of Government depended upon and demanded an "avalanche of printed numbers," which rendered the population calculable by turning it into inscriptions that were durable and transportable, that could be accumulated in the offices of officials, that could be added, subtracted, compared, and contrasted.

This has given rise to what Michael Power calls the 'audit society.' McDonaldizing calculability, which now permeates every aspect of the English school system, is evident in target-setting (for pupils, teachers, schools, LEAs), league tables, examination and SAT results, quantitative OEDC comparative international 'research findings' which support the introduction of new initiatives, the 'Autumn package,' number of exclusions and pupil-unit funding mechanisms. Even after-school sports activities, renamed 'study support,' seem no longer valued primarily for their promotion of sportsmanship, school community or physical development: for the DfES, these activities are important because the 'overall effect of participation in study support is:

- three and a half grades on Best 5 score, or one more A–C pass at GCSE;
- half a grade in Maths and English GCSE;
- a third of a level in Maths SATs at KS3;
- three quarters of a level in Science SATs at KS3.

Enriching opportunities, previously considered distinctive from academic provision in schools, are now part of a straight-jacketing 'standards' agenda and defined solely in terms of calculable examination results. As with a narrow working interpretation of efficiency, the problem with this approach is that what comes to matter is that which is numerically calculable. So, for schools, calculable progress in the number of GCSE passes and improved SAT results for primary mathematics, English and science takes precedence over all else and comes to dominate a narrowed and restricting menu of priorities. For the state, enriching extracurricular activities, once an integral part of school life, are justified with reductivist psychometric indicators which appear blind to any sense of a wider professional mission or holistic educational project.

Predictability

. . . Hargreaves discerns in 'many parts of the world . . . a compulsive obsession with standardization' and we might argue that the UK state's standardization of school education in its quest for predictability began with the Education Reform Act, 1988, and the introduction of the National Curriculum steered through parliament by the Department of Education and Science minister, Kenneth Baker. At that time, as McCulloch et al. have noted, there was fear that this policy instrument constituted an attack on professionalism which would reduce teachers to 'mere technicians or functionaries, implementing orders that had been decided elsewhere.' Whatever motivation underpinned this statute, a common and compulsory National Curriculum has, as it was designed to do, led to predictability expressed through common educational provision and entitlement. As predictability helps managers at McDonald's, so it assists the running of a McDonaldized school system since effective national inspection systems are predicated upon predictability without which they are unable to arrive at contextualized judgments and produce comparative reports.

Part of McDonald's predictability armoury is the issuing of 'scripts' to a McDonaldized workforce in order to control interactions between employees and customers. So, a major national education policy theme of recent years has been the establishment of scripts and scriptwriters and managers to achieve this predictability and control . . . Across the education system, standardization has produced not only uniformity of curriculum content and pedagogic style, but predictable 'bastard leadership' where head teacher's cox rowers of educational boats whose fixed rudders steer the vessel to a centrally-determined mooring point.

There is undoubtedly merit in the idea of ensuring that citizens are entitled to receive a minimum standard of provision from the education service. The paradox here is that, whilst successive Governments claim to be promoting choice and diversity, standardization and predictability of provision renders such choice academic. Secretaries of State for Education are 'promoting diversity' and valuing schools' 'distinct identity' only insofar as teaching staffs deliver the same curriculum using the same teaching strategies.

Control

. . . Whilst there has been an attempt to expand marketization in higher education which has contributed towards 'the McDonaldization of Higher Education,' Furedi notes that 'Despite the attempt to subordinate the academy to the dictates of economic calculation, it is not market forces but a centralized system of bureaucratic auditing that dominates university life.' Similarly, whilst the UK school system has been subject to some limited degree of what Glennerster (1991) terms 'quasi-markets,' it is managerialist techniques rather than market forces which have lead to the McDonaldization of the school system and which here equate to Ritzer's 'control through non-human technology.' It is this public-sector adaptation of Ray Kroc's franchising principles, the new public management which has resulted in the primacy of the principles of efficiency, calculability and predictability in the education system. In the context of the UK education system, controlling technologies would include the measuring instruments which make the system calculable and determine its efficiency and the checking mechanisms represented by the efficiency police. As we have seen, control through legislative and non-statutory 'scripts' with their writers, managers and training agents is also evident in today's McDonaldized school system and helps to ensure predictability.

The nature and extent of the control over teachers' work is remarkable, for two reasons. First, the sheer number of controlling technologies of McDonaldizing scripts, measuring technologies and agencies managing and patrolling these demonstrates the pervasive extent to which centrally directed policy steers not just the structure of the education system but the work of those within it at an individual operational level. Second, and perhaps unique amongst public-sector professions, it is striking that not one of these controlling bodies involved in either the policing of efficiency or the management of scripts is a national professional body comprised of, or representing, professional practitioners.

There is, then, an overwhelming prima facie case that national education policy has reproduced McDonaldizing techniques of control which has generated and promoted an English school system whose structure is characterized by centralizing mechanisms engaged in script-writing to control the content of teaching professionals' work and selective performance measurement to ensure the scripts are efficiently employed. Some recent policy statements indicate that the British Government is aware of some of the problems associated with their controlling instruments and has begun to present slight shifts in policy as an attempt at what I have elsewhere called 'the re-enchantment of a McDonaldized profession.' An awareness of collective demoralization in an overloaded and over-controlled teaching profession with a sense that their political masters do not trust them (Bottery, 2003), perhaps provided the motivation for the sentiments stressed in the White Paper Excellence and Enjoyment (DfES, 2003) which makes much of releasing teachers from unnecessary bureaucratic tasks and encouraging initiative and innovation so as to make the school experience enjoyable for children by reinvigorating the professionalism of their teachers. Any optimism that this heralds the deMcDonaldization of the English school system is, however, shown to be misplaced on reaching paragraph 2.18 where it is decreed that 'The Secretary of State has said that testing, targets and tables are here to stay.' It is not only the measuring technologies which are here to stay. The literacy and numeracy scripts too will remain:

> We also need to make sure that we are building on the gains that have been made in literary and numeracy—developing the Strategies still further, and not losing sight of important fundamentals like the value of discrete literacy and mathematics teaching through the literacy hour and daily mathematics lesson.

However, it is precisely these measuring technologies and scripts which have produced a disenchanted McDonaldized system, a corrosive culture of performativity and a narrowing vision of the educational project. It may be true that teachers have 'much more freedom that they often realize to design the timetable and decide what and how they teach' but where this freedom lies in administrative trivia, such as timetable design, or is constricted to curriculum areas which have effectively been rendered peripheral because they are 'unmeasured,' this amounts only to granting McDonald's franchisees the freedom to serve breakfast time Egg McMuffins beyond 10 am and the mock creativity to vary 'have-a-nice-day' to 'have a-good weekend.'

Conclusion

We have seen that the British state has focused on an ambiguous conception of the knowledge economy in its interpretation of how globalizing pressures affect the economic well-being of the UK. Further, it has sought to mediate and respond to these pressures by attempting to position the UK in a globally competitive economic niche specializing in high-tech industries and services and its education and employment policies have been geared towards achieving this end. To subordinate the education system to this overarching policy objective, it has been necessary to steer and control not only the goals of the English education project but its methodologies too. The introduction of the new public management techniques required to do this has resulted in the McDonaldization of the English state school education system with a disproportionate stress on narrowly-defined efficiency, an obsession with calculability and measurement, and the power of the controlling mechanisms needed for imposition, policing and enforcement. The state education system has effectively been reconfigured in order to serve the markets of McWorld, but it is heavy-handed managerialism rather than the internal quasi-markets within the system that has led to McDonaldization. It is, or course, difficult to be optimistic about the potential for a rigidly directed education system producing a flexible, creative workforce. These 'epidemics of standardization and overregulation' may deliver an education fit for the inhabitants of consumerist McWorld but its appropriateness for nurturing participatory citizens for twenty-first century liberal democracies is rather more contestable.

The more Orwellian danger McDonaldization presents is what Bottery has called the 'limiting of vision' where debate about the wider purposes of education and its role within a western liberal democracy is suffocated beneath the heavy pillow of abstracted, managerialist 'objectivity' and global economics. Ball recognizes that in McSchools the focus on outputs means that beliefs and values take second place as the pernicious effects of performativity lead to intensification, contradictions, fabrications, alienation and 'values schizophrenia.' Where practice and the performance of practitioners are calibrated and adjudged against a limited range of statistically quantifiable performance indicators, then 'rationalized efficacy binds subjectivity to truth, and subjects to experts, in new and potent ways.' The current policy technologies might be seen as an example of how to govern 'at a distance,' or in an 'advanced liberal' way where the state operates through the promotion of mechanisms which encourage the self-regulation of subjects—not only does the state achieve its purposes but such methods provide 'a plethora of indirect mechanisms that can translate the goals of political, social and economic authorities into the choices and commitments of individuals.' As McSchools seek to regularize their staffs and their work, a further concern is the fate of teachers suffering from 'values schizophrenia' in a disenchanted McDonaldized profession whose immersion in deskilled, discretion-free labour may lead to a lack of job satisfaction, unhealthy morale, and superficial professional loyalty and commitment, resulting in high staff turnover, poor pay and conditions, and low status. If a McDonaldized state school system is an education for Barber's McWorld, itself an allegory for the predominance of a value-free ideology of materialistic consumption, then alienation born of a frustrated yearning for a return to 'the Golden Age of teacher control' might represent teachers' Jihad, where the mysticism of unaccountable professional autonomy was once both balanced and licensed by the public's belief in their commitment to the civic good.

In *Enchanting a Disenchanted World*, Ritzer explores potential avenues of enchantment for a McDonaldized world. If accommodation is to be reached between the globally-focused economic priorities of the UK state and what must now be regarded as an untenable Jihadic mysticism of unfettered professional autonomy in education, a way of re-enchanting a McDonaldized system must be found. If universities need to 'make the unspectacular spectacular,' education professionals in the school sector must find a way of making 'excellence' enjoyable, engaging and rewarding for both children and education workers within a context whose meaning they have helped define and which extends beyond the production of 'human capital' for the digital age and the knowledge economy. The paternalistic days of the omniscient, unaccountable professional are patently finished in the public sector. But the objectives and methods of state control over the school system, explored here through the heuristic of McDonaldization, has produced what Ball calls a system where 'value replaces values.' Rose observes that governmentality exploits the attempts of individuals to make life meaningful for themselves. Education professionals, then, both collectively and individually have responded to the technologies of control in a McDonaldized system with a compensatory set of 'techniques of the self' with the result that through 'self-inspection, self-problematization, self-monitoring, and confession, [they] evaluate [them]selves according to the criteria provided for [them] by others.' Education professionals need to reclaim, redefine and regovern their own collective subjectivity. They might begin by uniting and striving within their trade unions and professional councils for collective influence at the national level of policy-making so as to re-enchant a McDonaldized state school system fit for engagement with something bigger than McWorld.

Thinking Critically

1. What role does the state in Great Britain play in creating a far more McDonaldized educational system than in the US?

2. What is it about American society and American education that has allowed it to avoid the extremes of McDonaldization found in Great Britain and British education?

3. How does McDonaldization assist in educating children?

4. How would the involvement of professional associations reduce the degree of McDonaldization?

5. How can the everyday activities of a school made to be magical, enchanting?

Nathan Jurgenson applies the concept of McDonaldization to the Internet, especially Web 1.0 and Web 2.0. He finds the application useful, especially to Web 1.0. However, while Web 1.0 continues to exist, the momentum on the Internet is in the direction of Web 2.0 (e.g. Wikipedia, Facebook, blogs). McDonaldization applies far less well to Web 2.0 (see Chapter 38 for a related discussion of ebay and the issue of whether ebayization is now a better paradigm than McDonaldization for the contemporary world). Indeed, Jurgenson argues that what we might be seeing is a broader trend in the direction of deMcDonaldization with Web 2.0 being the vanguard of this process. What transpires on Web 2.0 is less efficient, more unpredictable, less calculable, less subject to external control and therefore more humanized. As a result, Web 2.0 is less subject to the irrationalities of rationality than Web 1.0 or McDonaldized systems in the material world. The key differences on Web 2.0 compared to the material world are digitality and a lack of scarcity. It is these factors that make deMcDonaldization possible on Web 2.0. This essay clearly leads to a questioning of the grand narrative of ever-increasing McDonaldization, but it also suggests that we may see a bifurcation between the McDonaldized material world (which is not digital and is characterized by scarcity) and the de-materialized world that exists on the Internet.

15

The De-McDonaldization of the Internet

Nathan Jurgenson

The rapidly changing Internet raises the issues of both how to theorize it in general as well as its most recent developments. One strategy is to use longstanding theories and theoretical concepts and to see to what degree they apply to, and illuminate, these new realities. There are, of course, innumerable theoretical ideas, and a large number of theories, from which to choose. To make this manageable, we will focus here on one traditional social theory—the theory of rationalization, in particular its most recent manifestation in the concept of McDonaldization. Applying the latter idea to the Internet is no easy matter, especially since the Internet is in the midst of dramatic changes, one of which is the move from Web 1.0 to Web 2.0 as described below. Thus, one issue is whether the principles of McDonaldization apply, and apply equally well, to both Web 1.0 and Web 2.0. A second is whether the ongoing change is reflective of a process of increasing McDonaldization. That is, the McDonaldization concept, and the underlying theory, would predict an increase in the McDonaldization over time as it moves more toward Web 2.0; it would also predict that Web 2.0 is more McDonaldized than Web 1.0.

Editor's Note: This chapter was written especially for the third edition of *McDonaldization: The Reader.*

To anticipate the conclusion, it is argued here that while McDonaldization and its sub-dimensions can be usefully applied to both Web 1.0 and 2.0, the latter is *not* more McDonaldized than the former and that the Internet has *not* undergone a process of increasing McDonaldization. This leads to several issues: Does this finding indicate that the concept of McDonaldization is of declining utility? Does it serve to contradict the general thesis of the increasing McDonaldization of society? Or, is there something about the Internet in general, and Web 2.0 in particular, that distinguishes it from the rest of society, which continues, as a general rule, to undergo increasing McDonaldization? These issues will be dealt with in the final section of this essay, but first we need to take a closer look at the Internet and its continuing transformation, specifically of Web 1.0 and 2.0, and then seek to apply the dimensions of McDonaldization to both of them, as well as to the general trend away from Web 1.0 to Web 2.0.

Web 1.0 and 2.0

One could simply see Web 1.0 and 2.0 as indicating different time periods. That is, Web 1.0 as the Internet that existed before the dot-com bubble burst, or as the first decade of the Internet (the 1990s), and that which exists at the present, or the Internet's second decade (the 2000s), as Web 2.0 (and whatever the Internet has in store in the future as the tentatively labeled Web 3.0). Another way to contrast the two is by the change in connectivity speed, where Web 1.0 was most likely to be experienced through dial-up connections and Web 2.0 by high-speed connections. Yet another view of this move from Web 1.0 to Web 2.0 focuses on the shift of the Internet from existing exclusively on a computer screen towards other, often mobile, platforms, such as laptops, cell phones, and other Internet-capable devices.

However, this essay rejects views of Web 1.0 and 2.0 being completely distinct. Here, the two are seen as overlapping phenomena. Not only have Web 1.0 and 2.0 always coexisted, they continue to coexist to this day. This essay deals mainly with the emerging importance of Web 2.0, and *it is the explosion of user-generated content that defines Web 2.0 and differentiates it from the provider-generated content of Web 1.0.* To put this another way, Web 2.0 is a bottom-up system, while Web 1.0 is centrally conceived and more top-down.

Web 1.0

Web 1.0 encompasses websites of the past that had not yet taken advantage of the user-generated content that is popular today as well as today's sites that remain top-down. Examples of Web 1.0 include:

- Switchboard.com and YellowPages.com, which centrally conceive how users find people and businesses through the framework of the sites.
- The Apple Store and other shopping sites that dictate the content and users' browsing (i.e., shopping).
- Online consumption of news on Web 1.0 was relatively more centrally conceived than today's popular news sites that allow users to "comment," or allow communities to direct user searches through the use of the "most emailed," "most blogged," or "most searched" lists. News sites in the past that did not have these features, as well as those news sites that have not incorporated them to this day, are examples of Web 1.0.
- The creators of Fodors.com use their own tastemakers to point tourists to various hotels, restaurants, activities, and so forth. More general information is searched for on sites like about.com, whose creators employ "experts" to help users find information, again, exemplifying the centrally conceived nature of Web 1.0.

It is very tempting to offer a "grand narrative" of a shift over time from a top-down Web 1.0 to a bottom-up Web 2.0. However, not only are such grand narratives passé, but like all grand narratives, this one would be far too simplistic. First, we recognize that the degree to which users can produce content on a site is not a dichotomous variable, but rather represents a continuum where some sites are further toward one end of the 1.0–2.0 spectrum than others. At least some user-generation occurs on many Web 1.0 sites and some top-down structures exist on Web 2.0 (e.g., the format of articles on Wikipedia or the profile pages on Facebook). Second, the "cyber-libertarian" ideology behind Web 2.0 that seeks to keep the Internet free and open (including to inputs by users) was present in Web 1.0, indeed, at the very beginning of all thinking about the Internet's possibilities. The Internet, much like many other technologies, was conceived by some as a revolutionary, if not utopian, development that would bring great increases in freedom for those involved. In spite of such great hopes and grand ambitions, the Internet has not fully resisted corporate structures, hierarchies, and control. Companies like AOL and Microsoft sought to control many Internet technologies with their own products and to purchase online real estate much in the same way this occurs in the material world. In this way, Web 1.0 came to lose many of its libertarian ideals as corporate entities began to control it and to create centrally conceived Internet products that structured and greatly limited the ways in which individuals used them.

Of course, at the time, this was not how many saw the Internet. It is with the benefit of hindsight that we can conceive of the Internet as once having been a more top-down system. In other words, Web 1.0 is a largely retrospective label created and used in order to contrast it to the new technologies that emerged later, remembering the general point that remnants of Web 1.0 continue to exist today. While the Internet today is increasingly a place where users are able to produce content, it was not always this way. Web 1.0 was an attempt to reposition online traditional business and organizational models. At the time, this did not seem, as it might now, overtly top-down or constraining to much of the business community or to many users. Web 1.0, heavily supported by venture capital, was a major force in the emergence of the dot-com bubble of online businesses in the late 1990s. In 2000, that bubble burst due to the frantic expenditure of money on business models that were simply incapable, at least at the time, of being profitable.

However, the cyber-libertarian ideals that predated Web 1.0 had not disappeared. Those who bought into these ideals saw the bursting of the Web 1.0 bubble as an opportunity, as having the potential for "creative destruction." According to Joseph Schumpeter, the essence of capitalism is its continual ability to destroy the old in order to make way for the new. In this case, the destruction of Web 1.0 (or at least some aspects of it) was seen as a needed prerequisite for the emergence of Web 2.0. To put it in other terms, the possibility of the emergence of a "flat world" free of competitive advantage, lay under the ruins of hierarchies that were at the base of Web 1.0. Here existed the opportunity to attempt again the actualization of the libertarian project online. This time it was fueled by, amongst other factors, the failure of the Internet to produce the expected profits and, more positively, the power of new high-speed technologies that enabled infinitely more users to interact online. The Internet as fast, accessible, useable, and as something that is always on, akin to other utilities, opens the door to a new kind of richly social and more humanized online experience.

Web 2.0

In contrast to Web 1.0, which is defined as being largely centrally conceived and controlled, Web 2.0 accords far less power to the creators of these systems and much more to their users; Web 2.0 sites, or at least the material on them, are, to a large extent, user-generated. In addition to the Web 1.0 experience of reading, browsing, and consuming online content, Web 2.0 *also* allows for writing and producing this content. It also permits the greatly increased ability to network with others in a very social sense. One way of describing this is to see the implosion of the consumer and the producer on Web 2.0 into the "prosumer," that is, on Web 2.0, users produce that which they consume (e.g., users both produce and consume the profiles and networks on Facebook) . . . Because of their user-generated content, sites on Web 2.0 are by and large more humanized and exist in a state of flux, as opposed to the more static Web 1.0.

Major examples of Web 2.0, and of the centrality of user-generation on them, include:

- Wikipedia, where users generate articles and constantly edit, update, and comment on them;
- Facebook, MySpace, and other social networking websites, where users create profiles composed of videos, photos, and text; interact with one another; and build communities;
- Second Life, where users create the characters, communities, and the entire virtual environment;
- The blogosphere, blogs (Web logs), microblogging (Twitter), and the comments on them are produced by those who consume them;
- eBay and Craigslist, where consumers rather than retailers create the market;
- YouTube and Flickr, where mostly amateurs upload and download videos and photographs;
- Current TV, where viewers create much of the programming, submit it via the Internet, and decide which submissions are aired;
- Linux, a free, collaboratively built open-source operating system, and other open-source software applications, like Mozilla Firefox, are created and maintained by those who use them;
- Amazon.com, whose consumers do all the work involved in ordering products and write the reviews;
- Yelp!, whose users create an online city guide by ranking, reviewing, and discussing various locations and activities in their area;
- The GeoWeb, which consists of online maps where, increasingly, users are creating and augmenting content with Google, Microsoft, and Yahoo tools (Helft 2007). Google Maps users, for example, can fix errors; add the locations of businesses; upload photos; link Wikipedia articles to; and blog about their experiences with, or reviews of, places on the map, thereby creating social communities.

This explosion of user-generated content has massively transformed the Internet. There are many different ways to describe this shift, to describe what is new and unique about Web 2.0, including the populist notion that many minds are better than one (the "wisdom of the crowds"), the view that emphasizes the productivity and originality of mass self-expression, or the cyber-libertarian notion of the advantages that accrue from breaking down barriers and structures online (creating a "flattened world"). It is likely that these views, and many others, are important in thinking about the shift from Web 1.0, where the user experience was best characterized as "looking stuff up" preset by others, to a Web 2.0 experience of production in addition to consumption (prosumption) and the increasingly humanized and social nature of the web by way of networking, and collaborating that proliferation of prosumption allows. It is with this understanding of the Internet and changes that have taken place on it that we can apply the theoretical framework of McDonaldization and the concepts that are its essence.

McDonaldization

Here, we move to a discussion of the relationship between McDonaldization and the Internet. On the one hand, of interest is the issue of whether the ideas associated with McDonaldization help us to better understand Web 1.0 and 2.0, as well as the general trend in the direction of the predominance of the latter over the former. On the other hand, we need to address the issue of whether the concept and the theory of McDonaldization need to be revised, or even abandoned, in light of the changing realities online, as well as differences between them and the more material realities such as the fast food restaurant (keeping in mind the point that the Internet is not divorced from physical reality, and is perhaps increasingly merging with the physical, a point that will be touched upon at the conclusion of this essay). Rethinking McDonaldization is made especially pressing since the general argument to be made below is that the move from Web from 1.0 to 2.0 tends to be in the direction of *less* rather than more McDonaldization. This, of course, stands in opposition to Ritzer's general argument about a society-wide, if not global, trend toward increasing McDonaldization (to say nothing of Weber's similar argument about increasing rationalization).

McDonaldization is defined by Ritzer in terms of its basic dimensions—efficiency, predictability, calculability, and control by *non*human rather than human technology. Like material realities such as fast food restaurants, Web 1.0 was, and is, highly McDonaldized. As previously described above, Web 1.0 websites are centrally conceived, that is, they are constructed in a one-size-fits-all model, and from the point of view of those who own, control or work on them, this makes the sites highly efficient to create and to maintain. They are also highly efficient from the point of view of users largely because they are created and designed with such efficiency in mind. There are, of course, slip-ups and failures in this regard, but they can be fixed relatively easily.

User efficiency is enhanced by the predictability of websites on Web 1.0; they are more or less identical from one time or place to another because content follows a predictable top-down pattern. The ubiquity of Web 1.0

sites like Yahoo! or the services of AOL served to eliminate inefficiencies associated with having to deal constantly with different or changing website content. Because user choices are limited or non-existent in the Web 1.0 environment, there is also great predictability for those in control of the websites. The major source of unpredictability in any McDonaldized system—human behavior—is largely eliminated from these websites, especially relative to Web 2.0. Furthermore, once a website is created, it can remain in place indefinitely, further enhancing predictability from the perspective of the website's owner and controllers. Calculability is *easy* on Web 1.0 since those in control of the sites can *easily* monitor their use and calculate precisely things like the number of users and how the sites are used. Similarly, users can compare available sites to assess which ones allow them to use their time on them most efficiently.

Web 1.0 is, of course, dominated almost completely by the websites that are, in effect, nonhuman technologies. Once in place, these websites control what users do on them and give them few options. Since the websites are largely static, and the goal is to keep them that way, control is exercised over those who produce content on the sites. Indeed, Web 1.0 is largely distinguishable from Web 2.0 precisely because the former is far less *human* than the latter.

Thus, a strong argument can be made that Web 1.0 is McDonaldized to a high degree. However, anything that is McDonaldized to such a degree is subject to the irrationality of rationality. One such irrationality that stands out in this case is dehumanization. On the one hand, the humans who work on, or for, Web 1.0 websites are highly limited in what they can do; they cannot fully exploit their creative human capacities to improve the sites, or respond as fully as possible to user needs and complaints. In addition, these websites are largely dehumanized from the point of view of their users. If they want to use a site, people must use it in the way its designers and operators intended. They cannot use their skills and abilities to alter the site or to use it in highly creative ways. Further, the sites are structured in ways that are relatively uncollaborative and much less social than what we see on Web 2.0. This is irrational, an irrationality of rationality, in the sense that Web 1.0 squanders its ability to make use of the skills and abilities of both those who work for the sites and those who use them. It is especially in the latter case that Web 2.0 has a huge advantage of 1.0. In one sense, Web 2.0 has reduced or eliminated the irrationality of rationality associated with Web 1.0. In another sense, it could be argued that it has greatly heightened the rationality of these systems by figuring out how to get the most out of the people who use the sites without allowing them to compromise the basic functioning of the system. In this way, while Web 2.0 can be viewed as a rational next step, often in line with profit-based motives, it exists as such partially outside the principles outlined by the McDonaldization thesis, and thus Web 2.0 is argued to have, to some degree, *de*-McDonaldizing tendencies. This constitutes an important segue into a fuller discussion of Web 2.0 and its relationship to McDonaldization.

De-McDonaldizing the Web

In many ways Web 2.0 is less efficient than Web 1.0 (and material realities such as fast food restaurants), especially for the users. The amount of time and energy users spend producing content on social networking sites (often, users have more than one, including MySpace, Facebook and others), as well as blogging and microblogging (e.g., Twitter), writing comments on other's blogs, writing reviews on sites like Amazon and so on far exceeds the amount of user-generation that existed on Web 1.0. If efficiency is defined as the amount of output relative to the amount of input, then the massive amount of input that the user-generation of Web 2.0 allows tends not be as efficient as a centrally conceived structure, like Web 1.0. As Web 2.0 is defined by the ability for the masses to create content online, this general abundance of profiles, reviews, comments, opinions, news, photos, videos, and much else would be seen as wasteful in an efficient system, but is embraced on Web 2.0. How many users that ultimately contribute, or how much time they spend (for example, editing a Wikipedia entry), matters little; instead, the focus is on the quality of what they produce (leaving aside the debate on the actual quality of Web 2.0 content such as Wikipedia entries). That Web 2.0 involves a focus on output irrespective of the amount of input is an example of its relative inefficiency.

All of this also means that there is far more unpredictability on Web 2.0 sites than on Web 1.0 sites. The basic structure of many sites on Web 2.0 are predictable (e.g., the nature of a Facebook, YouTube, or Yelp! page), but what does or does not find its way onto that page is largely unregulated and unpredictable. There are limits that vary by site, but they are quite wide, with the result that users are unable to predict what they will find every time they log on to a site.

It is also much harder to quantify, to calculate, exactly what is transpiring on a 2.0 site. In part, this is because there is so much more going on and it takes so many different forms. More importantly, while Web 1.0 sites tended to be restricted to objective matters (did one order something? how much was paid for it?), Web 2.0 sites allow, and are even defined by, much more subjective inputs such as personalized messages, photos, and the like. Such things are harder, if not impossible, to quantify.

There are certainly nonhuman technologies involved in Web 2.0—for example computers, the web sites themselves—but human users are, by definition, much more able to manipulate content than on Web 1.0. While Web 1.0 sites are centrally conceived, prestructured, and largely immune to manipulation and alteration by users, Web 2.0 sites are based on the whole idea that users can, indeed must, manipulate and alter the sites in innumerable ways. In other words, humans have been put back in charge of technologies that in Web 1.0 totally controlled them. As a result, it is erroneous to describe the technologies involved in Web 2.0 as nonhuman technologies. While there are certainly technologies there, humans, especially human users, are to a large extent in control of them. Web 2.0 is far more than the wires and circuits that comprise the infrastructure of the Internet; it is also the intersection of machines with human production—of their creativity, identities, and socializing. To a great degree, machines and culture have merged on Web 2.0.

This discussion of the dimensions of McDonaldization leads into the issue of the irrationality of rationality and to the conclusion that Web 2.0 serves to reduce or eliminate such irrationalities, especially dehumanization, in comparison to Web 1.0, to say nothing of irrationalities associated with material realities (e.g., the fast food restaurant). Web 2.0 is clearly a far more humanized technology than Web 1.0. Indeed, in more fully utilizing the skills and abilities of users, it could be argued that Web 2.0 is a far more "reasonable" system than Web 1.0. On Web 2.0, human users remain human, and are valued for their unique contributions. User behavior is not directed, as is the case with Web 1.0, but, instead, is more creative in nature.

Further, we can ask whether the content on Web 2.0 sites such as Flickr or YouTube is McDonaldized? Is the content like McDonald's highly McDonaldized food, for example, with a chicken "McNugget" replacing a home-cooked bird, or like McFalafel in Israel versus the authentic variety? Even a casual examination of the Flickr or Picasa photo sites reveals no evidence of McDonaldized photography. Photos are not created to please as many people as possible. The photos are human and enchanted and are not created in a mechanized, standardized, calculable, or efficient way. On the other hand, the presentations of the pictures are standardized across these sites. But, is this of great consequence? There may be a point to be made about capitalism and profiting from art on Flickr, but Flickr does not seem to be McDonaldizing photography. Because Flickr does not create centrally conceived processes by which the content is created, we can see this example of Web 2.0 as, in general, having *de*-McDonaldizing tendencies (keeping in mind the point of the standardization of the way the photos are presented and consumed).

Overall, then, Web 2.0 represents a process of the *de*-McDonaldization of the Internet, at least in comparison to Web 1.0. In that sense, it contradicts Ritzer's underlying argument about ever-increasing McDonaldization. Through the proliferation of user-generated content, Web 2.0 loses something with respect to calculability, efficiency, predictability and control through nonhuman technologies; but these dimensions, and McDonaldization more generally, have not disappeared completely on Web 2.0. Although content might be personalized and creatively produced on Web 2.0 sites like eBay in the realm of consumption and Facebook in terms of identity and socialization, McDonaldization continues to exist on those sites. For example, efficiency is manifest in Facebook's (and other Web 2.0 companies') profit models that are based on the utilization of the efficient creation of value by an unpaid workforce. In this way, much of Web 2.0 excels at allowing mass collaboration to occur much more efficiently than has been previously possible by creating value through the unpaid labor of their users with little to no special effort required of the owners of these sites.

Facebook also exerts control, and in fact constitutes an unprecedented intrusion of technology into socializing and selfhood, through the application of nonhuman technologies to these processes. Facebook, for instance, structures social networking through dictating the look and behavior of the profiles. Interaction itself, on Facebook, follows preset and centrally controlled principles and structures. For example, the Facebook-created mechanisms like writing on someone's "wall" or the constant feed of updates on everything your Facebook 'friends' are doing with their profiles. Identity is chosen from selecting from Facebook-determined options and checkboxes, with the result that the profile pages look very similar. MySpace, on the other hand, has lost much market share to Facebook by giving users who are not expert in web design the ability to customize and personalize their digital presentations of self to a far greater degree than has Facebook. The resulting MySpace profiles are often difficult to navigate. Facebook, however, has much more uniform profiles, where everyone's page has a very similar look and behavior. By making the content more strictly structured, Facebook has provided a clean interface that is user-friendly and promotes growth. Further, one can assume that if Facebook is monetarily dependent on the databases that it is building through interaction, then it has some incentive to structure those databases accordingly. In structuring the processes of online social networking and the digital presentation of self, we might argue that, on Facebook, socializing itself has been McDonaldized. However, this is not to downplay the importance of the customization that Facebook allows, which is much different than the highly predictable Big Mac sold at nearly *all* McDonald's. But if something like socializing can be structured under a set of principles, then we have seen a replication online of what is at the heart of the McDonaldization thesis: the routinization of another very personal part of life.

While I have discussed the ways in which Facebook McDonaldizes socialization, we should also recognize that Facebook is *de*-McDonaldizing the web experience. Facebook, as an example of Web 2.0, makes the web more human through increased social interaction. This makes the experience highly unpredictable since one is interacting with humans. It is difficult, if not impossible, to quantify such interactions. Facebook makes keeping in touch with friends that are distant more efficient. However, it also is highly inefficient in that it also facilitates *more* socialization through the maintaining of social ties one might have lost in the past. And it is inefficient because of the constant and habitual way in which many people use these sites. The time spent on the site to upload pictures and to socialize online hardly seems an activity aimed at efficiency. Overall, while Web 2.0 is not without its McDonaldized elements, it is certainly less McDonaldized than Web 1.0. Does the theory of McDonaldization (and rationalization) need to be revised in light of this?

Conclusion

There are several conclusions to be derived from this analysis. First, it demonstrates the utility of thinking about the Internet, especially Web 1.0 and 2.0, from a theoretical perspective, in this case, the McDonaldization of society. Using that theory has proven useful in thinking about the differences between Web 1.0 and 2.0, as well as their differences (and similarities) with more material realities.

Second, it constitutes a kind of test of McDonaldization as a "grand narrative" and the idea that we are likely to see an ever-increasing McDonaldization of society. To the degree that Web 2.0 constitutes a later stage in the development of the Internet than 1.0, and of increasing relevance in society in general, it would be predicted that 2.0 would be *more* McDonaldized than 1.0. That this is not the case, and in fact Web 2.0 is far *less* McDonaldized than 1.0, casts considerable doubt on McDonaldization as a grand narrative.

Third, some crucial factors were uncovered that help to account for the *de*-McDonaldization associated with the move from Web 1.0 to 2.0. It is argued here that the principles behind de-McDonldization begins with digitality (and the replicability this implies), which exists on both Web 1.0 and 2.0. However, it is Web 2.0 that also has profoundly changed the way this digital content is created. Web 2.0 is defined by users producing that which they consume (and, as such, are prosumers) leading to a general abundance, rather than scarcity. In sum, giving users the ability to create information, identities, and social networks online has led to an explosive humanization of the web.

In this post-scarce digital environment, this humanization sits comfortably next to the structuring of user-generated content mentioned previously in the context of Facebook. And it is because of this humanization that the McDonaldization process is of diminishing applicability, at least to this digital content. Thus, this theoretical analysis underscores Neustadtl and Kestnbaum's previous point that "for those inclined to resist the McDonaldization of the Internet, we suggest going forth and producing content!"

While this analysis might lead one to the conclusion that the McDonaldization thesis needs to be abandoned, at least as a grand narrative, there are other trends that lead us to be cautious about leaping to that conclusion. One is the fact that the digital realities on Web 2.0 are coming to be integrated more and more with material realities, for example with the rise in popularity of "smart," internet-capable cell phones and 'mobile social networking.' Mobile social networking would be the use of social networking applications (like Facebook) on the cell phone, always on and always connected to the Web. With these devices, online social interaction can take place on the move in many different geospatial environments with technologies that locate one's device in relation to others in physical space. While it is not the objective of this essay to explicate this fully, one might further the argument made in this essay—that digital content resists McDonalidization—to mobile social networking. If and when social networking moves to cell phones, we might see a McDonaldization of this interaction since material realities are easier to McDonaldize. Alternatively, instead of viewing mobile social networking as the physicalization of digital realms, we might view it as the digitization of the material world, and, as such, a further possibility for *de*-McDonaldization. The applicability of the McDonalidization thesis diminishes as the ubiquity of our interaction with digital content increases, something that Web 2.0 has promoted, and that smart cell phones will undoubtedly promote to a far higher degree.

Thinking Critically

1. Are there benefits to McDonaldized interaction, especially online?

2. Where has McDonaldization continued to persist online?

3. Will the Internet become less McDonaldized in the future?

4. Will social networking sites also become widely used cell phone applications, and how might this apply to the McDonaldization thesis?

5. Does this critique of McDonaldization as an ever-expanding process mean that the theory is of declining utility?

The process of McDonaldization has led to the creation of a large number of McDonaldized jobs, or as they have come to be called—"McJobs." Jos Gamble studied the issue of McJobs in UK and Japanese retailers in China through hundreds of interviews and questionnaires with service workers in these settings. He is critical of the idea of McJobs, especially the negatives that tend to be associated with the idea such as seeing the jobs as dehumanizing, degrading, deskilled, and leading to a dead-end. Gamble focuses mainly on the workers' perceptions of their jobs rather than the structure of the jobs. That is, for example, he looks at the workers' perceptions of whether they acquired more skills on the job rather than looking at the job itself and asking whether it required less skills than jobs like it did in the past. He did find that the work in the Japanese stores was more McDonaldized structurally than in the UK stores, but even there employees felt that they had acquired new skills on the job. It is argued that there are specific aspects of these retailers, and the Chinese context in which they exist, that make it less likely that service work will be McDonaldized (although this could just be a transitional development) in those settings. However, it should be borne in mind that this study focuses on workers' self-perceptions, which could well be, and frequently are, distorted and idealized. A more fully adequate study would need to examine both self-perceptions and the structure of jobs, especially as they have changed over time.

16

Multinational Retailers in China

Proliferating 'McJobs' or Developing Skills?

Jos Gamble

Introduction

There has been extensive debate on the extent to which workers are either upskilled or deskilled in contemporary workplaces. During the 1970s and 1980s, most attention focused on the manufacturing sector. In the 1990s, the service sector came under increasing scrutiny, with call centres a recent focus for study. Absent in this debate, though, has been any exploration of the issues involved in non-Western contexts. Additionally, within the service sector the economically important and socially significant retail sector has been neglected. This paper reviews the debate on skills and then presents findings from empirical research conducted at multinational retail firms in China.

Editor's Note: From Gamble, J., "Multinational Retailers in China: Proliferating 'McJobs' or Developing Skills?," *Journal of Management Studies* 43:7 November 2006. Blackwell Publishing Ltd. Used with permission.

China provides an ideal locus for such research given the immense influx of foreign direct investment (FDI) in recent years . . . Study in China then not only allows us to broaden the debate on skills formation but also to explore the impact that service sector investment might have on human resources development in a transitional economy. Additionally, this study enables us to examine the variables that might explain why skill enhancement occurs in some country contexts and deskilling in others.

The Debate on Skill Formation

Much of the initial debate on skills development and utilization centred upon the manufacturing sector and the impact of technology on the labour process. Kerr et al. anticipated that technological development would lead to more complex types of work task and therefore rising levels of skill and responsibility. By contrast, Braverman saw technology as contributing to an increasing division of labour that condemned the masses to 'labor from which all conceptual elements have been removed and along with them most of the skill, knowledge, and understanding of production processes.'

Later there was renewed optimism over a range of 'new paradigms' that linked advanced manufacturing systems with increased utilization of skilled labour. However, critics questioned the assumed link between skill and work arrangements such as just-in-time and modular production. These practices might involve a broader range of tasks, but they did not necessarily require higher skills. In a survey of UK labour markets, Gallie reported an increasing polarization of workforce skills. He found a strong link between those who worked with advanced forms of technology and skill levels, while skill levels of those without this possibility tended to be unchanged.

Skills in the Service Sector

While Braverman devoted most attention to the manufacturing sector he perceived the degradation of work as a structural feature of the capitalist mode of production. He argued that, if anything, 'the worst examples of the division of labor' were to be found in those processes that remained unmechanized. Braverman took this to be the prevailing situation in service occupations and the retail trade, and described work in them as characterized by 'lack of developed skill, low pay, and interchangeability of person and function.'

Building on the work of Max Weber and F. W. Taylor, George Ritzer focused on 'McDonaldization.' He perceives this as a rationalization process manifest in all realms of the social world, with the work world a particularly important sphere that influences and is influenced by wider society. Ritzer details in particular the implications for customer service jobs . . .

For employees in McDonaldized workplaces Ritzer's conclusions parallel Braverman's bleak assessment; where the latter depicts the 'degradation of work' he perceives a proliferation of increasingly Taylorized dead-end 'McJobs.' Ritzer and Stillman argue that 'most customer service jobs have been deskilled, transformed into *McJobs* . . . These require little training and little skill to perform them.' In such workplaces, 'employees are forced to work in duhumanizing jobs.' For Ritzer, the increasing use of scripts to engender predictability in interactive workers' encounters with customers 'leads to new depths in the deskilling of workers'; in the same way as technology removes workers' manual skills, so scripts usurp their verbal and interactive skills.

The McDonaldization thesis has been subject to various criticisms. A recurring critique is the limited empirical underpinning of Ritzer's work. The impact of McDonaldization on employees is largely abstracted and 'read-off' from management trends, with little attention to the subjective experiences of actual workers. McDonaldization ignores the creativity of both workers and customers to fashion anew and find their own meanings in what is presented before them. There is also a tendency to overestimate the power of managers to exert detailed control . . .

This paper explores employees' perceptions of their skills acquisition and development through interview based case studies and underpins this with a broader questionnaire survey. The focus on local employees' perspectives provides a basis from which to interrogate assumptions derived from Western contexts . . .

Japanese and UK retail firms were selected for this study since they have developed in differing institutional contexts. Where Japanese firms are generally presumed to make substantial investments in human resources, UK firms have been considered to provide minimal training opportunities. The expectation, not supported in the research, was that this distinction would be replicated in retail firms from these two countries.

Research in China was undertaken in 1999, 2000, 2002 and 2003 at six stores owned by a British multinational retailer, 'UKStore.' One hundred and seventeen semi-structured interviews were conducted with a cross-section of local employees and expatriate staff. Background research was conducted at one of the firm's UK stores. Research on two Japanese-invested retailers was carried out in 2002, 2003 and 2004. Visits were made to six stores in four different cities, and 97 interviews were conducted with local and expatriate staff . . .

A questionnaire survey was undertaken of 799 employees at four Japanese-invested stores, three UK-invested stores in China and a parent country store of this firm in London, and a Chinese state-owned store in Beijing . . .

Company Backgrounds

In June 1999, UKStore opened a decorative materials warehouse store in Shanghai. Up to April 2005 a further 21 stores had opened in various cities. For the first year of operations, two expatriate managers filled the store manager and assistant store manager roles, subsequently all store-level roles were localized. JStore1 is a leading Japanese general merchandize retail firm. By 2005, it had five stores in China, the first opened in 1997. JStore2 is a major Japanese department store, with two subsidiaries in China. Compared to UKStore, the Japanese firms made greater use of expatriates with most senior positions held by Japanese staff. All the multinationals had more employees per store than comparably sized parent country stores. Customer numbers were also comparatively high; up to 40,000 per day made purchases at one JStore1 and 1500 at a UKStore . . .

Training and Skills Development in the Multinational Stores

> In the UK it's about money, not learning about the job. In China they want to know everything . . . Everyone in China wants to learn, and this is central to the business. (UKStore expatriate project manager)

New recruits at UKStore undertook a three-day induction programme; this included an introduction to the company and its management system, health and safety, customer service, operating procedures and display principals. Post-induction training included courses on product knowledge, procedures, customer service and demonstration skills. A decoration department deputy supervisor contrasted UKStore to his previous employer, a rival state store:

> At UKStore, there's an emphasis on the long-term. There's a strong company culture because we have a training department. I've learnt a lot here. People make progress every day.

This employee explained that many domestic retailers, such as his former store, did not have a training department. In contrast to Fröbel et al.'s expectations, these foreign firms had helped introduce the concept of training to China's retail sector.

Customer service training was often taught using role-play exercises in which employees took the part of customers. UKStore had a light touch in terms of scripting customer service interactions. The company's training manager stated that:

Generally speaking employees judge according to their own experience what they should say.

Encounters with customers were difficult to reduce to a script, not least since the potential range of questions was great.

UKStore also sought to enhance employees' product knowledge. Each trading department had an average of over 2000 product lines. The expatriate assistant manager recalled:

When we opened, product knowledge was virtually non-existent.

In a subsequent interview he commented:

I was staggered at how much people learnt in a year. Customers ask different questions every time; you need experience to deal with this.

A timber department deputy supervisor considered:

You can know enough about the product after 1–2 months, but to be an expert needs about one year.

Even employees on the refund section, recruited mainly for their social skills, aesthetic attributes and temperament, needed product knowledge to be able to determine whether returned items were faulty or damaged.

Training by vendors, either in-store or at their factories, was a key method to increase product knowledge. Informally, sales staff also took advantage of visits by vendors when they delivered stock to improve this knowledge. Additionally, during 2000 a system of gold, silver and bronze product knowledge certificates was introduced. The bronze certificate involved an hour-long written test on product knowledge and required about one month's preparation time. The silver certificate was awarded on the basis of product knowledge and a DIY demonstration to an audience. By 2003, all new recruits were expected to pass the bronze test within three months, and deputy supervisors and supervisors should pass the silver test.

The criteria for the gold certificate included both the elements required for silver plus a decoration test. For the latter, participants were given a notional budget and the plan of an empty room and must produce a design to decorate this space. The requirements of this certificate involved all the elements of 'theoretical knowledge, creativity, and use of analytical and social skills' that Frenkel et al. perceive as the hallmark of a tendency towards 'knowledge work.'

Daily storewide morning briefing sessions were also used to provide training on store procedures, product knowledge and customer service. Skills and knowledge grew not only from company provided training, but also incrementally from sharing knowledge and experience with co-workers. A decorative materials department supervisor enjoyed introducing products 'as customers can ask difficult questions. This time you can't answer, but the next time you can.' There was also potential to learn from customers with particular expertise and experience.

In September 2000, UKStore began a Fast Track Management Scheme. Up to 60 employees took part in each six-month long course to ensure a constant stream of suitably qualified local supervisors and managers. The shortage of qualified employees ensured that promotion was frequently more rapid than in UK stores or local firms. It was common to be promoted to deputy supervisor within one year, and to supervisor within two years.

The Japanese multinationals' approach to customer service interactions was more prescriptive and detailed than UKStore's; they required more intense provision of emotional labour than UKStore, with scripted polite phrases, bowing, and smiling. Correspondingly, training was more intensive and extensive, and more likely to be provided by Japanese expatriates. Japanese staff were said to have a 'coaching' (*zhidao*) role. JStore1's Managing Director prioritized politeness to customers (*daike de limao*) as the key means to attract and retain customers. Recruits appointed before store openings underwent three months' training, with attention to company history and policies, product knowledge, team-building, job content, dress and appearance, use of the 'six polite phrases' (such as 'please wait a moment' and 'I'm sorry'), appropriate gestures and behaviour, and bowing. Strict disciplinary and dress codes applied and a detailed employee handbook laid down the penalties for infringements.

Post-induction training included product knowledge, dealing with complaints, display skills and stocktaking. A personnel manager remarked:

> We're a training school (*peixun xuexiao*) since we need to keep training and to check constantly that employees are doing what they're supposed to do.

As at UKStore, role-plays were used to convey customer-orientated values. After each promotion to deputy supervisor and supervisor level, employees received two weeks' concentrated training. JStore1 also encouraged Japanese-style job rotation between departments.

At JStore2, training before store openings lasted 10–15 days. Training was also undertaken during daily departmental briefing sessions. As with JStore1, employees were encouraged to gain experience through job rotation in different departments. After each promotion, employees received half a day of training. Supervisors received annual training of about two hours per day, once a week, spread over two months. Each year, three or four supervisors were sent to Japan for a week's training. Supervisor level staff might also make short visits to Beijing or Shanghai for training.

Post-induction training included a smiling contest and monthly campaigns such as the '*arigato undo*' (being thanked) campaign. The store manager believed:

> We learn through these contests, we try to analyse why customers say 'thank you.'

Product knowledge was also considered important. JStore2 relied heavily on fashionwear sales and employees were taught about products' composition, use and maintenance. They visited factories to learn how garments were manufactured and received instruction on new seasons' products and fashion trends. There were also training courses on displays and colour coordination.

As mentioned above, the multinationals employed more staff in China than in their parent country stores. Despite this at UKStore, for instance, staff costs per store were roughly half their UK equivalent. Lower labour costs allowed greater use of full-time employees. In China, all UKStore's employees were full-time while at the company's London store 30 per cent were part-time. Low-cost labour permitted more concentration on training than in the UK where tight manning precluded staff taking time off for training. In the UK, for instance, UKStore did not operate the product knowledge certificate system. Survey evidence from UKStore showed that almost 72 per cent of employees in China received over four days' training compared to just over 42 per cent in the UK.

Employees' commitment to upgrade their knowledge and skills was enhanced by the prospect of promotion and career development. This was particularly evident at UKStore as the company expanded rapidly across China. The company adopted a 'conveyor belt' approach; employees recruited at one store were trained and groomed for promotion and progression to new stores. Promotion at the Japanese stores was slower, but still more rapid than in Japan itself.

Employees' Perceptions
of Skills Development

The majority of employees in the multinationals considered that they could learn a lot of new knowledge from their job. Almost 86 per cent agreed that this was the case; just 14 employees out of 575 disagreed. Even at the SOE, though, almost 62 per cent of employees agreed that they could learn new knowledge in their job, while less than 10 per cent actively disagreed . . . These figures are difficult to square with the McDonaldization thesis. The multinationals also provided an environment in which the majority of workers considered that they were encouraged to learn new skills . . .

Those at deputy supervisor level and above described how they had learned about the management of people and products and sales promotion techniques, and how to deal with interpersonal relations and customer complaints. A female clothing section floor manager at JStore2 remarked:

> I've learnt a lot, I was straight from school and didn't know anything.

When asked what she liked most about working at JStore2 she added:

> The company gives you many opportunities to develop your abilities.

Another floor manager commented:

> I've learnt too much! When I came to JStore2 I didn't know anything. Now I understand the whole process of garments, from their manufacture, sourcing, sales and storage.

Additionally, in all the firms employees learnt to provide a form of customer service that appealed to customers. The clothing section floor manager reflected:

> Previously all department stores were state-owned and customer service was terrible. We look at things from the customers' viewpoint.

It might provide few surprises that those with managerial or supervisory responsibilities developed skills in such firms. What though of those at the lowest level in the hierarchy? . . . The three lowest grades of employee at UKStore and JStore1. These included checkout staff whose work appeared to be particularly Taylorized and warehouse employees, a category of worker Braverman referred to as amongst those who perform 'simple labor in service of a complex machine,' in jobs of 'sheer and mindless drudgery.' Imputations by outside observers do not appear to concur with employees' self-assessment of their work; over 80 per cent felt they could learn in these roles, while no more than 6.1 per cent actively disagreed.

Inevitably the skills and competencies required and developed depended upon the departments in question. However, most employees stated that their social skills and sales skills or technique (*xiaoshou jiqiao*) had developed. At UKStore a paint department assistant previously employed on a factory production line described:

> A big difference to my old firm, there it was like being a machine. Here my ability to express myself has increased, as each customer is different.

The nature of work at JStore1 matches more closely than UKStore the McDonaldized workplaces described by Ritzer. Japanese stores especially prized the key dimensions of McDonaldized work: efficiency, calculability and predictability. The latter dimension in particular was evident as employees were expected to learn and then utilize scripts in their encounters with customers. However, when asked what they had learnt since joining the firm every employee could readily cite at least one or two aspects. These included practical skills; for instance, food section employees learnt about different varieties of fish and meat and their origin, preparation techniques and cooking methods. Many employees considered they had developed interaction skills. An underwear and socks section assistant contrasted her current job with that at a state retail firm:

> Here it's a large extended family that tempers people. In my previous job I couldn't develop, everything depended on personal connections (*guanxi*). Here it depends on your ability. So you can develop your ability here, it has tempered me.

Similarly, a cook in the fast food restaurant commented:

> I came to JStore1 because it has good welfare benefits and you can improve yourself (*duanlian ziji tigao*) as there are many types of customers.

An in-store baker explained that he not only made but also had to sell bread, for this:

> You have to use your experience to introduce products' taste and contents. We also develop new products.

A cosmetics section assistant highlighted the need for tact in dealing with customers. Although she had learnt to recognize different skin types she emphasized that:

> To sell a product you must start from the customer's viewpoint and understand their needs. You can't just say, 'Do you want to cover that blemish?'

She received some training, but much of her new knowledge derived from colleagues:

> People here are very warm. When I first came here I didn't know anything at all, but they [her colleagues] were very patient in teaching me.

A temporary worker in the female clothing section liked the fact that:

> I can develop my own special skill (*fahui ziji de techang*).

Echoing Thompson et al.'s comments on the importance of 'endurance skills' she added that:

> You can learn to get used to difficult situations.

A checkout assistant appreciated the Japanese management style and had:

> Learnt how to get on with people and to deal with complaints efficiently.

A service desk assistant liked dealing with customer complaints since:

> You can develop your ability (*duanlian nengli*).

Employees at the Japanese firms valued job rotation. A daily products section assistant stated:

> I like the chance to move to different departments and learn more. It gives a feeling of newness and a sense of challenge. You can develop your own talents (*fahui ziji de caizhi*).

A women's clothing section assistant welcomed such moves:

> Because you can learn new things.

He explained that following such transfers:

> You learn from other sales assistants, it takes time and the accumulation of experience.

A fish counter assistant had previously worked in a state factory. He joined JStore1:

> Because it's a foreign-invested firm you can learn a lot, so I should be able to improve myself. In a state-owned enterprise you couldn't learn this kind of knowledge.

Expanding on what he had learnt he commented:

> The work attitude is one that before I could never even have imagined. We were indolent/negligent (*lansan*). Here it's very strict and full of competition, it lets you develop yourself.

Some of this worker's colleagues were rural migrants and first generation employees in modern industry. JStore1 provided them with an introduction to and socialization in the discipline and habits that are essential for the capitalist style development China has embarked upon.

JStore1's checkout had the highest level of labour turnover, a reflection of the physically and emotionally demanding nature of the work. However . . . even in this routine and Taylorized role most employees still found material to learn from. A checkout assistant acknowledged that:

> The work is very simple, we just receive money.

However, she added that since they worked on different floors each day and there were different requirements on each that:

> It's necessary to understand all the floors.

Another checkout assistant commented:

> As a foreign enterprise, the company brings a lot of new things, so you can learn a lot. Working here you can learn constantly (*buduan de xuexi*).

She explained that:

> Even though the job itself is simple, you can see how the displays are done to raise the customer's desire to purchase, also we use POP (Point of Purchase) displays—these were rarely used in [this city] before.

Even awkward customers provided a learning opportunity:

> With unreasonable customers, you should analyse (*fenxi*) why they are like this.

Various observational and psychological skills were useful, and there was ample chance to develop these. For instance, emotional management skills and 'active listening' abilities were required to pacify irate customers. According to a UKStore hardware department deputy supervisor employees needed 'to listen to them, and then to stand in their viewpoint.' The ability to judge customers' income levels allowed employees to introduce appropriately priced products. It was also useful to detect who made buying decisions; a gardening department deputy supervisor described how:

> When customers come we observe and assess who asks the most questions to see who decides.

Sales staff could also save time and effort by learning to discern which customers came to buy and which just to browse . . .

Serving non-local customers provided employees with opportunities to practice and improve their standard Chinese (*putonghua*). Improved *putonghua* could enhance career prospects and facilitate upward mobility. In banks and other official workplaces, for instance, use of *putonghua* is required. Foreign customers could provide chances to practice foreign language (usually English) skills. UKStore's local managers had incentives to improve their English ability. This would enable them to interact directly with expatriate staff and to respond more easily to head office communications that arrived in English. Beyond the firm, English is a common requirement for the best paid and most prestigious jobs. Similarly, Japanese proficiency was useful at the Japanese multinationals, and could help secure employment at other Japanese enterprises in China.

Ritzer and Stillman argue that 'workers are unable to augment their own social capital in *McJobs,* ensuring slim prospects of future job mobility.' However, workers employed by the three multinationals overwhelmingly perceived skills developed at them as valuable in seeking alternative employment. Employees were asked whether they knew of other employers where they could make good use of what they had learnt at their company. The results indicate whether skills were firm specific or more generic and transferable . . . Whilst most men in SOEs and FIEs felt confident that their workplace derived skills would enable them to find another job (SOE, 80%; JStore1, 87%; UKStore, 88%) female employees at the multinationals were almost three times more likely than SOE counterparts to see these skills as 'very useful.' This suggests that these FIEs play a particularly positive role in enhancing female employees' skills.

Discussion

Retailers such as UKStore certainly aim to reduce the need for craftsman-type work; to maximize profits their ideal would be a Taylorized workplace. Indeed, the firm's senior expatriate described his ideal store as one in which customers selected goods directly from a catalogue. However, in China's low trust retail environment this would be difficult for customers to accept. Additionally, home decoration requires a reasonable level of skill, and skilful workers were needed to train and advise inexperienced customers and to answer questions posed by professional decorators. Employee-customer interactions were also relatively resistant to McDonaldization. The variety and unpredictability of customers' questions made it difficult to reduce responses to a script. And, in a highly competitive market, the firm's success depended upon staff being 'experts' and skilful in the 'drama of persuasion.'

DIY skills and product knowledge are widely dispersed in the UK; many employees possess such capabilities before they join the company. In China, UKStore could not recruit these skills so readily and employees start from a lower baseline in this respect. In Britain, training provides incremental advances in these dimensions; in China it often involved qualitative increases in skill levels. Moreover, the skill levels required of sales staff were probably higher than those needed by their counterparts in Britain. In part this relates to the social skills needed in an environment where transactions are more akin to 'negotiating.' The demanding nature of 'untrained' customers, and their bifurcation into amateurs with negligible DIY experience and professional builders also fostered the need for skilful assistants.

It could be argued that UKStore's business is rather novel, and the related skills development accordingly uncharacteristic of the retail sector. By contrast, both the Japanese stores, and especially JStore1, sold products that were usually familiar to local customers. In addition, compared to both UKStore and local stores, the Japanese firms placed greater emphasis on predictability in employee-customer interactions. However, even in the most rationalized roles at JStore1 workers still considered there was much they could learn.

The findings suggest that the Chinese context promotes skill enhancement. Several institutional factors related to the nature of labour and consumer markets might account for this. With respect to the former, China provides good basic education to its population; numeracy and literacy rates are high especially in urban areas. Secondly, the ample labour supply allows firms to select carefully employees who match their requirements. Thirdly, foreign multinationals often offer better salaries, training prospects and promotion opportunities compared to local firms; consequently they can recruit relatively well-educated and committed employees. Fourthly, lower labour costs enabled firms to devote greater emphasis to training than in their parent country stores.

In addition, by virtue of their alien status and high visibility multinationals have an extra motivation to offer good pay, benefits, training and working conditions in order to maintain cordial relations with the authorities. Foreign retailers were excluded from China for four decades and, in a one party state, WTO rules notwithstanding, the government maintains diverse bureaucratic powers over permits and operating licenses. Foreign firms are also seeking to enter a fiercely competitive market; customer service, which depends upon enthusiastic and skilful workers, is a valuable means of differentiation.

Chinese employees are, arguably, more amenable to training than those in the UK. Potential explanations to account for their apparent readiness to learn include the rapid commercialization of the economy and the withdrawal of state supports such as guaranteed jobs for life and extensive welfare benefits. In such an environment, learning and developing new skills constitutes an important maximizing strategy. China's booming economy creates immense demand for skilled employees and the rewards for those who upskill can be substantial. Allied to this, education has long been culturally valued and a key means of social mobility. China's job seekers might also be less reluctant to rule out work in the service sector than their British counterparts; in particular the paucity of welfare benefits means less likelihood of a 'benefits trap.'

Chinese customers' expectations constitute 'demand side' pressures for an upskilling of interactive service workers; their demanding nature can be understood in the institutional context of local consumer markets. With consumer law and market regulation both poorly developed, China's marketplace is characterized by low trust. The only reliable means for customers to ensure satisfaction is to drive a hard bargain and be confident of products' quality and fitness at the point of sale. Secondly, China's urban consumers are increasingly sophisticated and generally well-educated; this increases demand for knowledge-intensive service from retailers. Thirdly, consumers' expectations and the resultant demands on foreign firms are higher than those placed upon local firms. Allied to this is the awareness that multinationals are more susceptible to consumer pressure with respect to protection of their brand image. This is particularly significant in China with its history of nationalistic consumer boycotts against foreign products.

Theoretical and Methodological Implications

The social skills, characteristics and competencies distinguished as important in frontline service sector work in Western contexts were equally vital in China. The findings of this paper contrast sharply with those that would "implicitly . . . belittle such social 'skills.'" The evidence indicates that Chinese service workers could, like their Western counterparts, be conceptualized as active and skilled emotion managers. However, as with call centre employment, retail work does not constitute a monolithic category; the nature of individual roles and the associated skills and competencies required vary substantially.

For Ritzer, the expansion of the service sector is characterized by the growth of a poorly qualified workforce condemned to routine, repetitive and 'dehumanizing' work. However, human beings have the capacity to create their own meanings from the least nourishing fare. In shifting the gaze from that of external observers to workers' own self-assessment of their skills development this paper has indicated that even in sometimes seemingly barren terrains they perceived themselves to develop and acquire skills. External, supposedly objective, measures of the skills required in any particular job must be treated with caution. Imputations by outside observers do not appear to concur with participants' self-assessment; even highly Taylorized roles could allow space for the development of product knowledge, and organizational and social skills.

. . . neo-Marxists link skill with freedom from control. In such conceptions, researchers take the presence of rules and routine as prima facie evidence for the absence of skills . . . This has the ironic consequence of reproducing dominant social constructions of what is and is not skill. Ritzer's notion of McDonaldization matches closely this situation. Classification of particular jobs as deskilled or 'McJobs' has to be suspect not only as condescending but also as liable to misrepresent workers' subjective experience. Moreover, China is in a transitional stage with considerable social mobility; notions of what constitute 'McJobs' are both less settled and divergent.

The data highlight the extent to which skill is a subjective phenomenon, and the complexities involved in defining and measuring skill in service sector roles. Objective measures such as task complexity or average time cycle fail to capture the potential for employees to learn from their jobs. Typically, proxies such as educational qualifications or the extent of formal training courses have been used to distinguish and assess skill formation. However, these 'traditional signifiers' reveal little about the complex mixture of skills, competencies and personal characteristics that individuals develop or perceive themselves to develop. Equally hard to quantify is the informal transmission of values, attitudes and behavioural patterns through contact with expatriates.

Even when employee provided training was relatively limited, employees regularly cited significant learning from interaction with customers, vendors, fellow employees and managers. Workers' self-assessment of the time taken to learn to do their jobs is instructive in this regard. At UKStore, for instance, 50.8 per cent of workers stated that it had taken them between one week and one month to familiarize themselves with their job, and 29.2 per cent claimed it had taken over one month. This period is consistently longer than the formal training workers received.

This disjuncture indicates that a simple input model focusing on company training would fail to capture a substantial proportion of the learning that takes place. At JStore1, for instance, it was apparent that the works canteen provided a valuable forum for workers both to discharge tensions and to share and learn from colleagues how to deal with situations encountered on the shopfloor. It was also common for younger, unmarried staff to meet for social activities outside work; these too provided an informal learning forum. The extent of learning from colleagues, suppliers and customers indicates the need for more nuanced and sensitive means both to assess and foster skills development and acquisition. The findings add empirical support to Attewell's argument for the 'necessity of a thorough study of workers before categorizing their abilities and knowledge, a level of scrutiny that far exceeds current brief encounters with survey researchers or job raters.'

Characterizing other people's work as 'McJobs' helps support existing social hierarchies, and scarcely enhances these workers' status or self-esteem. Belt reports how women employed in call centres developed a sense of confidence about the social skills they developed. A similar raised consciousness was apparent amongst employees in China; workers not only developed social skills but also an awareness of and confidence in these skills. There was evidence of this with respect to their behaviour as 'knowing' consumers. Workers were customers in other contexts and they could utilize their professional skills both to judge other retail firms and to learn from these experiences. They described instances where they purposefully visited famous or new stores during vacation visits to other cities with just such an intention in mind. These activities mirror Alferoff and Knights' (2002) study of telesales workers who, in the capacity of customer, made calls to utilities in order to compare the presentation to the service with that they themselves delivered at work. As other researchers have observed, revealing the complexities involved in service workers' roles does not mean that the social value attached to these jobs or their remuneration is likely to increase. However, delineating and acknowledging the skills involved might be an important first step to challenging current reward structures.

Implications for HRD in China

Frenkel et al. consider that the trend towards knowledge work has implications for control, with workers' power likely to increase in relation to management. There was scant evidence to support this notion in the stores, managerial prerogatives held sway. However, the skills and competencies workers developed did enable them to secure jobs that they find meaningful. Prospects for rapid promotion also offered employees opportunities to move up the hierarchy and into managerial jobs, raising their incomes and future prospects in the process. In contrast to Ritzer and Stillman's assessment that service sector jobs offer minimal prospects of future job mobility, workers overwhelmingly perceived skills developed at these multinationals as valuable in other workplaces. This dimension is important both for the individuals concerned and for China's economic development since through labour turnover skills could be transferred to other host country firms. Significantly, female employees, typically seen as particularly vulnerable in the face of multinational capital, were more confident than their SOE counterparts that workplace-derived skills enhanced their career prospects.

The extent of learning and skills development outlined in this paper contradicts Fröbel et al.'s expectation that FIEs do little to benefit human resources development in host countries. Indeed, foreign retailers appear to have been instrumental in introducing the concept of training to China's retail sector. Moreover, the proportion of 'value-added' to Chinese employees might be greater than in investors' parent countries. The model of skills training provided by multinational retailers is also being copied by local firms. Market-seeking investment might have different consequences for skills formation compared to export-orientated investment. Multinational retailers are not inserted into the international division of labour delineated by Fröbel et al.; stores aim to tap local markets and replicate parent country operations. Further investigation might determine whether firms that invest in local market-seeking operations tend generally to engage in more extensive training than FDI in manufacturing plants located in global commodity chains. Ironically, China has favoured export-orientated FDI, but market-seeking firms might increase skill levels more.

Conclusion

This study of multinational retailers in China has provided data that illuminate the nature of skills in the retail sector. Additionally, the focus on multinational enterprises in a developing country has indicated the extent to which such firms contribute to human resource development in host countries. The data gathered indicate several unexpected conclusions. Firstly, foreign investment in a sector often characterized as providing deskilled jobs with minimal opportunities appears to provide meaningful work and valuable opportunities to upskill. Secondly, a UK firm provided at least as much opportunity in this respect as Japanese firms. Moreover, both the UK and the Japanese firms offered more opportunities than a comparable indigenous firm. The study further indicates that a number of presuppositions need to be questioned, and in particular when applied to non-Western contexts . . . This paper provides a further dimension of the notion that theories and empirics from developed economies may not be directly applicable in emerging economies. It might be necessary, for instance, to rethink assumptions about the nature of skills in the service sector and the expectation that upskilling is to be found primarily in technologically demanding jobs. Technology had a limited impact on sales staff's work; despite this employees reported substantial learning opportunities. This paper also illuminates the methodological imperative for specifics of skills in different occupations to be analysed in context . . . , and especially so in the service sector where unquantifiable 'intangible' skills often predominate.

Ritzer claims that the principles of McDonaldization are 'spreading from its source in the United States to affect more and more societies around the world.' Evidence from the Chinese context lends support to the notion of a global spread of rationalization. However, the data indicate that workers were not dehumanized by this work, nor were they forced to accept situations they deemed intolerable, quit rates were high in the most demanding and demoralizing roles. One might add that the Japanese firms' practices were more McDonaldized than those of the UK firm (which has consciously borrowed elements from an American firm in its business sector) suggesting, perhaps, that the locus of rationalization might need to be de-centred from its supposed heartland in the United States. The potent iron cage metaphor might also be inappropriate; the 'cage' if cage there be, appears more porous and less constraining than Ritzer suggests. Often, the container appeared less akin to prison bars than to a supporting structure that could foster growth and development.

One could argue that the current upskilling in these multinational retailers constitutes a transient phase, a one-off skills enhancement peculiar to this stage of China's transition from a planned to a market-driven economy. Relevant factors include the development of China's legal system; strengthening consumers' rights and means of redress might increase trust among customers. While the status of retail sector work is not high in China, employment in multinationals, and especially firms from America and Europe, is regarded as prestigious. This could change as these entrants' growth slows and career advancement prospects diminish. As labour market skill levels rise, firms' incentive to train staff might reduce. Set against this, increased competition encourages stronger customer focus. The evidence presented in this paper does not preclude the presence of a transitional skills boost, although recognition of such an effect is of intrinsic interest and worthy of further investigation. The host context's specific political economy and cultural values will also ensure that local configurations of skills and skill requirements continue to differ from those found in Western countries.

Thinking Critically

1. What is a McJob?

2. Would you like to have a McJob? Why or why not?

3. What are the positive contributions of McJobs to society?

4. What are the negatives associated with McJobs?

5. Can you find out whether a job is a McJob merely by asking those that have them their perceptions of them? What other information would you need?

As Andrew Knight shows in the following chapter, written especially for this volume, both industrial agriculture and meat processing have grown increasingly McDonaldized. All sorts of trends are associated with the McDonaldization of agriculture including the growing size of farms, their increasing specialization (monoculture), their increased reliance on chemicals and biotechnology, crop simplification, increased productivity, greater precision, more predictable products, more perfect products (at least in terms of their appearance to the consumer), and even efforts to control the weather to make it more predictable (e.g., more rain, less hail). Perhaps the strongest examples of McDonaldization in agriculture relate to bioengineered seeds that farmers must purchase from large corporations each year rather than saving their own seeds. There are even plans for so-called terminator seeds that automatically become sterile after a year so that the farmer must purchase new ones from the biotechnology company.

Although agriculture is increasingly McDonaldized, or more likely because of it, there are increasing irrationalities associated with it. These include enormous pollution, waste of great quantities of water in a highly water-intensive industry and in a society in which water is in increasingly short supply, physical dangers to those who work in the industry, high costs and marginal profitability often traceable to the McDonaldization of farming, and an overabundance of relatively inexpensive food (leading to problems such as overconsumption and obesity).

Meat processing has been McDonaldized to at least the same, if not a greater, degree. Large feedlots, assembly-line disassembling of steers, massive chicken and hog farms, and the like all reflect and exemplify this trend toward increasing McDonaldization. Many irrationalities are associated with this including animal cruelty, increased resistance (among animals and the humans who eat parts of these disease-resistant animals and therefore ingest the traces of antibiotics that exist in their meat) to antibiotics, and an increased risk of food poisoning.

17

Supersizing Farms

The McDonaldization of Agriculture

Andrew J. Knight

With the introduction and advancement of chemicals, machinery, and breeding, industrial agriculture and meat processing have been bought into the McDonaldization process. Today, the agriculture industry is driven to become more efficient, calculable, predictable, and to control humans and nature through technological means. This chapter details how McDonaldization relates to industrial agriculture and describes the irrationalities that this system has produced. The first section of this chapter focuses on the McDonaldization of agriculture, followed by how the meat processing industry has applied the McDonaldization process. The next section discusses how the organic movement developed as an alternative to the industrial model. Questions surrounding the future of the McDonaldization of agriculture are raised in the final section.

The McDonaldization of Agriculture

For many farmers today there is only one way of farming—get big or get out. Large farms have dominated the agricultural landscape for more than

---

Editor's Note: This chapter was written for the second edition of this volume.

40 years and are thought to be more efficient than their smaller counterparts. Although the acreage of farmland only decreased modestly from 1945 to 1998, farm size has increased dramatically over this period. The average farm size in 1940, for example, was 135 acres; in 1998, it was 435 acres. At the same time, the number of farms has declined from approximately 6.1 million in 1940 to 2.2 million in 1998.

Farming techniques and practices began to change dramatically after World War II. Modern farms tend to specialize in one cash crop, whether it be corn, cotton, rice, soybeans, tobacco, wheat, beef, chicken, dairy, or pork. Monoculture farming, where the same crop is grown year after year in the same field, or very simple rotations are used, is deemed more efficient because specialized large farms enable the farmer to use machinery, which allows farmers to harvest more crops in less time and to specialize in a single cash crop.

Without chemical inputs, monoculture farming would be impractical. Fertilizers add nutrients to the soil to aid crops grow faster and replenish the soil so that land can be used annually for growing crops. Traditional methods of leaving land out of production to allow land to replenish itself or of rotating crops became obsolete, and land is better used for production purposes. Pesticides allow the farmer to control insects and, thus, enhance efficiency by reducing crop damage. They also enhance efficiency by saving time because other methods of pest control, such as organic or integrated pest management, require more time, knowledge, and management.

The biotechnology revolution also enhances farm efficiency by streamlining the process. Today many food crops in the United States and Canada have undergone some sort of genetic modification. According to Pew Initiatives on Food and Biotechnology, 85% of soybeans, 45% of corn, and 76% of cotton grown in the United States in 2004 were genetically modified. An estimated 54% of all canola and 50% of all papayas grown in 2001 were genetically modified. Other genetically modified crops currently grown in the United States include squash, sugar beets, potatoes, and sweet corn, although these crops have not been as widely adopted.

The large majority of these engineered crops are what can be termed "first wave" bioengineered agricultural products, where specific traits are added or enhanced in plants to increase yields through making plants pest and disease resistant, hardier, and less energy intensive. These plants are marketed as having many advantages over traditional plants such as increasing yields, reducing capital inputs, and saving time and energy, which in turn increase farm profitability. They also allow land previously deemed marginal for agricultural purposes to be used.

Several "second wave" bioengineered agricultural products are now available. These products are referred to as "nutraceuticals" or "functional foods," where specific traits are added or enhanced in plants to increase nutrients or taste in food crops. They are being marketed as providing healthier and better tasting food to consumers. For example, tomatoes are designed to produce more lycopene to lower cholesterol levels, golden rice was designed purportedly to enhance the level of vitamin A in rice to reduce the risk of blindness, and research is being conducted to reduce the bitterness in citrus fruits.

"Third wave" bioengineered agricultural products comprise crops that are grown for nonfood purposes such as plants grown for pharmaceutical, cosmetic, and industrial by-products that will then be harvested and processed into drugs, chemical compounds, and plastics. Often referred to as "plant molecular farming," these plants will produce vaccines, antibodies, or other pharmaceuticals or industrial enzymes or bioplastics in greater quantity and at lower costs than traditional methods.

Advances in science and technology increase efficiency by simplifying the product. Although grocery stores or supermarkets may provide an illusion of variety, a further examination of produce sections quickly reveals the lack of choice. Only a few varieties of lettuce, tomatoes, cucumbers, apples, and oranges are available for purchase. On closer inspection, much of what is presented as variety by food companies is mostly clever packaging of similar products. With the advent of machinery, it became more efficient to grow crops that are hardier and travel better. As Jim Hightower, a former Texas Agriculture Commissioner, would lament, "hard tomatoes" rule the grocery shelves at the expense of their more tasty heirloom varieties. Today, many consumers do not understand how their food is produced and lack knowledge about modern agricultural practices. Although the fast-food industry continuously strives for efficiency to reduce or replace labor, farms rely primarily on technology to replace labor as consumers are cut off from the farm process.

Specialization is more difficult on farms than in food processing plants because the farmer must be involved in almost every aspect of farm life from purchasing seeds and chemical inputs to crop management to harvesting, storage, selling, and transportation of products. Also, land on farms may be unsuitable or marginal for agricultural production. Although biotechnology may ease these production concerns by developing less intensive and hardier plants, second and third wave biotechnology crops will likely add more variety and value-added products, which may increase the complexity and management of crops.

With advances in agricultural technology, agriculture has been able to calculate many aspects of farm life. The "hay days" of farming would be the late 1960s and 1970s when the United States focused on production for the export market, partially as a result of the need to feed Europe after World War II and the world thereafter. For the first time ever, the focus was on agricultural productivity and globalization rather than on emphasizing meeting regional consumers' demands. Maximum production policies have succeeded in increasing agricultural productivity growth. From 1948 to the mid 1990s, for instance, agricultural productivity growth has increased approximately 2.5 times.

The emphasis on productivity or—to be consistent with the process of McDonaldization—quantity is a major factor behind the specialization or monoculture of farms, increased size of farms, and the decline in variety of crops. Although some agricultural pundits fear that agricultural production has stagnated and will begin to decline, proponents of biotechnology see genetic engineering as a method to heighten agricultural productivity. In the controversial case of rBGH, for example, the genetically engineered synthetic version of the natural bovine growth hormone was designed to increase milk yields by 10% to 20%. By injecting cattle with rBGH, they are able to produce a greater amount of milk in a shorter time period.

The use of rBGH is a classic example of quantity over quality because there was no milk shortage before the advent of rBGH, and the demand for milk has been relatively stagnant. Also, the quality of milk has not increased. Critics claim that rBGH may pose health hazards, particularly to children and to cattle, and that farmers will bear the cost of the hormone, the inconvenience of administering daily injections to dairy cattle, and the economic implications of increased milk production. Despite these concerns, rBGH was approved for commercial use by the Food and Drug Administration in 1994.

With increased technology has also come more precise measurement of time, products, and processes. Precision farming allows farmers to use global positioning satellite (GPS) technology to manage soil and land quality at increasingly finer scales. This technology enables farmers to break down their fields into small plots, monitor yields, and apply chemicals as needed to these particular plots. For instance, with chemicals, precision farming should enable a farmer to conduct soil tests on a small plot of land, perhaps a 2.5- or 3.3-acre grid cell, and apply chemicals in the dosage necessary to that plot instead of applying chemicals to an entire field. Critics are concerned that precision farming is only another method to increase farmer dependence on off-farm suppliers and purchasers of farm products, as they provide the means for agribusiness to become integrated into field and farm-level production activities.

Predictability is relevant to the actual farming process. Industrial farms use the same practices and growing methods, and contract farming forces farmers to adopt similar methods. Industrial farming urges monoculture crops to be planted, irrigated, and sprayed with chemicals, and machines to be used to harvest crops. One cotton, soybean, or rice field appears to be identical to another.

Another aspect of predictability is creating predictable products and processes. Ideally, fruits, vegetables, and dairy and meat products would look the same, have the same shape, the same nutritional content, and the same taste. A pear, for instance, grown on one farm would be identical to another pear grown on another farm. Clearly, this ideal is not realistic as each pear is likely to vary in some way from other pears. Still, this ideal is approached particularly through breeding and the use of chemicals. Traditional breeding techniques have been relatively unsuccessful in achieving entirely predictable results, although the idea has been to work with limited varieties to come closer to this goal. The real hope for predictability lies with biotechnology. Biotechnology optimists portray a future where plants produce uniform crops. As well, cloning is hyped as a method to ensure that animals will have similar traits, and to ensure that each animal exhibits the best traits.

A final element of predictability is to minimize danger and unpleasantness. Although biotechnology optimists suggest bioengineered foods will be safer, tastier, and better for us, other methods have also been used (e.g., pesticides, irradiation) to protect the consumer. Pesticides are not only used to prevent loss of crops, but also limit pests from damaging fruits and vegetables aesthetically. Consumers will often search the produce bin for the perfect looking fruit or vegetable, and leave behind blemished ones. Scarecrows are used not only to scare away birds from eating produce but also to prevent them from damaging crops. The increased consumer distance from farm production has only exacerbated consumer desire for aesthetically pleasing foods.

Irradiation has been proposed as a method to not only ensure the pleasant appearance of fruits and vegetables, but also prevent spoilage. The consumption of spoiled food is a leading cause of food-borne illnesses. As well, the irradiation of meat kills potentially dangerous bacteria such as *Salmonella* and *E. coli* in meats. Another benefit of irradiation is less regulation of meat and produce industries because unsanitary practices in meat processing plants or on farms would not affect human safety. Costly recalls would be a thing of the past.

Farming remains unpredictable because it is heavily dependent on the whims of nature. Drought, wind, rain, the amount of sunshine, soil differences, and acts of God can all make farming unpredictable from one season to the next. Humans, however, appear to be endeavoring to make the weather more predictable. A quick search on weather modification on Yahoo.com yields various weather modification companies and projects in the United States. A popular method appears to be cloud seeding to suppress hail and enhance rain. According to William Cotton, funding for weather modification peaked in the 1970s, but weather modification programs exist in approximately 22 countries worldwide, and in any given year, there may be as many as 40 operational seeding projects in the United States.

Throughout history, humans have attempted to control nature and their surrounding environment through the use of technology. The only difference today from that of our forbearers is the extent to which we can and plan to control nature through technological advancements. At its core, industrial agriculture requires human transformation and control of nature, which is only feasible if certain elements of nature can be controlled.

Traditional farming methods required rotating crops and fallowing to allow soils to replenish. One reason monoculture farming was impracticable was because plots of land used to grow one crop decrease soil quality. Under the industrial model, fertilizers are added to the soil to replenish nutrients and keep land in production.

Livestock and crops require water to survive and grow. Large farms, particularly ones located on marginal agricultural lands, require vast irrigation systems to water livestock and crops. Once again, nature is controlled or altered in order that livestock and crops have a steady and predictable supply of water.

Biotechnology methods increase control over nature and farmers to a much greater extent than traditional breeding methods because individual genes can be manipulated to be less vulnerable to the whims of nature. Cloning increases control of nature as we continue to develop methods to clone specific characteristics of animals or enhance nature through the addition of selected genes. (One of the major arguments for cloning animals is to reduce disease.)

Bioengineered seeds allow agribusiness more control over farmers by forcing farmers to sign license agreements to use their seeds. Often these seed agreements prevent farmers from saving seeds and reusing them the following year and place limits on how the seeds can be used. Because the seeds are formulated to be resistant to certain chemicals, farmers must also purchase pesticides from the same seed company. Monsanto Roundup Ready seeds, for instance, require that Roundup pesticides be applied because these plants are only resistant to Roundup.

Another aspect of controlling the farmer with biotechnology seeds is that the farmer loses the ability to choose seed characteristics and may have to pay a higher price for characteristics he does not want. Take the case of a farmer whose farm is located next to a lake with prevailing winds that act as a control mechanism for pests. This farmer, because of a more moderate climate, only seeks a hardier corn plant. However, the bioengineered seed is hardier and resistant to particular pesticides. The farmer must purchase this seed from the company that owns that specific patent and pay a premium for a characteristic he does not want or need.

Perhaps the most controversial method to control farmers by agribusiness was the development of the terminator seed, which is genetically engineered to prevent germination after a specific period of time and eliminate any option of seed saving. These seeds become sterile so that leftover seeds cannot be planted the following year. In March 1998, the U.S. Department of Agriculture and Delta & Pine Land Co. developed and patented these seeds to prevent unauthorized seed saving by farmers to protect patented seed technologies. The terminator seed patent was acquired by seed giant Monsanto in May 1998 when it purchased Delta & Pine. Terminator seeds, however, have not been marketable because of fierce opposition by numerous special interest groups and nongovernmental organizations.

Consumers are also controlled because biotechnology-derived products are considered similar to those created by traditional methods, making them exempt from labeling. Thus, consumers cannot distinguish between genetically modified foods (GMFs) and non-GMF products. Only by purchasing certified organic products are consumers able to limit purchases of bioengineered foods.

Agriculture is in many ways an irrational system and attempts to rationalize it are likely to produce irrational results. This section demonstrates how the negative effects or irrationalities of industrial agriculture may lead to its eventual decline. Perhaps the most irrational aspects of industrial agriculture are environmental because industrial agriculture is one of the most, if not the most, pollution-generating industries. An agricultural system based on monoculture is heavily dependent on chemicals, which have been linked to many negative effects. Although the effects of pesticides on humans is contested, some pesticides have been linked to groundwater contamination and numerous health problems, including birth defects, nerve damage, and cancer. Pesticide resistance has led to the development of even more potent pesticides, and genetically modified pesticide-resistant crops have not as of yet significantly decreased chemical use.

There is evidence that soils are degraded, and some suggest that productivity will decline as topsoil is continually eroded.

Over-irrigation and -fertilization of land have resulted in the salinization of soil and eutrophication, a process where bodies of water receive excess nutrients that stimulate excessive algae and plant growth. The Gulf of Mexico, for instance, has an increasing dead zone as nitrogen from fertilizer and soil run-off chokes out aquatic life through oxygen depletion.

Agriculture is the second most water-intensive industry in the United States. As water becomes an evermore precious commodity, it is likely that conflict between farmers and residents will increase as demonstrated in several recent events. In Maine, cottage owners accused the blueberry industry of lowering lake levels. In Lakefield, Michigan, residents banded together against farms because their wells are going dry. In the Southwest, some farmers with water rights sell them to cities at an enormous profit, although their agricultural land remains fallow.

Industrial agriculture is extremely resource intensive, particularly relying on nonrenewable energy sources, such as fossil fuels. The reliance on monoculture farming, mechanization, and chemicals has also decreased biodiversity and affected wildlife negatively.

Technological advances have also been detrimental to farmers, farmworkers, and consumers. Not only has machinery reduced the need for many farm laborers, but farming and meat processing jobs are two of the most dangerous and low paying jobs in the United States. According to the Alabama Cooperative Extension System, more than 700 deaths occurred in farm-related activities in 2003, and another 150,000 agricultural workers suffered disabling work-related injuries. It is estimated that the number of deaths per 100,000 workers in agriculture has remained near 50 for the past 20 years. Approximately 68% of these farm-related deaths can be traced to machinery.

The case of rBGH may serve as an example of what is to come for farmers who adopt biotechnology. Although some farmers have experienced milk-yield increases, those farms have not become more profitable. As bioengineered foods become more commonplace, so have debates surrounding the ethicalness of biotechnology and its impact on biodiversity, wildlife, animal, and human health. Even some farmers are beginning to question biotechnology as evidenced by farmer opposition to genetically modified wheat in Canada. As contract farming has increased, critics argue that it has diminished knowledge and independence to the point where farmers have become wage laborers. Often, so-called technological advances require more management from farmers and are more capital intensive than traditional means. Still, the solution to all of these ills is more technology. This solution itself appears to be tautological and irrational as any technology is likely to spur additional side effects.

The cost of chemicals and capital inputs, such as machinery, has made farming an expensive business, and these costs have hindered the profitability of farms. Farming by nature is a risky business. Weather can affect crops, and productivity varies year by year. Farmers must also compete on world markets where prices fluctuate. In the late 1990s, more than half of all farms were in good financial health, but 45% of the small, noncommercial farms were financially vulnerable. U.S. Department of Agriculture data reveal that the farm debt-to-asset ratio is increasing, although it is still much lower than in the early 1980s during the farm crisis. Although the average annual income of farm households in 1997 was $52,300, approximately 89% of the average farm operator's income came from off-farm sources. Although the motto "Get Big or Get Out" applies, getting big does not guarantee farm survival, but may hasten or only delay the inevitable failure of many farms.

As a consequence of these trends, the federal government passed the largest farm bill in U.S. history in 2002 totalling $246.8 billion over the next decade. Farm subsidies have averaged more than $20 billion a year since 1999 with most of these funds benefiting the largest and wealthiest farms and agribusinesses. Eighty percent of the farm subsidies between 1998 and 2000 were to offset low prices, primarily to corn, cotton, rice, soybean, and wheat farmers.

As cities expand, farmland is threatened by development. Aside from agricultural values and practices conflicting, increased land values are a death knell for farmers, and it becomes unfeasible economically to leave the farm to their children in their wills. Perhaps because of this, the capital intensive nature of industrial agriculture, and the risky nature of agriculture, fewer students are enrolling in agricultural colleges.

Another irrationality of industrial agriculture is that it has led to an overabundance of food. According to Marion Nestle, the United States supplies a daily average of 3,800 calories per capita, nearly twice the amount needed to meet the energy requirements of most women, one-third more than needed by most men, and much higher than that needed by babies, young children, and the sedentary elderly. The overproduction of food results in waste and is a contributor to obesity. The American choice of a meat-laden diet also increases the amount of waste, as animal carcasses must be destroyed, and requires more energy to produce than a nonmeat diet.

A final irrationality of industrial agriculture is the belief that large monoculture farms are more efficient and productive than small farms. Despite the concentration of agribusinesses and the growth of large farms, small farms still constitute about 60% of all farms, although the larger farms are responsible for most of the agricultural output. Numerous studies have shown that smaller farms are more efficient at using resources than larger farms, and if total output per unit area is used instead of total yield as a measure of productivity, small farms are more productive than larger farms. There is also evidence that small farms are more beneficial for communities than large farms, and adopt more innovative marketing strategies. The trends of larger farms and concentration of ownership in agriculture have also been shown to be detrimental to rural economies.

McDonaldization of Meat Processing

In the processing of beef, cattle are corralled in overcrowded supersized lots close to the slaughterhouse, where large numbers of cattle are herded together in pens to maximize space. This housing method is much more efficient than conventional ranching styles, where cattle roam on the plains eating grass. This process also eliminates waste, because instead of putting dairy cattle that are beyond their milking days out to pasture, they are slaughtered for human consumption, and space is made for younger dairy cattle.

Cattle ready to be processed enter the slaughterhouse on conveyor belts, and on entry, are quickly killed by workers with the sole responsibility of cutting their throats. As the carcasses continue on the assembly line, each worker is responsible for one task in the disassembly process. Waste is reduced through the use of machines that attempt to take every morsel of meat from the carcass. This factory assembly-line approach is also used in the hog and poultry industries.

Contract farming has increased the need for calculability. In this system, processors outsource animals to farmers who are contracted to raise them for a specific period of time. Although only approximately 12% of farmers sell their products through production contracts, there has been an increase in contract farming in the United States. Almost all broiler chickens are raised under contract. Although cattle and hog industries are less integrated into the contract system, contract farming in the hog industry is becoming increasingly common.

In the chicken industry, processors drop off chicks on a farm close to the poultry processing plant to lower transportation costs. Farmers then raise the chickens for a specified period of time and according to the terms provided in the contract. This system places a focus on calculability because farmers are paid a specified number of cents per pound and provided incentives and penalties related to performance and quality standards. Typically, growers receive day-old chicks from the processors that can mature to four or five pounds in seven to eight weeks. Growers are only paid for live chickens. Similarly, beef and hog growers are also paid by weight gained.

Farm contracts with Tyson illustrate how farmers are controlled by agribusinesses. Farmers usually sign a four-year contract with Tyson (or other similar regional firms) that makes Tyson the sole provider of the chicks to be raised, the feed, and veterinary services. The company is also the sole determiner of the number, frequency, and type of chicks provided. Tyson then collects the mature birds after seven weeks, at a date and time of their own determination, providing the scales on which the birds are weighed, and the trucks take them away. The farmer provides the labor, the buildings in which the chicks are raised, and the land on which the buildings stand. The detailed control of inputs and farming practices are entirely in the hands of Tyson. Moreover, the farmer must adhere to the Company's "Broiler Growing Guide" and a failure to do so puts the farmer into "Intensified Management" status under the direct supervision of the Company's "Broiler Management and Technical Advisor."

Contract farming has been linked to the growth of larger farm size and fewer farms. In the hog industry, for example, the number of hog farms in the United States has decreased dramatically, although the number of hogs sold has increased. In particular, the fastest growth of hog farms is from super hog farms (50,000 to 500,000 hogs per year) and mega hog farms (greater than 500,000 hogs per year).

Farmers are controlled and are increasingly becoming more dependent on a few agribusinesses that sell inputs to farmers and then purchase their crops or livestock. This oligopoly of agricultural chemical companies and food processors determines the price of farm crops and controls the cost of seeds and chemicals. At the same time, vertical integration among processors has increased to the point where only a few companies control the food supply. ConAgra provides an example of the extent of both horizontal and vertical integration by agribusiness. ConAgra is one of the largest distributors of agricultural chemicals and fertilizers in North America, and has developed partnerships with seed companies. It is the largest turkey producer and second largest broiler producer in the United States, manufactures poultry and livestock feeds, owns and operates hatcheries, and processes foods. From farm to table, a significant proportion of the food system is owned and controlled by ConAgra.

Attempts to rationalize the meat processing industry have led to numerous irrationalities. Large feedlots have come under greater scrutiny for environmental, aesthetic, and health reasons. Animal-rights groups, such as People for the Ethical Treatment of Animals, have launched public relations campaigns against fast-food giants, such as McDonald's, on the issue of animal cruelty in food processing plants. Political conflicts between neighboring residents and large feedlots and meat processing plants have increased as residents concerned about air quality, waste, and property values attempt to shut down, relocate, or prevent the construction of large feedlots and meat processing plants.

A problem of large feedlots is the health of animals. In the case of beef, in order for large feedlots to be viable, cattle are fed grain instead of grass. This diet allows cattle to gain weight much faster than a traditional grass diet, and corn is often sold to meat processors below market value. The problem is that cattle's digestive systems are not designed to digest grains. Also, the concentration of cattle in a small area poses health problems as cattle eat and live where they defecate. To control the rate of disease infection, grain feed often contains antibiotics. This process has been linked to increased antibiotic resistant illness in humans.

Although the Department of Agriculture reassures the public that the U.S. food system is one of the safest in the world, the industrialization of food processing has heightened the risk of food contamination, particularly by bacteria such as *Salmonella, E. coli,* and *Listeria.* Although feeding livestock ruminants animal parts was banned in 1997 in response to the outbreak of Mad Cow disease in Europe, the recent discovery of a case in the United States highlights this irrational, inefficient process. Still, the food processing industry is primarily responsible for regulating itself. Although contract farming provides guaranteed pricing, contract farming does not appear to be a system that enriches farmers. Few contract farmers are able to eliminate debt, and that concentration of ownership within the industry has created a financial crisis among growers.

Rebelling Against the McDonaldization of Agriculture

The most vocal opponent of industrial agriculture is the organic movement. As people have become increasingly concerned about the environmental and health tolls of industrial agriculture, the organic industry has undergone massive growth. In 2001, organic foods represented a $5 billion industry, and by some industry estimates, sales have increased by 20% annually since 1990. Still, organic products represent only 2% of all food sales. Organic agriculture is in many ways the complete opposite of industrial agriculture. According to the U.S. Department of Agriculture, organic production systems emphasize the use of renewable resources and the conservation of soil and water to enhance environmental quality for future generations. Animals that are raised organically are not given antibiotics or artificial growth hormones. Organic food is produced without the use of most conventional pesticides, synthetic fertilizers, biotechnology, and irradiation. Organic farmers, handlers, and food processors must be inspected by government-approved certifiers to ensure that all organic standards are met.

The organic movement is more than just an agricultural production system, however. One slogan of the organic movement is food with a face, a taste, and a place. It strives to be a fully integrated food system that connects farmers, local communities, and consumers, particularly through farmer's markets and community-supported agriculture. The organic movement shares many agrarian values as it espouses values of self-empowerment, social justice, economic gain, environmental health, creativity, autonomy, individualism, localism, and smallness. The challenge for organic agriculture, however, is whether these values can be maintained with growth, particularly as agribusinesses turn their attention to the growing organic industry.

The Future of the McDonaldization of Agriculture

This chapter has demonstrated that, with a few exceptions, industrial agriculture is becoming increasingly McDonaldized, in that it seeks to make agriculture more efficient, calculable, and predictable, particularly through the use of nonhuman technologies, even though agriculture remains to a great extent an irrational industry. The analysis, however, has focused only on the production side of agriculture. Ritzer correctly points out that the McDonaldization process does have advantages, particularly for consumers. One advantage of industrial agriculture has been the production of an abundance of cheap food. Today's consumers, compared to previous generations, spend little of their disposable income on food. However, if one includes subsidies and the costs of the irrationalities of industrial agricultural production in the price of products, the actual price of food is much higher. And, it remains to be seen whether industrial agriculture can sustain the current level of productivity in the future. Another advantage of industrial agriculture and the globalization of food is the availability of products year round. Consumers are no longer tied to local and seasonal availability of foods.

Jean Kinsey noted several trends driving U.S. food demands, some of which favor the McDonaldization process and some of which may favor alternative methods of food production. Consumers demand more variety, homogeneous products worldwide, convenience, services from the public sector, environmentally friendly foods, and healthier foods. It remains to be seen whether the industrial model, particularly through the use of biotechnology, can make some of these demands become a reality or whether alternate food production systems, such as organic farming, will become mainstream.

The trend toward the McDonaldization of agriculture is not limited to the United States. Like other industries, agriculture is becoming increasingly international. Just how far can the reach of McDonaldization be extended? In the case of agriculture, the answer to this question will likely be determined by the success or failure of biotechnology, and how well the ever-increasing irrationalities caused by the McDonaldization of agriculture can be addressed. The future of industrial agriculture seems to be putting all of its future eggs into one basket. Could it be that the long arm of McDonaldization may be reaching too far?

Thinking Critically

1. What are the advantages of McDonaldizing farms?

2. What are the disadvantages of McDonaldizing farms?

3. If you were a farmer, would you prefer to work on and/or own a McDonaldized or a non-McDonaldized farm?

4. If you were a farm animal, would you prefer to exist on a McDonaldized or a non-McDonaldized farm?

5. On balance, is McDonaldization good or bad for the consumer of U.S. farm products?

As was true in the preceding chapter's analysis of farms, this chapter continues to extend the McDonaldization thesis from its natural home in consumption and the city to areas of production such as farms and rural areas. Morris and Reed study the McDonaldization of ecological movements on farm areas in England. One would not expect to find such movements McDonaldized, but they are, although the authors also discuss the emergence of alternative, less- or non-McDonaldized movements of this type. They focus specifically on an environmental movement in England—"agri-environment schemes" (AEs)—which is concerned with landscape and wildlife/habitat conservation on British farms. In general they find that such conservation efforts are McDonaldized and there is significant evidence that all of the dimensions of McDonaldization can be found in them. AEs have been found to be a rational method of conservation, even though their goals such as improved biodiversity and landscape character relate more to a non-McDonaldized characteristic—"quality"—rather than to the "quantity" that is usually associated with McDonaldization. Nevertheless, there are a series of irrationalities of rationality associated with the McDonaldization of AEs (e.g., the deskilling of land management and the dehumanization of such work). The McDonaldization of conservation is in many ways paradoxical—e.g., the effort to standardize the wild elements of nature—and it also has produced local resistance. However, Morris and Reed conclude by wondering whether the resistance, too, will end up being McDonaldized.

18

From Burgers to Biodiversity?

The McDonaldization of On-Farm Nature Conservation in the UK

Carol Morris and Matt Reed

Introduction

The conservation of rural nature has become an issue of increasing public and political concern over the past few decades, particularly in the UK. Unlike North America, where highly prized natural locations are often located within reserves and national parks (i.e., the so-called "wild" areas beyond agriculture), similar areas in the UK and other parts of Europe are largely located **within** agricultural spaces. The farming community, therefore, by necessity has been involved in the debate about the need to conserve rural nature, although some parts of this community remain stubbornly

Editor's Note: From Morris, C. and Reed, M., "From Burgers to Biodiversity? The McDonaldization of On-Farm Nature Conservation in the UK," in *Agriculture and Human Values* 24: 207–218 (2007). Kluwer Academic Publisher, with kind permission of Springer Science and Business Media.

resistant to the environmental agenda. Particularly in the UK, the debate about on-farm nature conservation has been centered on landscape and wildlife/habitat conservation, the former being a peculiarly British preoccupation. The dominant method of on-farm nature conservation in the UK is the "agri-environment scheme" (AES), which represents the practical or operational face of "agri-environmental policy" (AEP). These schemes emerged in the early 1980s, due in no small part to the campaigning efforts of environmental organizations about the adverse impacts of modern agriculture on species, habitats, and landscapes. AESs are government initiatives that provide financial incentives to farmers and other land manangers to undertake a variety of actions and operations, benefiting on-farm nature. These include the extensive reinstatement and/or positive management of features such as hedgerows and wet areas . . .

This paper responds to this omission and seeks to develop a more critical analysis of AEP as it has been applied within the UK.

The chosen means of approaching this task is through George Ritzer's notion of McDonaldization, the socially transformative process of rationalization. This may seem an unlikely perspective given both the urban and consumption emphasis of much of Ritzer's work, but a number of reasons lead to its adoption. First, at one level, extending the McDonaldization thesis into the rural and, by extension, into the natural is simply tracking the burger-food chain to the place where the raw materials are produced. On another level, however, it is about the challenge that nature presents to social theory, particularly within sociology. Second, the analysis and discussion of contemporary European agriculture has placed undue emphasis on various forms of neo-Marxist political economy or post-structural perspectives. At the same time, the analytical possibilities provided by neo-Weberian perspectives, including rationalization, have been largely neglected. This neglect represents another reason to consider and utilize Ritzer's ideas in this context. Third, AEP is a rationalized approach to the management of rural nature, and so an analytical framework that deconstructs and questions rationalization provides an important means of critically approaching these initiatives. Fourth, for the largely urban-oriented audiences, applying the McDonaldization thesis to the analysis of AEP provides a means of demonstrating how the management of rural nature is far from antithetical to the rationalization of urban space . . .

The McDonaldization Thesis

Ritzer's McDonaldization thesis has gained currency as a quickly and readily deployable heuristic device, one that is not only familiar but has analytical incisiveness. Ritzer has always acknowledged his debt to other theorists and, through his recent incorporation of concepts from Bourdieu, Foucault, and Baudrillard, explicitly accepts that his social theorizing is a synthetic project that weaves together a range of insights about the ongoing project of rationalization in modernity . . .

It is reasonable to assume, therefore, that the social processes surrounding the management of rural nature have also been subject to rationalization. Indeed, in the subsequent sections, evidence is presented to support the contention that AESs represent a McDonaldized approach to the conservation management in the UK. Key to this analysis is realization that McDonaldized systems typically lead to a set of irrational outcomes (indeed, Ritzer argues that irrationality is the fifth defining characteristic of McDonaldization) that, in turn, can induce profound disenchantment for those caught up within them.

The McDonaldization of On-Farm Nature Conservation Through Agri-Environment Schemes

The arguments of other neo-Weberians, such as Beck and his risk society thesis, can be used to interpret the emergence of AESs as the latest manifestation of a longer-term process of rationalization within agriculture. Beck highlights the effects of technology that "boomerangs back" onto society through its unintended and unknowable side-effects. This leads to the tools of science, including that of critique, being turned on science itself, "targeted not only as a source of solutions to problems, but also as a cause of problems." Thus, the unintended consequences of earlier rationalization projects come to undermine present society. In most of Beck's examples, the interface where these risks arise is between science and (an a-rational) nature (in our case, science as it is applied to agriculture, and rural nature). Beck is compelled to conclude that society has begun to advance not because of the positive benefits of modernity but through its "bads." In short, one round of rationalization, or McDonaldization, inevitably leads to another, as the irrationalities from these earlier rounds become evident. This is apparent in the emergence of nature conservation initiatives such as AESs which have been designed and implemented to deal with the adverse environmental consequences, or irrationalities, of the post-war rationalization project in agriculture. AEP can therefore be conceptualized as the latest round of McDonaldization within the agricultural sector and it is to the operational detail of AEP and AESs that the paper now turns.

Hanley et al. define agri-environmental policy as "any policy implemented by farm agencies or ministries, for which funding comes out of agricultural support budgets, and which is concerned mainly with encouraging or enforcing the production of environmental goods, as joint products with food and fibre outputs." Agri-environment schemes were initially piloted in 1983, as the "Halvergate experiment," in a wetland area in Eastern England known as the Norfolk Broads. Here, a system of flat rate hectarage payments from the public purse were offered to farmers who agreed to undertake positive conservation actions. That the scheme successfully recruited the majority of farmers in the area has been attributed to a number of factors. First, it was a voluntary rather than a regulatory approach to nature conservation, the ideal form of agricultural governance from the point of view of the agricultural community and one that the agricultural lobby had long and successfully campaigned for. Second, it offered a standardized application procedure and a set of management prescriptions that, in theory, were relatively straightforward to put into practice. Finally, the financial incentive was of a sufficient amount to attract farmers but was not designed to cover all costs or loss of profits.

The Halvergate model was applied to the development of the first full-blown agri-environment scheme, the Environmentally Sensitive Area (ESA) scheme, which was implemented in the UK in 1987. This was followed by the introduction of a series of other agri-environment schemes throughout the 1990s. The Countryside Stewardship Scheme (CSS) was significant among these in terms of numbers of farmers and area of land involved. In England, effort has been made to simplify and consolidate the system into one "mega" agri-environment scheme, known as Environmental Stewardship, initiated in 2005.

In order to demonstrate how the four dimensions of McDonaldization are evident within the design and operation of agri-environment schemes (and, by doing so, how this approach to on-farm conservation is by no means ideal), this paper draws on various forms of empirical material . . .

Efficiency

The tens of thousands of farmers who have signed up for AESs can be interpreted as a sign of the efficiency of this system of nature conservation (i.e., it has been able to recruit relatively large numbers of farmers into conservation management for relatively little cost). The system adopted in AESs uses a flat rate hectarage payment for land management and set financial contributions for "capital works" (e.g., restoring boundary features such as hedges or stone walls). This has not only proved attractive to farmers but also has been welcomed by bureaucrats who recognize the financial savings of the system when compared with the previous, site-based approach to nature conservation, which paid farmers on an individually-negotiated, profits foregone basis. That AESs have recruited many more farmers into conservation than perhaps would have been the case through less rational means reflects the observation by Ritzer that among the positive changes brought about by McDonaldization is "a wider range of goods and services . . . available to a much larger proportion of the population than ever before." However, the cost dimension of AESs is only one aspect of its efficient approach to conservation. Crucial in Ritzer's analysis of efficiency in rationalized systems is the use of rules and regulations.

> The people who work in McDonaldized organizations are also controlled to a high degree. They are trained to do a limited number of things in precisely the way they are told to do them. The technologies used and the way the organization is set up reinforce this control. Managers and inspectors make sure that workers toe the line.

Rules and regulations abound within the implementation of AESs and both impact the scheme staff, notably the project officers who provide guidance and information to farmers and the schemes' principal "customers"— the farmers and land managers. The scripts of the staff serving burgers in a fast food restaurant are replaced in a conservation context by an extensive set of guidelines for how project officers should process scheme applications and how they should proceed on farms when they undertake advisory and compliance visits. This of course is a great deal less tightly scripted than in the fast food situation, but nevertheless the "Project Officer Operating Instructions" heavily prescribe the rules of the conservation game.

Likewise, agreement holders themselves are subject to numerous rules and regulations once they have signed up for a scheme. Management prescriptions represent the scientific rules underpinning AESs. These prescribe the management actions to be undertaken in order to realize the desired conservation outcomes. They not only determine what a farmer should do, but also the timing of his/her actions, as AESs specify, for example, the dates when hay meadows should be cut or when sheep should be removed from moorland grazing areas. One typical illustration of this is the grazing management guidelines for Heather Moorland and Coastal Heath habitat within the Exmoor ESA scheme.

To ensure that overgrazing does not occur, you will be asked to keep within prescribed stocking levels. In summer (April 16 to October 31) this will be the equivalent of 1.5 ewes/hectare—or cattle equivalents—(0.225 livestock units (LU) per hectare), and in winter (November 1 to April 15) up to one ewe per hectare with no cattle (pony grazing may be allowed but needs approval in winter) . . .

Nationally devised management prescriptions make little allowance for local variation in the timing of such agricultural activities. Should farmers not follow these management rules, they are faced with the legal repercussions, because they are contravening the terms of a legally binding contract with the state. A system of "care and maintenance" and "compliance" visits by project officers is designed to ensure that farmers keep to the task . . .

Farmers' legal obligations also include allowing regular monitoring exercises (by independent third party organizations) on their agreement land . . .

Control

. . . Control within the context of AESs is manifested within the records held by DEFRA on each AES agreement. Each file contains a copy of all the paperwork relating to that agreement, including correspondence between the applicant agreement holder and project officer or between the project officer and other environmental experts, farmer claims for their scheme payments, applications for derogations, and other related materials. While these agreement files serve as important records, basic information about agreements is also entered into and held on a national electronic database. Analysis of the paper files reveals the extent to which agreement holders are controlled (albeit indirectly and remotely) through an elaborate system of electronic mechanisms. When a farmer applies to an AES, this triggers a number of procedures, all of which entail the deployment of a variety of nonhuman technologies. Aerial photographs of the particular farm and its surrounding area are used to identify the location of the proposed agreement. Farm maps (supplied by the applicant) are entered into and processed through a geographical information system (GIS) and those aspects of the farm subject to conservation management are represented by color-coded symbols and shading. An Integrated Arable Control System (IACS) "reconciliation exercise" is undertaken to ensure that the proposed area of land corresponds with the farm's IACS area. Meanwhile, under the new Environmental Stewardship Scheme, farmers now have the option of making their applications over the Internet, thereby reducing the amount of paperwork. Although scheme participants surveyed in monitoring exercises frequently complained about the amount of paperwork involved, the use of nonhuman technologies within the conservation management of nature is by no means universally welcomed by farmers. Indeed, monitoring studies of AESs have revealed that farmers actually appreciate working one-on-one with a person—a project officer or equivalent environmental expert—during the application process and when they are trying to implement their scheme agreement.

Calculability

Intertwined with the other dimensions of McDonaldization, calculability involves counting and quantifying. Numerical standards are set for both processes and end results with an emphasis on speed and size, respectively (Ritzer, 2000). At first sight, it would appear that nature and its management have little to do with quantification. Indeed, in the following quote, which explicitly contrasts the modern theme park such as Disney World (an epitome of McDonaldization) with nature, Ritzer suggests our experience of nature has a strong affective or emotional dimension. This is likely to work against or contradict a McDonaldized approach to nature management, in particular systems that attempt to quantify or reduce nature to numbers and targets.

> There is a form of enchantment at the Disney Worlds, but it's a very different, mass-produced, assembly-line form, consciously fabricated and routinely produced over and over rather than emerging spontaneously from the interactions among visitors, employers, and the park itself, and especially rather than emerging spontaneously from an actual encounter with . . . nature.

Nevertheless and therefore somewhat paradoxically, the calculability that is evident within AESs is perhaps the most strongly defined feature of this McDonaldized approach to nature conservation. The first thing that greets the visitor to DEFRA's "England Rural Development Programme" web site (http://www.defra.gov.uk/rural/rdpe/index.htm) is a list of figures detailing the uptake, in hectares of land, of its various agri-environment schemes. Setting quantifiable targets for the AES, in terms of the numbers of farmers and areas of land, has always been a concern of DEFRA and its predecessor, the Ministry of Agriculture, Food and Fisheries. For the Environmental Stewardship Scheme, this target figure is 75% of all farmers in England. Previously, ESAs targets were set at different levels for each of their designated areas. Increasingly, the number of environmental outputs DEFRA wishes to see resulting from the environmental management has grown in importance

importance (e.g., the numbers of farmland birds and other UK Biodiversity Action Plan species). That there is an increasing emphasis on points and targets as AESs have developed is demonstrated by the new Environmental Stewardship scheme in which prospective participants are

> required to meet a "points target" for the land you enter into the Scheme, which will be calculated at the rate of 30 points per hectare (except for Less Favoured Area land within parcels of 15 hectares or more which will be calculated at the rate of 8 points per hectare). You will be able to choose from over 50 simple management options, each of which is worth a certain number of "points" to reach your "points target." There are options to suit most farm types.

Management options also are all highly quantified, as the schemes specify lengths of wall and other boundary features, widths of arable field margins, and grassland areas to be managed in acres or hectares. Completed applications to the CSS are then subject to a "scoring system" that is administered by project officers as a means of evaluating whether or not the applicant is likely to meet the scheme objectives and its targets.

According to Ritzer (2000), a further aspect of the calculability of McDonaldization is the emphasis on keeping costs and prices as low as possible. Within the context of AESs, there is an emphasis on ensuring value for money across the entire operation of the program. Furthermore, the importance of the payments offered through the schemes as opposed to their environmental objectives, is a particularly significant factor in explaining farmers' involvement . . . Balancing the books is, therefore, the critical determinant in shaping whether or not a farmer becomes a customer within this McDonaldized system of conservation.

Predictability

The widely valued diversity and associated spontaneity of nature suggests that it is not predictable, nor could its management be made predictable. Although this aspect of the rationalization process may appear to be the one that fits AESs the least well, a tendency toward making nature's management predictable is nonetheless apparent. As outlined above, after the inception of the first AES in 1987 (the Environmentally Sensitive Area Scheme), numerous other AESs were introduced, some of which dealt with specific environmental management challenges (e.g., protection and enhancement of hedgerows (the Hedgerow Incentive Scheme) or the management of highly valued sites of special scientific interest). Nevertheless, since all the schemes were designed and operated in much the same way—voluntary entry, flat rate payments, prescribed management—they made the process of conservation management more predictable. A rather universal scheme format means that farmers know what to expect no matter where or what they are farming. It is predictability, according to Ritzer, that makes the consumer of McDonaldized systems feel safe. The recent consolidation of AES schemes into one mega-scheme intended to recruit the overwhelming majority of farms in England (literally a one size fits all approach) is the latest phase of making nature management more predictable for potential participants. Likewise, the management prescriptions of individual AESs are designed to ensure a predictable conservation outcome, suggesting that to prescribe is to predict. As Burgess et al. explain in their account of the Wildlife Enhancement Scheme, the science underpinning AES prescriptions seeks to control and make predictable the nature to which it is applied.

> The scientific knowledge of nature is the guide to its manipulation, for the universal products of science can be expertly brought to bear on any local arena. And nature needs this manipulation. For the most part, it must be controlled in order to conserve and enhance habitats, and to promote particular species wherever these occur.

However, AESs do not only make nature conservation predictable to farmers. There are other consumers involved in these schemes, notably the general public, who are encouraged to visit the sites being managed. Indeed, farmers can receive payments for providing additional public access routes across their AES agreement land. Where this occurs, DEFRA provides standardized signage systems informing consumers of the McDonaldized countryside what to expect; in other words, what they should look for in terms of wildlife, their habitats, and also any features of historic interest. It also instructs them where they should walk. In this way, the schemes make the public's experience of the countryside more predictable and less spontaneous. Signs and route ways also provide the means of controlling them.

While Ritzer and others express profound concerns about rationalized systems, their analyses highlight how, at the same time, McDonaldization has been enormously popular and successful. Ritzer himself regards the process as both enabling and constraining, although he chooses to emphasize its "dark side." Many people visit fast food restaurants and other McDonaldized institutions on a regular basis and appear to enjoy the experience. Likewise, the agri-environment program has been welcomed by numerous organizations with nature conservation and environmental interests. Scientific monitoring of AES also suggests that the schemes have been successful in at least stemming the tide of environmental decline and, in some cases, successful in leading to environmental enhancement. Indeed, CSS agreement holders (when interviewed for a monitoring exercise) were able to point to "an increase in the number of birds on the holding," "more wildlife in the hedges," "improvements in flora as a result of grazing and controlling access," and "the maintenance of floristically diverse pastures."

For the farmers involved it would appear, ostensibly at least, that they have been persuaded by the benefits of joining an AES and indeed survey evidence shows that the experience of participating can be both rewarding and educational . . . This evidence provides some support for Weberian and neo-Weberian ideas that rational systems, in spite of their constraints, "paradoxically and simultaneously serve to create their own kinds of enchantment." The delight associated with the reassertion of nature under AESs suggests that this approach to conservation can be enchanting for their primary consumers. It is doubtful, however, that such an approach allows these same consumers to live out their (environmental) fantasies, as Ritzer observes, in the context of other rationalized, but enchanted, consumption contexts such as shopping malls.

The Irrationality of Rationalized On-Farm Nature Conservation

. . . Of particular significance are the limits of rationalized AESs (indeed of any rationalized system) in being able to deal with ecological variability. The creation within AESs of a "menu" of natural items to be managed through a set of carefully delineated prescriptions is designed to create predictable conservation outcomes, wherever they are applied. However, this approach to nature conservation breaks down all too easily because nature itself is by no means always so reliable and compliant. Discussions with the agreement holders of CSS agreements reveal just a few of the ways in which nature is uncontrollable and unpredictable. Weed problems, particularly ragwort and thistles, and difficulties controlling scrub are often mentioned. Where scheme rules prohibit conventional (typically chemical) methods of weed control and restrict grazing densities, AHs frequently are at a loss for how to tackle invasive plant species. In one case, a West Kent farmer complained that the prescribed management guideline of bi-annual mowing of his CSS field margins was "already leading to problems of weed control." Another farmer in West Sussex argued for more flexibility in "weed control and scheduling [as] the control of thistles and docks is a big bug-bear in the margins and grass fields." He described how the CSS arable margins had "encouraged magpies and jackdaws to pull down the wheat," something that had not previously been a problem. Both difficulties had led this AH to apply technological solutions, with a weed wiper purchased to deal with the first and an automated bird "banger" to address the second.

Other difficulties encountered by farmers included problems with establishing areas sown to grass (e.g., field margins), sometimes because of weed problems or because wet weather had delayed the CSS work program. For example, one farmer in Buckinghamshire described how the prescribed grass seed mix used on his arable reversion land "didn't grow at all. . . . It was a complete waste of money." Likewise, an Essex based farmer reported how his CSS grass strips "didn't establish in the first year," and was concerned they will not "take" in the future either. In a number of cases, CSS agreements entailed the "wetting up" or flooding of areas, typically to effect changes in the composition of the sward, leading to improvements in bird habitat. However, agreement holders pointed to problems of accessing the necessary water for these tasks because of unpredictable weather conditions (e.g., lower rainfall).

Further evidence of the irrationality of rationalized AES is found in the disenchantment expressed towards these schemes not only by those who resist participating but also among agreement holders. In the context of the fast food industry, disenchantment arises among both the people using and working within McDonaldized systems, particularly restaurant employees who become frustrated with their scripted procedures, and customers who become fed up with queuing and the standardized product offerings. For the agreement holder of CSSs, disenchantment is evident in their reactions to the Scheme's prescriptions and, implicitly, to the science underpinning them. Instead they assert their own understandings of how the land to which the CSS agreement applies needs to be managed, based on many years of working that land. Agreement holders made reference to the weakness of the scheme's "blanket prescriptions," questioning the logic of having one set of prescriptions that is applied in any situation or land use context. For example, one Buckinghamshire farmer asserted that the scheme was "too regimented . . . the rules apply to the whole country that may well apply to some parts of the country better than others—more local flexibility is needed." In this and other cases, farmers were advancing the importance of "local knowledge" and expressing concern that this was being disregarded in the implementation of the scheme. As Burgess et al. have observed, "the listened to voice, when it comes to knowledge, understanding, and action, is that of the conservationist." AESs, which are underpinned by scientific knowledge, can be seen as riding roughshod over the situated, local knowledge held by the farmers and other land managers participating in these schemes.

AES prescriptions limit the creativity of farmers and point to the deskilling that is characteristic of McDonaldized systems. Many examples were found of how the "universalizing prescriptions and practices of professional nature conservationists were very much at odds with the farmers' intense, contextual, specific knowledge and experience of the land." A farmer in County Durham described how his CSS agreement had underestimated the time needed for hedge trees to grow to an appropriate height before being laid. He explained that, "this is a very exposed site on the North East coast. It takes longer for trees to grow up here than elsewhere. This was not accounted for in the advice and scheduling or timetabling of the hedging." He went on to add that he would have "preferred advice from a local person with more experience of hedge laying, to enable them to prepare a more realistic schedule and timetable, one that accounted for the local conditions and how these impact on hedge shrub growth, etc."

Partly as a result of their frustration with the centralized, inflexible, and bureaucratized AESs, some agreement holders expressed a desire for a return to the more locally designed, managed, and flexible schemes that some of them had experienced prior to their participation in the ESA scheme or CSS. This suggests that there are (or can be) non-McDonaldized approaches to nature conservation, something that is considered in the final section of the paper.

Discussion and Conclusions

It has been the purpose of this paper to critically examine the UK's agri-environment program through the lens of Ritzer's version of rationalization—McDonaldization. Although AESs are not the only means of managing rural nature on UK farms—others can and indeed do exist (Colman et al., 1992)—it is our contention that a McDonaldized version has become the dominant form of nature conservation management in this context, just as it has become almost universal in food and other retailing situations. We acknowledge that the particular agricultural policy of the UK, combined with distinctive cultures of land use, mean that our claim may not apply in other contexts, particularly in those with less state intervention in the agricultural sector and where there are greater levels of cooperation among members of the agricultural community. Nevertheless, in the UK, AESs have come to be viewed as the best or most efficient way of moving from a poorly managed countryside, in nature and landscape conservation terms, to a better or optimally managed countryside. While the outputs of nature conservation management—improved biodiversity and landscape character—can be understood as "quality products," "quality and McDonaldization are not inimical."

This analysis has demonstrated how AESs represent a rationalizing approach to conservation—efficient, predictable, calculable, and controlling. These dimensions of McDonaldized systems have undesirable consequences on their own, but it is the irrationality of rationality that carries the greatest potential for disenchantment among the farmer participants and other "customers" of McDonaldized on-farm conservation. Indeed, the irrationalities associated with this rationalized approach to on-farm conservation raise serious questions about the ability of rationalized systems to deal with ecological variability and unpredictability, the marginalization of land manager knowledge, and the de-skilling that this implies. Perhaps because they fear being caught up in the iron cage of rationalized conservation management, many farmers continue to resist AES in spite of on-going government attempts to enroll them into the program. As Ritzer has commented, in spite of the ubiquity of McDonaldization, it is possible to develop strategies of resistance. In the context of AESs, it is not always easy to disentangle the extent to which this resistance is a product of a perceived infringement of property rights or a reaction to their rationalized character.

The interpolation of rationality and irrationality abounds within agri-environmental schemes in ways that are often deeply paradoxical. Certainly the impact of McDonaldization in rural areas is not as intense as it is in urban contexts and it could be argued that the AES have re-introduced variety back into the countryside. This variety, as discussed above, is not spontaneous but measured and standardized. Only close ecological observation can apprehend this standardization, but we cannot deny that it is present. Equally, the natural entities that are promoted, favored, or re-introduced by these schemes, while wild, are not quite as wild as they were when they were the "accidental" (rather than planned-for) by-products of farming systems. As the product of a McDonaldized scheme, these natural entities are now the product of a deliberate intervention to preserve, quantify, and monitor them. This is perhaps just the next stage in this co-evolution, but its very intentionality marks it as distinct from the processes that preceded it. By becoming problematized, and later becoming the subject of a remedial bureaucratic system, much of the autonomy that characterized this form of nature has been lost. Nevertheless, as Ritzer suggests this system retains the power to enchant. Farmers, as we have seen, enjoy and welcome the return of this more diverse flora and fauna to their holdings. Those who implement and manage the schemes are similarly convinced of the value and wider importance of the program, including many of the social and natural scientists who monitor the policies.

Moreover, there appears to be a degree of reflexivity, which suggests that the limits of, and the disenchantment associated with, a McDonaldized approach to nature conservation have been recognized within policy circles. Here there is some evidence of a shift away from the universalizing, bureaucratic, and rationalized AES-type approaches to more locally oriented, farm and rural community-lead approaches, such as those piloted under the Countryside Agency's Land Management Initiatives (LMI) program and the European Union's LEADER schemes. Likewise, the proliferation of food branding and labeling schemes that are based on a valorization of on-farm nature may also represent a less rationalized approach to conservation. These new interventions may offer opportunities through which the practice of nature conservation can become re-enchanted. Alternatively, they may be the next evolutionary stage in the process of rationalization, as the techniques involved in managing nature become more refined and subtle. Indeed, as Ritzer pessimistically concludes, "in the natural world . . . we find not only much that is fostering the [McDonaldization] process but also a number of barriers to it. However, while such barriers exist, none are likely in the near future to stem the tide in the direction of McDonaldization or reverse it and lead to de-McDonaldization" (2000: 199, emphasis added). Whether the more localized approaches to nature conservation represent the next round of McDonaldization or a means of resisting it is, at present, an open question . . .

Thinking Critically

1. Are you surprised to find the environmental movement McDonaldized? Why or why not?

2. What is the great paradox involved in this process?

3. How can the resistance to this McDonaldization of the environmental movement succeed?

4. What are the irrationalities of rationality associated with the McDonaldization of the environmental movement?

5. In what ways can McDonaldization help the environmental movement?

This chapter contains a recent essay in which John Drane extends the arguments of The McDonaldization of Society. *Drane concludes that the church is indeed highly McDonaldized and that this is one of the key sources of the crisis facing the church today. In fact, the church has a history of increasing rationalization that predates the advent of the fast-food restaurant by centuries; it is traceable to the earliest history of the church. A good example of the McDonaldization of the church, and an indicator of its current crisis, is the mega-church movement. Indeed, the church and McDonald's are seen as growing in tandem with one another and more alike over the last few decades. The culmination of this was the opening in 2001 of the first McDonald's franchise in a church—naturally, a mega-church. More generally, instead of offering spirituality and liberation, the church is seen as processing churchgoers in much the same way that fast-food restaurants process customers or hamburgers. Ironically, what is ostensibly the most human of social institutions has, like many other institutions, grown increasingly dehumanized.*

19

From Creeds to Burgers

Religious Control, Spiritual Search, and the Future of the World

John Drane

W hen I first read George Ritzer's pioneering work *The McDonaldization of Society,* I was—like many others—struck by the way in which his iconic notion of 'McDonaldization' captures so poignantly the sense of anxiety and futurelessness felt by people who struggle with life in an increasingly rationalized world, and it seemed an obvious step to speculate as to whether his insights could also add to our understanding of the predicament of the church in post-modern society. It soon became evident that McDonaldization, with its fourfold foundation of efficiency, calculability, predictability, and control, did indeed describe the way that many people experience the church, even if they are not values that all church leaders would self-consciously espouse as their guiding principles. Ritzer's description of the dehumanizing effects of McDonaldization expressed what many people who abandon the church—and not a few who remain in it—complain about:

Editor's Note: From Drane, J. "From Creeds to Burgers," in *Theorising Religion: Classical and Contemporary Debates,* Beckford, J. A., & Wallis, J. (Ed.). Copyright © 2006, reprinted with permission from Ashgate Publishing.

'Human beings, equipped with a wide array of skills and abilities, are asked to perform a limited number of highly simplified tasks over and over . . . forced to deny their humanity and act in a robot-like manner.'

More recently, Alan Jamieson's study of people who leave the church has provided empirical confirmation of what for me was originally no more than an informed guess. He reports countless conversations with leavers for whom the McDonaldized nature of church had been a significant catalyst—if not the major underlying reason—in their decision to abandon the institution, many of them claiming that this was a necessary part of their spiritual growth and development because, just as the fast-food industry had apparently devalued the experience of eating, so the church had become an unhelpful distraction in their desire to live out the Christian faith with integrity. One of Jamieson's interviewees (a former church minister) expressed this sense of spiritual frustration in terms that are almost a textbook summary of Ritzer's analysis of the angst felt by so many in relation to society at large:

> The person last night was essentially saying that their spirituality had dried up, and they wanted to get out of the church. They were saying they go through this rote every week. They come to church twice on Sundays, sing the songs and listen to the messages but their spirituality has dried up. They want to get out and get to something, not just another church, but something that brings their spirituality alive again. That really means something to them, with a deep conviction. It is not just a routine you go through . . .

I was not taken aback by this, because I had already argued that Ritzer's four marks of McDonaldization were present in the structures and attitudes of most churches. What did surprise me, however, was Ritzer's own surprise when he included my analysis in the first edition of *McDonaldization: The Reader* and posed the rhetorical question, 'Who would ever have thought that the church . . . could have been thought of as McDonaldized?' Though my original study highlighted the detail of everyday life in the average church— things like the conduct of worship, the collection of statistics, marketing strategies, the presentation of beliefs, and so on—there are many other aspects of contemporary church life that connect very directly with both the philosophical concepts behind McDonaldization and also the pragmatism of the fast-food industry which provided the source of the model. I shall suggest below that the cultural strands which together constitute the fabric of a McDonaldized society are in fact much older and more deeply rooted in Western civilization than has generally been acknowledged, while recognizing that some of the most striking examples of the McDonaldization of the church have developed in parallel with ostensibly 'secular' trends, specifically that entrepreneurial mindset which has characterized the can-do culture of southern California since the 1950s and 1960s. The growth of the fast-food industry during that period has a number of uncanny parallels with the history of the church in the same time frame, including some overtly religious overtones to the way in which fast food has been packaged and promoted, as well as the adoption of McDonaldized marketing strategies by some churches.

One of the most noticeable developments in church life over the past fifty years has been the emergence of large churches with thousands of members and attenders (the so-called 'mega-church'). It is largely an American phenomenon, though one that is increasingly admired, if not copied, by churches in other parts of the world. The period of rapid growth of such churches during the 1990s matches the development of the fast-food industry, which is unlikely to be a coincidence as they both tend to develop following the same formulaic pattern: entrepreneurial mavericks step outside the box of cultural conformity to imagine new ways of doing things, which then become rationalized in such a thoroughgoing way that the organization actually inhibits the kind of free thinking that led to its emergence in the first place. According to Charisma News Service (www.charisma.com) in 1970 there were only ten such mega-churches in the United States, rising to 250 by 1990, and not far short of 800 by 2004 with many more aspiring to such status. The early promotion of the McDonald's restaurant chain incorporated so many echoes of both the language and underlying ideology of the church, particularly in its American free-market version, that it is hard to think that founder Ray Kroc was not consciously modeling his business on the religious attitudes which were familiar from the cultural matrix in which he operated. Like the founder of a new faith, he often insisted that franchisees sever ties with other business enterprises, and offered them a restaurant well away from their homes so as to encourage them to leave behind other commitments and be single-minded in their devotion. In his memoirs, Kroc invokes overtly religious language to describe the processes of food preparation, so that cooking fries becomes 'a ritual to be followed religiously.' Even the golden arches apparently convey a quasi-spiritual nurturing message as a portrayal of 'mother McDonald's breasts,' while a cartoon character on the McDonald's Web site in 1998 told children that Ronald McDonald, like God, was 'the ultimate authority in everything.' It was therefore almost inevitable that sooner or later church and McDonald's would come together, the only surprise being that it took until 2001 before what was hailed as the world's first McDonald's franchise to be situated within a church complex opened at Brentwood Baptist Church in Houston, Texas—itself a mega-church.

The irony of such a development has not passed unnoticed. James L. Evans is a Baptist leader whose vision of Christian faith is clearly somewhat different from that offered at Brentwood:

It's a development rich in irony. Christianity began as a home-based religious movement. Now the faith boasts of mega-churches that actually draw people out of their homes and into buildings called "family life centers," or in Brentwood's case, "community life centers." Christianity began as a movement of hope symbolized by the sharing of a simple fellowship meal of wine and bread. Now the faith has become a complex corporate-like affair, with such heavy demands on members that fast food must be provided so everyone can get to their meetings.

Moreover, he proposes that there is something intrinsically incompatible between this and what he regards as authentic Christian values: 'If we are where we eat, we are alone, watching without touching other diners as we all hurry off to our next meeting. It's sad if we think about it. The meal used to be the meeting.' In other words, McDonaldization and church do not mix: to embrace the one, the other is forced to deny its core values.

This is the same criticism that is increasingly now leveled at the fast-food industry itself. While the advertising images depict happy families spending quality time together, there is a growing recognition that the reality for many is uncontrollable obesity and declining health, if not an early death—something that even the food companies are now taking seriously, with a switch to menus offering 'healthier' portions and even vegetarian options. But the application of an ideology based on efficiency, calculability, predictability, and control is by no means restricted to fast food. On the contrary, it is virtually ubiquitous throughout Western culture, and the more it spreads the more dangerous the world becomes. This is not the time or place for it, but in due course it will be interesting to apply this thesis to the events surrounding the toppling of Saddam Hussein from power in Iraq in 2003, or for that matter to the concerns about asylum-seekers that have dominated the domestic British headlines throughout the early years of this century. Difference and diversity are no longer regarded as a cause for celebration—nor even for natural curiosity about other people's ways of being—but traits to be ironed out and replaced by the bland canvas of homogeneity. Schlosser puts into words what many intuitively feel when he comments that 'An economic system promising freedom has too often become a means of denying it, as the narrow dictates of the market gain precedence over more important democratic values.'

If we were to substitute 'religious' for 'economic,' 'institution' for 'market,' and 'gospel' for 'democratic,' we would have a statement which for many people encapsulates the predicament in which the church now finds itself. For those who prefer to be 'spiritual' rather than 'religious,' the church—like much in contemporary Western culture—appears to have denied its own core values, and has ended up processing people rather than liberating them, even imprisoning God in prescriptive propositional formulas rather than recognizing that, whoever or whatever 'God' might be, it is certainly a contradiction in terms to conceive of him or her in terms of anything that is remotely connected to the four marks of McDonaldization. Like the prevailing culture, the church is still to a remarkable degree in a state of denial about this reality. Contemporary hymn books are full of songs declaring that Christians are 'taking ground' and 'claiming the land' and happy-clappy worshipers sing them with gusto—while their churches are dying on their feet! This is the same kind of self-delusion as restaurant owners who manage to ignore the true cost of their practices by refusing to contemplate the environmental and human cost of the farming and employment methods that they have encouraged over recent decades. Even a sympathetic observer like Peter Brierley, commenting on the declining level of church involvement in England, paints a bleak picture: 'I am a statistician, not a theologian. The numbers in this book show a haemorrhage akin to a burst artery. The country is littered with people who used to go to church but no longer do. We could well bleed to death. The tide is running out. At the present rate of change we are one generation from extinction.'

The ease with which what are increasingly perceived as dehumanizing trends in the marketplace can be paralleled within the churches is a major challenge for those Christians who believe they have a contribution to make to the future well-being of the planet and its people. To put it simply, if the church merely offers more of the same McDonaldized way of being, then why would any reasonable person want to connect with it? Not all Christians think about these questions, of course, but among some who do there is a tendency to imagine that the problems now being encountered have come about as a result of what they like to label the 'secularization' of the church, by which they generally mean its adoption of values and attitudes that in some way are intrinsically 'un-Christian,' usually identified with 'the Enlightenment.' Not only is 'the Enlightenment' itself a disputed category, but we also need to take seriously the insights of Weber and the likelihood that the tendency toward rationalization (of which McDonaldization is just a particular, exaggerated form) derives, at least in part, from the legacy of the Protestant Reformation, particularly in its Calvinist manifestation. That being the case, if the church is to escape the effects of McDonaldization, it will be required to engage in a more far-reaching self-examination. For if, in some measure, the church has contributed to the store of raw materials out of which the iron cage has been constructed, it was probably inevitable that sooner or later it would come to be regarded not as part of the solution, but as part of the problem.

Because of the neat fit between McDonaldization and cultural trends since the 1960s, it is often assumed that these tendencies emerged only in the second half of the 20th century or, at most, were the natural outcome of the assembly-line mentality associated with Fordism a few decades earlier. . . .

. . . The signs of McDonaldization are not hard to find more or less throughout the history of the church. The ideology of the British empire owed a good deal to the memory of Christendom, which in turn had been modeled on the Roman empire and from which it took its philosophical and techno-logical inspiration. When viewed within this frame of reference, enterprises such as the Crusades can be understood as a manifestation of the same orga-nizational tendencies so neatly encapsulated in Ritzer's emphasis on effi-ciency, calculability, predictability, and control. Even further back, one might use the same perspective to understand the many internal ecclesiastical battles that took place between the second and the fourth centuries, leading to the definition of a clear canon of sacred scripture, centralization of power in the hands of bishops, and eventually the formalized statements of Christian belief known as the creeds—all of which put together had the effect of creating a monolithic, McDonaldized institution with clear definitions of who could do what, and how and when. Though Ritzer is surely correct in proposing that in its present form McDonaldization would not have emerged without the development of scientific technology, in terms of the impact that an imposed rationalization has on the human spirit, it might plausibly be argued that these episodes in the life of the church promoted a McDonaldized spirituality in a more extreme form than anything we have witnessed in recent decades. In more ancient times, all roads led to Rome, which also means they led from Rome and facilitated the dissemination of such a one-world ideology. McDonald's Hamburger University in Oak Brook, Illinois, is only a pale reflection of the educational powerhouse of ancient Rome.

Thinking Critically

1. Assuming you are a religious person, would the McDonaldization of the church attract or repel you?

2. Why should we not be surprised that the church has McDonaldized?

3. What might a non-McDonaldized church look like? Are there any examples?

4. What religious goals are facilitated by McDonaldization?

5. What religious goals are impeded by McDonaldization?

Politics occupies our attention in Chapter 20. Bryan Turner discusses the ways in which McDonaldization leads to "thin"/"cool" politics: that is, political activity that is thin—"superficial, transient, and simple" and cool—the opposite of hot politics that involve "hysteria, effervescence, mystical trances, and spiritual possession" (see Chapter 25, "Jihad vs. McWorld," in Part III). Modern hot loyalty and thick solidarity are associated with the kinds of ethnic political conflicts that we associate with Northern Ireland, Kosovo, Afghanistan, and Iraq. Most modern societies, however, are characterized by "cooler modes of identification and thinner forms of solidarity." The latter might be described as "drive-in democracy" with cool assumptions about how committed people should be to political causes. Turner also associates the latter with "ironic liberalism." Ironic liberals refuse to be committed to grand political visions and ambitious efforts at social reform. They are opposed to inflicting pain in the name of a political cause. Their political detachment is related to Turner's notion of "drive-in democracy."

Given this argument, Turner points to the positive side of McDonaldization, at least in the political sphere. That is, he views hot loyalty and thick homogeneity in politics as hazardous in the contemporary world. They are likely to lead to dangerous conflagrations at the local level that have the potential to become much wider conflicts. Instead, Turner urges that we turn to McDonald's for our political models. A McDonaldized model of politics would lead to "cool cosmopolitans with ironic vocabularies" who would not only be averse to actions that might lead to political conflagration but would in fact serve as preventives to such conflagrations. Thus, Turner comes down, at least ironically, on the side of "global McCitizenship."

20

McCitizens

Risk, Coolness, and Irony in Contemporary Politics

Bryan S. Turner

While Ritzer's position is [not] overtly political, I want to suggest . . . that his approach to McDonaldization might present us with a fruitful and important perspective on the requirements of citizenship (as a form of cultural lifestyle) in globalized social systems. . . .

I want therefore to suggest a more interesting reading of Ritzer by an examination of eating styles in McDonald's as a metaphor for political commitments in a global and multicultural environment. There is obviously an important difference between eating and its social role in modern societies by contrast with traditional societies. In presenting this difference between a continuum that ranges from the orgy to a McDonald's snack, I draw upon . . . the emergence of the reflexive self with the growth of consumerism, because the modern self is produced through the notion of unlimited consumption. The consuming self with its insatiable desires is elaborated through and by

---

Editor's Note: From Turner, B., "McCitizens: Risk, Coolness, and Irony in Contemporary Politics," in Smart, B. (Ed.), *Resisting McDonaldization*, copyright © Bryan Turner 1999, reprinted with permission of Sage Publications, Ltd.

the consumer industry. Changing patterns of food consumption are an important part of this evolving self. In traditional societies, the self was closely bound into the rituals of social solidarity, associated with festival. The ritual meal sacrifice in the Abrahamic religions was the basis of the bond between God and humans and between people. Eating together was a fundamental basis of social order in which the exchange of gifts (especially food) took place. In Christianity, the bread and wine are exchanged as symbols of the sacred gift of body and blood.

If we treat McDonaldization as a secularization of religious patterns of friendship and familiarity associated with sacred meals, then the McDonald's snack represents a privatized and individualistic pattern of consumption which does not aim to build bonds of belonging. Brand loyalty does not lead to the creation of societies. McDonaldization involves a limited menu, precise measurements of food, the standardization of taste, and the elimination of surprises; it stands at the opposite end of a continuum from ritualized orgy.

I wish to argue that . . . we can compare and contrast these traditional and religious patterns of eating with the modern fast-food restaurant in terms of two dichotomies: thick/thin solidarity and hot/cool commitments. Traditional religious festivals generate a thick solidarity, characterized by its intensity, duration, and complexity; ritualized meals take place within and produce patterns of social solidarity such as brotherhoods, tribes, and communities. The social solidarity of eating in McDonald's is superficial, transient, and simple. McDonaldization produces global identities and images (the Big M), but these create thin communities. At the same time, the commitments of tribal festivals are hot; they involve hysteria, effervescence, mystical trances, and spiritual possession.

Eating in McDonald's requires the participants to be cool. Customers form short queues and assemble quickly to give their orders, they retire to their tables in well-regulated movements, and they sit quietly eating their standardized and predictable meals. There are no expectations that the meal will receive an applause. The regulated patterns and general silence are punctuated only by the occasional children's birthday parties where party uniforms are issued to small groups of children. These social forms are thin and cool. In terms of conventional sociology, participation in McDonald's outlets has many of the features . . . of "role distance," where social actors learn techniques of subjective neutrality. University professors out with their children for Saturday lunch at McDonald's learn to show to others that they are not really there. These patterns of coolness of commitment and thin solidarity offer a model of social interaction which perfectly conforms to the emerging patterns of global citizenship.

We can briefly trace the development of Western citizenship through four broad historical stages. In medieval society, the status of citizen in the city-state was more or less equivalent to denizen. It involved minimal privileges of immunity and a limited range of obligations. Although there was considerable pride in civility within the city walls, there was little notion of city identity and membership (cool commitments and identity). There was, however, a density of social involvement within the narrow confines of the city (in the guilds, for example) which resulted in thick membership. Modern citizenship as we know it really started with the nation-state, which through doctrines of nationalism in the 19th century encouraged hot nationalist commitment in order to create a homogeneous community as the base of the state. The nation-state attempted to overcome internal divisions within civil society (religion, ethnicity, and regional membership) to forge patterns of thick solidarity. These patterns of involvement were threatened by class divisions, but under welfare capitalism the welfare state functioned to reduce class divisions and to enhance commitment to the state. Finally, with the growth of a world economy and the globalization of cultures, the increase in migration, trade, and tourism creates a more diverse culture and multiple political loyalties. For example, there is an increase in dual citizenship. With globalization, the traditional forms of hot loyalty and thick solidarity become irrelevant to modern citizenship forms; indeed, hot loyalties of a national or local variety can often become dangerous in a world system which needs tolerance as a functional basis of political interaction. The ethnic conflicts of Eastern Europe, Russia, and Northern Ireland can be understood in terms of the negative consequences of hot nationalist loyalties in societies which require cooler modes of identification and thinner forms of solidarity. Global citizenship, organized around high levels of labor migration, might form a cultural pattern which is parallel to McDonald's—political loyalties should be formed on the assumption of high mobility in which citizens would enjoy the privileges of a drive-in democracy, which in turn had cool assumptions about the level of political commitment.

These assumptions also fit the . . . view of "private irony and liberal hope." An ironist is a person who believes that his or her "final vocabulary" is always open to criticism and revision. Ironists are nominalists and historicists, and as a result they do not believe there is a natural order to which language approximates. An ironist is skeptical about the legitimacy of "grand narratives" and hence there is a similarity between varieties of postmodernism and language theory. In political terms, the latter is also minimalistic—liberals support "bourgeois freedoms" as a basic level for social consensus not because liberalism is true but simply because it offers opportunities for self-creation and personal liberties. Ironic liberals do not commit themselves to a grand vision of history and social reform. Their basic assumption is that the worst thing we can do to another person is to inflict pain by an act of intentional cruelty. In short, ironists are cool about their commitment to political systems, they do not feel that thick solidarity is necessarily helpful in the realization of personal freedoms, and their detachment from traditional ideologies (especially nationalism) has an elective affinity with the concept of a drive-in McDemocracy.

. . .

The quest for community has been particularly powerful in the imagination of political philosophers where the legacy of a small Greek democracy continues to haunt the debate about democratic participation. Now Greek democracy, like Protestant sects, requires hot commitments and thick solidarities; modern democracy, as we know, presupposes large nation-states, mass audiences, ethnic pluralism, mass migrations, and globalized systems of communication. Hot democratic identities are probably dangerous in such an environment; where, to continue with this metaphor, nationalist fervor can fan the coals of ethnic hatred and difference. Bosnia, Cambodia, and Algeria are contemporary examples of the quest for thick homogeneity and hot loyalty in societies which are in fact subject to forces of global diversification. If we were to seek out a metaphor for modern citizenship, we may be better to look neither to Athens nor Jerusalem . . . but to McDonald's for our political models of association. Modern societies probably need cool cosmopolitans with ironic vocabularies if they are to avoid the conflagration of nationalistic versions of political authenticity and membership.

Thinking Critically

1. In what ways is the world threatened by non-McDonaldized politics?

2. In what ways is the world threatened by McDonaldized politics?

3. What are the links between McDonaldized/non-McDonaldized politics and 9/11?

4. If we are moving toward a drive-in democracy, what does that auger for the future of democracy in the United States?

5. Can you envision a world in which the major division is between those governments that are McDonaldized and those that are not?

The issue of consumption in general, and as it relates to McDonaldization, is closely tied to production and work in many ways (e.g., the earlier discussion of consumers as workers). However, it is important to keep these topics distinct, especially because of the increasing importance of consumption in the contemporary world and because the idea of McDonaldization has such strong roots in the world of consumption. This chapter offers an excerpt from my 2005 book, Enchanting a Disenchanted World: Revolutionizing the Means of Consumption. *Means of consumption (also called "cathedrals of consumption") are settings or places that allow people to consume goods and services. The focus is on the "new" means of consumption, those created in the United States in the half century after the close of World War II. Of course, the chains of fast-food restaurants (1955) are one of the new means, as are fully enclosed shopping malls (1956), megamalls (1981), superstores (e.g., Toys "R" Us, 1957), theme parks (1955), cruise ships (1966), and casino-hotels (1946). One central point is that all the cathedrals of consumption, not just the fast-food restaurants, are highly McDonaldized (or rationalized), and they all produce a variety of irrationalities of rationality.*

What is new here is the discussion of the link between these McDonaldized systems and disenchantment. That is, rationalized systems seek to remove all magic, mystery, and enchantment from their operations. For example, to operate efficiently, McDonaldized systems seek to eliminate any form of enchantment that impedes the efficient operation of the system. Or predictability is anathema to any sense of enchantment that, almost by definition, must be unpredictable.

Interestingly, although McDonaldization leads to disenchantment, there is a sense in which McDonaldization can be enchanting. For example, the efficiency of McDonald's or FedEx can seem quite magical as consumers marvel over how quickly their meals arrive or packages are delivered. On the FedEx Web site, one can see the various stops a package makes en route to its destination and find out the precise time of its arrival. Consumers can be similarly amazed that the Big Mac they ate in New York today is identical to the one they had in Tokyo the day before. Perhaps no aspect of McDonaldization is more seemingly magical than the nonhuman technologies. Thus, the modern cruise ship appears to be a technological marvel encompassing so many different things and so many passengers and crew that it is a wonder it can even float, let alone provide so many different types of entertainment (and so much food) to so many people.

21

Cathedrals of Consumption

Rationalization, Enchantment, and Disenchantment

George Ritzer

O ne of the concepts used to describe the settings of concern . . . is *means of consumption*. These settings, as means, allow us to consume a wide range of goods and services. . . . These places do more than simply permit us to consume things; they are structured to lead and even coerce us into consumption. . . .

The *new means of consumption* are, in the main, settings that have come into existence or taken new forms since the end of World War II and that, building on but going beyond earlier settings, have dramatically transformed the nature of consumption. Because of important continuities, it is not always easy to clearly distinguish between new and older means of consumption.

The concept . . . *cathedrals of consumption* . . . points up the quasi-religious, "enchanted" nature of these new settings. They have become locales to which we make "pilgrimages" in order to practice our consumer religion. . . .

Editor's Note: "Enchanting a Disenchanting World: Revolutionizing the Means of Consumption," by George Ritzer. In *McDonaldization: The Reader* 2/e by George Ritzer. Copyright © 2006 Sage Publications.

This . . . chapter is divided into two sections. First, I will link rationalization (McDonaldization) to the disenchantment of these settings. Second, I will deal with the degree to which rationalized systems can, themselves, be enchanting. Overarching all of this is the problem of continuing to attract, control, and exploit customers. Rationalization is needed to accomplish these objectives on a large scale, but the resultant disenchantment can have the opposite effect. . . .

Linking Rationalization to Disenchantment

. . . The process of rationalization leads, by definition, to the disenchantment of the settings in which it occurs. The term clearly implies the loss of a quality—enchantment—that was at one time very important to people. Although we undoubtedly have gained much from the rationalization of society in general, and the means of consumption in particular, we also have lost something of great, if hard to define, value.

Efficient systems have no room for anything smacking of enchantment and systematically seek to root it out of all aspects of their operation. Anything that is magical, mysterious, fantastic, dreamy, and so on is apt to be inefficient. Enchanted systems typically involve highly convoluted means to whatever end is involved. Furthermore, enchanted worlds may well exist without any obvious goals at all. Efficient systems, also by definition, do not permit such meanderings, and designers and implementers will do whatever is necessary to eliminate them. The elimination of meanderings and aimlessness is one of the reasons that rationalized systems were, for Weber, disenchanted systems.

. . . One major aspect of efficiency is using the customer as an unpaid worker. It is worth noting that all of the mystery associated with an operation is removed when consumers perform it themselves; after all, they know exactly what they did. Mystery is far more likely when others perform such tasks, and consumers are unable to see precisely what they do. What transpires in the closed kitchen of a gourmet restaurant is far more mysterious than the "cooking" that takes place in the open kitchen of a fast-food restaurant, to say nothing of the tasks consumers perform in such settings.

The same point applies to employees of rationalized systems. Their work is broken down into a series of steps, the best way to perform each step is discovered, and then all workers are taught to perform each step in that way. There is no mystery in any of this for the employee, who more or less unthinkingly follows the dictates of the organization. There is little or no room for any creative problem solving on the job, much less any sense of enchantment.

With regard to *calculability*, in the main, enchantment has far more to do with quality than quantity. Magic, fantasies, dreams, and the like relate more to the inherent nature of an experience and the qualitative aspects of that experience than, for example, to the number of such experiences one has. An emphasis on producing and participating in a large number of experiences tends to diminish the magical quality of each of them. Put another way, it is difficult to imagine the mass production of magic, fantasy, and dreams. Such mass production may be common in the movies, but magic is more difficult, if not impossible, to produce in settings designed to deliver large numbers of goods and services frequently and over great geographic spaces. The mass production of such things is virtually guaranteed to undermine their enchanted qualities. This is a fundamental dilemma facing the new means of consumption.

Take, for example, the shows that are put on over and over by the various new means of consumption—the "Beauty and the Beast" show at Disney World, the sea battle in front of the Treasure Island casino-hotel in Las Vegas, or the night club shows on cruise ships. The fact that they must be performed over and over tends to turn them into highly mechanical performances in which whatever "magic" they produce stems from the size of the spectacle and the technologies associated with them rather than the quality of the performers and their performances.

. . .

No characteristic of rationalization is more inimical to enchantment than *predictability*. Magical, fantastic, or dream-like experiences are almost by definition unpredictable. Nothing would destroy an enchanted experience more easily than having it become predictable.

The Disney theme parks sought to eliminate the unpredictability of the midway at an old-fashioned amusement park such as Coney Island with its milling crowds, disorder, and debris. Instead, Disney World built a setting defined by cleanliness, orderliness, predictability, and—some would say—sterility. Disney has successfully destroyed the old form of enchantment and in its place created a new, highly predictable form of entertainment. As the many fans of Disney World will attest, there is enchantment there, but it is a very different, mass-produced, assembly-line form, consciously fabricated and routinely produced over and over rather than emerging spontaneously from the interaction among visitors, employees, and the park itself.

. . .

Both *control* and the *nonhuman technologies* that produce it tend to be inimical to enchantment. As a general rule, fantasy, magic, and dreams cannot be subjected to external controls; indeed, autonomy is much of what gives them their enchanted quality. Fantastic experiences can go anywhere;

anything can happen. Such unpredictability clearly is not possible in a tightly controlled environment. It is possible that tight and total control can be a fantasy, but for many it would be more a nightmare than a dream. Much the same can be said of nonhuman technologies. Such cold, mechanical systems are usually the antitheses of the dream worlds associated with enchantment. Again, it is true that there are fantasies associated with nonhuman technologies, but they too tend to be more nightmarish than dream-like.

An interesting example of the replacement of human with nonhuman technology is currently taking place in Las Vegas. Shows in the old casino-hotels used to feature major stars such as Frank Sinatra and Elvis Presley. One could argue that such stars had charisma; they had an enchanted relationship with their fans. Now the emphasis has shifted to huge, tightly choreographed (i.e., predictable) extravaganzas without individual stars. For example, the Rio Hotel and Casino features "ballet dancers who bounce, toes pointed, from bungee cords, hooked to the casino ceiling . . . [and] a mechanical dolphin that dives from aloft with a rider playing Lady Godiva." The focus is on the nonhuman technology (which controls the performers) and not on the individuals performing the acts. The performers in such extravaganzas are easily replaceable; they are interchangeable parts.

The point of this section has been to argue that increasing rationalization is related to, if not inextricably intertwined with, disenchantment. However, as we shall see, there are aspects of rationalization that actually heighten enchantment.

Rationalization as Enchantment

There is no question that although rationalized systems lead in various ways to disenchantment, they paradoxically and simultaneously serve to create their own kinds of enchantment. We should bear in mind that this enchantment varies in terms of time and place. Because these settings are now commonplace to most of the readers of this book, few of them (especially fast-food restaurants) are likely to be thought of as enchanting. However, it should be remembered that they still enchant children, as they did us for some time (and, in many cases, may still); it is certainly the case that they enchanted our parents and grandparents; and they are found enchanting in other societies to which they are newly exported. It is also worth remembering that there are degrees of enchantment; Disney World and Las Vegas are undoubtedly seen by most as more enchanting than Wal-Mart and the Sears catalog.

Reflect for a moment on the highly rationalized, and therefore presumably disenchanted, setting of Sam's Club and other warehouse stores. What could be more disenchanting than stores built to look like warehouses—comparatively cold, spare, and inelegant? Compare them to the "dream worlds" of early department stores like Bon Marché. Great effort was made to make the latter warm, well-appointed, and elegant settings that helped enflame the consumer's fantasies—in a word, enchanting. Sam's Club has gone to great lengths in the opposite direction; it seems to have sought to create as rationalized and disenchanted a setting as possible. It comes strikingly close, in the realm of retailing, to Weber's image of the rational cage.

Yet this disenchanted structure produces another kind of fantasy—that of finding oneself set loose in a warehouse piled to the ceiling with goods that, if they are not free, are made out to be great bargains. It is a cold, utilitarian fantasy, but a fantasy nonetheless. As a general rule, disenchanted structures have not eliminated fantasies but, rather, replaced older fantasies with more contemporary ones. The new, rationalized fantasies involve getting a lot of things at low prices rather than the fantasies associated with the older department stores that might involve imagining what it would be like to wear elegant clothing or to surround one's self with luxurious home furnishings.

. . .

Perhaps the ultimate in the capacity of the rationalization of the new means of consumption to enchant us comes from their advanced *technologies*. Although at one time enchantment stemmed from human wizards or magicians, it now stems from the wizardry of modern robotic and computerized technology. Ultimately, it is the technology of the modern cruise line, the Las Vegas casino, and Disney World that astounds us, not the humans who happen to work in these settings or the things they do. Our amazement can stem from the technologies themselves or from what they produce. We can, for example, marvel over how McDonald's French fries always look and taste the same. Or we can be impressed by the fact that Wal-Mart's shelves are always so well-stocked.

. . .

Are the contemporary fantasies associated with rational systems as satisfying as those conjured up in the past? This is a complex and highly controversial issue. Clearly, the huge number of people who flock to the new means of consumption find them quite magical. However, it is fair to wonder whether rationally produced enchantment is truly enchanting or whether it is as enchanting as the less rational, more human, forms of enchantment that it tends to squeeze out. We might ask whether one of the *irrational* consequences of all of this is that these contemporary fantasies come closer to nightmares than did their predecessors. After all, it is far harder to think of a nightmare associated with an elegant department store than with a warehouse. In any case, it is clear that rationally produced enchantment is deemed [by many to be] insufficient. . . .

Thinking Critically

1. Can you think of places like shopping malls as cathedrals?

2. Can you conceive of consumption as a kind of religious activity?

3. Do you find the cathedrals of consumption enchanting? In what ways?

4. What devices do those cathedrals employ to make themselves seem enchanted?

5. Do you find rationalization/McDonaldization enchanting? In what ways?

Like much else in the global tourist business ("McTourism"), cruise ships, especially those that are "supersized," tend to be highly McDonaldized. Adam Weaver found much that was McDonaldized on cruise ships including

- *the use of debit cards to make consumption efficient;*
- *lots of data collection on customers yielding considerable calculability about them from the perspective of those who run the cruise ships;*
- *itineraries that make cruises highly predictable as does the fact that many of the cruise ships themselves are nearly identical;*
- *rules onboard, as well as the structure of the ships, that serve to control what passengers do;*
- *irrationalities of rationality such as harm to the environment by the ships as well as the boredom often experienced by passengers.*

While Weaver finds much to support the applicability of the McDonaldization thesis to cruise ships, he is critical (incorrectly) of the thesis for not dealing with the "mass customization" that one finds on many of these ships that serves to counter McDonaldization, at least to some degree. More importantly, he critiques it (more correctly) for exaggerating the importance of predictability and for ignoring the risks, the unpredictabilities, associated with cruises such as fire at sea and the threat of disease. Weaver does not see these unpredictabilities as contradicting the McDonaldization thesis, but rather as adding greater nuance to it.

22

The McDonaldization Thesis and Cruise Tourism

Adam Weaver

. . . Pleasure travel by ship, once considered the preserve of the wealthy elite, became comparable in price to mass-market resort holidays. The development of mass-market air travel enabled tourists from across the United States to reach cruise-ship disembarkation points swiftly and affordably. There is a certain irony that characterizes this relationship between air travel and cruise tourism. The rise of commercial air travel in the 1960s offered a faster alternative to ship travel, after transcontinental ship travel virtually disappeared as tourists opted to travel by airplane. However, by the 1970s and 1980s, a marked "popularization" of cruise tourism was underway, a process that has continued to the present time, as total capacity within this sector increases. In 2002, 37 new cruiseships were on order.

In the 1980s and 1990s, several companies started to build "supersized" cruiseships that could accommodate over 2,000 (and sometimes as many as 3,000) tourists at once. Over 40 currently in operation worldwide can accommodate 2,000 or more passengers. These enormous (and mobile) vacation enclaves contain casinos, exercise facilities, health spas, performance halls,

Editor's Note: Excerpts from "The McDonaldization Thesis and Cruise Tourism" by Adam Weaver (2005), *Annals of Tourism Research, 32*(2), 346–366. Used with permission.

bars, restaurants, discotheques, and boutiques. Travel writers have compared them to theme parks, Wal-Mart stores, and McDonald's restaurants. This restaurant chain is, in fact, the namesake of the McDonaldization thesis that is discussed and critiqued in this paper. Developed by Ritzer, it represents one way to interpret the nature of production and consumption on board super-sized cruiseships . . .

. . . This paper examines the production and consumption of cruise vacations. It explores a particular class of cruiseships and the extent to which vacations on board have become McDonaldized.

The supersized cruiseship is perhaps indicative of a broader trend. There are many tourism-oriented domains (supersized ships, theme parks, casinos, and enclave resorts) that promote and stimulate consumption in a rationalized manner. Such provision of pleasure appears to be popular with many consumers. It also facilitates efforts made by corporations to earn more revenue from consumers. While the thesis may have certain flaws, it does speak to the carefully orchestrated nature of "pleasure production" on board supersized ships (and within other tourism-based environments).

The sector spans the world. Cruiseships visit ports of call in the Caribbean, the Mediterranean, Asia, Alaska, Northern Europe, and Antarctica. The supersized ships examined in this paper mostly operate in Caribbean waters and primarily serve the North American market. In many ways, they exemplify the principles that underpin Ritzer's thesis. While companies that offer McDonaldized cruise vacations, at present, mostly cater to North American tourists, there are also some supersized vessels that visit Mediterranean and Asian ports of call and, as a result, mainly serve European and Asian markets, respectively. It is possible, then, to cruise within a McDonaldized "tourist bubble" in areas of the world other than the Caribbean.

This study of cruise tourism uses qualitative data as evidence. The research methods used to obtain data included participant observation and the study of cruise-oriented texts . . .

The McDonaldization Thesis

. . . Ritzer's Weberian approach has been criticized because it emphasizes rationalization but not the commodification process (a Marxian critique) and the notion that commodities possess value as a result of the symbols and emblems that they bear (a postmodern critique). A number of commentators have also indicated that the McDonaldization thesis is insensitive to variations across different countries and cultures. This paper offers a different critique of the thesis. Risk and post-Fordism customization are identified as tendencies that affect the nature of production and consumption on board supersized ships and that are, in some ways, at variance with certain principles that underpin the McDonaldization thesis. The main contention here is that the cruiseship sector exhibits some qualities which are easily reconciled with this thesis and other qualities that are more at odds with it. Ritzer does examine the notion that rationalization has irrational consequences (the "irrationality of rationality"), but there are some serious omissions from his work. The McDonaldization thesis does address how production and consumption within a variety of tourism- and pleasure-oriented realms have become more systematized. At the same time, however, it must be understood that rationally structured systems are tempered by processes and tendencies that run counter to them.

Ritzer does not explicitly discuss risk in his work. On occasion, risk may exemplify his notion that rationalization has irrational outcomes. Unanticipated events and circumstances can undermine how efficiency, predictability, calculability, and control manifest themselves within built environments. As rational systems become more complex, risk sometimes becomes more of a concern for both corporations and consumers. It is evident, too, that certain types of risk can be controlled. Rationalization has reduced and even eradicated certain types of risk. Of course, accidents and certain hazards have not disappeared completely. Risk does endure; it often exists in tandem with rationalization.

Post-Fordist customization is perhaps more difficult to reconcile with McDonaldization. While Ritzer emphasizes that the thesis is oriented around mass production and mass consumption, other commentators contend that there has been a broad shift within modern society whereby uniformity and predictability have been supplanted by variety and choice. Post-Fordist customization is a concept that can account for product diversity within the cruiseship sector and the enormous number of choices and options available to tourists on board supersized vessels. This concept conflicts with Ritzer's belief that products and services have become more uniform and standardized.

The McDonaldization thesis has been used to interpret broad trends and tendencies across the tourism industry and the way in which Disney themeparks operate. A number of tourism-oriented environments exhibit traits consistent with the principles that underpin Ritzer's thesis. The corporations, for example, that own and operate themeparks and enclave resorts try to provide consumers with efficiently produced products and services that possess relatively standardized features. This standardization ensures consistency, predictability, and certainty, so that tourists often receive precisely the experiences they anticipate. When they visit a themepark or an enclave resort, efforts are made to "contain" and control them in ways that increase onsite purchases. Various control mechanisms are also used within tourism-oriented workplaces: service employees are required to abide by certain scripts and perform tasks in a prescribed order. It is no accident that many McDonaldized spaces are popular with tourists. Their popularity and profitability can be directly attributed to careful market research which renders tourists calculable. Their desires are, in a sense, "written into the texts" of consumption-based environments.

The McDonaldization thesis addresses the structured and ordered nature of production and consumption within realms that are supposed to evoke pleasure and earn profit. In many ways, cruiseships are similar to themeparks, casinos, and enclave resorts . . . Ritzer has described these domains as "cathedrals of consumption." A tension exists between rationalization and enchantment within these cathedrals. On the one hand, they operate in a rationalized manner and are oriented around commerce. The way in which they function is discussed and determined in corporate boardrooms; their ability to earn revenue is monitored and measured. On the other hand, cathedrals of consumption provide tourists with an opportunity to escape from the rationalized world, with simulated (and often themed) environments that seem far removed from calculated concerns. Rationalization and enchantment also exist in concert and in tension with each other on board supersized cruise ships; these vessels contain consumption-oriented realms that enchant tourists and simultaneously possess attributes consistent with the five core principles of McDonaldization. These principles will be discussed in turn.

McDonaldization and the Cruiseship Sector

. . . For Ritzer, efficiency involves the selection of the optimum means to achieve a desired end. Expediency and convenience are desired by many consumers. As a result, many companies within the retail and tourism sectors try to ensure that consumers achieve satisfaction as swiftly as possible. Efficiency is typically shaped by institutionalized rules and broader social structures, helping individuals to select—or determine—certain courses of action. Efficiency, then, can circumscribe choice; the rules and structures that ensure it may also restrict an individual's choice of means to ends.

One way that cruiseship companies have increased the efficiency of the retail transactions on board is via debit cards issued to tourists when they embark. They are required to use these cards (which also serve as room keys and shipboard identification) for onboard purchases. Before receiving their debit card, they must provide the company with their credit card number. Purchases made with the debit card are then billed directly to the credit card.

The debit cards make shipboard consumption seem far removed from the actual expenditure of cash. As a result, this technique maximizes expenditure because it stimulates consumption that may not otherwise take place.

These debit cards provide other efficiency-related benefits. For instance, there is no need for these companies to pay for cash custody and cash security. The use of debit cards also means that cruiseship cashiers do not have to handle different currencies; opportunities for employee-perpetrated crime are reduced, thus eliminating the possibility of cash theft.

Perhaps the facility on board a cruiseship that best exemplifies the concept of efficiency is the kitchen. On board supersized ships that can accommodate as many as 2,000 or 3,000 tourists, the kitchen is an elaborate food preparation factory. There are usually over 100 kitchen employees. The food preparation process to which the kitchen staff must adhere has a strict timetable:

> Everything must be done by the book with no room for exceptions. The dishes are timed to be cooked just before they are served, so that if the first sitting is at 6:30 pm, the servers will have the orders in to the galley by 6:45 pm and begin serving the appetizers. The first of the main entries will start coming off the line at 6:55. By 7:30 the first dirty dishes will be coming in (to be immediately washed and reused for the second sitting) and desserts and coffee will be coming out. By 8 pm people will begin to leave (they have to if they want to catch the first show—a graceful way to empty the dining room)! This leaves time for the servers to reset the tables with clean linen and tableware for the second sitting at 8:30

A serious deviation from this timetable can disrupt the entire food preparation system and even prompt customer complaints. To ensure that food is prepared in a timely fashion, production quotas are sometimes implemented. The kitchen workers of Royal Caribbean International, for example, are required to plate and serve over 1,000 meals in approximately 22 minutes. Efforts to achieve efficiency often involve the imposition of strict production benchmarks.

For Ritzer, calculability addresses the notion that size and measurement are important to both corporations and consumers . . . Quantity, then, is quite often a proxy for quality. By the same token, cruiseship companies emphasize the sheer scale of their supersized vessels in their brochures, indicating that there are a wide array of activities and facilities on board. In fact, there is considerable competition between cruiseship companies in terms of the amenities they offer to tourists. This competition could be seen as a type of one-upman "ship."

The concept of calculability can be extended to encompass efforts made by corporations to collect information about (prospective) consumers. Within the service sector, for instance, many corporations obtain data from consumers via questionnaire cards (usually referred to as comment cards) and telephone surveys. Such surveys enable corporations to understand and "calculate" the preferences of their customers. The evaluations and comments are used to "fine-tune" their vacation products. One executive interviewed by the author stated that comment cards are taken very seriously by the company for which he works; in fact, he claimed that data from comment cards "run the business."

Beyond quality control, cruiseship companies compile data about their customers for purposes of product development. In 1999, Royal Caribbean collected data about current and future customers when it commissioned a market research company to interview 1,000 Americans about their vacation preferences. The resulting data demonstrated that Americans want access to a variety of facilities and amenities on board. In order to satisfy this preference for choice and variety, the company commissioned the construction of several enormous and elaborate ships that can accommodate over 3,000 passengers. These vessels have a wider selection of onboard services and activities than those owned by the main competitors.

Predictability is tied to the imposition of order, systematization, routine, and consistency . . .

The way cruise vacations are scheduled is meant to ensure that tourists have predictable vacation experiences. A supersized ship will typically travel the same itinerary (usually three-, five-, or seven-day) for several consecutive months or even years. The circuit itinerary is usually described and mapped in cruise-vacation brochures. As a result, tourists can determine in advance which port destinations the ship will visit and when.

Predictability is also reflected in the types of cruiseships that are currently built. Many ships are built from nearly identical sets of architectural plans. This practice enables companies to benefit from economies of scale. It also ensures product uniformity. With similarity in size and onboard services and facilities, a cruiseship company can provide its customers with consistently similar vacation experiences.

There are three cruiseships within the fleet owned by Carnival Cruise Lines that are practically identical to each other: Carnival Destiny, Carnival Triumph, and Carnival Victory, which are referred to as the Destiny-class ships. They each accommodate over 2,600 passengers. The economies of scale and replication achieved by Carnival are substantial. One business writer has noted that this company reduces costs considerably because it standardizes its ships "down to the bedspreads and barstools."

It is not only Carnival that commissions the construction of cruise-ships "cloned" from a prototype. Three within the fleet owned by Princess Cruises are essentially identical vessels: Grand Princess, Golden Princess, and Star Princess. Each can accommodate over 2,600 passengers. Many smaller companies have commissioned the construction of smaller "cloned" vessels almost identical to each other.

Finally, control is necessary in order to ensure efficiency, calculability, and predictability . . . A number of researchers have examined how control is often exercised over tourists, including the way they behave and consume. For example, tourists are usually not permitted to purchase alcohol ashore and then consume it on board. When they board with bottles of alcohol purchased ashore, they must turn them over to the shipboard employees who monitor the embarkation ramps. The alcohol is then stored in a secure room until the end of the cruise. This practice ensures that passengers purchase alcohol from shipboard bars.

The "soft" control that is sometimes exercised over tourists resembles persuasion and enticement rather than coercion. This type of control is subtle, but it does manipulate human behavior and prompt certain actions that would perhaps otherwise not occur. Interior spaces on board are constructed and positioned in ways meant to induce certain types of behavior. Typically, casinos, bars, and boutiques are situated in areas close to frequently used pedestrian walkways. The sheer number of bars is also meant to prompt consumption.

> Good ship designs incorporate a lot of bars and serving stations. The idea is that you should be able to get a drink wherever and whenever you want it. Equally important, designers recognize that since the sale of drinks is as often an impulse buy as it is a planned purchase, bars need to be situated in high-traffic areas. In a well-executed ship design, the most convenient way to go from your cabin to the dining room should take you past a lounge of some sort, where you can stop for a cocktail before dinner or a drink afterwards. And because most ships sail in warm waters, you also need a highly visible bar by the pool—or even in it! In fact, one can argue that there should be a bar everywhere! Some lines even station waiters near the library in case people want a drink while browsing.

The placement of bars and other concessions is not haphazard. Onboard facilities that offer extra-fee products and services are positioned in ways that are meant to maximize revenue.

Ritzer addresses the notion that the rationality of the system imposed by McDonaldization spawns irrational tendencies . . .

A number of irrational tendencies manifest themselves on board supersized cruiseships. Passengers produce an enormous amount of waste. "Rationally" structured holiday pleasure can harm the environment, which is a rather irrational consequence of shipboard hyper-consumption. It is commonplace on board supersized ships for people to queue at buffets and when they disembark and reboard at ports of call. If McDonaldized systems are so efficient, why do tourists have to wait so often? There are then serious paradoxes that can impair the smooth operation of McDonaldized institutions. The rationalization process may even threaten the mystery, romance, and sentimentality that are sometimes associated with the cruise-vacation experience. That banality and routinization may stifle fantasy and enchantment possibly means that companies will have to reenchant those elements of the cruise vacation which rationalization and McDonaldization have disenchanted.

The McDonaldization Thesis: A Critique

There is ample evidence to demonstrate that vacations on board supersized cruiseships have been McDonaldized in a variety of ways. This thesis aptly addresses the ordered and structured nature of service provision and consumption on board these ships. It has been demonstrated in this paper that there are numerous aspects of cruise tourism that are consistent with the five key principles that underpin McDonaldization. The enchantment that supersized ships offer exists in concert with the rationalization process.

Ritzer's thesis is not immune to criticism, however. While he does address certain irrational tendencies that run counter to the other four principles that underpin McDonaldization, risk and uncertainty are simply not mentioned in Ritzer's oeuvre. His thesis, too, only examines variety and diversity in Western economies in a very cursory fashion. The notion that production and consumption have become more standardized deserves scrutiny.

. . . That theorists such as Beck and Giddens consider risk and uncertainty to be widespread is inconsistent with Ritzer's contention that Western societies have become more predictable in nature. Many researchers have noted that risk and uncertainty affect the tourism industry.

The concept of post-Fordist customization can be used to temper Ritzer's view that rationalization, standardization, and routinization completely dominate contemporary Western economies. Post-Fordist customization and McDonaldization should not be viewed as mutually exclusive processes. The ascendancy of McDonaldization is far from absolute. A number of cruiseship companies demonstrate an extraordinary ability to identify and serve different market niches. The thesis, as articulated by Ritzer, cannot account for the existence of niche markets and customization practices that are post-Fordist in nature. When Ritzer writes about McDonaldization, he emphasizes its capacity to promote and spread uniformity. He does not discuss the way in which institutions that possess such qualities actively strive to offer variety and choice. In this paper, the concepts of risk and post-Fordist customization will be addressed in succession.

Risk and Accidents

There are numerous types of risk that can pose problems for cruiseship companies; some are provoked by nature, others are caused by human activity and by the complex nature of supersized ships. These ships possess many features that can intensify certain risks. For example, a common feature on board many supersized cruiseships constructed since the 1990s is a multi-storey atrium. There have been some concerns about these atriums because they could potentially promote the spread of a shipboard fire. When a fire occurs on board, the first safety precaution is to contain it. But it is impossible to close off an atrium deck by deck. A fire could potentially travel its way up an atrium as if the atrium was a chimney. While there have been many cruiseship fires in recent decades, there is no documented case of a fire that has actually spread to (and up) an atrium. This scenario, however, has been discussed and studied by safety experts. In order to produce more profit and more spectacular ships, companies may actually create seaborne environments that could be unsafe.

A fire at sea is one of the most hazardous situations that cruiseship tourists and employees can encounter. When a ship is distant from shore, it may be quite far from other ships that could provide assistance if a fire occurred on board. There have been numerous fires in recent years. In summer 1998, one occurred aboard Carnival Ecstasy. There were no fatalities, but 60 tourists and crew-members were hospitalized and treated for smoke inhalation. The ship was removed from service for several weeks and repaired at a cost of $15 million. Other ships that have had onboard fires in recent years include Carnival Celebration, Carnival Tropicale, Carnival Victory, and Carnival Destiny.

The problems posed by fire are intensified by the sheer size of supersized ships. It remains uncertain if a cruiseship that accommodates so many people can be evacuated quickly and safely at sea. For the most part, supersized ships have elaborately built and complexly structured interior environments that could potentially disorient and confuse tourists in a hurry to evacuate. There is the potential for even more complications to arise. Once the evacuation takes place, how quickly can other ships reach the scene of the accident and rescue evacuees? The sheer size could therefore make evacuation and rescue extraordinarily difficult.

When accidents and mishaps take place on board, it is usually not the causal connections between events and consequences that create surprise, but the occurrence of certain events (fires, disease outbreaks, and mechanical breakdowns, for instance) at particular places and times. Business executives within the cruiseship sector are quite aware that such situations happen. Even many tourists realize that cruiseships are not immune to risk. While, in a very broad sense, it is anticipated that such events will occur, the probability of a particular occurrence is so small that it is still a surprise when it does occur.

Terrible accidents take place despite efforts to prevent them. Efforts to identify and control risk can never be comprehensive; human error and system malfunctions will never completely disappear. Even with the best of preparations and precautions, risk and McDonaldization are inescapably intertwined; they exist in tension with each other. On the one hand, McDonaldization can minimize, neutralize risk, even "tame" risk and the uncertainties that are often associated with it. On the other hand, the process cannot eliminate risk and uncertainty entirely, which in some instances may even be more pronounced within McDonaldized environments. Indeed, certain types of risk have become a more serious concern as cruiseships increase in size.

The Threat of Disease

A company strives to ensure that the ships within its fleet are clean and sanitary environments. On occasion, however, cruiseships are sites of disease outbreaks, efforts to prevent these outbreaks are not entirely successful. A company can only act in response to these outbreaks not predict exactly when and where they may occur.

In 2002, many tourists and employees on board several ships owned by Carnival Cruise Lines, Holland America Line, and Disney Cruise Line were infected with a Norwalk virus. The name "Norwalk" is actually applied to a class of viruses (named after a small town in Ohio, where the first identified outbreak of a Norwalk virus occurred in 1968). Afflicted individuals experience severe nausea, abdominal pain, severe dehydration, and diarrhoea; they may also vomit repeatedly. The confined quarters of a cruiseship provide exemplary conditions for Norwalk viruses to multiply and be transmitted. While a cruiseship is a "tourist bubble" that shields people from certain perceived hazards, its insularity can also pose a potential threat if a disease outbreak occurs on board.

Several companies temporarily removed ships from service for disinfection, sacrificing revenue while their ships were inactive. Even when disinfected, disease outbreaks still occurred; several ships were the site of more than one outbreak. It was eventually concluded that outbreaks of the

Norwalk virus were not due to inadequately disinfected washrooms and kitchens on board. Rather, tourists were infected by these viruses even before they boarded the ships. Once on board, they spread the virus to both tourists and employees. Perhaps the noteworthy aspect of these outbreaks was not that a Norwalk virus can spread rapidly, but that it did so within a controlled environment where it was believed that sufficient precautions had been taken.

Risk and the Consumer

The production of commodities and commodified experiences often involves risk. A particular product or service will not necessarily be popular with consumers. Indeed, some view certain products and services with suspicion and even fear. Many consumers, for instance, are hesitant to take a cruise vacation.

There are several reasons for this hesitancy. First, some consumers believe that cruiseships are excessively circumscribed holiday environments. They are afraid that they will experience a form of entrapment while on board a ship. The bounded and controlled enclave environment that offers various "creature comforts" may actually be a potential source of boredom or anxiety. Second, there are those who have concerns about seasickness, perhaps being afraid that this ailment will ruin their holiday. Third, consumers have expressed concerns about medical facilities on board, worried that they will receive poor medical treatment should they have a health problem or accident.

Efforts made by companies to address the concerns of (potential) customers demonstrate that they do not act passively when confronted by risk. In fact, they have actively responded to the hesitancy of some first-time consumers. These responses include the incorporation of statements and descriptions into brochures that will supposedly ease certain concerns. For instance, brochures typically emphasize that cruiseships are holiday environments that have many onboard activities and facilities, described in detail in order to preempt worries about boredom. Brochures also downplay the frequency of seasickness. In response to concerns that cruiseships cannot provide adequate medical care, companies mention that their ships have on-duty medical staff and well-equipped facilities.

Post-Fordist Customization and Product Differentiation

Ritzer contends that efficiency and predictability have caused standardization and uniformity to increase within contemporary economies; this proposition is debatable. There are still tourism-oriented businesses that clearly benefit from and exploit economies of scale. It is also apparent, that product variety within the industry has increased considerably in recent years. Economies within Western countries are not nearly as uniform as Ritzer seems to believe. In fact, they have become complex combinations of diverse activities and production forms.

It is Ritzer's contention that many consumers seek predictability and want the products and services that they purchase to be the same over time and across many places. There is some truth to his observation; often consistency is viewed as an important determinant of quality. This desire for consistency does not mean that consumers do not want choice and diversity. In fact, there is considerable choice available to those who want a vacation on board a supersized ship.

The ships operated by Carnival Cruise Lines have whimsical and fanciful decor oriented around particular themes, which has been described as "party-hearty." In contrast, ships operated by Royal Caribbean International and Princess Cruises have more muted ornamentation and offer an onboard experience quieter and more sedate than ships within Carnival's fleet. Those using Holland America Line have been described as "fairly sedentary, 55-plus North American couples." Carnival's Clientele is considered to be more boisterous.

Many companies that operate supersized ships are currently owned by Carnival Corporation. This acquisition of certain cruiseship companies has made some consumers nervous. When Carnival Corporation purchased Holland America in 1989, there were concerns expressed by consumers that Holland America would become "Carnivalized," meaning that it would offer a cruise-vacation product similar to Carnival Cruise Lines. The Chief Executive Officer of Carnival Corporation has stated, however, that he has been careful to preserve different brand identities. Indeed, he is aware that he could ruin the reputation of a particular brand if he does not preserve its distinctiveness and autonomy.

The McDonaldization thesis, as it is set forth by Ritzer, assumes that tastes and preferences have become standardized across the world. This (supposedly increased) standardization of tastes and preferences is understood to mean that more consumers in more countries desire predictable sameness and consistency. Ritzer, however, does not take into account that there are important variations in tastes and preferences across different countries and cultures. Indeed, some cruiseship companies own ships that are built to serve certain national markets. One owned by P&O Cruises, Oriana, can accommodate over 1,800 tourists and caters mostly to the British market. On board, the breakfast buffet features a number of popular British "delicacies": kippers, smoked haddock, and baked beans. That afternoon tea is served on board reinforces the ship's British extraction. The dinner menu features quite essentially British fare such as steak and kidney pie and roast beef.

Of course, the claim could be made that Oriana is merely a McDonaldized cruiseship that possesses certain British attributes. The vacation experience that is offered on board is in many ways similar to what is offered by Carnival Cruise Lines. One could certainly make the case that variation and diversity have perhaps been McDonaldized to the point where different companies offer consumers a circumscribed set of bland choices. It could be said that post-Fordist customization only accounts for minor deviations from a standardized norm. This view would probably be endorsed by many who are disaffected with and alienated by present-day hyper-consumption.

It is possible, however, to interpret variation and diversity in another way. There are important palpable and worthy differences between Oriana and ships owned by Carnival. Ritzer's thesis underestimates the importance of trends and processes that run counter to standardization. While individual market niches may possess McDonaldized qualities, market niches are distinct from each other—and the sheer existence of different niches within the cruiseship sector demonstrates that it is not a uniform entity. Ritzer's thesis bluntly conceptualizes diversity as a manifestation of standardized sameness. This connection between diversity and sameness is rather crude because it depicts post-Fordist customization as a process purely subordinate to McDonaldized standardization. Instead, McDonaldization and post-Fordist customization should be viewed as processes that influence each other in a reciprocal fashion.

Variety and Choice

A recent trend within the cruiseship sector has been the introduction of various extra-fee services and facilities. While casinos and bars on board have traditionally offered tourists extra-fee products and services, companies have built ships that feature even more extra-fee facilities. These facilities include extra-fee restaurants, duty-free shops, hair salons, and health spas. Tourists can, to some extent, customize and individualize their cruise vacations with the purchase of various extra-fee items, serving the interests of both cruiseship companies and tourists, providing the former with additional sources of revenue. In fact, when a cruiseship is at sea, the tourists on board become "captive consumers." Various extras provide tourists with more choice and access to more than a standardized bundle of products and services. Research conducted by companies indicates that many tourists prefer choice and variety, even if they come at a price. Many, it would seem, do "buy into" the notion that supersized ships are places where they can purchase extra-fee products and services. Their availability seems to contradict Ritzer's belief that many tourism-oriented environments simply provide standardized and uniform holiday experiences.

Tourists can also customize their cruise holiday when they reserve a stateroom that possesses certain attributes or is of a certain size. A supersized ship often has many different types of accommodation on board: staterooms without windows or balconies, staterooms with windows, staterooms with both windows and balconies, and even multi-room suites. Other factors that vary include bed and bathroom sizes. On board supersized ships owned by Carnival Cruise Lines, Royal Caribbean International, and Princess Cruises, there may be as many as 20 different stateroom classes. Tourists clearly have some choices in terms of onboard accommodation.

The ability that companies have to mass produce diverse and "destandardized" products and services is perhaps best conceptualized as an example of "mass customization." In essence, mass customization is a hybrid process by which a company creates particular products and services that can be produced in abundance but are customized at the same time. Both mass customization and McDonaldized standardization promise efficiency and economies of scale. Within the cruiseship sector, companies that own supersized ships can serve an enormous volume of tourists and simultaneously cater to diverse tastes. Ritzer mentions mass customization in his work, but he addresses it in only a cursory fashion. This paper indicates that his thesis requires some revision in the context of more customized production methods (and increased demand for more tailor-made products and services), an opinion that has been reached by other commentators.

Conclusion

The McDonaldization thesis is a recently conceived interpretation of contemporary society that deserves more consideration from tourism researchers. It offers an innovative but ultimately incomplete interpretation of production and consumption on board supersized cruiseships. While this thesis does address the ordered and structured nature of shipboard production and consumption, it does not satisfactorily examine tendencies that may run counter to McDonaldization. A more complex and nuanced view of society (and cruise tourism) would account for these tendencies. The purpose of this paper has not been to discredit Ritzer's thesis. Instead, the paper has demonstrated that supersized ships possess some attributes easily reconciled with this thesis and others that are more difficult to reconcile.

Risk is compatible with Ritzer's notion that rationality often has irrational consequences, but he does not provide a comprehensive analysis of it. There are instances when risk undermines certain elements of the rationalization. Ritzer also understates the pervasiveness of post-Fordist customization. His thesis overemphasizes the extent to which consumption-oriented realms offer consumers sameness and uniformity. When McDonaldization is considered in tandem with the concepts of risk and post-Fordist customization, it offers a more complete interpretation of developments and practices within contemporary society.

An issue that deserves more study from tourism researchers is how tourists experience McDonaldization on board cruiseships. Ritzer himself concedes that individuals do not react uniformly to McDonaldized environments. A variety of research questions arises from his concession. Why do some tourists choose to take holidays within McDonaldized environments? Why do others avoid these environments with such vehemence? How do tourists perceive various risks and hazards on board? To what extent do they believe that cruiseships offer a diverse array of products and services? To date, research that examines their experiences within enclosed holiday environments is rare.

Tourists, it should be noted, are not the only individuals who experience McDonaldization. Onboard employees are often required to behave in accordance with the principles that underpin the thesis. The way in which they perform their work merits attention. How do they both adapt to and resist McDonaldized work routines? To what extent do they improvise their interactions with tourists despite the control that is exercised over them in the workplace? Research addressing these questions would enhance the ability of researchers to understand how shipboard service employees experience the McDonaldization process.

The measures that cruiseship company executives adopt in order to address risk could also be explored in more detail. Without doubt, these executives are aware of risk. They understand that it can affect the production and consumption of the cruise-vacation product. What sorts of "rational" schemes, then, have these executives deployed in order to minimize risk? Do these schemes necessarily achieve their intended aims? To what extent are there trade-offs among different types of risk? Risk is a variable that can be influenced (but not necessarily eradicated) by corporate decision makers.

The research discussed in this paper is restricted in scope as it only examines cruise tourism and, more particularly, supersized cruiseships. Other sectors of the tourism industry do possess features that are consistent with the principles that underpin the McDonaldization thesis. However, researchers who examine the McDonaldization process should also be conscious of tendencies that are not clearly compatible with it. Theoretically robust scholarship that explores complexity and contradiction offers a more nuanced way to understand contemporary tourism and society.

Thinking Critically

1. What is mass customization and in what ways is it McDonaldized?

2. What is the relationship between predictability and risk?

3. Can McDonaldized systems ever completely eliminate risk?

4. When people are on vacation, do they want McTourism? Why? Why not?

5. Discuss the ways in which McTourism has the potential to destroy tourism.

As the following essay shows, it is important to examine and understand the architecture of any consumption setting, including McDonald's. The author, Kristine P. Jerome, connects the similarity in the structure of McDonald's restaurants throughout the world to globalization. That is, in order to expand globally, McDonald's and many other chains have to provide a good deal of "sameness" across the globe. Places like McDonald's are where the global intersects with the local in order to reproduce globalization, especially a globalization based on consumption and profit-making (rather than, for example, greater sociality). In addition to taking a detailed look at the typical structure of a McDonald's restaurant, Jerome is also interested in the ways in which the structure conceals what it is up to, seduces people into misinterpreting homogenization as a good thing, as well as fooling them into thinking that consumption can be equated with personal happiness. This misrecognition and the control exercised by such settings is what Jerome, following the work of Pierre Bourdieu, calls "symbolic violence." Because they believe that there is more to be gained by accepting than contesting this locally produced world, consumers are complicit in the creation of McDonaldization and, more broadly, globalization. This essay is very useful not only in bringing architecture into the discussion about McDonaldization, but also placing it, at least implicitly, into the broader theory of structure (of the global as well as of individual McDonald's restaurants) and agency (of McDonald's customers).

23

A Case of McDonald's Restaurant

The Built Environment and the Perpetuation of the Phenomenon of Globalisation

Kristine Peta Jerome

Introduction

McDonald's restaurant is taking large unprecedented risks through the built environment. This is because the interior setting of McDonald's is where its patrons are required to participate in everyday practices embedded in the social institution of globalisation. For this process to operate with relative ease and maintain financial growth the spatial domain must facilitate the experience of 'sameness' across the globe. Ensuring this occurs also requires

---

Editor's Note: From Jerome, K. (2007). "A Case of McDonald's Restaurant: The Built Environment and the Perpetuation of the Phenomenon of Globalisation" Used with permission.

the built environment to perpetuate a set of relations founded on domination and control. In order to understand this, a discussion of a particular McDonald's restaurant is provided. This demonstrates the significance of producing particular kinds of environments in the maintenance of the new world order of globalisation.

By utilising the concepts of social order and symbolic violence it is possible to unpack the way the social institution of globalisation is constructed at an everyday level and the role of the spatial setting in this process. The site of McDonald's restaurant is used to explore this relationship and, more broadly, demonstrate how organisations produce commonsense worlds and the risk associated with explicitly using the built environment in this way. This business corporation takes a great risk in constructing a particular kind of setting designed to homogenise experience in order to remain intimately tied to the phenomenon of globalisation.

Social Order: Symbolic Violence and the Built Environment

. . . In order to understand the significance of the concept of symbolic violence the following description of a reception room in a mental hospital is explored. This description describes the construction of a commonsense world and emphasises the significance of the spatial domain.

> [t]he visiting room in some total institutions is important here. Both décor and conduct in these places are typically much closer to outside standards than are those that prevail in the inmate's actual living quarters. The view of inmates that outsiders get thus helps to decrease the pressure these outsiders might otherwise bring to bear on the institution. It is a melancholy human fact that after a time all three parties—inmate, visitor, and staff—realize that the visiting room presents a dressed-up view, realize that the other parties realize this, too, and yet all tacitly agree to continue the fiction.

In this instance, 'the visiting room' is effective because the social reality it depicts is recognised as fiction and then negotiated and misrecognised by participating members in order to produce a social world of commonsense. This is because there is more to be gained by sustaining this performance than fracturing it. The décor of the space, and subsequent conduct, help to construct the system of relations equating to misrecognition and symbolic violence. It is worth noting at this point that Bourdieu and Wacquant define these concepts and their interrelatedness as:

[s]ymbolic violence, to put it tersely and simply as possible, is the *violence which is exercised upon a social agent with his or her complicity*. . . . To say it more rigorously: social agents are knowing agents who, even when they are subjected to determinisms, contribute to producing the efficacy of that which determines them insofar as they structure what determines them. . . . I call mis-recognitions the fact of recognizing a violence which is wielded precisely inas-much as one does not perceive it as such. What I put under the term 'recognition,' then, is the set of fundamental, prereflexive assumptions that social agents engage by the mere fact of taking the world for granted, of accepting the world as it is, and of finding it natural because *their mind is constructed according to cognitive structures that are issued out of the very structures of the world.*

The social and spatial relations of the visiting room described by Goffman, encapsulate the act of symbolic violence because they manage to sustain interaction and a continuance of the everyday. That is, the social and spatial relations of the visiting room operate to create a social reality at a local level that is recognised as fiction but reinterpreted by participants and *misrecognised* in order to manage a performance, construct a commonsense world and sustain social order. Therefore, the participants who partake in this act of symbolic violence sanction the practices of this institution as legit-imate. In this instance, the spatial domain helps to guarantee the complicity of social relations and functioning of symbolic violence.

This example demonstrates the way the spatial domain is embedded in practices of social control. It highlights that the built environment is a sig-nificant constituent in the perpetuation of practices of domination. It is also clear that the operational success of these practices is reliant upon partici-pants recognising and then *misrecognising* what the physical environment is attempting to do. That is, in order for the mental hospital to perpetuate a code of conduct founded on relations of domination great risk is taken in instituting this process throughout the physical domain because it relies, in part, on participants willingly engaging with a space that operates to ensure that "power is exercised and simultaneously disguised." *Thus, a crucial component in the success of perpetuating social order is often the way the spatial domain contributes to perpetuating acts of symbolic violence.* It is argued here that the institutional structure of globalisation, which is based upon the ideology that economic growth and consumer capitalism are the path to happiness, also relies upon the spatial domain to maintain acts of symbolic violence and perpetuate a commonsense world. This relationship is explored through a case of McDonald's restaurant because this is a site which relies heavily on a particular kind of spatial setting to perpetuate prac-tices of globalisation.

Ritzer states that in order for McDonald's to make a profit it is essential that it employs the principles of efficiency, predictability, calculability, and control at all levels of its operations. These principles are practiced to ensure standardisation, which is a crucial component in the financial stability of this corporation. It is argued here that the process of standardisation is, in part, managed through the *homogenisation of experience,* and the spatial domain is very significant in ensuring that this kind of experience is maintained. This is why McDonald's restaurants are generally consistent in supplying an interior setting that facilitates the provision of a standard experience across the globe. These settings share a commonality of encouraging consumption in the pursuit of personal wellbeing in order to maintain a commonsense world. Here, the built environment helps to disguise the fact that the practice of homogenising experience is used to strengthen economic growth and perpetuate globalisation. It is argued in this paper that the built environment is a crucial component in maintaining symbolic violence and McDonald's takes great risk in using the built environment as a means to standardise experience and maintain economic growth.

Globalisation and the Homogenising of Experience

Globalisation is a worldwide phenomenon that has spread and colonised many areas of the world. It holds a very specific ideology that is based on the belief that human wellbeing is intimately tied to consumption. This ideology emphasises the importance of the volume and quality of goods and services in the achievement of personal happiness.

As a consequence of this worldwide adoption of an ideology founded on the accumulation of wealth, the instrumental trades of globalisation "opening up of trade, the emergent power of financial markets, the transnationalisation of corporations and international economic co-ordination" have been afforded a privileged place in the construction of everyday life. Activities and policies that promise an increase in the rate of economic growth in order to service the ideology of "consumption as the foundation lifestyle" are a priority and this prioritisation is re-enacted at a global and local level on a daily basis.

It is argued here that one of the methods that the phenomenon of globalisation relies upon to maintain its increasing presence in the construction of a commonsense world is the frequent inclusion of acts of symbolic violence. As previously discussed, these seduce people, to whatever degree, from

> . . . having grievances by shaping their perceptions, cognitions and preferences in such a way that they accept their role in the existing order of things, either

because they can see or imagine no alternative to it, or because they see it as natural and unchangeable, or because they value it as divinely ordained and beneficial.

As a mechanism of governance it enforces a new world order. Globalisation invites and engages with the production of homogenising experience in order to sustain a commonsense world that is largely underpinned by the "economics of profit rather than the economics of sociality." The homogenisation of experience is what tends to drive the individual on the endless pursuit of consumption in anticipation of happiness. This kind of ritual becomes misrecognised as a positive form of progress and embodied as an acceptable way of engaging with everyday life because of its link with human wellbeing. This set of relations is what enables the ideology of globalisation and its affiliated practices to recreate and construct a commonsense world that rejoices in consumerism.

It is at the point of certain built spaces, which actively reproduce the phenomenon of globalisation, such as McDonald's restaurant, that provides an opportunity to unpack the way the homogenisation of experience is maintained at a local level. These kinds of sites also highlight the way symbolic violence is embedded in the process of constructing a social institution. In order to comprehend the way the spatial domain of McDonald's encourages participants to partake in the 'pursuit of happiness through consumption' a description of one particular interior setting of McDonald's is provided. As a result of this description it is then possible to describe the way the spatial domain is embedded in the production of a commonsense world.

The McDonald's Experience

Upon entering McDonald's you are greeted by a tiled floor of muted browns and earth tones. This formula is repeated on the vinyl panels that cover the wall to rail height. Deep blue laminate panels cover the wall to picture rail height. To the right of the entrance are waste disposal bins separated by bench seating at window sections. To the left of the entrance are two parallel rows of fixed rectangular tables with fixed stools. Along the back wall of the restaurant, bench seating invites larger groups to partake in the ritual of dining. Adjacent to this area are toilet facilities. These are serviced through an enclosed communal space, which is screened by glass doors. Dark blue vinyl covers all the seating and the table and bench tops are mottled brown granite.

Straight ahead of the entrance lies the service area. The counter is clear and the overhead signage is well illuminated with graphics displaying consumable items. To the rear of this service area is the food preparation section, barely visible behind the stainless steel kitchen items. Beside the service area is another section nominated for the provision of coffee, teas and condiments. On the granite bench is a display cabinet with cakes, muffins and sweet biscuits. Behind the counter the display signage shows imagery of coffee mugs, cakes and milkshakes. In this area the lighting is notably softer—engaging with downlights as opposed to the fluorescent lighting used elsewhere. Adjacent to this area and in the centre of the restaurant are armchairs used for seating around fixed lowest granite tables. A dividing low-set wall of dark blue vinyl tiles and glass mosaic panels of bronze and blue tiles delineates this section from the other 'less cosy' areas throughout the space. Dining areas have fixed tables and chairs and are located along the perimeter of the restaurant. Loud music from the local radio station is consistent throughout the space.

Streamlining activities through the positioning of fitted and unfitted furniture, defining zones through lighting and décor and minimising distracting design features, help to achieve the operational principles of efficiency, predictability, calculability, and control that underpin McDonald's restaurant. Collectively, these operate to ensure standardisation. In this context participants are required to participate in the consumption of standardised food in a standardised way in a standardised environment. As Robin Leider describes

> McDonald's pioneered the routinization of interactive service work and remains an exemplar of extreme standardization. Innovation is not discouraged ... at least among managers and franchisees. Ironically, though, "the object is to look for new innovative ways to create an experience that is exactly the same no matter what McDonald's you walk into, no matter where it is in the world."

The success of this practice relies very heavily on the built environment. In most instances the interior setting operates to standardise the 'act of dining' and offers 'sameness' as a component of consumption and the pursuit of happiness. In the case described here this is managed through techniques such as providing a sterile backdrop and harsh lighting along with regimenting the arrangement of the furniture within an open plan that clearly delineates zones of activities such as: servicing area, eating area, toilet area. These design solutions ensure that the act of dining is a public event and because of this participants are encouraged to police their own actions as well as those of others in the pursuit of personal wellbeing. By engaging the built environment in this way and homogenising experience, participants are more likely to recognise and misrecognise this process as a good thing.

Arguably, the success of operations of McDonald's also requires participants to willingly, if only temporarily, acquire a set of dispositions to act and think in a local context whilst drawing upon global forms of cultural knowledge underpinned by the notion of homogenisation. Participants must recognise and then misrecognise what the physical environment is attempting to do in order to perpetuate codes of conduct founded on the economics of profit and the maintenance of social order. In order for McDonald's to perpetuate these great risk is taken in instituting this process through the physical domain. This is partially because it relies on participants willingly engaging with a space that operates to maintain relations of domination and control. McDonald's also takes a great risk in this procedure because it veers away from traditional corporate business strategies of diversification. That is, whilst McDonald's recognises that 'diversity' is a key method in managing risk, evidence suggests that comprehending the extent of diversification manifest in the built environment is crucial for maintaining economic security. This is because all forms of 'diversity' do not guarantee the homogenisation of experience.

As demonstrated, one of the ways McDonald's manages to seduce its patrons into *misrecognising* that the homogenisation of experience is a good thing is through the inclusion of design outcomes such as an efficient thoroughfare, predictable seating arrangements and easily identifiable and accessible service areas that ensure a locally produced order is maintained. It is important that these characteristics remain consistent in McDonald's settings to sustain movement and the commonsense world it manufactures for economic profit. Across the globe the spatial domain and the practice of the homogenisation of experience facilitates processes of standardisation to ensure that the phenomenon of globalisation is entrenched on a daily basis.

. . . The corporate business strategy of using the built environment to minimise diversification is a crucial business method. This strategy must recognise how the spatial domain can produce 'sameness' and respond to cultural design trends in order to guarantee the maintenance of relations intent on reproducing codes of conduct underpinning the social institution of globalisation.

What is interesting is that the sameness of the facilities and the activities it generates is compatible to participants willing to partake in the belief that consumption equates with personal happiness. This relationship suggests that participants are content to misrecognise the way the built environment maintains the ideology of globalisation. This is important. It is proposed that this process of misrecognition is recognised by the vast majority of participants who choose to participate in this social world and conform to the actions the space prescribes. This is because there is more to be gained by sustaining and interacting in this locally produced world according to the dominant commonsense understandings of it, than by disputing it.

As demonstrated at the site of McDonald's restaurant, it is a certain kind of physical environment that perpetuates the homogenisation of experience in order to drive consumers to consume more and more in the pursuit of happiness. This kind of experience is misrecognised as a significant aspect in achieving a lifestyle of personal wellbeing. This is how symbolic violence comes to be reflexively related to the built environment and the way it is embedded in the construction of the institutional structure of globalisation.

Discussion

In this instance a particular spatial domain of McDonald's restaurant is explored because it is representative of the significance of space in the reproduction and perpetuation of acts pertaining to globalisation . . . This paper explores the way McDonald's employs the spatial domain in the construction of a commonsense world and the production of globalisation. It is only through a detailed observation of the locally produced order that it is possible to comprehend the precision McDonald's requires in producing a setting that institutes a particular code of conduct in order to maximise consumption and maximise profit. It is only through an investigation of the daily operations of a particular McDonald's restaurant that it is possible to understand the reflexive relationship between space and symbolic violence and social order.

As demonstrated, the spatial design plays a very important role in maintaining the global principles of calculability, control, efficiency, and predictability aligned with McDonald's financial success. Employer training, the same equipment, back-lit menus, formula food and beverages are constant. Although the built environment responds to cultural design trends it constantly and strategically cloaks acts of symbolic violence by employing a variety of generic design features associated with the act of dining in order to homogenise experience. What is interesting in this case is that when McDonald's employs the strategy of 'diversification' to the built environment it runs the risk of no longer cloaking the processes of symbolic violence that are in operation to maintain the reproduction of the social institution of globalisation. Demystifying these cloaking processes through the built environment does not minimize risk.

Ritzer notes that the kinds of 'cloaking processes' employed by McDonald's on at an everyday level tend to disenchant the world; they have a wide range of dehumanizing effects on people as workers and consumers as well as on human relationships; and they tend to have an homogenizing effect that often serves to make life far less interesting and exciting.

By deliberately employing techniques that focus action on the activity dining consumers are seduced into consuming more and more in the hope of acquiring happiness. What has been demonstrated here is that a particular kind of spatial setting is a crucial component in the operational success of McDonald's. That is, the spatial domain is a key constituent in the successful operation of this global company, which strategically aligns itself with the ideology that consumption is intimately tied to personal wellbeing through the experience of homogenization.

In order to ensure that this ideology is produced at a local level the homogenisation of experience is introduced, operationalised and maintained throughout the built environment. It is emphasised that McDonald's restaurant takes great risk in perpetuating the social institution of globalisation in this way because it relies very heavily on particular kinds of built environments to do this. Specifically, it minimises risk in this area by ensuring realms of activities are clearly delineated and that dining is a public event whilst injecting subtle forms of design diversification relevant to cultural trends. These processes of standardisation are reflected in and through the built environment. As demonstrated when design diversification disrupts the experience of 'sameness' this commonsense world struggles to sustain itself. This is because the likelihood of experiencing homogenisation is reduced, which decreases the possibility of participants misrecognising what the restaurant is about and therefore disputing the apparent 'order of things.'

Conclusion

The relevance of understanding the way the built environment contributes to the construction of a commonsense world and production of social order is demonstrated through an exploration of one setting of McDonald's restaurant. Undertaking this kind of examination and unpacking the layers of everyday life reveals the significance of the built environment in the construction of social institutions like globalisation. In this instance McDonald's restaurant is used as a case study to comprehend the way the spatial domain reinforces acts that impose meaning and legitimise actions founded on "the ideology of growth and consumer capitalism in the pursuit of personal happiness." McDonald's must minimise its risk in the environment by providing a setting that clearly delineates zones and activities to ensure the experience of 'sameness' is sustained whilst including design features that respond to cultural trends. These features must not distract the participant from the primary intent of the space—ensuring that actors navigate moral codes of economic rationalism. Thus, McDonald's must steer away from injecting too much diversity in and through the built environment if a particular kind of commonsense world is to be maintained and economic growth is to be sustained.

Understanding the intricacies of this relationship is important. First, it provides great insight into the way the physical environment contributes to the construction of social institutions like globalisation. Second, it highlights the role the built environment plays in the disguise of practices intent on dominating and controlling populations. Third, it offers an opportunity to comprehend why this particular kind of setting is successful in achieving a commonsense world in some instances and not in others. Understanding these relationships are very important for the design fields because this kind of knowledge is generally absent. Descriptions that unpack the way the spatial setting maintains institutionality and constructs social order are crucial for designers. As this discussion highlights, failure to take into account the logic behind the appropriation of particular design strategies employed by corporations like McDonald's can lead to professionals naively participating in the construction of a new world order.

Thinking Critically

1. How does architecture contribute to McDonaldization? Globalization?

2. Think about the architecture of settings other than fast food restaurants and the ways in which they contribute to McDonaldization.

3. Describe an architectural structure which would reduce or limit McDonaldization.

4. In what ways are customers complicit in the process of McDonaldization?

5. Even if the structures are very much the same, aren't there great differences in what goes on in a fast food restaurant?

Remaining within the realm of consumption, the final essay of Part II is an excerpt from another of my books, Expressing America: A Critique of the Global Credit Card Society *(1995). I analyze one of the keys to the modern consumer society, the credit card, from the point of view of the McDonaldization thesis. The credit card has McDonaldized the consumer loan business and it, in turn, has led to the rationalization of other types of loans, such as automobile and home equity loans. More generally, it has played a central role in McDonaldizing the entire banking business with, for example, a nonhuman technology, the ATM, progressively replacing human tellers as a source of cash. The bulk of this excerpt is concerned with analyzing the credit card from the perspective of each dimension of McDonaldization, as well as from the vantage point of the irrationality of rationality.*

24

Credit Cards, Fast-Food Restaurants, and Rationalization

George Ritzer

The credit card, like the fast-food restaurant, is not only a part of this process of rationalization but is also a significant force in the development and spread of rationalization. Just as McDonald's rationalized the delivery of prepared food, the credit card rationalized (or "McDonaldized") the consumer loan business. Prior to credit cards, the process of obtaining loans was slow, cumbersome, and nonrationalized. But obtaining a modern credit card (which can be thought of as a collateralized consumer loan) is now a very efficient process, often requiring little more than filling out a short questionnaire. With credit bureaus and computerization, credit records can be checked and applications approved (or disapproved) very rapidly. Furthermore, the unpredictability of loan approval has been greatly reduced and, in the case of preapproved credit cards, completely eliminated. The

Editor's Note: Excerpts from "Credit Cards, Fast-Food Restaurants, and Rationalization" by George Ritzer, pp. 129–156, in *Expressing America: A Critique of the Global Credit Card Society* by George Ritzer. Copyright © 1995 by Pine Forge Press.

decision to offer a preapproved card, or to approve an application for a card, is increasingly left to a nonhuman technology—the computer. Computerized scoring systems exert control over credit card company employees by, for example, preventing them from approving an application if the score falls below the agreed-on standard. And these scoring systems are, by definition, calculable, relying on quantitative measures rather than qualitative judgments about things like the applicant's "character." Thus, credit card loans, like fast-food hamburgers, are now being served up in a highly rationalized, assembly-line fashion. As a result, a variety of irrationalities of rationality, especially dehumanization, have come to be associated with both.

It is worth noting that the rationalization of credit card loans has played a central role in fostering the rationalization of other types of loans, such as automobile and home equity loans. Automobile loan approvals used to take days, but now a loan can be approved, and one can drive off in a new car, in a matter of hours, if not minutes. Similarly, home equity loans can now be obtained much more quickly and easily than was the case in the past. Such loans rely on many of the same technologies and procedures, such as scoring systems, that are used in decision making involving credit cards. Thus, just as the process of rationalization in society as a whole has been spearheaded by the fast-food industry, it is reverberating across the banking and loan business led by the credit card industry. We can anticipate that over time other types of loans, involving larger and larger sums of money (mortgages and business loans, for example), will be increasingly rationalized. Virtually every facet of banking and finance will be moving in that direction.
    . . .

Calculability: The All-Important Credit Report

. . . A particularly revealing example of quantification in the credit card industry is the use of "credit scoring" in determining whether an applicant should be issued a credit card (or receive other kinds of credit). Of course, in the end the majority of applicants are approved by one credit card firm or another because the profits from the credit card business are extraordinarily high. Credit card firms can afford to have a small proportion of cardholders who are delinquent in paying their bills or even who default on them. Nonetheless, it is obviously in the interest of the card companies to weed out those who will not be able to pay their bills.

Credit scoring is usually a two-step process. First, the application itself is scored by the credit card company. For example, a homeowner might get more points than a person who rents. If an application scores a sufficient number of points, the lender then buys a credit report on the applicant from a credit bureau. The score on the credit report is key to the decision to issue a card. Said a vice president of a company in the business of designing scoring models for lenders: "You can have an application that's good as gold, but if you've got a lousy credit report, you'll get turned down every time." In other words, it is the numbers, not qualitative factors, that are ultimately decisive.

Scoring models vary from one locale to another and are updated to reflect changing conditions. Despite great variation from report to report, the following items usually receive the most weight:

- Possession of a number of credit and charge cards. . . .
- Record of paying off accumulated charges. . . .
- Suits, judgments, and bankruptcies involving the applicant. . . .
- Measures of stability. . . .
- Income. . . .
- Occupation and employer. . . .
- Age. . . .
- Possession of savings and checking accounts. . . .
- Homeownership. . . .

Scoring systems clearly quantify the decision-making process. In doing so, they reduce human qualities to abstract quantities. That is, they reduce the individual quality of creditworthiness to a simple, single number that "decides" whether or not an applicant is, in fact, worthy of credit. The more human judgment of an official of a credit card firm is then considered unnecessary. One banking consultant claims that "the character of an individual is much more important than [a credit score]. You can't decide who to lend to by using a computer." However, with a crush of applicants brought in large part by active recruiting efforts, credit card firms are increasingly relying on computerized scoring systems and paying more attention to quantifiable scores.

. . .

Efficiency: The Faster the Better

. . . The credit card is a highly efficient method for obtaining, granting, and expending loans. Applicants need do little more than fill out a brief application, and in the case of preapproved credit cards, even that requirement may be waived. In most cases, the customer is granted a line of credit, which is accessed and expended quickly and easily each time the card is used.

Assuming a good credit record, as the credit limit is approached it will be increased automatically, thereby effortlessly increasing the potential total loan amount.

Furthermore, the credit card tends to greatly enhance the efficiency of virtually all kinds of shopping. Instead of carrying unwieldy amounts of cash, all one needs is a thin piece of plastic. There is no need to plan for purchases by going to the bank to obtain cash, no need to carry burdensome checkbooks and the identification needed to get checks approved. With their credit cards, consumers are no longer even required to know how to count out the needed amount of currency or to make sure the change is correct.

Credit (and debit) cards are also more efficient from the merchant's point of view. . . . Although it might be a tad slower than cash at the checkout counter, a card transaction is ultimately far more efficient than a cash deal because it requires little from the merchant except the initial electronic transmission of the charge. Handling cash is, as one supermarket electronic banking services executive points out, "labor intensive. From the time it leaves the customer's hands to the time it hits the bank, cash may get handled six to eight different times, both at the store and at the bank level." All these steps are eliminated in a charge (or debit) transaction.

. . .

Predictability: Avoiding Those Painful Lulls

. . . The credit card has made the process of obtaining a loan quite predictable as well. Consumers have grown accustomed to routine steps (filling out the questionnaire, for example) that lead to the appearance of a new card in the mail. After all, many people have gone through these same steps many times. In the case of preapproved credit cards, the few remaining unpredictabilities have been eliminated because offer and acceptance arrive in the very same letter.

. . .

The credit card also serves to make consumption in general more predictable. Before credit cards, people had to spend more slowly, or even stop consuming altogether, when cash on hand or in the bank dipped too low. This unpredictability at the individual level was mirrored at the societal level by general slowdown in consumption during recessionary periods. But the credit card frees consumers, at least to some degree, from the unpredictabilities associated with cash-flow and the absence of cash on hand. It even frees them, at least for a time, from the limitations of depleted checking and savings accounts. Overall, the credit card has a smoothing effect on consumption. We are now better able to avoid "painful" lulls when we are unable to participate in the economy because of a lack of ready cash. Most generally, the credit card even allows people to consume, at least to some degree, during recessionary periods. For the purveyors of goods and services, the availability of credit cards makes the world more predictable by helping to ensure a steadier stream of customers during bad times as well as good ones.

Nonhuman for Human Technology: No Visitors, No Staff

. . . The credit card is itself a kind of nonhuman technology. More important, it has given birth to technologies that intervene between buyer and seller and serve to constrain both. Most notable is the vast computerized system that "decides" whether to authorize a new credit card and whether to authorize a given purchase. Shopkeeper and customer may both want to consummate a deal, but if the computer system says no (because, for example, the consumer's card is over its credit limit), then there is likely to be no sale. Similarly, an employee of a credit card firm may want to approve a sale but be loath, and perhaps forbidden, to do so if the computer indicates that the sale should be disapproved. The general trend within rationalized societies is to take decision-making power away from people (customers, shopkeepers, and credit card company employees alike) and give it to nonhuman technologies.

With the advent of smart cards, the card itself will "decide" whether a sale is to be consummated. Embedded in the card's computer chip will be such information as spending limits, so the card itself will be able to reject a purchase that is over the limit.

Not only do some aspects of our credit card society take decision making away from human beings, but other of its elements eliminate people altogether. Thus, widespread distribution of the smart card may eliminate many of the people who now operate the credit card companies' extensive computer systems. Today, ATMs have been increasingly replacing bank tellers. A bank vice president is quite explicit about the substitution of ATMs for human beings: "This might sound funny, but if we can keep people out of our branches, we don't have to hire staff to handle peaktime booms and the like. That drives down costs." A similar point can be made about debit cards, which involve far less human labor than do the checks that they are designed to replace. The growth of debit cards has undoubtedly led to the loss of many bank positions involved in clearing checks. Similarly, because credit cards are designed to be used in place of cash, the increasing use of such cards has led to the loss of positions involved in a cash economy (for example, bank tellers needed to dole out cash).

. . .

Irrationality of Rationality: Caught in the Heavy Machinery

The irrationality of rationality takes several forms. . . . Credit cards are supposed to offer greater efficiency but sometimes are quite inefficient. Take, for example, the Discover Card's program to allow its cardholders access to Sprint's long-distance service. To make a long-distance call with the card, "all you need do is dial Sprint's 11-digit access number. Then 0. Then a 10-digit phone number. Then the 16-digit account number from your Discover Card. Then a four-digit 'Personal Access Code.'" A highly inefficient string of 42 digits must be entered just to make one long-distance telephone call. To take another example, the credit card companies are supposed to function highly predictably. Thus, for example, our bills should be error free. However, billing errors do find their way into monthly statements. For example, there may be charges that we did not make or the amount entered may be incorrect.

. . . The credit card world is also highly dehumanized because people generally interact with nonhuman technologies, with such products as bills or overdue notices, or with people whose actions or decisions are constrained if not determined by nonhuman technologies. Horror stories abound of people caught in the "heavy machinery" of the credit card companies. Pity the poor consumers who get charged for things they did not buy or who are sent a series of computer letters with escalating threats because the computer erroneously considers them to be delinquent in their payments. Then there are the many complaints of people who get turned down for credit because erroneous information has crept into their credit reports. Trying to get satisfaction from the technologies, or from their often robot-like representatives, is perhaps the ultimate in the dehumanization associated with a rationalizing society.

. . . Computerized credit approval is associated with a greater likelihood of delinquency and default than when financial institutions employ more traditional methods. Credit card companies are willing to accept these risks because of the relatively small amounts involved in credit card loans and the fact that credit cards in general are so profitable. Such losses are hardly noticeable.

. . .

Perhaps the most persistent and reprehensible activities of the credit card companies . . . are their efforts to keep interest rates high even when interest rates in general are low or declining. Of course, there are many other irrationalities of the rationalized credit card industry. . . the tendency of credit card companies to engage in practices that lead people to spend recklessly, the secrecy of many aspects of the credit card business, the invasion of the privacy of cardholders, and the fraudulent activities engaged in by various players in the credit card world. . . .

Thinking Critically

1. In what ways have credit cards, and the McDonaldization process that stands at their base, improved your life?

2. In what ways has your life been adversely affected by credit cards and their McDonaldization?

3. How do you feel when you "interact" with an ATM?

4. Why do the credit card companies charge interest rates several times the rate that is charged for other loans (mortgage, car)? Is such a rate defensible?

5. Do you pay off your credit card balance in full in each month? If not, should you?

PART II

Pedagogical Questions

1. How do the elements of McDonaldization operate in the legal justice system? Draw parallels to its effects in the education and health systems in the United States.

2. What does the McDonaldization of social services mean for ethnic, religious, and racial minority groups in the society? How does the irrationality of rationality affect the daily practices of these minority groups?

3. Think about the dialectical relationship of agency and McDonaldization. Does the power of individual agency increase or decrease in a McDonaldized system? Does it lead to ever-increasing alienation in society?

4. Visit the Web sites of the political parties in the United States. Examine their agendas on social issues. To what extent are their solutions McDonaldized?

5. Not only is the Internet changing the way people think about politics, but it is one more way to motivate them to get involved in politics. Discuss the ways in which McDonaldization turns the Internet into the foremost political medium.

6. In what ways is your body McDonaldized? Would you like it to be more McDonaldized? How would you go about McDonaldizing your body further?

7. In your experience, have you noted the effects of McDonaldization on your sex life? Do you find the emphasis on the standardization of sex life oppressive? If so, in what ways?

8. While there are clearly disadvantages associated with McSchools, what are their advantages?

9. Given the high rate of divorce in the United States, would it be more appropriate to view divorce as the irrationality of rationality?

10. Describe how your experiences on Web 2.0 sites such as Facebook, YouTube, or Second Life exhibit de-McDonaldization. In what ways are they still McDonaldized?

11. Describe one of the McJobs you have held. What, if any skills, were involved? In what ways did it help you to develop new skills?

12. How does McDonaldization affect ecology? Discuss its effects on the ecosystem with reference to monoculture farming, genetically engineered seeds, chemicals, and mechanization.

13. Is McDonaldization only applicable to Christianity? Are other world religions McDonaldized as well? How does McDonaldization change the beliefs, rituals, and experiences of those faiths?

14. Would McDonaldized politics lead to public alienation about social problems? How does it adjust public involvement in gender, environmental, and class politics?

15. Discuss the notions of political commitment and global citizenship in supranational political organizations such as the UN, G-8, and NATO. Does modern democracy necessarily require "hot" commitment?

16. How does McDonaldization relate to the enchantment and disenchantment of the modern world? What is the relationship between rationalization and disenchantment?

17. Why, when you are going on a vacation to "get away from it all," would you want to have a McDonaldized experience on, for example, a cruise? In what ways does such a cruise help you get away from your day-to-day life? How does it simply reinforce it?

18. Think of IKEA which, in point of origin, is a Swedish firm. In what ways does its nature as a built environment perpetuate globalization? How do its products relate to globalization?

19. Are credit cards really helpful in periods of economic recession? Do they inflate the economy artificially?

PART III

Cross-Cultural Analysis, Social Movements, and Social Change

In Part III of the book, we deal with a wide range of subjects that relate McDonaldization to cross-cultural developments and social change, including an issue—Jihad—that is very much in the headlines as I write, along with the hotly debated topic of globalization (see Part IV).

The first essay in Part III is a now-famous, and extraordinarily prescient (it was published in 1992), article by Benjamin Barber titled "Jihad vs. McWorld." Barber developed his idea of McWorld independently of my concept of McDonaldization, but there are obvious similarities between them (including the use of McDonald's as a model), and for the purposes of this book, they will be treated as being essentially the same idea. Barber treats McWorld as one of the dominant processes in the world, but his work is unique (he is a political scientist, not a sociologist) in that he juxtaposes it to another important process throughout much of the world—Jihad. The term "Jihad" (literally "struggle") is derived from Islam (where it is seen as battles against those who threaten the faith), but it is clear that Barber is not restricting it to the Islamic world; he discusses many different nations that are experiencing Jihad-like movements (e.g., Spain and even Switzerland). What is so prescient about Barber's work, however, is that it seemed to anticipate the cataclysmic events of September 11, 2001; the U.S. attacks on the Taliban in Afghanistan; the war against the terrorist organization Al Qaeda; and the declaration of a Jihad against the United States by the leadership of the Taliban and Al Qaeda. In the early 21st century, we are involved in a struggle that is well described as Jihad versus McWorld.

Barber looks at what he considers a clash between two global forces. One, McWorld, is quite clear to us, at least to the degree that it overlaps with McDonaldization. The other, however, needs clarification. Here is the way Barber defines "Jihad":

> subnational factions in permanent rebellion against uniformity and integration . . . they are cultures, not countries; parts not wholes; sects, not religions; rebellious factions and dissenting minorities at war not just with globalism but with the traditional nation-state . . . people without countries, inhabiting nations not their own, seeking smaller worlds within borders that will seal them off from modernity.

While McWorld seems to have most of the advantages (the fruits of McDonaldization, especially a massive number and diversity of military weapons), the passion behind Jihad makes it a formidable and dangerous opponent.

25

Jihad vs. McWorld

Benjamin R. Barber

The two axial principles of our age—tribalism and globalism—clash at every point except one: they may both be threatening to democracy.

Just beyond the horizon of current events lie two possible political futures—both bleak, neither democratic. The first is a retribalization of large swaths of humankind by war and bloodshed: a threatened Lebanonization of national states in which culture is pitted against culture, people against people, tribe against tribe—a Jihad in the name of a hundred narrowly conceived faiths against every kind of interdependence, every kind of artificial social cooperation and civic mutuality. The second is being borne in on us by the onrush of economic and ecological forces that demand integration and uniformity and that mesmerize the world with fast music, fast computers, and fast food—with MTV, Macintosh, and McDonald's, pressing nations into one commercially homogenous global network: one McWorld tied together by technology, ecology, communications, and

---

Editor's Note: Published originally in *The Atlantic Monthly,* March 1992 as an introduction to the *Jihad vs. McWorld* (Ballantine paperback, 1996), a volume that discusses and extends the themes of the original article.

commerce. The planet is falling precipitantly apart *and* coming reluctantly together at the very same moment. . . .

The tendencies of what I am here calling the forces of Jihad and the forces of McWorld operate with equal strength in opposite directions, the one driven by parochial hatreds, the other by universalizing markets, the one re-creating ancient subnational and ethnic borders from within, the other making national borders porous from without. They have one thing in common: neither offers much hope to citizens looking for practical ways to govern themselves democratically. If the global future is to pit Jihad's centrifugal whirlwind against McWorld's centripetal black hole, the outcome is unlikely to be democratic—or so I will argue.

McWorld, or the Globalization of Politics

Four imperatives make up the dynamic of McWorld: a market imperative, a resource imperative, an information-technology imperative, and an ecological imperative. By shrinking the world and diminishing the salience of national borders, these imperatives have in combination achieved a considerable victory over fractiousness and particularism, and not least of all over their most virulent traditional form—nationalism. . . .

The Market Imperative . . . All national economies are now vulnerable to the inroads of larger, transnational markets within which trade is free, currencies are convertible, access to banking is open, and contracts are enforceable under law. In Europe, Asia, Africa, the South Pacific, and the Americas such markets are eroding national sovereignty and giving rise to entities—international banks, trade associations, transnational lobbies like OPEC and Greenpeace, world news services like CNN and the BBC, and multinational corporations that increasingly lack a meaningful national identity—that neither reflect nor respect nationhood as an organizing or regulative principle.

The market imperative has also reinforced the quest for international peace and stability, requisites of an efficient international economy. Markets are enemies of parochialism, isolation, fractiousness, war. Market psychology attenuates the psychology of ideological and religious cleavages and assumes a concord among producers and consumers—categories that ill fit narrowly conceived national or religious cultures. Shopping has little tolerance for blue laws, whether dictated by pub-closing British paternalism, Sabbath-observing Jewish Orthodox fundamentalism, or no-Sunday-liquor-sales Massachusetts puritanism. In the context of common markets, international law ceases to be a vision of justice and becomes a workaday framework for getting things done—enforcing contracts, ensuring that governments abide by deals, regulating trade and currency relations, and so forth.

Common markets demand a common language, as well as a common currency, and they produce common behaviors of the kind bred by cosmopolitan city life everywhere. Commercial pilots, computer programmers, international bankers, media specialists, oil riggers. entertainment celebrities, ecology experts, demographers, accountants, professors, athletes—these compose a new breed of men and women for whom religion, culture, and nationality can seem only marginal elements in a working identity. Although sociologists of everyday life will no doubt continue to distinguish a Japanese from an American mode, shopping has a common signature throughout the world. Cynics might even say that some of the recent revolutions in Eastern Europe have had as their true goal not liberty and the right to vote but well-paying jobs and the right to shop (although the vote is proving easier to acquire than consumer goods). The market imperative is, then, plenty powerful; but, notwithstanding some of the claims made for "democratic capitalism," it is not identical with the democratic imperative.

The Resource Imperative. Democrats once dreamed of societies whose political autonomy rested firmly on economic independence. . . .

But the rapid depletion of resources even in a country like ours, where they once seemed inexhaustible, and the maldistribution of arable soil and mineral resources on the planet, leave even the wealthiest societies ever more resource-dependent and many other nationals in permanently desperate straits.

Every nation, it turns out, needs something another nation has; some nations have almost nothing they need.

The Information-Technology Imperative. Enlightenment science and the technologies derived from it are inherently universalizing. They entail a quest for descriptive principles of general application, a search for universal solutions to particular problems, and an unswerving embrace of objectivity and impartiality.

Scientific progress embodies and depends on open communication, a common discourse rooted in rationality, collaboration, and an easy and regular flow and exchange of information. Such ideals can be hypocritical covers for power-mongering by elites, and they may be shown to be wanting in many other ways; but they are entailed by the very idea of science and they make science and globalization practical allies.

Business, banking, and commerce all depend on information flow and are facilitated by new communication technologies. The hardware of these technologies tends to be systemic and integrated—computer, television, cable, satellite, laser, fiber-optic, and microchip technologies combining to create a vast interactive communications and information network that can potentially give every person on earth access to every other person, and make every datum, every byte, available to every set of eyes. If . . . electronic telecommunication and information systems are an ideology at 186,000 miles per second—[that] makes for a very small planet in a very big hurry. Individual cultures speak particular languages; commerce and science increasingly speak English; the whole world speaks logarithms and binary mathematics.

Moreover, the pursuit of science and technology asks for, even compels, open societies. Satellite footprints do not respect national borders; telephone wires penetrate the most closed societies. . . . In their social requisites, secrecy and science are enemies.

The new technology's software is perhaps even more globalizing than its hardware. The information arm of international commerce's sprawling body reaches out and touches distinct nationals and parochial cultures, and gives them a common face chiseled in Hollywood, on Madison Avenue, and in Silicon Valley. . . . This kind of software supremacy may in the long term be far more important than hardware superiority, because culture has become more potent than armaments. What is the power of the Pentagon compared with Disneyland? Can the Sixth Fleet keep up with CNN? McDonald's in Moscow and Coke in China will do more to create a global culture than military colonization ever could. It is less the goods than the brand names that do the work, for they convey lifestyle images that alter perception and challenge behavior. They make up the seductive software of McWorld's common (at times much too common) soul.

Yet in all this high-tech commercial world there is nothing that looks particularly democratic. It lends itself to surveillance as well as liberty, to new forms of manipulation and covert control as well as new kinds of participation, to skewed, unjust market outcomes as well as greater productivity. The consumer society and the open society are not quite synonymous. Capitalism and democracy have a relationship, but it is something less than a marriage. An efficient free market after all requires that consumers be free to vote their dollars on competing goods, not that citizens be free to vote their values and beliefs on competing political candidates and programs. The free market flourished in junta-run Chile, in military-governed Taiwan and Korea, and, earlier, in a variety of autocratic European empires as well as their colonial possessions.

The Ecological Imperative. The impact of globalization on ecology is a cliché even to world leaders who ignore it. We know well enough that the German forests can be destroyed by Swiss and Italians driving gas-guzzlers fueled by leaded gas. We also know that the planet can be asphyxiated by greenhouse gases because Brazilian farmers want to be part of the twentieth century and are burning down tropical rain forests to clear a little land to plough, and because Indonesians make a living out of converting their lush jungle into toothpicks for fastidious Japanese diners, upsetting the delicate oxygen balance and in effect puncturing our global lungs. Yet this ecological consciousness has meant not only greater awareness but also greater inequality, as modernized nations try to slam the door behind them, saying to developing nations, "The world cannot afford *your* modernization; ours has wrung it dry!"

Each of the four imperatives just cited is transnational, transideological, and transcultural. Each applies impartially to Catholics, Jews, Muslims, Hindus, and Buddhists; to democrats and totalitarians; to capitalists and socialists. The Enlightenment dream of a universal rational society has to a remarkable degree been realized—but in a form that is commercialized, homogenized, depoliticized, bureaucratized, and, of course, radically incomplete, for the movement toward McWorld is in competition with forces of global breakdown, national dissolution, and centrifugal corruption. These forces, working in the opposite direction, are the essence of what I call Jihad.

Jihad, or the Lebanonization of the World

OPEC, the World Bank, the United Nations, the International Red Cross, the multinational corporation . . . there are scores of institutions that reflect globalization. But they often appear as ineffective reactors to the world's real actors: national states and, to an ever greater degree, subnational factions in permanent rebellion against uniformity and integration—even the kind represented by universal law and justice. The headlines feature these players regularly: they are cultures, not countries; parts, not wholes; sects, not religions; rebellious factions and dissenting minorities at war not just with globalism but with the traditional nation-state. Kurds, Basques, Puerto Ricans, Ossetians, East Timoreans, Quebecois, the Catholics of Northern Ireland, Abkhasians, Kurile Islander Japanese, the Zulus of Inkatha, Catalonians, Tamils, and, of course, Palestinians—people without countries, inhabiting nations not their own, seeking smaller worlds within borders that will seal them off from modernity.

A powerful irony is at work here. Nationalism was once a force of integration and unification, a movement aimed at bringing together disparate clans, tribes, and cultural fragments under new, assimiliationist flags. But as

Ortega y Gasset noted more than sixty years ago, having won its victories, nationalism changed its strategy. In the 1920s, and again today, it is more often a reactionary and divisive force, pulverizing the very nations it once helped cement together. The force that creates nationals is "inclusive," Ortega wrote in *The Revolt of the Masses*. "In periods of consolidation, nationalism has a positive value, and is a lofty standard. But in Europe everything is more than consolidated, and nationalism is nothing but a mania. . . ."

This mania has left the post-Cold War smoldering with hot wars; the international scene is little more unified than it was at the end of the Great War, in Ortega's own time. There were more than thirty wars in progress last year, most of them ethnic, racial, tribal, or religious in character, and the list of unsafe regions doesn't seem to be getting any shorter. Some new world order!

The aim of many of these small-scale wars is to redraw boundaries, to implode states and resecure parochial identities: to escape McWorld's dully insistent imperatives. The mood is that of Jihad: war not as an instrument of policy but as an emblem of identity, an expression of community, an end in itself. Even where there is no shooting war, there is fractiousness, secession, and the quest for ever smaller communities. Add to the list of dangerous countries those at risk: In Switzerland and Spain, Jurassian and Basque separatists still argue the virtues of ancient identities, sometimes in the language of bombs. Hyperdisintegration in the former Soviet Union may well continue unabated—not just a Ukraine independent from the Soviet Union but a Bessarabian Ukraine independent from the Ukrainian republic; not just Russia severed from the defunct union but Tatarstan severed from Russia. Yugoslavia makes even the disunited, ex-Soviet, nonsocialist republics that were once the Soviet Union look integrated, its sectarian fatherlands springing up within factional motherlands like weeds within weeds within weeds. Kurdish independence would threaten the territorial integrity of four Middle Eastern nations. Well before the current cataclysm Soviet Georgia made a claim for autonomy from the Soviet Union, only to be faced with its Ossetians (164,000 in a republic of 5.5 million) demanding their own self-determination within Georgia. The Abkhasian minority in Georgia has followed suit. Even the good will established by Canada's once promising Meech Lake protocols is in danger, with Francophone Quebec again threatening the dissolution of the federation. In South Africa the emergence from apartheid was hardly achieved when friction between Inkatha's Zulus and the African National Congress's tribally identified members threatened to replace Europeans' racism with an indigenous tribal war. After thirty years of attempted integration using the colonial language (English) as a unifier,

Nigeria is now playing with the idea of linguistic multiculturalism—which could mean the cultural breakup of the nation into hundreds of tribal fragments. . . .

The passing of communism has torn away the thin veneer of internationalism (workers of the world unite!) to reveal ethnic prejudices that are not only ugly and deep-seated but increasingly murderous. Europe's old scourge, anti-Semitism, is back with a vengeance, but it is only one of many antagonisms. It appears all too easy to throw the historical gears into reverse and pass from a Communist dictatorship back into a tribal state.

Among the tribes, religion is also a battlefield. ("Jihad" is a rich word whose generic meaning is "struggle"—usually the struggle of the soul to avert evil. Strictly applied to religious war, it is used only in reference to battles where the faith is under assault, or battles against a government that denies the practice of Islam. My use here is rhetorical, but does follow both journalistic practice and history.) Remember the Thirty Years War? Whatever forms of Enlightenment universalism might once have come to grace such historically related forms of monotheism as Judaism, Christianity, and Islam, in many of their modern incarnations they are parochial rather than cosmopolitan, angry rather than loving, proselytizing rather than ecumenical, zealous rather than rationalist, sectarian rather than deistic, ethnocentric rather than universalizing. As a result, like the new forms of hypernationalism, the new expressions of religious fundamentalism are fractious and pulverizing, never integrating. This is religion as the Crusaders knew it, a battle to the death for souls that if not saved will be forever lost.

The atmospherics of Jihad have resulted in a breakdown of civility in the name of identity, of comity in the name of community. International relations have sometimes taken on the aspect of gang war—cultural turf battles featuring tribal factions that were supposed to be sublimated as integral parts of large national, economic, postcolonial, and constitutional entities.

Thinking Critically

1. Is there such a thing as McWorld?

2. Is there such a thing as Jihad?

3. Are you afraid of McWorld?

4. Are you afraid of Jihad?

5. Are you afraid of what might happen if the tensions between McWorld and Jihad increase?

The potential for danger discussed by Barber came to fruition on September 11, 2001. In the next essay, I deal with the relationship between the spread of fast-food restaurants, credit cards, and the cathedrals of consumption, and the kind of terrorism that occurred that day. I am certainly not arguing that the worldwide expansion of these phenomena caused these events. Nor am I condoning the acts of September 11 (they cannot be condoned) or condemning the United States. However, we do have to recognize that the attacks were aimed at national symbols, and the World Trade Center was a dramatic symbol of America's worldwide economic power. While America's economic power takes many forms, it is most visible to many people around the world in the realm of consumption. Thus, it could be argued that the attack on the World Trade Center was, in part, an attack on a symbol that stood for the incursions of symbols of the American economy, including those associated with consumption, into the lives of many people around the world.

The main thrust of this essay is to argue that fast-food restaurants, credit cards, and cathedrals of consumption bring with them American ways of doing business, American ways of consuming, and powerful American icons (such as the "golden arches" of McDonald's). Let us be absolutely clear: The vast majority of people in most nations welcome these incursions. However, others are, to varying degrees, offended by them. They have their own ways of doing business and of consuming, and American ways may be seen not only as different but also as offensive. In addition, for those who resent these things, there are the seemingly omnipresent symbols of the icons of these incursions, such as those of McDonald's, Visa, and Wal-Mart. They serve as highly visible and constant reminders of these American ways of doing things and of the perceived insults to indigenous practices. They also serve as a backdrop for a wide range of expressions of outrage against the United States.

The clearest support for this argument involves the case of "Carlos the Jackal," a terrorist linked to a variety of skyjackings, bombings, and machine-gun attacks. A Venezuelan, Carlos was reported to have worked for a number of Islamic leaders. Carlos was eventually captured and convicted of murder in France. He is serving a life sentence for his crimes. In his closing speech before sentencing, Carlos spoke of "world war, war to the death, the war that humanity must win against McDonaldization."

26

September 11, 2001

Mass Murder and Its Roots in the Symbolism of American Consumer Culture

George Ritzer

On September 11, 2001, the terrorists not only killed thousands of innocent people and destroyed buildings of various sorts, they also sought to destroy (and in one case succeeded) major symbols of America's preeminent position in the globalization process: The World Trade Center was a symbol of America's global hegemony in the economic realm, and the Pentagon is obviously the icon of its military preeminence around the world. In addition, there is a widespread belief that the fourth plane, the one that crashed in Pennsylvania, was headed for the symbol of American political power—the White House. Obviously, the common element in all these targets is that they are, among other things, cultural icons, with the result that the terrorist attacks can be seen as assaults on American culture. (This is not, of course, to deny the very material effects on people, buildings, the economy, and so on.) Furthermore, although symbols, jobs, businesses, and lives

---

Editor's Note: This chapter was written for *McDonaldization: The Reader* (2002).

were crippled or destroyed, the main objective was symbolic—the demonstration that the most important symbols of American culture were not only vulnerable but could be, and were, badly hurt or destroyed. The goal was to show the world that the United States was not an invulnerable superpower but that it could be assaulted successfully by a small number of terrorists. One implication was that if such important symbols could be attacked successfully, nothing in the United States (as well as in U.S. interests around the world) was safe from the wrath of terrorists. Thus, we are talking about an assault on, among other things, culture—an assault designed to have a wide-ranging impact throughout the United States and the world.

In emphasizing culture, I am not implying that economic, political, and military issues (to say nothing of the loss of life) are less important. Indeed, these domains are encompassed, at least in part, under the broad heading of culture and attacks on cultural icons. Clearly, many throughout the world are angered by a variety of things about the United States, especially its enormous economic, political, and military influence and power. In fact, this essay will focus on one aspect of the economy—consumption—and its role in producing hostility to the United States. . . .

By focusing on America's role in consumption and its impact around the world, I am not condoning the terrorist attacks (they are among the most heinous of acts in human history) or blaming the United States for those attacks. Rather, my objective is to discuss one set of reasons that people in many different countries loathe (while a far larger number of people love) the United States. Indeed, it is a truism that, often, love and hate coexist in the same people. However, needless to say, those involved in these terrorist acts had nothing but hatred for the United States.

Consumption

American hegemony throughout the world is most visible and, arguably, of greatest significance, in economic and cultural terms, in the realm of consumption. On a day-to-day basis in much of the world, people are far more likely to be confronted by American imperialism in the realm of consumption than they are in other economic domains (American factories and companies are far less obvious than the consumer products they offer for sale throughout the world), the military (U.S. troops and advisers are far less visible throughout the world than they used to be and certainly less than Nike shoes or McDonald's hamburgers), and the polity (American political influence is most likely to be covert in terms of its impact within the governments of most nations around the world). While the firing of American cruise missiles into sovereign nations such as Somalia may have provoked occasional demonstrations and intense outbursts of anger, the ubiquitousness of American consumption sites (e.g., McDonald's restaurants) and products (Nike shoes) is likely to be, at least for some, a long-running provocation that leads in the end to great animosity toward the United States and its intrusion into the everyday life of many cultures (of course, to many others they are irresistible attractions). In other words, we need to pay at least as much attention to everyday perceptions (in the realm of consumption and elsewhere) of provocations and insults as we do to the far more dramatic, but distant and intermittent, economic, political, and military actions.

Rather than focus on consumption in general, I will discuss three of its aspects of greatest concern to me: fast-food restaurants, credit cards, and "cathedrals of consumption" (for example, discounters such as Wal-Mart). Before getting to these, it is important to point out that they, and many other components of our consumer culture, are not only physical presences throughout the world, they are media presences by way of television, movies, the Internet, and so on. Furthermore, even in those countries where these phenomena are not yet material realities, they are already media presences. As a result, their impact is felt even though they have not yet entered a particular country, and in those countries where they already exist, their impact is increased because they are also media presences.

I want to focus on the ways in which, from the perspective of those in other nations and cultures, fast-food restaurants, credit cards, and cathedrals of consumption bring with them (a) an American way of doing business, (b) an American way of consuming, and (c) American cultural icons. I will examine why some may react negatively to one, two, or all three of these things. However, it is important to remember that the vast majority of those in most, if not all, nations throughout the world not only welcome these forms of Americana but actively seek them out and work hard to make them part of their country. In fact, the majority of people in nations that lack some or all of these (and who are aware of them) feel deprived by their absence and are eager to do what is necessary to bring them to their country. Again, in our focus on problems and negative effects and perceptions, we must never lose sight of the advantages and the great attraction to most people everywhere of these and many other aspects of our consumer culture.

Fast-Food Restaurants

Let us begin with fast-food restaurants, particularly the paradigmatic chain of fast-food restaurants, McDonald's. . . .

As it moves into each new nation, it brings with it a variety of American ways of doing business. In fact, in more recent years, the impact of its ways of doing business was surely felt long before the restaurant chain itself became a physical presence. McDonald's has been such a resounding success, and has offered so many important business innovations, that business leaders in other nations were undoubtedly incorporating many of its ideas almost from the inception of the chain. Of course, the major business innovation here is the franchise system. Although the franchise system predated McDonald's by many years (Singer Sewing Machine was involved in franchising prior to the Civil War, retailers such as Rexall and IGA were franchising by the 1930s, and in the fast-food industry A&W Root Beer was the pioneer in 1924), the franchise system came of age with the development of the McDonald's chain. Kroc made a number of innovations in franchising (he retained centralized control by refusing to grant blocs of regional franchises to entrepreneurs, and he based the corporation's income not on high initial fees but on a relatively large and continuing percentage of all sales); McDonald's also owned the real estate on which its restaurants were built and continued to earn rent as well as having the advantage of the increasing value of its real estate holdings that served to make it a far more successful system. The central point, given the interests of this essay, is that this system has been adopted, adapted, and modified by all sorts of businesses not only in the United States but throughout the world. In the case of franchise systems in other nations, they are doing business in a way that is similar to, if not identical with, comparable American franchises.

The fact that indigenous businesses (e.g., Russkoye Bistro in Russia, Nirulas in India) are conducting their business based, at least to a large degree, on an American business model is not visible to most people. However, they are affected in innumerable ways by the ways in which these franchises operate. Thus, day-to-day behaviors are influenced by all this, even if consumers are unaware of these effects.

What is far more obvious, even to consumers, is that people are increasingly consuming like Americans. This is clear not only in American chains in other countries but in indigenous clones of those chains. In terms of the former, in Japan, to take one example, McDonald's has altered long-standing traditions about how people are expected to eat. Thus, although eating while standing has long been taboo, in McDonald's restaurants, many Japanese eat just that way. Similarly, long expected not to touch food with their hands or drink directly from containers, many Japanese are doing just that in McDonald's and elsewhere. Much the same kind of thing is happening in indigenous clones of American fast-food restaurants in Japan such as Mos Burger.

These and many other changes in the way people consume are obvious, and they affect the way people live their lives on a daily basis. Just as many Japanese may resent these incursions into, and changes in, the ways in which they have traditionally conducted their everyday lives, those in many other cultures are likely to have their own wide-ranging set of resentments. However, these changes involve much more than transformations in the way people eat. . . . Almost no sector of society is immune from McDonaldization, and this means that innumerable aspects of people's everyday lives are transformed by it.

Finally, the spread of McDonald's and other fast-food chains around the world has brought with it a range of American cultural icons. Of course, McDonald's itself has become such an icon, as has its "golden arches," Ronald McDonald, and many of its products—Big Mac, Egg McMuffin, and so on. Other fast-food chains have brought with them their own icons—Burger King's Whopper, Colonel Sanders of Kentucky Fried Chicken, and so on. These icons are accepted, even embraced, by most, but others are likely to be angered by them. For example, traditional Japanese foods such as sushi and rice are being replaced, at least for some, by Big Macs and large orders of French fried potatoes. Because food is such a central part of any culture, such a transformation is likely to enrage some. More important, perhaps, is the ubiquity of the McDonald's restaurant, especially its golden arches, throughout so many nations of the world. To many in other societies, these are not only important symbols in themselves but have become symbols of the United States and, in some cases, even more important than more traditional symbols (such as the American embassy and the flag). In fact, there have been a number of incidents in recent years in which protests against the United States and its actions have taken the form of actions against the local McDonald's restaurants. To some, a McDonald's restaurant, especially when it is placed in some traditionally important locale, represents an affront, a "thumb in the eye," to the society and its culture. It is also perceived as a kind of "Trojan Horse," and the view is that hidden within its bright and attractive wrappings and trappings are all manner of potential threats to local culture. Insulted by, and fearful of, such "foreign" entities, a few react by striking out at them and the American culture and business world that stands behind them.

Credit Cards

The modern, "universal" credit card (Chapter 24) can be used in a variety of settings throughout the United States and, increasingly, the rest of the world. This is another American invention (circa 1950), although it was preceded by many years by various other forms of credit and even specific credit cards that could be used in department stores and gasoline stations. It took a decade or two for the credit card to take off in the United States, but in the last three decades, its use has skyrocketed as has the number of cards in existence, the amount of credit card expenditures, and the total credit card debt. Credit cards were slower to gain acceptance in other parts of the world, but in more recent years, credit card use has exploded in many countries. Even Germany, long seen as averse to credit instruments, has in the last few years embraced the credit card. Although credit cards are issued by innumerable local banks throughout the United States and the world, they almost always issue American cards, especially Visa and MasterCard. A few other cards are available (e.g., JCB in Japan), but the world market for credit cards is dominated by American brands and credit card companies. With the American market for credit cards approaching saturation levels, those companies have shifted much of their attention to obtaining the new business available through the exportation of their cards to the rest of the world.

The credit card represents an American way of doing business, especially a reliance on the extension of credit to maintain and to increase sales. Many nations have been dominated, and some still are, by "cash-and-carry" business. Businesses have typically been loathe to grant credit, and when they do, it has usually not been for large amounts of money. When credit was granted, strong collateral was required. This is in great contrast to the credit card industry, which has granted billions of dollars in credit with little or no collateral. In these and many other ways, traditional methods of doing business are being threatened and eroded by the incursion of the credit card.

Once again, although the business side of this transformation is not obvious to most people, its flip side in the realm of consumption is abundantly clear. That is, increasing numbers of people have been, and are, changing the way they consume from cash to credit card transactions. They are aware of this not only on a day-to-day basis as they consume but also quite pointedly (and sometimes alarmingly) at the end of each month when they must confront their credit card bills and, possibly, accumulating interest charges. As in the United States, those in other nations who can pay their bills in full each month are quite happy with their credit cards and the many advantages they offer. However, those who cannot pay those bills and must wrestle with large balances and exorbitant interest charges are apt to become increasingly discomforted by credit cards. Given this state of discomfiture, when they look at their bills and their cards what they see are the names and the logos of the American credit card companies that can easily be blamed for their plight. After all, it is easier to blame credit card companies than oneself. It is not a great leap from blaming the American credit card firms to blaming America itself.

But there is a more important issue here, one that will be also dealt with later. That is, credit cards are perceived as playing a key role in the development and expansion of consumer culture, a role characterized by hyper-consumption. Although many are overjoyed to be deeply immersed in consumer culture and others would dearly love to be so involved, still others are deeply worried by it on various grounds. One of the concerns, felt not only in the United States but perhaps even more elsewhere in the world, is the degree to which immersion in the seeming superficialities of consumption and fashion represents a threat, if not an affront, to deep-seated cultural and religious values. For example, many have viewed modern consumption as a kind of religion, and I have described malls and other consumption settings as cathedrals of consumption. As such, they can be seen as alternatives, and threats, to conventional religions in many parts of the world. At the minimum, the myriad attractions of consumption and a day at the mall serve as powerful alternatives to visiting one's church, mosque, or synagogue.

Finally, credit cards in general, to say nothing of the major brands—Visa and MasterCard (as well as the "charge card" and its dominant brand, American Express)—are seen as major icons of American culture. While these icons are similar to, say, McDonald's and its golden arches, there is something quite unique and powerful about credit cards. Although one who lives outside the United States may encounter a McDonald's and its arches every day, or maybe every few days, a Visa credit card, for example, is *always* with those who have one. It is always there in one's wallet, and it is probably a constant subconscious reality. Furthermore, one is continually reminded of it every time one passes a consumption site, especially one that has the logo of the credit card on its door or display window. Even without the latter, the mere presence of a shop and its goods is a reminder that one possesses a credit card and that the shop can be entered and goods can be purchased. The credit card is a uniquely powerful cultural icon because it is with cardholders all the time and they are likely to be reminded of it continually.

Cathedrals of Consumption

Cathedrals of consumption, many of which are also American innovations, are increasing presences elsewhere in the world. There is a long list of these cathedrals of consumption (see Chapter 21), but let us focus on two—shopping malls and discounters, especially Wal-Mart. American-style fully enclosed shopping malls are springing up all over the world (a good example is the abundance of such malls on Orchard Road in Singapore). Most of these are indigenous developments, but the model is the American mall. Discount stores are experiencing a similar proliferation, but this is taking the form of indigenous versions as well as the exportation of American representatives such as Wal-Mart to many parts of the world.

These, of course, represent American ways of doing business. In the case of the mall, this involves the concentration of businesses in a single setting devoted to them. In the case of discounters, it represents the much greater propensity of American businesses (in comparison with their peers around the world) to compete on a price basis and to offer consumers deep discounts. Although appealing to many people, resentment may develop not only because these represent American rather than indigenous business practices but because they pose threats to local businesses. As in the United States, still more resentment is likely to be generated because small local shops are likely to be driven out of business by the development of a mall or the opening of a Wal-Mart on the outskirts of town.

Again, more obvious is the way consumers are led to alter their behaviors as a result of these developments. For example, instead of walking or bicycling to local shops, increasing numbers are more likely to drive to the new and very attractive malls and discounters. This can also lead to movement toward the increasing American reality that such trips are not just about shopping; such settings have become *destinations* where people spend many hours wandering from shop to shop, having lunch, and even seeing a movie or having a drink. Consumption sites have become places to while away days, and as such, they pose threats to alternative public sites, such as parks, zoos, and museums. In the end, malls and discounters are additional and very important contributors to the development of hyperconsumption and all the advantages and problems associated with it. Settings such as a massive shopping mall with a huge adjacent parking lot and a large Wal-Mart with its parking lot are abundantly obvious to people, as are the changes they help to create in the way natives consume.

Settings such as these are perceived as American cultural icons. Wal-Mart may be second only to McDonald's in terms of the association of consumption sites with things American, and the suburban mall is certainly broadly perceived in a similar way. Furthermore, malls are likely to house a number of other cultural icons, such as McDonald's, the Gap, and so on. And still further, the latter are selling yet other icons in the form of products such as Big Macs, blue jeans, Nike shoes, and so on. Many of those icons will be taken from the malls and eaten, worn, and otherwise displayed in public. Their impact is amplified because their well-known logos and names are likely to be plastered all over these products. Again, there is an "in-your-face" quality to all of this, and although many will be led to want these things, others will react negatively to the ubiquity of these emblems of America and its consumer culture and that these emblems tend to supplant indigenous symbols.

The argument here is that the recent terrorist attacks can be seen as assaults on American cultural icons—specifically the World Trade Center (business and consumption), the Pentagon (military), and potentially, the White House (political). That cultural icons were the target is further reflected by the closing of Disney theme parks, the restrictions put in place around Las Vegas casinos, the enormous loss of business for cruise lines, the suspension of major league baseball for a week, the cancellation of National Football League games for the week, and so on. Now, of course, there are pragmatic factors involved here; all of these involve large numbers of people in a single location, but beyond that, they were perceived as potential targets because of their symbolic importance.

Although I have focused on three American cultural icons in this essay and their worldwide proliferation, in vast portions of the world they are of minimal importance or completely nonexistent. Even where they are not physical presences, however, they are known through movies, television, magazines, and newspapers, and even by word of mouth. Thus, their influence throughout the world far exceeds their material presence in the world.

Their media presence leads to another problem. When those in most other countries get a glimpse of American consumer culture in the media, it is usually one that underscores that no matter how far (or little) their own consumer culture has advanced, it lags far behind that in the United States. Specifically, there are far more fast-food restaurants, credit cards, and cathedrals of consumption and the consumer products they offer for sale in the United States than anywhere else in the world. This is likely to be especially galling to those in nations that offer little more than a subsistence economy, if that. Media images of American affluence—sparkling fast-food restaurants, people with credit cards in hand rushing about in the Mall of America, the incredible sites of Las Vegas and gamblers betting more on one roll of the dice than people in many nations in the world will earn in their lifetimes—anger some in impoverished nations who may not know where their next meal will come from. Thus, the phenomena discussed in this essay do not even have to exist in a given nation for there to be a great deal of hostility toward them and the American society that is their source and center.

Although there is clearly a link between the phenomena just discussed and hostile reactions around the world (this is evident in several of the essays that follow in this volume), what is the case for relating them to events such as those of September 11? Afghanistan had no McDonald's restaurants, and Osama Bin Laden has never been quoted (to my knowledge) as expressing anger over credit cards, fast-food restaurants, or Wal-Mart. In fact, some of those involved in the September 11 attacks used credit cards to finance some of their actions and were known to frequent McDonaldized settings. Bin Laden, Al Qaeda, and the Taliban are Islamic fundamentalists who are hostile to the United States (and other nations) because of the threat it poses to basic Islamic beliefs and modes of life. In terms of our interests here, they see no place for fundamentalist Islam in fast-food restaurants and, more generally, in a world dominated by indebtedness and consumerism made possible and incited by credit cards and cathedrals of consumption.

Islamic fundamentalists such as Bin Laden are mainly motivated by animus to the presence of American political and military might in Islamic nations, by the leadership of Saudi Arabia (which permits tens of thousands of non-Muslims to live there, to say nothing of accepting an American military presence), and by Israel (which, interestingly, one observer views as "like a giant McDonald's franchise in the Middle East") and its relationship to the Palestinians. However, the kinds of concerns discussed in this essay are linked to, and are everyday reminders of, American influence in the Islamic world. Thus, in the wake of the American war on the Taliban in Afghanistan, and its effort to hunt down Bin Laden and Al Qaeda, Islamic protests broke out in various parts of the world. For example, in Indonesia, the world's largest Muslim nation, the protesters bombed a Kentucky Fried Chicken restaurant and shook their fists at the golden arches of a McDonald's restaurant in Jakarta situated close to the American embassy. Whenever a protest approached, employees of the restaurant responded by raising a banner saying "This store is owned by a Muslim."

However, the clearest example for the link being made in this essay involves "Carlos the Jackal," a terrorist linked to a variety of skyjackings, bombings, and machine gun attacks. Carlos (a Venezuelan) was reported to have worked for a number of Islamic leaders, including Mohammar Qaddafi (Libya), Saddam Hussein (Iraq), Hafez Assad (Syria), and George Habash (Popular Front for the Liberation of Palestine). Carlos was eventually captured and convicted of murder in France. He is serving a life sentence for his crimes. In his closing speech before sentencing, Carlos spoke of "world war, war to the death, the war that humanity must win against McDonaldization." More generally, the argument being made here is that there are many around the world, including a number within the Islamic world, who are waging war against McDonaldization and American-style consumerism.

Responding to the Crisis

It is interesting to note that some notable responses to the crisis of September 11 occurred in the realm of consumption. The mayor of New York, Rudolph Giuliani, was quickly heard and seen urging the citizens of the city, as well all of America, to get back to their normal routine, especially by going shopping. Similar calls soon came from President Bush. A quick reaction to these calls came from former Secretary of Labor Robert Reich, who penned an essay on the front page of the *Washington Post*'s Outlook section titled, "How Did Spending Become Our Patriotic Duty?"

The answer to Reich's rhetorical question is that the demand that we spend and shop has been with us for some time, and it has been growing more powerful. One measure of this is the increasing attention and importance given to data associated with consumption, especially the index of consumer confidence. In the past, production data were of greatest importance to the stock market, but more recently, it seems that consumption-related data have become as important, if not more important. Declines in consumption, as well as consumer confidence, are viewed as harbingers of big trouble to corporations and their profits, as well as increases in unemployment rates. With traditional production industries (steel, autos, textiles) declining or even disappearing in the United States, it is little wonder that consumption is gaining ascendancy. Furthermore, the nation's economy as a whole is increasingly tied to consumption, and a recession seems to be increasingly tied, at least in part, to recalcitrant consumers. Thus, to Americans, it *has* come to seem that they have a duty to the nation, the economy, corporations, and their fellow workers to spend and consume.

Another interesting aspect of the aftermath of September 11 is the sense that Americans can protect themselves from various threats by buying the right product. The answer to the threat of some form of gas being released into the environment is to buy gas masks, even though one is unlikely to have one at hand if such an attack were to occur, let alone even know that gas has been released. The answer to the mini-outbreak of anthrax was the antibiotic Cipro, with the result that many called their doctors, or exploited other less legal methods, to get a supply on hand *in case* they contracted the disease. As other crises emerge, other consumables will emerge as solutions.

Not only are such actions unnecessary in almost all cases, but they also support the widespread view throughout the world that Americans are the world's most affluent consumers. In many nations in the world, there is not enough to eat or there are few, if any, medications, even for those who are already quite ill and likely to die without them. The latter cannot obtain Cipro even if it could be of help, and it is certainly too costly for the vast majority of other people in less developed countries. In those nations, as well as among the disenchanted within developed nations where hostility to America and its affluence already exists, we are likely to see an exacerbation of that hostility as people watch Americans endeavoring to spend their way into some measure of safety from both real and imagined dangers. The great capacity of Americans to spend and consume is *both* a great source of national strength *and* the nation's Achilles heel in that it has helped to create a hostility that found expression on September 11 and beyond and may well find other ways of expressing itself in the years to come.

Conclusion

Wars are always about culture, at least to some degree, but the one we have embarked on seems to reek with cultural symbolism. We live in an era—the era of globalization—in which not only cultural products and the businesses that sell them but also the symbols that go to their essence are known throughout the world. In fact, some—Nike and Tommy Hilfiger come to mind—are *nothing but symbols;* they manufacture nothing (except symbols). Although we deeply mourn the loss of life, the terrorists were after more. Surely, they wanted to kill people, but mainly because their deaths represented symbolically the fact that America could be made to bleed. But they also wanted to destroy some of the American symbols best known throughout the world; in destroying them, they were, they thought, symbolically destroying the United States. Interestingly, the initial response from the United States was largely symbolic—American flags were displayed everywhere; the sounds of the national anthem wafted through the air on a regular basis; red, white, and blue ribbons were wrapped around trees and telephone poles; and so on. Of course, the response soon went beyond symbols: Missiles have been launched and bombs dropped, special forces are in action, and people are dying. However, should the mastermind of the terrorist acts—Osama Bin Laden—be caught or killed, he will quickly become an even greater cultural icon than he is at the moment (his likeness already adorns T-shirts in Pakistan and elsewhere). Destroying his body may be satisfying to some, but it may well create a greater cultural problem for the United States, one that might translate into still more American citizens killed and structures destroyed.

Returning to my central point, the emphasis here has been on the peculiar power of consumption and the icons associated with it to arouse both admiration and hatred in many parts of the world. The symbols of our business, political, and military influence throughout the world are likely to be half-hidden, and when they become clear, it is usually only on an intermittent basis and for a short period of time. They are not highly involved, at least in any way that is apparent to most, with the day-to-day lives of most people around the world. Certainly, their impact is often indirect and quite powerful, but people on a daily basis are at best only half-conscious of that impact and power. It is quite a different matter in the realm of consumption, particularly in terms of the phenomena of concern here—fast-food restaurants, credit cards, and cathedrals of consumption. In the many nations of the world in which they have become prominent, their impact is clear for all to see, continuous, and long lasting. They are obvious both to those who long for them and those who hate them. They surround these people, and they are on their person—T-shirts, Nike shoes, jeans with a Visa card in the wallets in their pockets.

Of course, such representatives of American consumer culture have long been objects of antiglobalization forces. For example, McDonald's restaurants have been boycotted and picketed, had manure dumped in front of them, and have been destroyed. Nike and its sweatshops in Southeast Asia and elsewhere have also been favorite targets. The terrorists of September 11, 2001, however, were after even bigger symbolic game. McDonald's is a major symbol, but it is dispersed across more than 30,000 settings throughout the world. Aiming a plane at one McDonald's restaurant, or even at one corporation (say, McDonald's headquarters outside Chicago), is not likely to have the impact of crashing planes into twin towers that represent not only such businesses but many others as well. I am not equating the forces opposed to globalization with the terrorists, but they do share the goal of symbolic assault.

In conclusion, the focus of this chapter on key symbols of American consumer culture is not to denigrate the importance of other symbols, much less that of the material realities associated not only with that culture but with the United States as a whole. Furthermore, a focus on consumption is not to deny the importance of other economic symbols and material realities or those associated with politics, the military, and the polity. The symbols, as well as American consumer culture in general, are important not only in themselves but also because of their very distinctive capacity to influence the day-to-day lives of people throughout the world. Many welcome this influence, even want more of it, but a few are enraged by it (and many other things associated with the United States) and want to destroy it and its source—the United States. This certainly does not excuse the heinous acts of September 11, 2001, but it does help us to analyze at least one of the root causes of such terrorism.

Thinking Critically

1. Is there a global war against McDonaldization?

2. Was 9/11 part of it?

3. Are American consumption patterns offensive to those in other nations?

4. Are they objectionable within an American context?

5. Is spending and consumption our national duty?

The next three essays deal with several examples of collective behavior/social movements in various parts of the world (especially Great Britain, France, and Italy) that target McDonald's as well as the larger process of McDonaldization. In Chapter 27, the McSpotlight group offers a summary of the now infamous McLibel trial. This is a one-sided perspective on the trial, but it is presented here because it represents the viewpoint of the social movement against McDonald's that emerged from the trial. The facts are that McDonald's sued two activists involved in London Greenpeace for passing out a leaflet critical of McDonald's on a variety of grounds. The trial began in 1994 and ultimately became the longest running trial in British history. While McDonald's "won" the case (although the judge found for the defendants on several grounds), it was a public relations disaster for the company. The case continued on with a series of appeals undertaken by the defendants.

The trial and its history are important in themselves, but of greatest interest to us here is the formation of the group known as McSpotlight, which now is in the forefront not only of anti-McDonald's activity but also in opposition to many different multinational corporations. Of greatest importance is its Web site, which has become the international center for communicating and finding out about activities being mounted against McDonald's and other corporations around the world. The McSpotlight group is a social movement as well as a spur to other such movements.

27

The McLibel Trial Story

McSpotlight

Handing out leaflets on the streets was one of the main activities of the small activist group London Greenpeace, who'd been campaigning on a variety of environmental and social justice issues since the early 1970s. (The group predates the more well known Greenpeace International and the two organizations are unconnected.)

In 1978, local postman Dave Morris worked alongside London Greenpeace activists in protests against nuclear power. By 1982 he had started attending the group's meetings.

London Greenpeace campaigned on a wide range of issues from nuclear power and third world debt to anti-traffic actions and the Miners Strike. In the mid 1980s, the group began a campaign focusing on McDonald's as a high-profile organization symbolizing everything they considered wrong with the prevailing corporate mentality. In 1985, they launched the International Day of Action Against McDonald's, which has been held on October 16 ever since. In 1986, they produced a 6-sided fact sheet called "What's Wrong With McDonald's? Everything They Don't Want You to Know." The leaflet attacked almost all aspects of the corporation's business, accusing them of exploiting children with advertising, promoting an unhealthy diet, exploiting their staff, and being responsible for environmental damage and ill treatment of animals.

Editor's Note: Excerpts from "The McLibel Trial Story" available online from McSpotlight (www.mcspotlight.org/case/trial/story.html).

But the group also continued with other campaigns, and in 1987, 21-year-old gardener Helen Steel went along to meetings to get involved with protests in support of Aboriginal land rights at the time of the reenactment of the First Fleet sailing to Australia.

Meanwhile, McDonald's were busily suing (or threatening to sue) almost everyone who criticized them—from the BBC and *The Guardian* to student unions and green groups. . . .

In 1989, as the campaign grew and was taken up by more and more groups around the world, McDonald's produced their own "McFact cards" detailing their position on many of the accusations made in the leaflet. They also decided to take extreme action against London Greenpeace.

McDonald's hired two firms of private investigators and instructed them to infiltrate the group in order to find out how they operated, who did what, and, most importantly, who was responsible for the production and distribution of the leaflet.

Since London Greenpeace was an unincorporated association, if McDonald's wanted to bring legal action to stop the campaign it would have to be against named individuals—which meant the company needed to find out people's names and addresses. Seven spies in total infiltrated the group. They followed people home, took letters sent to the group, got fully involved in the activities (including giving out anti-McDonald's leaflets), and invented spurious reasons to find out people's addresses. One spy (Michelle Hooker) even had a 6-month love affair with one of the activists. Another, Allan Claire, broke into the office of London Greenpeace and took a series of photographs.

At some London Greenpeace meetings there were as many spies as campaigners present and, as McDonald's didn't tell each agency about the other, the spies were busily spying on each other (the court later heard how Allan Claire had noted the behavior of Brian Bishop, another spy, as "suspicious").

Not all the spies were unaffected by the experience: Fran Tiller "felt very uncomfortable" doing the job and "disliked the deception, spying on people and interfering with their lives." She later gave evidence for the defendants in the trial, stating "I didn't think there was anything wrong with what the group was doing" and "I believe people are entitled to their views."

In 1990, McDonald's served libel writs on five volunteers in the group over the "What's Wrong With McDonald's?" leaflet. They offered a stark choice: retract the allegations made in the leaflet and apologize or go to court.

There is no legal aid (public money) for libel cases, but the five did get two hours' free legal advice, which boiled down to: the legal procedures in libel are extremely complex and weighted against defendants, you'll incur huge costs, with no money or legal experience you'll have no chance against

McDonald's legal team, you probably won't even get past the legal obstacles before the full trial. In short: back out and apologize while you've got the chance. One of the barristers that they met at this time, Keir Starmer, said that if they decided to fight he would back them up for free.

Three of the five took the advice and reluctantly apologized. Which left Helen Steel and Dave Morris. Dave's partner and his very young son had a bad accident and he was nursing them single-handed (he and his partner later split up and Dave became a full-time single father). He said he would go along with whatever Helen decided.

"It just really stuck in the throat to apologize to McDonald's. I thought it was them that should have been apologizing to us—well not us specifically, but to society for the damage they do to society and the environment"—Helen Steel.

Unlike anyone McDonald's had ever sued for libel before, Helen and Dave decided that they would stand up to the burger giants in court. They knew each other well from their involvement in community-based campaigns in their local North London neighborhood and felt that although the odds were stacked against them, people would rally round to ensure that McDonald's wouldn't succeed in silencing their critics.

Long before you get to trial, there are an enormous number of preliminary hearings and procedures that have to be completed. First, Helen and Dave had to prepare their defense—a detailed response to McDonald's Statement of Claim. Then there were several rounds of "Further and Better Particulars of Justification and Fair Comment" to complete.

Meanwhile, the McLibel Support Campaign was set up to generate solidarity and financial support for Helen and Dave. Over the next few years they would raise more than £35,000 to pay for witness airfares, court costs, expenses, and so on—every penny coming from donations from the public. Helen and Dave would only claim some travel and administration expenses (photocopying, phone calls to witnesses, etc.)—they were determined that they would never take a penny for themselves.

In 1991, the defendants took the British government to the European Court of Human Rights to demand the right to legal aid or the simplification of libel procedures. Paradoxically, the court ruled that, as the defendants had put up a "tenacious defense," they could not say they were being denied access to justice. They lost the application.

Meanwhile, back in the UK High Court, legal battles were raging between the two sides over McDonald's refusal to disclose all the relevant documents in its possession. McDonald's barrister argued that the defense case was very weak, that Helen and Dave would not be able to produce evidence to support it, so large parts of it should be dismissed and therefore there was no need for McDonald's to hand over the documents. The judge overturned normal procedures (whereby documents are disclosed before exchange of witness statements) and ruled that the defendants had three weeks to produce witness statements.

To everyone's surprise, Helen and Dave came back with 65 statements. McDonald's then took the unusual step of bringing in a top lawyer at this pretrial stage: employing Richard Rampton QC, one of Britain's top libel lawyers for a reputed fee of £2,000 a day plus a 6-figure briefing fee. Their legal team now comprised Rampton, his junior barrister, solicitor Patti Brinley-Codd, at least five solicitors and assistants from [the] leading city law firm Barlow, Lyde, and Gilbert, and even someone to carry Rampton's files. Helen and Dave were representing themselves, with occasional backup from Keir Starmer. At this time, Mr. Justice Bell, who ultimately presided over the full McLibel trial, took over the pretrial hearings. . . .

In late 1993, Richard Rampton started to prove why he is paid so much money. He applied for the trial to be heard by a judge only, arguing that the scientific evidence necessary to examine the links between diet and disease are too complicated for the ordinary people of a jury to understand. This was despite the obvious fact that the defendants themselves were ordinary people with no scientific training.

The judge ruled in favor of McDonald's, saying that it would be too complex for lay people to adjudicate some of the issues, and it could be tried more "conveniently" without a jury. The trial would now be heard by a single judge: a major blow to the defendants as it was very likely that a jury would be more sympathetic. They may even have been outraged that the case was ever brought at all.

McDonald's also applied for an order striking out certain parts of the defense on the grounds that the witness statements gathered by the defendants did not sufficiently support those areas of the defense. The judge agreed to strike out the entire rainforest section and many of the pleadings relating to trade union disputes in other countries around the world.

Dave Morris and Helen Steel applied unsuccessfully to the Court of Appeal and the House of Lords to reinstate the jury. However, in a landmark legal decision, the Court of Appeal restored all parts of the defense struck out by the judge, on the basis that the defendants are entitled to rely on not only their own witnesses' statements but also those from McDonald's witnesses, the future discovery of McDonald's documents, and what they might reasonably expect to discover under cross-examination of the company's witnesses.

Steel and Morris prepared to prove that the statements in the allegedly libelous leaflet were true or fair comment. Defendants are required under

British libel law to provide "primary sources" of evidence to substantiate their case. This means witness statements and documentary proof rather than press reports, common knowledge, or even scientific journals.

Just before the trial proper was due to start, in March 1994, McDonald's produced 300,000 copies of a leaflet to distribute to their customers via their burger outlets. The leaflet stated that "This action is not about freedom of speech; it is about the right to stop people telling lies." The company also issued press releases in a similar vein. In a neat legal move, Helen and Dave issued a counterclaim against McDonald's over the accusation that the company's critics (including them) are liars. This meant that, as well as the defendants having to prove that the criticisms made in the "What's Wrong With McDonald's?" leaflet are true, McDonald's would now have to prove they are false (and that the defendants knew they were false) if they wanted to win the counterclaim. As it turned out, however, the judge did not run the trial in this way.

June 28, 1994, and the full libel trial finally started in Court 35 of the Royal Courts of Justice, London. It was presided over by Mr. Justice Bell, a new judge with almost no experience of libel.

The contested allegations made in the leaflet can be divided into seven broad categories: nutrition, rainforests, recycling and waste, employment, food poisoning, animals, and publication (i.e., did Steel and Morris publish the leaflet?). . . .

Meanwhile, questions were being asked in the UK parliament. Labor MP Jeremy Corbyn sponsored two Early Day Motions called "McDonald's and Censorship" in which he said that "this House opposes the routine use of libel writs as a form of censorship" and that "apologies and damages have been obtained under false pretences after McDonald's lied about their practices." Serious stuff.

The nutrition section of the case got off to a flying start with a contrast between McDonald's internal company memo—"We can't really address or defend nutrition. We don't sell nutrition and people don't come to McDonald's for nutrition"—and one of their public leaflets—"Every time you eat at McDonald's, you'll eat good, nutritious food." Defense witness Tim Lobstein testified that McDonald's concept of a balanced diet is "meaningless." "You could eat a roll of cellotape as part of a balanced diet," he said.

Classic Court Moment Number 1 came on September 12, 1994, when McDonald's expert witness on cancer, Dr. Sydney Arnott, inadvertently admitted that one of the most contentious statements made in the leaflet was a "very reasonable thing to say."

Around this time the defendants received a most unexpected message: McDonald's wanted to meet them to discuss a settlement. . . . McDonald's said they would drop the suit and pay a substantial sum to a third party if the defendants agreed never to publicly criticize McDonald's again. Helen and Dave said they wanted an undertaking from McDonald's not to sue anyone for making similar criticisms again and for the company to apologize to those they've sued in the past. No deal, so back to court.

By Autumn 1994, the court was listening to evidence on McDonald's advertising techniques, and part of their confidential *Operation Manual* was read out in court: "Ronald loves McDonald's and McDonald's food. And so do children, because they love Ronald. Remember, children exert a phenomenal influence when it comes to restaurant selection. This means you should do everything you can to appeal to children's love for Ronald and McDonald's."

On Day 102 in court—March 13, 1995—McLibel became the longest ever UK libel trial. . . .

Around this time an Australian documentary team received a leaked confidential McDonald's Australia memo, which detailed their strategy for dealing with media interest in the McLibel case. It included such gems as "we could worsen the controversy by adding our opinion" and "we want to keep it at arm's length—not become guilty by association."

Meanwhile, McDonald's shareholders were getting upset. At the annual general meeting in Chicago, Michael Quinlan, Chair and Chief Executive, said the case would be "coming to a wrap soon." It actually lasted two more years.

June 28, 1995, and the trial celebrated its first anniversary, with a birthday cake and picket outside the court.

Before the trial started, McDonald's had made an agreement with the judge and with Helen and Dave to pay for daily transcripts of the trial to be made, and to give copies to all parties. In July 1995, they said that they were withdrawing this agreement unless the defendants agreed to stop giving quotes to the press. Helen and Dave considered this to be a crude attempt by McDonald's to stop the swell of negative publicity based on quotes from the transcripts—especially admissions obtained during their cross-examination of McDonald's witnesses. McDonald's said that it was to stop Helen and Dave distorting what their witnesses had said. The McLibel Support Campaign launched an appeal to raise the £35,000 needed to pay for transcripts for the remainder of the trial (£425 per day). . . .

In June 1995, at McDonald's request, the two sides met again for more settlement negotiations. . . . McDonald's repeated that they can't possibly agree to never sue anyone again. Helen and Dave repeated that they couldn't possibly agree not to criticize McDonald's anymore. The talks failed, and the trial continued.

By October 1995, the court was listening to evidence on McDonald's employment practices—over 30 ex-employees and trade union officials and activists from around the world would be called. Media highlights included allegations of racism, cooking in a kitchen flooded with sewage, watering down products, illegal hours worked, underage staff employed, fiddling of time cards, and obsessive anti-union practices. . . .

McLibel notched up another one for the record books on December 11, 1995, as it became the longest civil case (as opposed to criminal case) in British history.

The greatest moment of the whole case, campaign, and possibly the history of the planet came on February 16, 1996, when Helen and Dave launch the McSpotlight Internet site from a laptop connected to the Internet via a mobile phone outside a McDonald's store in Central London. The Web site was accessed more than a million times in its first month, of which 2,700 were from a computer called "mcdonalds.com."

Between February and April of that year the court heard evidence on one of the most controversial allegations in the leaflet: that McDonald's were responsible for the destruction of rainforests in Central and South America to make way for cattle pasture. Witness Sue Brandford, appearing for the Defense, testified that she visited one of the particular areas in Brazil under contention 20 years ago and that it was rainforest then. The judge said that it was the most important evidence heard so far on this issue.

The defendants were by now completely exhausted but were refused an adjournment for rest.

Around this time, the judge denied the defendants leave to appeal his decision to allow McDonald's to change their Statement of Claim (original case against Morris and Steel) regarding the issues of nutrition and animal welfare. The Court of Appeal also refused them leave to appeal.

After rainforests came publication. Did Helen and Dave produce or distribute the fact sheet? If McDonald's did not manage to prove this, then their whole case would fall apart.

The majority of McDonald's case on publication relied on the spies who had been paid to infiltrate the London Greenpeace meetings in the 1980s. Four of them came to give evidence for McDonald's. But, in one of the great twists of the trial, another one, Fran Tiller, appeared on behalf of Helen and Dave. She testified that she "did not think there was anything wrong with what the group was doing." Three of the spies admitted distributing the leaflet, and so the defendants claimed McDonald's had consented to its publication.

In June, the trial celebrated its second anniversary with a Ronald McDonald cake outside court.

On July 17, 1996, the court closed with all the evidence completed. Each side now had just three months to write their closing speeches—analyzing 40,000 pages of documentary evidence, 20,000 pages of transcript testimony, and dealing with many complex legal arguments and submissions—in order to present their final case. . . .

In fact, the corporation was receiving increasingly bad publicity now, and as the trial progressed, campaigners were stepping up their protests against McDonald's worldwide. In particular, "What's Wrong With McDonald's?" leaflets were becoming probably the most famous and widely distributed protest leaflets in history.

The two sides returned to court in October to start the closing speeches. The judge turned down the defendants' request either for more time to prepare or for McDonald's to go first with the closing speeches. The defendants argued that they were unprepared and couldn't hope to analyze even half the testimony in the time available. They also argued that they had no experience in what should be included and since McDonald's were represented by experienced lawyers they should go first. The judge said no, and a few weeks later, the Court of Appeal refused to give the defendants leave to appeal against the judge's ruling.

Helen and Dave started their closing speeches on October 21 and carried on for a massive 6 weeks. This surely had to be one of the longest speeches ever made in history, not least because . . . two weeks later, on November 1, 1996 (Court Day 292), McLibel became the longest trial of any kind in English history. . . . The *Guinness Book of Records* took note.

Richard Rampton QC, for McDonald's, decided to present his closing speech in written form and handed his 5-volume document to the judge on November 28, 1996. All that remained was a few days of legal arguments. The defendants argued that the UK libel laws are oppressive and unfair, particularly (in this case) the denial of legal aid and a jury trial and that multinational corporations should no longer be allowed to sue their critics in order to silence them over issues of public interest. They cited European and U.S. laws which would debar such a case and also recent developments in UK law debarring governmental bodies from suing for libel. It was further argued that the McLibel case was beyond all precedent, was an abuse of procedure and of public rights, and that there was "an overriding imperative for decisions to be made to protect the public interest."

December 13, 1996, was the last day of final submissions. Mr. Justice Bell said, "I will say now that I propose to reserve any judgment. It will take me some time to write it. I don't mean to be difficult when I say I don't know when I will deliver it because I don't know." He denied newspaper reports that his ruling would come at the beginning of 1997 or early 1997, adding "It will take me longer than that."

The media frenzy continued as the judge deliberated, with Channel 4 TV news stating that the McLibel case was considered to be "the biggest corporate PR disaster in history." . . .

But things were going well for the corporation too: In April, they announced that "systemwide sales exceeded $30 billion for the first time, and net income crossed the $1.5 billion threshold."

Despite the build-up in the preceding weeks, no one had any inkling of the scale of the media attention on Judgment Day—June 19, 1997. . . .

Mr. Justice Bell took two hours to read his summary to a packed courtroom. He ruled that Helen and Dave had not proved the allegations against McDonald's on rainforest destruction, heart disease and cancer, food poisoning, starvation in the third world, and bad working conditions. But they had proved that McDonald's "exploits children" with their advertising, falsely advertise their food as nutritious, risk the health of their most regular, long-term customers, are "culpably responsible" for cruelty to animals, are "strongly antipathetic" to unions, and pay their workers low wages.

. . ."Not proved" does not mean that the allegations against McDonald's are not true, just that the judge felt that Helen and Dave did not bring sufficient evidence to prove the meanings he had attributed to the leaflet. The judge ruled that Helen and Dave had libeled McDonald's, but as they had proved many of the allegations, they would only owe half of the claimed damages: £60,000.

Helen eloquently summarized the defendants' response: "McDonald's don't deserve a penny and in any event we haven't got any money." McDonald's had 4 weeks to decide whether they were going to pursue their costs and the injunction which they had originally set out to obtain back in September 1990.

Press interest was at a peak around the day of the verdict. McSpotlight was accessed 2.2 million times. . . .

Two days after the verdict Helen and Dave were leafleting outside McDonald's again, in defiance of any injunction McDonald's may serve. They weren't alone: Over 400,000 leaflets were distributed outside 500 of McDonald's 750 UK stores, and solidarity protests were held in over a dozen countries. . . .

McDonald's dropped their claim for damages as well as their intention of getting an injunction (meaning that if Helen and Dave continued to distribute the leaflets it would be contempt of court, for which they could be jailed). Although this was a sensible move, PR-wise (as the defendants had already stated that they would defy any injunction) it signaled a clear admission of defeat. The securing of damages and an injunction had been the corporation's two aims in starting proceedings. . . . They are now claiming that they were only interested in establishing the truth (for example, that they exploit children).

Two months after the verdict, the defendants' appeal was safely lodged. Helen and Dave argued that the trial was unfair and the libel laws oppressive, that the defense evidence on all of the issues was overwhelming, and that in any case Mr. Justice Bell's findings against the corporation were so damaging to McDonald's reputation that the case should have been found in the defendants' favor overall.

After a short break to recover from the stress of the trial, the defendants would have to start extensive preparation anew.

Meanwhile, the global protests and the distribution of London Greenpeace leaflets continued to grow—including a week of action around Anti-McDonald's Day in October 1997.

Pre-appeal hearings—and legal arguments and disputes—took place throughout 1998 in front of three Lord Justices. The appeal itself finally started on January 12, 1999, ending on March 21, 1999. . . . The defendants represented themselves, opposed by the usual McSuspects on the other side of the room. . . .

McDonald's on the other hand, did not appeal against any of the rulings made against them. In fact, they had conceded in writing on January 5, 1999, that the trial judge had been "correct in his conclusions." . . .

On March 31, 1999, Lord Justices Pill, May, and Keane announced their verdict on 309 pages. The controversy continued as they added to the findings already made against McDonald's. They ruled that it was a fact that McDonald's food was linked to a greater risk of heart disease and that it was fair comment to say McDonald's workers worldwide suffer poor pay and conditions.

The defendants felt that, although the battle with McDonald's was now largely won, it was important to continue to push for an outright victory and for changes in the libel laws. On July 31, 1999, they lodged a 43-point petition to the House of Lords for Leave to Appeal further. Should this petition fail they were planning to take the British government to the European Court of Human Rights. While the legal dispute continued, opposition to McDonald's did likewise—during 1999 . . . dramatic protests by local residents, French farmers, and the first unionization of a McStore in North America. On October 16, 1999, there were protests in 345 towns in 23 countries. . . . After the House of Lords, the defendants plan to take their fight to the European Court of Human Rights, where they will argue that, because they had to represent themselves and there was no jury, the whole trial was unfair and the verdict should be overturned.*

Thinking Critically

1. What was the McLibel trial all about?

2. Was it a victory or loss for McDonald's?

3. Would you have persevered the way Dave Morris and Helen Steel did?

4. Do you think, as the judge did, that McDonald's exploits children?

5. Is the global opposition to McDonald's a good thing? A bad thing?

*In February 2005, the court ruled that Morris and Steel had been denied their human rights; they should have been given legal aid to pay for appropriate representation.

José Bové, a French sheep farmer and spokesperson for a large farmer's union, la Confédération paysanne, *achieved international fame in 1999 by leading a group that dismantled a McDonald's ("McDo") under construction in a small town in France. At his trial for his involvement in this action, Bové shouted "down with junk food." Bové's opposition to McDonald's is part of his broader opposition to globalization, especially neo-liberal globalization supported by the United States and the global organizations that it dominates such as the World Trade Organization (WTO). More specifically, he is deeply opposed to the globalization of food as an industrial commodity and the threat such food poses to traditional French food and culture. McDonald's, and fast food restaurants in general, have proliferated in France in spite of that nation's association with fine cuisine. Bové's actions were designed to oppose the "McDomination" of France, as well as many other parts of the world. It was also designed to counter the growing power of multi-national corporations and global capitalism. Bové is not only defending France's food traditions and its organizations, but it distinctive identity, as well. He is a charismatic individual who has come to serve as an icon for those opposed to McDonaldization and much else about globalization.*

28

José Bové vs. McDonald's

The Making of a National Hero in the French Anti-Globalization Movement

Wayne Northcutt

"*Lutter, c'est le plaisir!*"—*José Bové*

"*Une seule chose qui bouge en France, c'est José Bové!*"—*Francis Fukuyama*

J osé Bové, a sheep farmer/activist in Aveyron in the Midi-Pyrénées region of France, is a modern day Astérix, a mythical Gaul who drubbed foreign intruders centuries ago. In Bové's case, the intruder was McDonald's, the American fast food chain (referred to in a satirical way by Bové and his

Editor's Note: From Northcutt, W. (2003), "José Bové vs. McDonald's: The Making of a National Hero in the French Anti-Globalization Movement." Used with permission.

supporters as "McDo"). On 12 August 1999 Bové and his confrères from the Confédération paysanne, the second largest farmers' union in France, "dismantled" a McDonald's under construction in Millau, a town of approximately 20,000 inhabitants on the wind swept Larzac plateau. Earlier in January 1988 he and his comrades destroyed genetically modified maize in a grain silo in Nerac in the department of Lot-et-Garonne. While he received an eight month suspended sentence for the Nerac incident, the action in Millau brought Bové, the spokesperson for the Confédération paysanne, several weeks in jail but also national and international publicity. At his trial, an estimated 40,000 people from France and around the world showed up to support Bové and his cause.

What triggered Bové's attack on McDonald's in Millau was a dispute between the United States and its World Trade Organization (WTO) supporters on one side and Europe on the other. When the WTO backed the right of the U.S. to export hormone induced beef to Europe and the Europeans resisted, the U.S. imposed heavy duties on certain luxury products as a retaliatory measure. One of the items targeted by the U.S. was Roquefort cheese—the same cheese that Bové produced on his sheep farm. According to the Canadian journalist and activist Naomi Klein, Bové's actions in Millau represented an attack "against an agricultural model that sees food purely as an industrial commodity rather than the centerpiece of national culture and family life." Bové's counter-attack made him not only a hero in France, but one of the "celebrities" at the massive Seattle, Washington, protest in December 1999, which saw more than 50,000 people demonstrating against the WTO.

The year following the dismantling of McDonald's and the Seattle protest, Bové published a best selling book, *Le Monde n'est pas une marchandise,* that discussed his *altermondialiste* views. Since the McDonald's incident Bové has become a national hero in France and leader of the French anti-globalization movement due to several factors: 1) he is charismatic, articulate, and utilizes novel and creative tactics; 2) he taps into national concerns about the quality of the food supply in France; 3) he challenges a threat to French cultural identity; 4) he speaks out against U.S.-led multinational and WTO trade policies; 5) he is an interesting personality for the media, not just in France, but around the world and especially in English-speaking countries; 6) he employs powerful symbols; and 7) the government's commando style arrest of Bové in June 2003 only strengthened his reputation as an important *altermondialiste*. An examination of these factors will reveal how a contemporary David took on several international Goliaths and transformed himself into a key spokesperson for the anti-globalization movement both inside and outside of France.

Before examining the reasons for Bové's meteoric rise, we must first consider the term "globalization" and its meaning. What is globalization? Is it a reference to a new age of easy access to information, facilitated by fax machines, cell phones, computers and the Internet, paving the way for a revolution in production, communication, and trade? Or is globalization something more, an extension of capitalist relations throughout the world made possible by the technological revolution that we are now witnessing? In this regard, does globalization represent neo-liberal economic policies and a new age of imperialism? For Bové, globalization means an extension of capitalist relations, with both positive and negative aspects. Bové is an important personality because he has raised significant questions about the process of globalization, especially the production of food and WTO trade policy.

Bové's charisma, articulate manner, and creative and novel tactics are an important part of his popularity and success in the anti-globalization movement. His charisma stems in part from his interesting background and his appearance. Although Bové was born in Bordeaux in 1953, he spent the early years of his life, 1956–1959, in Berkeley, California, where his parents were researchers in biochemistry at the University of California. Ironically, his parents later went on to become researchers at the Institut national de la recherche agronomique (INRA). His father, originally from Luxembourg, even became regional director of INRA and a member of the Académie des Sciences. José Bové began his schooling in California and claims he learned to speak English before French. When the Bové family returned to France, the young José attended a bilingual primary school on the Avenue de la Bourdonnais in Paris. Later in life, he participated in several Parisian anti-war demonstrations aimed against American involvement in Vietnam. As a young man he seemed imbued with pacifist, anti-militarist, and anarchist ideas. He began his university studies at the University of Toulouse hoping to teach philosophy. He endured university life for only one year, dropping out and becoming involved in the ecology movement and left-wing politics.

In the early 1970s, after visiting Larzac by chance with his companion Alice Monier and witnessing the first large scale demonstration in an area that has now become a symbol of protest and resistance, this budding activist knew where he wanted to live. He moved to the department of Aveyron and began his life as a sheep farmer, settling in a small hamlet with just a few families. At this point he became involved in protesting the government's plan to create a large military base in Larzac. Later, in 1987, he cofounded the Confédération paysanne. Bové's activism was international even before 1999, the year that catapulted him into the global spotlight. In 1995, for example, he participated in Greenpeace efforts to stop French nuclear testing in the South Pacific, testing re-launched by the newly elected Gaullist president Jacques Chirac.

This interesting and varied background explains, to some extent, his charisma. But part of his charisma, too, is his appearance. He dresses in simple clothes, the clothes of a farmer, and looks like the French version of Lech Walesa, the Polish labor leader who challenged the Soviet government in the 1980s. Bové has short hair and a long drooping moustache, much like Walesa himself. Moreover, Bové's ever-present pipe suggests that he is a calm, thoughtful person, a key ingredient of his charisma.

The new French Astérix is known also for his articulate manner, both in French and in English, which has contributed to his success as an activist. One of the words which he coined and uses with great frequency is "*malbouffe*" (junk food). His book, *Le Monde n'est pas une marchandise* and his public statements also reveal a man who expresses himself easily and directly. His verbal directness and ability to counter arguments supporting the WTO, the food supply, genetic modification, and other issues helped to make him a spokesperson for many in France who worry about the impact of globalization on their country. Recently, he even debated Alain Madelin, Minister of Finance and the Economy in 1995 and now head of the Démocratie libérale party, part of Chirac's Union pour la majorité présidentielle (UMP), on French television. The image of an articulate sheep farmer confronting the issue of globalization and its corporate sponsors has helped to galvanize French opinion behind this activist.

His novel and creative tactics also have won him many adherents. On the day of his trial in Millau, for instance, he arrived in an oxcart with a large wheel of Roquefort cheese aloft. He shouted to the crowd, "We shall overcome—save our Roquefort and down with junk food." Then when he emerged from the courthouse following his trial, fully handcuffed, he raised his hands above his head showing the crowd his handcuffs and beaming a large, defiant smile. This was the image of Bové that appeared on the cover of his popular book. Other tactics, too, have aided his cause. For instance, on 19 June 2002 he reported to prison at Villeneuve-lès-Maguelone near Montpellier in an unusual way. He and a group from Confédération paysanne drove a cortege of tractors from his hamlet in Aveyron to the prison, a six-hour trek by tractor. A sign on the back of the labor leader's tractor read: "Chirac en prison, Bové a la maison." The drive to prison was a media event and newspapers and the electronic media showed Bové on his tractor with his sign, an image that captured the sentiments of many critical of Chirac and the WTO. Another creative strategy came after his release from prison in August 2003, an incarceration for destroying GM (genetically modified) crops near Montpellier. When the court refused due to parole related conditions to give him permission to travel to Cancun in early September of this year to protest the agricultural policy of the WTO, Bové announced that he would organize a demonstration in France in a small village with a name that sounded very similar to "Cancun"—Cancon in the Lot-et-Garonne. The *Midi Libre*, one of the key newspapers read in the Midi-Pyrénées and the Languedoc regions, published a photograph of Bové standing before the entrance to Cancon next to the sign with the name of the village. Bové's ability to devise media-catching tactics that often embody humor if not biting satire has greatly aided his visibility in and outside of France.

With respect to tactics, Bové sees himself as a French Gandhi, using nonviolent civil disobedience to call attention to injustices. Like Gandhi, Bové realized that time spent in jail would win him more followers. For instance, the year of his trial for dismantling McDonald's, Bové declared to the press, "If prison must be the consequences of action, it will be more difficult for those with economic and financial power than for those who must go to jail." At his trial in Millau, he quoted Gandhi directly, proclaiming that "Gandhi dismantled a British installation in the cause of peaceful resistance to British rule in India. Our action was non-violent resistance by citizens . . . against American provocation." His combination of direct nonviolent civil disobedience and humor aided his rise in stature. But unlike Gandhi, Bové has something at his disposal that he has used to his advantage—the Internet. His organization, the Confédération paysanne, has its own sophisticated web site that helps to keep Internet users informed about the organization and protests scheduled against the WTO, artificial food, genetic modification, and other relevant issues.

Despite his Gandhi-like tactics, Bové proclaims that he is an anarchosyndicalist. Bové once declared, "I am an anarcho-syndicalist. I am closer to Bakunin [the Russian anarchist] than Marx. My references are the Federation of Jaurès in the First International in the last century and the Spanish CNT of 1936." While he has professed a willingness to use violence, especially against companies or corporations, this violence is not aimed specifically against individuals. According to his French biographer, Denis Pingaud, Bové is ideologically closer to Ralph Nader than Arlette Laguiller, the Trotskyite leader of the Lutte ouvrière party. Thus, his unique tactics as well as his charisma and articulate manner have contributed to transforming a sheep farmer into a folk hero in France, the Daniel Cohn-Bendit of the new millennium.

One of the main reasons for Bové's success is that he tapped into deep fears concerning the safety of the food supply in France and on the continent. These fears have grown over the years and culminated with serious concerns in the European Community as a result of dioxin found in chicken, the recall of thousands of cases of Coca-Cola, mad cow disease, and hoof and mouth disease. In attacking McDonald's in Millau, Bové focused attention on the food supply, raising concerns about hormone induced beef used by McDonald's, artificial food, and genetically modified crops like corn. For example, according to Bové: "The greatest danger that genetically modified corn represents as well as other GM crops resides in the impossibility of evaluating the long term consequences and following the effects on the environment, animals, and humans." Referring to McDonald's food as *malbouffe*, he warned the French that they must control what they eat and not simply permit a U.S.-led multinational corporation to dictate how or what a nation consumes.

Another reason for his success is that he identified and challenged a threat to French cultural identity. France is a nation that is proud of its culinary tradition. Yet today in France there are more than 750 McDonald's, a company that has led the fast food charge in the U.S., France, and around the world. Shockingly, in Paris, once considered the culinary capital of the world, one out of four restaurants is now a fast food establishment! Bové understood the way that McDonald's penetrated France and its consequences and realized that "McDomination" would continue unless protests emerged.

Today, McDonald's has approximately 28,000 restaurants worldwide and opens about 2,000 new restaurants each year. McDonald's success rests on two pillars—the company produces inexpensive food even though it may be artificial, and it produces standardized food around the world, leading consumers to think that they know what they order regardless of the locale. Uniformity in food consumption and cheap meals often desired by people with little time or inclination to cook at home worry many in France who are proud of their nation's culinary tradition. Moreover, the rise of fast food restaurants makes it difficult for aspiring restaurateurs to open an establishment and make it successful. The cheap burger, fries, and play land at McDonald's attract customers who in earlier times preferred a true restaurant experience. Food is central to French cultural identity, yet what people consume and how they consume it are changing due to fast food establishments like McDonald's and the "branding" (the selling of brands rather than products) that is so much a part of the strategy of multinational companies in the consumer culture.

Bové's success, too, is due to the fact that he, like David against Goliath, stood up to a U.S.-led multinational corporation, not to mention the WTO. McDonald's is a huge corporation, as attested to by the worldwide number of establishments noted above and also by its economic clout in the nation where it originated, the U.S. In the United States McDonald's hires one million people, more than any other public or private corporation. It is the largest purchaser of beef, pork, and potatoes and the second largest purchaser of chicken. Furthermore, the McDonald's corporation is, surprisingly, the largest owner of retail property in the world, earning a majority of its profits not from selling food but from collecting rents. It spends more money on advertising and marketing than any other brand, replacing Coca-Cola as the world's most recognized brand.

According to Eric Schlosser, author of *Fast Food Nation: The Dark Side of the All-American Meal*, McDonald's and the fast food phenomenon launched what we now know as globalization, getting an early start on the phenomenon that is now upon us. Schlosser charges that "the fast food industry has triggered the homogeneity of our [American] society. Fast food has hastened the malling of our landscape, widening the chasm between the rich and the poor, fueled an epidemic of obesity, and propelled the juggernaut of American cultural imperialism abroad." Bové expressed many of these ideas himself in leading the attack on McDonald's in France. Moreover, since the French Revolution, challenging centralized authority, whether it be national or international, has been an important part of the French political tradition.

In challenging a large U.S.-dominated multinational, Bové tapped into French fears about the consequences of corporate mergers, acquisitions, and downsizing. There is a genuine concern in France and elsewhere that the battle of the twenty-first century may not be conflict among nations, or even international terrorism, but controlling the power of corporations. According to one author, "The history of the twentieth century was dominated by the struggle against totalitarian systems of state power. The twenty-first century will no doubt be dominated by a struggle to curtail corporate power." In France over the past few decades there has been a spate of privatizations and acquisitions despite the fact that the French are accustomed to a state that owns large sectors of the economy. The former socialist government of Lionel Jospin (1997–2002) sold off more state-owned assets than the five previous governments combined. Corporate power worries the French, and Bové's attack on a key symbol of international corporate power resonated well in France because the economic landscape is quickly changing and creating economic insecurities for French citizens, including farmers.

In challenging McDonald's, Bové also challenged the power of the World Trade Organization and fueled the fires in France against globalization carried out under the authority of the WTO. For Bové, the WTO is simply an expression of corporate power, an organization designed to benefit corporations and not necessarily citizens of the world. According to Bové:

The World Trade Organization can no longer function as before. This organization is going to be obliged to reconstruct its legitimacy, becoming a democratic institution. Democracy between countries is a must. When we look at the treatment inflicted on countries in the Southern hemisphere we can easily see that all countries are not treated equally. . . . [Also necessary] is the creation of an International Court, a permanent organization to verify if the rules of the World Trade Organization conform with all of the charters, notably the United Nations' . . . or ones on bio-diversity.

Interestingly enough, Ralph Nader's organization invited Bové to attend the protest against the World Trade Organization in Seattle. Bové accepted the invitation and smuggled into the U.S. a large piece of Roquefort cheese and displayed it at a rally where he spoke, in front of a McDonald's of course. At this rally, drawing on his knowledge of American history (i.e. the Boston Tea Party), he told the crowd that McDo's *malbouffe* must be "thrown into the sea." Subsequently, demonstrators broke the windows of the McDonald's near the site where he spoke. For Bové, the WTO is a Trojan horse working on behalf of international corporate power.

In France, McDonald's is a key target for those opposed to WTO-style globalization. While polls show that a majority of French believe that globalization boosts growth, many worry that it also threatens their identity and may lead to greater inequalities. Fifteen years ago foreign ownership of French firms stood at only ten percent; today, however, more than forty percent of the shares on the French Bourse are foreign owned, nearly forty-four percent of the CAC 40 is foreign owned, and thirty-six percent of state bonds are owned by non-residents.

Another ingredient that explains Bové's rise as a national hero is that he is an interesting personality who caught the attention of the media. He makes for good television and good photojournalism, especially given his background and appearance. An articulate sheep farmer using Gandhi and Martin Luther King-like tactics to challenge the power of McDonald's, the WTO, and genetic modification conjured up a powerful image for the media. Moreover, his ability to speak English made him and his movement accessible to the English-language press, often a twenty-four-hour-a-day press constantly seeking news stories. During his trial in Millau he appeared on the cover of the *Washington Post*, and CNN even rented an apartment near the courthouse in Millau to cover his court appearance. Coverage of Bové abroad only added to the star-like quality of this experienced activist. The image of a sheep farmer taking on an American-led international corporate power and doing it with great pizzazz, followed by the publication of his book which sold more than 100,000 copies, ensured Bové folk hero status, especially since he led a movement with anti-American overtones. The fear that an American corporation was dictating French tastes in food and that the World Trade Organization favored the U.S. at the expense of

Europe and the rest of the world played well in the French electronic and print media.

He has caught the attention of the media, too, because he has employed powerful symbols in his protests. An obvious example already mentioned is McDonald's, the most recognized brand in the word. Utilizing McDonald's as a target provided Bové with access to a vast economic system, namely global corporate capitalism. Bové also has cultivated the symbol of the small farmer from *la France profonde* to promote his cause. For many, *la France profonde* is still an idyllic place that represents the "good old days" of a France now confronting numerous challenges on both the domestic and international fronts. This activist with a global focus knows, too, that sixty percent of the word's population works in agriculture. Thus, the symbol of the small farmer confronting agribusiness corporations became a key symbol of the resistance to globalization. He has used also the Roquefort cheese produced in his region as a symbol. As previously mentioned, he "cheesed it up," so to speak, at his Millau trial and at the protest in Seattle. Another powerful symbol he has employed is Larzac itself, a longtime symbol of protest that dates back to the early 1970s. Bové's original motivation for moving to Larzac sprang from the budding protest movement he found in southern Aveyron in the early 1970s. He has mastered the art of using symbols to communicate his message . . .

In conclusion, while most would agree that globalization is an irreversible trend, critics like Bové call attention to the problems that must be addressed. For instance, Bové and others claim that globalization reduces standards. Corporations that can operate anywhere in the world often seek places with the lowest environmental standards and weakest labor laws. Thus, governments often compete to entice investors with ever weakening standards. Consequently, globalization may have a negative impact on the environment and may impoverish workers. Globalization, too, strips governments of their sovereign powers. For the critics, all of this means that globalization paves the way for global capitalism. Moreover, Bové insists that the WTO is not a democratic organization since members of this body are not elected but appointed, and the organization conducts its business in secrecy. According to Bové, the WTO favors the rich nations at the expense of the poor ones.

Moreover, those supporting free trade often argue that the trickle down effects from deregulation are positive, such as reductions in poverty. The experience of NAFTA, the North American Free Trade Association between the U.S., Canada, and Mexico, suggests that there is a poor record for the labor and environmental side of the agreement. Poverty, too, has not been reduced in a country like Mexico, where fifty-three million of the one hundred million inhabitants of the nation live in poverty. Since 1994, the beginning of NAFTA,

1.7 million Mexican workers in the agricultural sector have lost their jobs, and there has been an increased concentration of wealth, with the richest ten percent of Mexicans garnering forty-six percent of the total income. It is clear that globalization needs to be monitored and the rights of citizens protected against the greed sometimes associated with global corporate power.

In France, an interesting organization has emerged that is dedicated to combating globalization and liberalization, at least the negative aspects of these trends. The organization is called ATTAC—Association for the Taxation of Financial Transactions for the Aid of Citizens. ATTAC was inspired by Viviane Forrester's *L'Horreur économique*, first published in 1996, a book that became a best seller and was translated into numerous languages. ATTAC, which has several thousand members, calls for a tax on the flow of international capital, to be used to help poor countries. Bové supports ATTAC as a way of restoring ethics and democracy to corporations.

While Bové is not completely opposed to globalization, he maintains that it must be policed to prevent corporations and shareholders addicted to profits from reducing life to mere commodities and the "logic" of market exchange. Although Bové began his protest by attacking McDonald's and genetic modification of food, he has inspired many critics to speak out against what he sees as an undemocratic globalization process. To some small degree he contributed to the moral victory of the G 21 (a grouping of poor nations that included Brazil and China) at the September 2003 meeting of the WTO, where poor nations and the rich northern hemisphere failed to agree on such matters as agricultural subsidies paid to farmers in developed nations, which stifle agriculture in the Third World. What Bové undoubtedly hopes for is to give a human face to globalization to protect citizens' rights and national sovereignty. This sheep farmer from Aveyron has inspired an international protest movement that will surely continue to demand protection for human rights, including the right to control the supply and safety of one's food.

Bové and the phenomenon that he represents are products of factors that are internal and external to France. Like a Gandhi or a Martin Luther King, he has the charisma and the skills to lead a protest movement that has taken on international dimensions. Bové and the anti-globalization movement that he represents—perhaps a new "International" according to *Le Nouvel Observateur*—show us that activism is still very much alive in the western world and that unbridled capitalism is not necessarily the end of ideology. Bové has not only succeeded in uniting *le milieu populaire*, including farmers and intellectuals; he has also raised significant questions about the functioning of multinationals, the WTO, and the safety of the food supply, especially genetically modified crops. In France, Bové represents a post-*soixante-huitard* phenomenon and perhaps the rise of a new, new left. Bové's next challenge will be to shift the discussion from the negativism implied by the anti-globalization movement to a specific debate about democracy in France and elsewhere, convincing others that "another world is possible," a theme now used by the Confédération paysanne. While he has helped to create what some are calling "the movement of movements," this is a fragmented group of dissidents who sometimes have different agendas. Nevertheless, his neo-humanism has raised important questions about global economic power that need to be addressed in France and abroad. The contradictions inherent in the current globalization process, such as WTO agricultural policy, will ensure more protests and mass movements as concerned citizens around the globe attempt to improve the human condition and control the global economic forces that we now confront.

Thinking Critically

1. Do you think McDonald's deserves to be labeled "McDo"?

2. Are you afraid of McDomination?

3. Do you think that José Bové and others exaggerate the importance of food?

4. Are you concerned about junk food and more generally a junk food culture?

5. What is industrial food? Give specific examples beyond the fast food restaurant. Does the proliferation of industrial food concern you?

McDonaldization is a global phenomenon, and global responses are required to deal with it and its excesses. One of the most important of these oppositional movements is Slow Food and a brief history of it, and its founder, Carlo Petrini, is offered by Hielke S. Van Der Muelen in the following excerpt. While it had much earlier roots, a key development in the history of Slow Food was a 1985 protest against the opening of a McDonald's restaurant near the foot of the historic Spanish Steps in Rome. Van Der Muelen details a variety of stages in the history and development of Slow Food through 2005 (and it has continued to grow and expand its activities since then). In contrast to the globalized foods offered by McDonald's (and the decline in agro-diversity that such foods encourage and accelerate), Slow Food has focused its efforts on championing local foods and more generally the local in the face of the growing power of the global. While the focus on local foods, and the local in general, has limitations in the global age, it can succeed by taking advantage of what McDonaldized systems are hard-pressed to provide: "consumer preferences for personal proximity, local identity, and different tastes." While Slow Food is important and influential, we must remember how small it is compared to not only McDonald's, but the plethora of McDonaldized businesses throughout the world.

29

The Emergence
of Slow Food

Social Entrepreneurship,
Local Foods, and the Piedmont
Gastronomy Cluster

Hielke S. Van Der Meulen

Introduction

Slow Food has developed from a group of culturally engaged youngsters in the Langhe area of Piedmont, Italy, into an international movement for the enjoyment of 'good, clean and fair' food. Over the past three decades, the movement's agenda has shifted from local quality wines toward the broader matters of food education, the protection of traditional local foods, and the

Editor's Note: From Van Der Meulen, "The Emergence of Slow Food" in W. Hulsink and H. Dons (eds.), *Pathways to High-tech Valleys and Research Triangles: Innovative Entrepreneurship, Knowledge Transfer and Cluster Formation in Europe and the United States,* pp. 225–247 (2008). Springer-Verlag. Reprinted with permission from Springer Science and Business Media.

sustainability of global food chains. Its impact has been greater than the actual number of members (80,000) may suggest. Its force is in the dedication and intelligence of the leaders, in the mobilization of their civic homebase, and in the many local volunteers whom they have inspired. The Slow Food events and publications propose eye-catching alternatives to the mainstream agri-food sector, and manage to involve people and organizations from very different backgrounds . . .

Community and Communists: 1975–1990

Slow Food started in the 1970s with cultural activities organized by a couple of friends in the town of Bra, among them Carlo Petrini, visionary food writer and now the international president of Slow Food, Piero Sardo, now president of the Slow Food Foundation for Biodiversity, and Alberto Capatti, now dean of the University of Gastronomic Science.

Without the idealism, complete dedication, and intelligence of a few people, Slow Food would just not have existed today.

The essays Petrini wrote a few years ago provide an interesting retrospect on the emergence of the movement from a local community. Remarkable are his references to the old local associations and political networks on which he and his colleagues have capitalized, to gradually set in motion a social movement and build . . . new organizations. This use of 'social capital' appears throughout the activities described below.

Petrini starts off to describe the rise and fall of the leather-tanning factories that developed in the 19th century because of cattle breeding in the nearby plains of Cuneo, in combination with a longstanding tradition of clog and slipper makers in Bra. After World War II, the market declined and in response the production of tan, one of the ingredients of the leather industry, was set up; as appropriately observed by Petrini: "The penetrating smell sticks in the nose and makes the breath heavy with the stench of rot. [. . .] But the air of Bra contained more flavours, since every year in October the main street of Bra is full of the strong smell of must that rises from the deepest of every patio and cuts through swarms of flies. The people of Bra are making their wine. They all pick a few thousand grapes, drag them down from their tiny vineyards on top of a steep slope or hidden in a chasm in the clay hills, and turn them into wine at their homes. [. . .] An agrarian economy divided over many parcels, in a village that stumbles through a stage of a still artisan and paternalistic industry."

According to Petrini this marked the situation in the early 1970s. He points out that, in addition to the industrial architecture, another cultural element was left behind: a large number of cooperatives and associations of farmers, labourers, merchants, and soldiers, which had developed since 1900. Some of them still exist today, like the Società di San Crispino e Crispiniano (clog and slipper makers), and the Società dei Contadini (vegetable growers). "Seasonal guests and Sunday tourists are already there, but the atmosphere is that of a half-sleeping and half-hearted province town, a mix of cultures from the Alps and the Po valley. Who is born here, does not have Barolo [local wine] in his blood (rather the country wine from the inner courts of the town), but does possess the necessary sensitiveness to understand how precious the heritage of wine, agriculture and commerce is [. . .] in a period when most people thought the industry of Lombardy and Piedmont could be the only motor of modern development. [. . .]." Thus, in 1980 Petrini and his friends decided to found the Libera e Benemerita Associazione Amici del Barolo (Friends of Barolo Association).

At that time the promotion of wine and gastronomy was not common in Piedmont, so they started to organize wine tastings and group meals. "The gathering at the Palazzo dei Dogi in Mira was exemplary. [. . .] Massimo Martinelli, from the Cantine Ratti wine house, told about his wines and guided the tasting, while the Brezza family, of the restaurant in Barolo with the same name, served the local cuisine. [. . .] Or the beginner wine courses to students of the technical high-school Amedeo Avogadro in Turin. Or the Week of the Barolo and the Barbaresca, held in Bra after the courses we had just followed in the Bourgogne." For many curious gourmands in search of their cultural background and reliable information, the new association was a revelation. Within three years membership grew from 3,000 to 8,000.

In Bra, after the foundation of Friends of the Barolo, a cooperative was created to promote tourism and to distribute wines and other products. As a result of this, the Osteria del Boccondivino was opened, a restaurant around which Slow Food headquarters would develop. The name Slow Food had been evoked by a protest demonstration at the opening of the first McDonald's close to the Spanish Stairs in Rome in 1985. "But the real reason behind the name was a critical attitude towards the emerging globalisation," as Petrini emphasizes. In December 1989, the international Slow Food movement was founded in Paris, in the Opéra Comique.

In 1990 Slow Food Editore (editor) launched the movement's new name in its first publication: Osterie d'Italia. This guide revolutionized the restaurant world with concepts like region, tradition, simplicity, hospitality and reasonable prices. It meant the survival of hundreds of small, traditional restaurants and their suppliers. "We want to defend the richness in agricultural food products against the deterioration of the environment, protect consumers and high-quality products, stimulate research and promote gastronomic pleasure and eating together." . . .

The popular character of the Slow Food movement is manifest in its grassroots structure. As long as it follows the main philosophy, every group of local members can start a so-called convivium, choose its board members, and decide which activities it likes to organize: charity dinners, fairs, excursions, courses, informative websites, protection of local food specialties, etc.

However much inspired by social motives, the activities of Slow Food have been contested by both left-wing colleagues and conservatives. The former accused the movement of hedonism and a lack of attention to political matters, while the established gastronomes of the Academia Italiana della Cucina refused to be involved because they feared to lose their monopoly on gastronomic knowledge and corresponding social status. So, after the initial influx of "disillusioned lefties," people from varying backgrounds started to join in, all having one interest in common: good food, in a multiple sense.

Diversification and Internationalization: 1990–2005

After guiding the Langhe economy towards 'the other tan' (from leather to wine), Slow Food has initiated many other activities, from the above-mentioned publications to education programmes and international events. In the early 1990s, the first convivia outside Italy were set up, in Germany and Switzerland. At the 1994 congress in Palermo Slow Food decided to invest money in the international development of the movement, which it continues to do. Today, Slow Food has almost 1,000 convivia in over 60 countries, which constitute the basis of virtually every event. In 1993, the 'Week of Taste' was organized at Italian primary schools.

In 1994, member education was started, which later evolved into the Master of Food programme (in 2006 involving 9,500 participants in 400 courses). 'Education through taste' workshops, starting at the Vinitaly in 1994, have become an integral part of many Slow Food events. In 2002, several projects with students from the hotel management school were started.

The year 1996 was decisive to Slow Food's image and visibility. The first Slow Food magazine (The International Herald of Tastes) was sent to the members, and the first Salone del Gusto (Salon of Taste) was held, a bi-annual fair in the Lingotto halls in Turin. Today this fair is the largest of its kind in the world, focusing on traditional and other exclusive high-quality food products. It attracts 130,000 visitors in the course of four days, including consumers as well as many food writers, scientists and representatives of NGOs and public institutions. Besides the fair, hundreds of workshops, dozens of dinner dates and a number of 'taste theatres' are offered, with an increasingly international character.

At the first Salone the 'Ark of Taste' programme was launched, demonstrating the idealism behind the hedonism. Starting in Italy, dozens of almost extinct, traditional local food products—cheeses, meat products, rare breeds, indigenous vegetable and fruit varieties—had been identified and described and were now presented to the public.

Since these products are neither backed by strong companies or consortia, nor legally protected as geographical indications, a new protection structure was designed, the so called Presidium. A Presidium is a group of local producers who agree with coordinators of Slow Food on a stringent code of practice, defining aspects like husbandry system, type of feed, minimum age of slaughtering, sustainability, etc. Presidia are often supported by local governments, area management boards, etc.

Today, there are over 250 presidia around the world, almost 200 of which are located in Italy. They are at the centre of attention at both local and international events, like Cheese, a bi-annual fair in Bra that attracts about 180,000 visitors, which was started in 1997. In 2002, the first 30 'international' (non-Italian) Presidia were presented at the fourth Salone del Gusto. The Ark & Presidia programme has changed the image of Slow Food members from hedonists to heroes, saving cultural heritage, genetic patrimony and vulnerable ecosystems. Still, the combination of pleasure and good company with rescue and education, constitutes the movement's appeal and strength.

In 2000, the international focus of Slow Food became clear at the first Slow Food Award for Biodiversity event, held in Bologna. A jury of hundreds of food journalists and other experts from countries around the world had nominated an equal number of persons who had dedicated their lives to preserving traditional local food stuffs or rare breeds, but never received due recognition, like the women of the Moroccan Amal cooperative, which produces the delicate Argan oil, saving an excellent food and a unique tree species. The media attention that went along with these recognitions triggered awareness in countries where Slow Food was unknown before.

The 'No GMO wine' campaign and the 'manifesto for the defence of rawmilk cheese' were launched in 2001 in all countries where there are Slow Food members. It increased consumer awareness about food policy, as did the USA school gardens project, also launched in 2001. In 2003, the biannual fair Aux Origines du Goût (to the origins of taste) was started by Slow Food members in the south of Italy's jealous neighbouring country, France. In 2004, the Slow Food Foundation for Biodiversity was created, with financial support from the Italian Ministry of Agriculture and the Tuscan Regional Government. The foundation manages the Ark & Presidia programme and has a leading role in Terra Madre, which is a huge event parallel to the Salone del Gusto, in which representatives of thousands of 'food communities' (local specialty producers) in the world gather in Turin to share their experiences. In 2006, a thousand cooks and hundreds of scientists from sympathizing universities were added to the programme. In 2004, 75 bachelor students from 10 countries started the bachelor programme at the University of Gastronomic Sciences (UGS), housed in the Agenzia di Pollenzo, near Bra.

Finally, in 2004, the first Slow Fish fair (annual) was held at Genoa, featuring endangered and undervalued species, like the Oosterschelde lobster (Dutch) and Cornwall pilchards (UK).

Business Dilemmas to Slow Food

The internationalization of the Slow Food movement has created at least two major dilemmas. The first is whether small-scale local food production systems can solve global problems at hand . . .

Local Foods Versus Global Problems

Some of the global problems that the leaders of Slow Food have identified as relevant to their objectives are the decrease in agro-biodiversity, loss of cultural heritage, damage to the environment, degradation of rural areas, an increase in obesity, and persisting hunger.

These problems have been addressed at press conferences, events and political lobbies. But first of all the concerns have been translated into concrete local activities, many of which pivot around local foods; in taste lessons at primary schools, Master of Food courses, fairs, excursions for the students at the UGS, etc. Thus, local foods appear as a panacea to many generic and global problems.

In order to properly address the question how much local foods can contribute to the solution of large-scale problems, first a distinction must be made between the various categories of origin food. In Anglo-Saxon countries 'local food' usually refers to unprocessed, organically grown foodstuffs sourced by restaurants, box schemes and sometimes private consumers among farmers in their own area. Such examples of 'co-production,' i.e. involving consumers in primary production, have recently been advocated more by Slow Food in part caused by the fast increase of members in Anglo-Saxon countries. Local distribution channels offer farmers opportunities to escape the price squeeze in the bulk market by adding unique experiences to the food: personal attention, farm life, countryside, etc. Increasingly, newly invented processed farmhouse products are also offered, in farm shops, delicatessen stores, tourist shops and to distributors for Christmas baskets.

These initiatives are believed to be, and promoted as, more environmentally and economically sustainable.

In Latin-European countries, by contrast, local food usually refers to traditional food stuffs with special characteristics that are linked to a well-defined area or town of origin, which will be referred to here as 'regional typical.' Some of them are embedded in strong organizations and legally protected, but many minor regional typical food products are still unprotected, like the ones in the Ark of Taste programme of Slow Food. A third category of local foods can be called 'indigenous': crops and animals which are still traditionally produced, processed and consumed by many people in poorer countries, in particular in rural areas, but which lack the wider reputation and degree of organization of the Latin-European regional typical products. This category of indigenous local foods can be divided into common, daily food stuffs (for instance the Gari from Benin) and rare specialties (for instance Moroccan Argan oil and highland coffees). The latter are usually more processed and have the potential to develop into premium regional typical products . . .

. . . [A]mple reason to be sceptical about the problem-solving capacity of local food initiatives. However, the main argument to counter the criticism of marginality is that local food networks serve as an important signal and example to the mainstream, reflecting where society is going and where the new opportunities lie. "The actual practices do not represent a simple re-proposing of old traditional productions, rather they derive from a new reading of the internal and external environment based on the needs and characters of the modern consumer." Therefore, probably the largest gains are going to be realized by actors outside the initial networks. In the same vein, conspicuous consumption of local specialty food products by upper-class people will turn local foods into 'culture goods,' making them desirable to the middle and lower classes. Thus, the largest gains will be realized by the mass of second-instance buyers.

The trend-setting potential of local-food initiatives emphasizes their emancipating role. Local, indigenous products and know-how are upgraded by the Western cultural elite, and local producers acquire greater bargaining power in the market. This argument refutes the frequently heard criticism that 'slow food' is created by an elite that is "fetishizing cultural diversity and sentimentalizing struggles for cultural or economic survival." To neutralize the criticism, Petrini prefers to call Slow Food members an 'inclusive elite.'

A further argument in favour of the local-food movement is that generic solutions to large-scale problems are usually sub-optimal. In a sense, the industrialization of the agri-food sector and the accompanying standardization of flavours have produced a vacuum in which small-scale newcomers can find 'ecological' niches by exploiting neglected resources: consumer preferences for personal proximity, local identity and different tastes.

Although local foods will never serve the masses, by definition, they do serve people in specific market segments (craft, local) and specific areas (mountains) very much. In such areas, the impact of local-food initiatives is often higher than their direct net added value, because of synergies with other economic activities, notably tourism and landscape management . . .

Thinking Critically

1. What is the Slow Food movement?

2. Does it have any chance of succeeding against global giants like McDonald's?

3. Why do you think this movement arose in Italy (and José Bové came from France) rather than in the United States?

4. Would large numbers of Americans support the Slow Food movement? Why? Why not? Would you?

5. Do you want food that is more personal, is identified with a particular locale, and tastes "different"?

PART III

Pedagogical Questions

1. Benjamin Barber suggests that the four imperatives of the McWorld theory replace the premises of the nation-states that are based on territory and political sovereignty. Are these four imperatives as influential as the theory suggests? Evaluate the standpoints of world leaders on issues such as Middle Eastern politics, global warming, and AIDS.

2. To what extent are science and technology impartial? Do science and technology that provide the means for greater public voice necessarily compel global actors to better reflect the public interest? Are innovations in technology substitutes for real change in the economic and political structures of the global world?

3. Do you think limiting McDonaldization is necessary to secure our environmental future? Why or why not?

4. To what extent does McDonaldization correlate with Americanization? Are they really distinct processes? What are their common features?

5. Is the omnipresence of U.S. consumer products, images, and sounds around the world supported by U.S. corporate, political, or military power? How discrete are their agendas? Think about the recent overseas interventions by the United States and the reconstruction efforts in these countries.

6. In what ways have credit cards changed your and your families consumption patterns? Give examples of the irrationalities of rationality in your consumption patterns caused by the introduction of credit cards.

7. Does replacement of a local restaurant with a McDonald's restaurant imply an important political and economic transformation? Why or why not?

8. What does the domination of credit cards by U.S. brands and credit card companies indicate in terms of the global economy? How does individual consumption affect global economic dependence and interdependence?

9. Could the spread of consumer culture be perceived as a reflection of neo-imperialism?

10. What is the relationship between terrorism and national and global economies? Analyze the ever-growing national security industry. Do antiterrorism measures maintain local industries that serve government goals on national security?

11. Is it likely that the Slow Food movement can resist McDonaldization? Can it be successful? Does it necessarily lead to de-McDonaldization?

12. Keeping in mind that movements such as Slow Food might be restricted to a limited group of people who have higher income levels, how realistic do you think such anti-McDonaldization efforts are?

13. Modern agribusiness uses high-tech farming methods that involve new hybrid seeds, advanced irrigation methods, chemical fertilizers, and pesticides for insect control to raise agricultural yields in poor nations. Given the fact that global agribusiness is controlled by developed countries, discuss the role of those countries in global economic development.

14. Does the authority of multinational corporations over global agricultural production replicate colonial-style patterns? Is there a possibility for poor nations to develop industries of their own and also to trade with one another? Does McDonaldization block paths to development for poor countries?

PART IV

The Debate Over
the Relationship
Between McDonaldization
and Globalization

Jan Nederveen Pieterse identified three major paradigms in theorizing the cultural aspects of globalization, specifically on the centrally important issue of whether cultures around the globe are eternally different, converging, or creating new hybrid forms out of the unique combination of global and local cultures.

Cultural Differentialism. Those who adopt this paradigm argue that there are lasting differences among cultures that are largely unaffected by globalization. This is not to say that culture is unaffected by globalization, but that at its core, a culture remains much as it has always been. In this perspective, globalization only occurs on the surface with the deep structure of cultures largely, if not totally, unaffected by it. In one image, the world is envisioned as a mosaic of largely separate cultures. More menacing is a billiard ball image, with billiard balls (representing cultures) bouncing off others (representing other cultures). This is more menacing because it indicates the possibility of dangerous and potentially catastrophic collisions among and between world cultures.

Cultural Convergence. This paradigm is based on the idea of globalization leading to increasing sameness throughout the world. Those who support this perspective see cultures changing, sometimes radically, as a result of globalization. The cultures of the world are seen as growing increasingly similar, at least to some degree and in some ways. There is a tendency to see global assimilation moving in the direction of dominant groups and societies in the world. Those who operate from this perspective focus on such things as cultural imperialism, Americanization, and McDonaldization. At a global level, McDonaldization can be seen, at least in part, as a force in cultural convergence.

Cultural Hybridization. The third paradigm emphasizes the mixing of cultures as a result of globalization and the production, out of the integration of the global and the local, of new and unique hybrid cultures that are not reducible to either the local or the global culture. From this perspective, McDonaldization may be taking place, but it leads to largely superficial changes. Much more important is the integration of McDonaldization with various local realities to produce new and distinctive hybrid forms that indicate continued heterogenization rather than homogenization. Hybridization is a very positive, even romantic, view of globalization as a profoundly creative process out of which emerges new cultural realities and continuing, if not increasing, heterogeneity in many different locales.

30

Globalization and Culture

Three Paradigms

Jan Nederveen Pieterse

This is a . . . reflection on cultural difference that argues that there are three, and only three, perspectives on cultural difference: cultural differentialism or lasting difference, cultural convergence or growing sameness, and cultural hybridization or ongoing mixing. Each of these positions involves particular theoretical precepts and as such they are paradigms. Each represents a particular politics *of difference*—as lasting and immutable, as erasable and being erased, and as mixing and in the process generating new translocal forms of difference. Each involves different subjectivities and larger perspectives. The first view, according to which cultural difference is immutable, may be the oldest perspective on cultural difference. The second, the thesis of cultural convergence, is as old as the earliest forms of universalism, as in the world religions. Both have been revived and renewed as varieties of modernism, respectively in its romantic and Enlightenment versions, while the third perspective, hybridization, refers to a postmodern sensibility of traveling culture. . . . Arguably there may be other takes on cultural difference, such as indifference, but none have the scope and depth of the three perspectives outlined here.

Clash of Civilizations

In 1993 Samuel Huntington . . . published a controversial paper in which he argued that "a crucial, indeed a central, aspect of what global politics is likely to be in the coming years . . . will be the clash of civilizations. . . . With the end of the Cold War, international politics moves out of its Western phase, and its centerpiece becomes the interaction between the West and non-Western civilizations and among non-Western civilizations."

The imagery is that of civilizational spheres as tectonic plates at whose fault lines conflict, no longer subsumed under ideology, is increasingly likely. The argument centers on Islam: the "centuries-old military interaction between the West and Islam is unlikely to decline." "Islam has bloody borders." The fault lines include Islam's borders in Europe (as in former Yugoslavia), Africa (animist or Christian cultures to the south and west), and Asia (India, China). Huntington warns against a "Confucian-Islamic military connection" that has come into being in the form of arms flows between East Asia and the Middle East. Thus "the paramount axis of world politics will be the relations between 'the West and the Rest'" and "a central focus of conflict for the immediate future will be between the West and several Islamic-Confucian states." He therefore recommends greater cooperation and unity in the West, between Europe and North America; the inclusion of Eastern Europe and Latin America in the West; cooperative relations with Russia and Japan; exploiting differences and conflicts among Confucian and Islamic states; and for the West to maintain its economic and military power to protect its interests . . .

McDonaldization

The McDonaldization thesis is a version of the recent idea of the worldwide homogenization of societies through the impact of multinational corporations.

McDonaldization is a variation on a theme: on the classical theme of universalism and its modern forms of modernization and the global spread of capitalist relations. Diffusionism, if cultural diffusion is taken as emanating from a single center (e.g., Egypt), has been a general form of this line of thinking. From the 1950s, this has been held to take the form of Americanizations. Since the 1960s, multinational corporations have been viewed as harbingers of American modernization. In Latin America in the 1970s, this effect was known as Coca-colonization. These are variations on the theme of cultural imperialism, in the form of consumerist universalism or global media influence. This line of thinking has been prominent in media studies according to which the influence of American media makes for global cultural synchronization.

Modernization and Americanization are the latest versions of westernization. If colonialism delivered Europeanization, neocolonialism under U.S. hegemony delivers Americanization. Common to both is the modernization thesis, of which Marx and Weber have been the most influential proponents. Marx's thesis was the worldwide spread of capitalism. World-system theory is a current version of this perspective. With Weber, the emphasis is on rationalization, in the form of bureaucratization and other rational social technologies. Both perspectives fall within the general framework of evolutionism, a single-track universal process of evolution through which all societies, some faster than others, are progressing—a vision of universal progress such as befits an imperial world. . . .

Hybridization: The Rhizome of Culture

Mixing has been perennial as a process but new as an imaginary. As a perspective, it differs fundamentally from the previous two paradigms. It does not build on an older theorem but opens new windows. It is fundamentally excluded from the other two paradigms.

Hybridization . . . takes as its point of departure precisely those experiences that have been banished, marginalized, tabooed in cultural differentialism. It subverts nationalism because it privileges border-crossing. It subverts identity politics such as ethnic or other claims to purity and authenticity because it starts out from the fuzziness of boundaries. If modernity stands for an ethos of order and neat separation by tight boundaries, hybridization reflects a postmodern sensibility of cut 'n' mix, transgression, subversion. It represents, in Foucault's terms, a "resurrection of subjugated knowledges" because it foregrounds those effects and experiences which modern cosmologies, whether rationalist or romantic, would not tolerate.

Hybridization goes under various aliases such as syncretism, creolization, métissage, mestizaje, crossover. Related notions are global ecumene, global localization, and local globalization. . . . Hybridization may conceal the asymmetry and unevenness in the process and the elements of mixing. Distinctions need to be made between different times, patterns, types, and styles of mixing; besides mixing carries different meanings in different cultural settings.

Hybridization occurs of course also among cultural elements and spheres *within* societies. . . .

Intercultural mingling itself is a deeply creative process not only in the present phase of accelerated globalization but stretching far back in time. Cees Hamelink notes: "The richest cultural traditions emerged at the actual meeting point of markedly different cultures, such as Sudan, Athens, the Indus Valley, and Mexico." . . .

A schematic précis of the three paradigms of cultural difference is in Table 30.1.

Table 30.1   Three Ways of Seeing Cultural Difference

Dimensions	Differentialism	Convergence	Mixing
Cosmologies	Purity	Emanation	Synthesis
Analytics	Territorial culture	Cultural centers and diffusion	Translocal culture
Lineages	Differences in language, religion, region. Caste.	Imperial and religious universalisms. Ancient "centrisms."	Cultural mixing of technologies, languages, religions.
Modern times	Romantic differentialism. Race thinking, chauvinism. Cultural relativism.	Rationalist universalism. Evolutionism. Modernization. Coca-colonization.	Métissage, hybridization, creolization, syncretism.
Present	"Clash of civilizations." Ethnic cleansing. Ethnodevelopment.	McDonaldization, Disneyfication, Barbiefication, Homogenization.	Postmodern views of culture, cultural flows, crossover, cut 'n' mix.
Futures	A mosaic of immutably different cultures and civilizations.	Global cultural homogeneity.	Open-ended ongoing mixing.

Futures

The futures evoked by these three paradigms are dramatically different. McDonaldization evokes both a triumphalist Americanism and a gloomy picture of a global "iron cage" and global cultural disenchantment. The clash of civilizations likewise offers a horizon of a world of iron, a deeply pessimistic politics of cultural division as a curse that dooms humanity to lasting conflict and rivalry; the world as an archipelago of incommunicable differences, the human dialogue as a dialogue of war, and the global ecumene as an everlasting battlefield. The political scientist Benjamin Barber in *Jihad vs. McWorld* (Chapter 25) presents the clash between these two perspectives without giving a sense of the third option, mixing. Mixing or hybridization is open-ended in terms of experience as well as in a theoretical sense. Its newness means that its ramifications over time are not predictable because it doesn't fit an existing matrix or established paradigm but itself signifies a paradigm shift.

Each paradigm represents a different politics of *multiculturalism*. Cultural differentialism translates into a policy of closure and apartheid. If outsiders are let in at all, they are preferably kept at arm's length in ghettos, reservations, or concentration zones. Cultural communities are best kept separate, as in colonial "plural society" in which communities are not supposed to mix except in the marketplace, or as in gated communities that keep themselves apart. Cultural convergence translates into a politics of assimilation with the dominant group as the cultural center of gravity. Cultural mixing refers to a politics of integration without the need to give up cultural identity while cohabitation is expected to yield new cross-cultural patterns of difference. This is a future of ongoing mixing, ever-generating new commonalities and new differences.

Each paradigm involves a different take on *globalization*. According to cultural differentialism, globalization is a surface phenomenon only: the real dynamic is regionalization, or the formation of regional blocs, which tend to correspond with civilizational clusters. Therefore, the future of globalization is interregional rivalry. According to the convergence principle, contemporary globalization is westernization or Americanization writ large, a fulfillment in installments of the classical imperial and the modernization theses. According to the mixing approach, the outcome of globalization processes is open-ended and current globalization is as much a process of easternization as of westernization, as well as of many interstitial influences.

Thinking Critically

1. In what ways are cultures of the world growing increasingly different?

2. In what ways are cultures of the world growing increasingly the same?

3. Can cultures be simultaneously growing increasingly similar and different?

4. What are cultural hybrids and are you familiar with any? If so, can you describe them?

5. Would you rather live in a world characterized by cultural differentiation, convergence, or hybridity? Why?

Malcolm Waters is a key contributor to the literature on globalization, and from that perspective, he takes issue in Chapter 31 with the idea of McDonaldization (and Americanization). First, Waters contends that I argue that globalization must be seen as homogenization. This is not true. I argue that McDonaldization implies a large degree of homogenization, but I do not equate globalization with McDonaldization. I understand that McDonaldization can be seen as a subtype of globalization and that the latter is the broader concept that encompasses, among others, both McDonaldization and Americanization (as well as Jihad). However, Water's second point is more interesting and provocative. He argues that although McDonaldization may have homogenizing effects, it also can be used in local communities in ways that are unanticipated by the forces that push it. That is, it may be used in ways that further heterogeneity rather than homogeneity.

31

McDonaldization and the Global Culture of Consumption

Malcolm Waters

On the face of it . . . Ritzer offers a persuasive case that McDonaldization is an influential globalizing flow. The imperatives of the rationalization of consumption appear to drive McDonald's and like enterprises into every corner of the globe so that all localities are assimilated. The imperatives of such rationalization are expressed neatly:

> [C]onsumption is work, it takes time and it competes with itself since choosing, hauling, maintaining and repairing the things we buy is so time-consuming that we are forced to save time on eating, drinking, sex, dressing, sleeping, exercising and relaxing. The result is that Americans have taught us to eat standing, walking, running and driving—and, above all, never to finish a meal in favour of the endless snack . . . we can now pizza, burger, fry and coffee ourselves as quickly as we can gas our autos.

. . . The globalization of "McTopia," a paradise of effortless and instantaneous consumption, is also underpinned by its democratizing effect. It

Editor's Note: Excerpts from Waters, M. (1996). "McDonaldization and the Global Culture of Consumption." *Sociale Wetenschappen*, 1996, Issue 4. Used with permission.

democratizes by de-skilling, but not merely by de-skilling McWorkers but also by de-skilling family domestic labor. The kitchen is invaded by frozen food and microwaves so that domestic cooks, usually women, can provide McDonaldized fare at home. In the process, non-cooks, usually men and children, can share the cooking. Meals can become "de-familized" (i.e., de-differentiated) insofar as all members can cook, purchase, and consume the same fatty, starchy, sugary foods. Consequently, while "America is the only country in the world where the rich eat as badly as the poor," the appeal of such "gastronomic leveling" can serve as a magnet for others elsewhere.

However, we can put in perspective the alarmist in Ritzer's neo-Weberian suggestions that globalization will lead to a homogenized common culture of consumption if we expose them to the full gamut of globalization theory. Globalization theory normally specifies that a globalized culture is chaotic rather than orderly—it is integrated and connected so that the meanings of its components are "relativized" to one another but it is not unified or centralized. The absolute globalization of culture would involve the creation of a common but hyperdifferentiated field of value, taste, and style opportunities, accessible by each individual without constraint for purposes either of self-expression or consumption. Under a globalized cultural regime, Islam would not be linked to particular territorially based communities in the Middle East, North Africa, and Asia but would be universally available across the planet and with varying degrees of "orthodoxy." Similarly, in the sphere of the political ideology, the apparently opposed political values of private property and power sharing might be combined to establish new ideologies of economic enterprise. In the sphere of consumption, cardboard hamburgers would be available not only in Pasadena but anywhere in the world, just as classical French cuisine would be available not only in Escoffier's in Paris but anywhere. A globalized culture thus admits a continuous flow of ideas, information, commitment, values, and tastes mediated through mobile individuals, symbolic tokens, and electronic simulations. Its key feature is to suggest that the world is one place not because it is homogenized but because it accepts only social differentiation and not spatial or geographical differentiation.

These flows give a globalized culture a particular shape. First, it links together previously encapsulated and formerly homogeneous cultural niches. Local developments and preferences are ineluctably shaped by similar patterns occurring in very distant locations. Second, it allows for the development of genuinely transnational cultures not linked to any particular nation-state-society, which may be either novel or syncretistic. Appadurai's increasingly influential argument about the global cultural economy identifies several of the important fields in which these developments take place.

The fields are identified by the suffix "-scape"; that is, they are globalized mental pictures of the social world perceived from the flows of cultural objects. The flows include ethnoscapes, the distribution of mobile individuals (tourists, migrants, refugees, etc.); technoscapes, the distribution of technology; finanscapes, the distribution of capital; mediascapes, the distribution of information; and ideoscapes, the distribution of political ideas and values (e.g., freedom, democracy, human rights).

McDonaldization infiltrates several of these flows, including ethnoscapes, technoscapes, finanscapes, and ideoscapes. However, its effects are by no means universally homogenizing. The dynamics that are at work center on processes of relativization, reflexivity, and localization that operate against the assumed capacity of McDonaldization to regiment consumer behavior into uniform patterns. The return of agency that many authors have identified is not simply a series of isolated and individualized coping reactions of the type advocated by Ritzer in *McDonaldization* but a generalized feature of contemporary society that arises from the intersection of these globalizing flows. Indeed, such developments might be called the dysfunctions of McDonaldization in much the way that post-Weberian organizational theorists wrote of the dysfunctions of bureaucracy . . .

The term "relativization" . . . implies that globalizing flows do not simply swamp local differences. Rather, it implies that the inhabitants of local contexts must now make sense of their lifeworlds not only by reference to embedded traditions and practices but by reference to events occurring in distant places. McDonaldization is such an intrusive, neonistic development that it implies decisions about whether to accept its modernizing and rationalizing potential or to reject it in favor of a reassertion of local products and traditions. In some instances, this may involve a reorganization of local practices to meet the challenge. If we remain at the mundane level of hamburgers to find our examples, there is a story about the introduction of McDonald's in the Philippines that can illustrate the point:

> Originally, Filipino hamburger chains marketed their product on the basis of its "Americanness." However, when McDonald's entered the field and, as it were, monopolized the symbols of "Americanness," the indigenous chains began to market their product on the basis of local taste.

The relativization effect of McDonaldization goes of course much further than this because it involves the global diffusion not only of particular products but of icons of American capitalist culture. Relativizing reactions can therefore encompass highly generalized responses to that culture, whether positive or negative.

As people increasingly become implicated in global cultural flows they also become more reflexive. . . . Participation in a global system means that one's lifeworld is determined by impersonal flows of money and expertise that are beyond one's personal or even organizational control. If European governments cannot even control the values of their currencies against speculation, then individual lifeworlds must be highly vulnerable. Aware of such risk, people constantly watch, seek information about, and consider the value of money and the validity of expertise. Modern society is therefore specifically reflexive in character. Social activity is constantly informed by flows of information and analysis that subject it to continuous revision and thereby constitute and reproduce it. "Knowing what to do" in modern society, even in such resolutely traditional contexts as kinship or child rearing, almost always involves acquiring knowledge about how to do it from books, or television programs, or expert consultations, rather than relying on habit, mimesis, or authoritative direction from elders. McDonaldization is implicated in this process precisely because it challenges the validity of habit and tradition by introducing expertly rationalized systems, especially insofar as its capacity to commercialize and to commodify has never been in doubt.

The concept of localization is connected with the notions of relativization and reflexivity. The latter imply that the residents of a local area will increasingly come to want to make conscious decisions about which values and amenities they want to stress in their communities and that these decisions will increasingly be referenced against global scapes. Localization implies a reflexive reconstruction of community in the face of the dehumanizing implications of such rationalizing and commodifying forces as McDonaldization. The activist middle classes who mobilize civic initiatives and heritage preservation associations often stand in direct opposition to the expansion of McDonaldized outlets and hark back to an often merely imagined prior golden age.

Returning to more abstract issues, these three processes can assure us that a globalized world will not be a McWorld. It is a world with the potential for the displacement of local homogeneity not by global homogeneity but by global diversity. Three developments can confirm this hopeful prognosis.

First, one of the features of Fordist mass-production systems, of which McDonaldization might be the ultimate example, is that they sought to standardize at the levels of both production and consumption. Ultimately, they failed not only because they refused to recognize that responsible and committed workers would produce more in quantity and quality than controlled and alienated ones but because markets for standardized products became saturated. The succeeding paradigm of "flexible specialization" involved flexibly contracted workers using multiple skills and computerized machinery to dovetail products to rapidly shifting market demand. So consumer products took on a new form and function. Taste became the only determinant of their utility, so it became ephemeral and subject to whim. Product demand is determined by fashion, and unfashionable products are disposable. Moreover, taste and fashion became linked to social standing as product-based classes appeared as central features of social organization.

The outcome has been a restless search by producers for niche-marketing strategies in which they can multiply product variation in order to match market demand. In many instances, this has forced a downscaling of enterprises that can maximize market sensitivity. Correspondingly, affluent consumers engage in a restless search for authenticity. The intersection of these trends implies a multiplication of products and production styles. The world is becoming an enormous bazaar as much as a consumption factory. One of the most impressive examples of consumer and producer resistance to rationalization is the French bread industry, which is as non-McDonaldized as can be. . . . Consumers and producers struggled collectively against invasions by industrialized bakers, the former to preserve the authenticity of their food, the latter to maintain independent enterprises. Bread-baking is an artisanal form of production that reproduces peasant domestic traditions. About 80 percent of baking (Ritzer's *Croissanteries* notwithstanding) is still done in small firms. The product, of course, is the envy of global, middle-class consumers.

This diversification is accelerated by an aestheticization of production. As is well known, the history of modern society involves an increasing production of mass-cultural items. For most of this century, this production has been Fordist in character, an obvious example being broadcasting by large-scale private or state TV networks to closed markets. Three key features in the current period are the deregulation of markets by the introduction of direct-satellite and broadband fiber-optic technology; the vertical disintegration of aesthetic production to produce "a transaction-rich nexus of markets linking small firms, often of one self-employed person"; and the tendency of de-differentiation of producer and consumer within emerging multimedia technologies associated with the Internet and interactive television. The implication is that a very rapidly increasing proportion of consumption is aesthetic in character, that aesthetic production is taking place within an increasingly perfectionalized market, and that these aesthetic products are decreasingly susceptible to McDonaldization. An enormous range of individualized, unpredictable, inefficient, and irrational products can be inspected simply by surfing the Internet.

The last development that can disconfirm the thesis of a homogenized global culture is the way in which globalization has released opposing forces of opinion, commitment, and interest that many observers find threatening to the fabric of society and indeed to global security. One of these is the widespread religious revivalism that is often expressed as fundamentalism. Globalization carries the discontents of modernization and postmoderniza- tion (including McDonaldization) to religious traditions that might previ- ously have remained encapsulated. . . . Religious systems are obliged to relativize themselves to these global postmodernizing trends. This relativiza- tion can involve an embracement of postmodernizing patterns, an abstract and humanistic ecumenism, but it can also take the form of a rejective search for original traditions. It is this latter that has given rise to both Islamic fun- damentalism and . . . the New Christian Right.

Globalization equally contributes to ethnic diversity. It pluralizes the world by recognizing the value of cultural niches and local abilities. Importantly, it weakens the putative [relationship] between nation and state releasing absorbed ethnic minorities and allowing the reconstitution of nations across former state boundaries. This is especially important in the context of states that are confederations of minorities. It can actually alter the mix of ethnic identities in any nation-state by virtue of the flow of economic migrants from relatively disadvantaged sectors of the globe to relatively advantaged ones. Previously homogeneous nation-states have, as a consequence, moved in the direction of multiculturalism.

Conclusion

The paradox of McDonaldization is that in seeking to control consumers it recognizes that human individuals potentially are autonomous, a feature that is notoriously lacking in "cultural dupe" or "couch potato" theories of the spread of consumer culture. As dire as they may be, fast-food restaurants only take money in return for modestly nutritious and palatable fare. They do not seek to run the lives of their customers, although they might seek to run their diets. They attract rather than coerce so that one can always choose not to enter. Indeed, advertising gives consumers the message, however dubi- ous, that they are exercising choice.

It might therefore be argued, *contra* Ritzer, that consumer culture is the source of the increased cultural effectivity that is often argued to accompany globalization and postmodernization. Insofar as we have a consumer culture, the individual is expected to exercise choice. Under such a culture, political issues and work can equally become items of consumption. A liberal-democratic political system might only be possible where there is a culture of consumption precisely because it offers the possibility of election—even if such a democracy itself tends to become McDonaldized, as leaders become the mass-mediated images of photo opportunities and juicy one-liners, and issues are drawn in starkly simplistic packages. Equally, work can no longer be expected to be a duty or a calling or even a means of creative self-expression. Choice of occupation, indeed choice of whether to work at all, can be expected increasingly to become a matter of status affiliation rather than of material advantage.

Ritzer is about right when he suggests that McDonaldization is an extension, perhaps the ultimate extension, of Fordism. However, the implication is that just as one now has a better chance of finding a Fordist factory in Russia or India than in Detroit, it should not surprise us to find that McDonaldization is penetrating the furthest corners of the globe, and there is some indication that, as far as the restaurant goes, there is stagnation if not yet decline in the homeland. McDonaldization faces post-Fordist limits and part of the crisis that these limits imply involves a transformation to a chaotic, taste- and value-driven, irrational, and possibly threatening global society. It will not be harmonious, but the price of harmony would be to accept the predominance of Christendom, or Communism, or Fordism, or McDonaldism.

This chapter, then, takes issue with the position taken by Ritzer. . . . First, there is a single globalization-localization process in which local sensibilities are aroused and exacerbated in fundamentalist forms by such modernizing flows as McDonaldization. Even in the fast-food realm, McDonaldization promotes demands for authenticity, even to the extent of the fundamentalism of vegetarianism. Second, the emerging global culture is likely to exhibit a rich level of diversity that arises out of this intersection. Globalization exposes each locality to numerous global flows so that any such locality can accommodate, to use food examples once again, not only burgers but a kaleidoscope of ethnically diverse possibilities hierarchically ordered by price and thus by the extent to which the meal has been crafted as opposed to manufactured. Thus while it is not possible to escape the ubiquity of McDonald's in one sense, the golden arches are indeed everywhere, in another it certainly is, one can simply drive by and buy either finger food from a market stall or haute cuisine at a high priced restaurant. Ritzer is not wrong then to argue that McDonaldization is a significant component of globalization. Rather, he is mistaken in assuming first that globalization must be understood as homogenization and second that McDonaldization only has homogenizing effects.

Thinking Critically

1. What is the relationship between McDonaldization and Americanization?

2. What is the relationship between McDonaldization and globalization?

3. In what ways can McDonaldization foster heterogenization?

4. What do you think of the case being made in this essay for globalization leading to increasing heterogenization?

5. Are people around the world "cultural dupes"? Have you ever been duped?

James Watson draws a number of conclusions that tend to support Waters's position and the critique of McDonaldization. Although Watson recognizes that "McDonald's has effected small but influential changes in East Asian dietary patterns," his overriding conclusion is that "East Asian consumers have quietly, and in some cases stubbornly, transformed their neighborhood McDonald's into local institutions." In other words, McDonald's is not a force, or at least a successful force, for cultural imperialism.

One of Watson's most interesting contentions is that East Asian cities are being reinvented so rapidly that it is hard even to differentiate between what is local and what is global (or foreign). That is, the global is adopted and adapted so rapidly that it becomes part of the local. Thus, many Japanese children are likely to think that Ronald McDonald is Japanese.

Watson also does not see McDonald's as a typical transnational corporation with headquarters in the first world. Rather, to him, McDonald's is more like "a federation of semiautonomous enterprises" with the result that local McDonald's are empowered to go in their own separate directions, at least to some degree. Thus, Watson offers examples of the ways in which McDonald's adapts its menu to local tastes, although he also recognizes that its basic menu remains largely the same everywhere in the world. In the same way, locals have accepted some of McDonald's "standard operating procedures," but they have also modified or rejected others. McDonald's undergoes a process of localization whereby the locals, especially young people, no longer see it as a "foreign" entity.

While Watson takes this process of localization as a positive development, I find it more worrisome from the point of view of the concern with the growing McDonaldization of the world. If McDonaldization remains a foreign presence, it is easy to identify and oppose, at least for those concerned about it. However, if it worms its way into the local culture and comes to be perceived as a local phenomenon, it becomes virtually impossible to identify and to oppose.

32

Transnationalism, Localization, and Fast Foods in East Asia

James L. Watson

Does the spread of fast food undermine the integrity of indigenous cuisines? Are food chains helping to create a homogenous, global culture better suited to the needs of a capitalist world order?

. . . We do not celebrate McDonald's as a paragon of capitalist virtue, nor do we condemn the corporation as an evil empire. Our goal is to produce ethnographic accounts of McDonald's social, political, and economic impact on five local cultures. These are not small-scale cultures under imminent threat of extinction; we are dealing with economically resilient, technologically advanced societies noted for their haute cuisines. If McDonald's can make inroads in these societies, one might be tempted to conclude, it may indeed be an irresistible force for world culinary change. But isn't another scenario possible? Have people in East Asia conspired to change McDonald's, modifying this seemingly monolithic institution to fit local conditions?

Editor's Note: From Watson, J. (ed.), *Golden Arches East, McDonald's in East Asia,* copyright © 1997 by the Board of Trustees of the Leland Stanford Junior University. All rights reserved. Used with the permission of Stanford University Press, www.sup.org

. . . The interaction process works both ways. McDonald's *has* effected small but influential changes in East Asian dietary patterns. Until the introduction of McDonald's, for example, Japanese consumers rarely, *if* ever, ate with their hands; . . . this is now an acceptable mode of dining. In Hong Kong, McDonald's has replaced traditional teahouses and street stalls as the most popular breakfast venue. And among Taiwanese youth, French fries have become a dietary staple, owing almost entirely to the influence of McDonald's.

At the same time, however, East Asian consumers have quietly, and in some cases stubbornly, transformed their neighborhood McDonald's into a local institution. In the United States, fast food may indeed imply fast consumption, but this is certainly not the case everywhere. In Beijing, Seoul, and Taipei, for instance, McDonald's restaurants are treated as leisure centers, where people can retreat from the stresses of urban life. In Hong Kong, middle school students often sit in McDonald's for hours—studying, gossiping, and picking over snacks; for them, the restaurants are the equivalent of youth clubs. . . . Suffice it to note here that McDonald's does not always call the shots.

Globalism and Local Cultures

. . . The operative term is "local culture," shorthand for the experience of everyday life as lived by ordinary people in specific localities. In using it, we attempt to capture the feelings of appropriateness, comfort, and correctness that govern the construction of personal preferences, or "tastes." Dietary patterns, attitudes toward food, and notions of what constitutes a proper meal . . . are central to the experience of everyday life and hence are integral to the maintenance of local cultures.

Readers will note . . . class, gender, and status differences, especially in relation to consumption practices. One surprise was the discovery that many McDonald's restaurants in East Asia have become sanctuaries for women who wish to avoid male-dominated settings. In Beijing and Seoul, new categories of yuppies treat McDonald's as an arena for conspicuous consumption. Anthropologists who work in such settings must pay close attention to rapid changes in consumer preferences. Twenty years ago, McDonald's catered to the children of Hong Kong's wealthy elite; the current generation of Hong Kong hyperconsumers has long since abandoned the golden arches and moved upmarket to more expensive watering holes (e.g., Planet Hollywood). Meanwhile, McDonald's has become a mainstay for working-class people, who are attracted by its low cost, convenience, and predictability.

One of our conclusions . . . is that societies in East Asia are changing as fast as cuisines—there is nothing immutable or primordial about cultural systems. In Hong Kong, for instance, it would be impossible to isolate what is specifically "local" about the cuisine, given the propensity of Hong Kong people to adopt new foods. . . . Hong Kong's cuisine, and with it Hong Kong's local culture, is a moving target. Hong Kong is the quintessential postmodern environment, where the boundaries of status, style, and taste dissolve almost as fast as they are formed. What is "in" today is "out" tomorrow.

Transnationalism and the Multilocal Corporation

It has become an academic cliché to argue that people are constantly reinventing themselves. Nevertheless, the speed of that reinvention process in places like Hong Kong, Taipei, and Seoul is so rapid that it defies description. In the realm of popular culture, it is no longer possible to distinguish between what is "local" and what is "foreign." Who is to say that Mickey Mouse is not Japanese, or that Ronald McDonald is not Chinese? To millions of children who watch Chinese television, "Uncle McDonald" (alias Ronald) is probably more familiar than the mythical characters of Chinese folklore.

We have entered here the realm of the transnational, a new field of study that focuses on the "deterritorialization" of popular culture. . . . The world economy can no longer be understood by assuming that the original producers of a commodity necessarily control its consumption. A good example is the spread of "Asian" martial arts to North and South America, fostered by Hollywood and the Hong Kong film industry. Transnationalism describes a condition by which people, commodities, and ideas literally cross—transgress—national boundaries and are not identified with a single place of origin. One of the leading theorists of this new field argues that transnational phenomena are best perceived as the building blocks of "third cultures," which are "oriented beyond national boundaries."

Transnational corporations are popularly regarded as the clearest expressions of this new adaptation, given that business operations, manufacturing, and marketing are often spread around the globe to dozens of societies.

At first glance, McDonald's would appear to be the quintessential transnational. On closer inspection, however, the company does not conform to expectations; it resembles a federation of semiautonomous enterprises. James Cantalupo, former President of McDonald's International, claims that the goal of McDonald's is to "become as much a part of the local culture as possible." He objects when "[p]eople call us a multinational. I like to call us *multilocal*," meaning that McDonald's goes to great lengths to find local suppliers and local partners whenever new branches are opened.

. . . McDonald's International retains at least a 50 percent stake in its East Asian enterprises; the other half is owned by local operators.

Modified Menus and Local Sensitivities: McDonald's Adapts

The key to McDonald's worldwide success is that people everywhere know what to expect when they pass through the Golden Arches. This does not mean, however, that the corporation has resisted change or refused to adapt when local customs require flexibility. . . . McDonald's restaurants in India serve Vegetable McNuggets and a mutton-based Maharaja Mac, innovations that are necessary in a country where Hindus do not eat beef, Muslims do not eat pork, and Jains (among others) do not eat meat of any type. In Malaysia and Singapore, McDonald's underwent rigorous inspections by Muslim clerics to ensure ritual cleanliness; the chain was rewarded with a *halal* ("clean," "acceptable") certificate, indicating the total absence of pork products.

Variations on McDonald's original, American-style menu exist in many parts of the world: chilled yogurt drinks (*ayran*) in Turkey, espresso and cold pasta in Italy, teriyaki burgers in Japan (also in Taiwan and Hong Kong), vegetarian burgers in the Netherlands, McSpagetti in the Philippines, McLaks (grilled salmon sandwich) in Norway, frankfurters and beer in Germany, McHuevo (poached egg hamburger) in Uruguay. . . .

Irrespective of local variations (espresso, McLaks) and recent additions (carrot sticks), the structure of the McDonald's menu remains essentially uniform the world over: main course burger/sandwich, fries, and a drink—overwhelmingly Coca-Cola. The keystone of this winning combination is *not*, as most observers might assume, the Big Mac or even the generic hamburger. It is the fries. The main course may vary widely (fish sandwiches in Hong Kong, vegetable burgers in Amsterdam), but the signature innovation of McDonald's—thin, elongated fries cut from russet potatoes—is ever-present and consumed with great gusto by Muslims, Jews, Christians, Buddhists, Hindus, vegetarians (now that vegetable oil is used), communists, Tories, marathoners, and armchair athletes. . . .

Conclusion: McDonaldization Versus Localization

McDonald's has become such a powerful symbol of the standardization and routinization of modern life that it has inspired a new vocabulary: McThink,

McMyth, McJobs, McSpiritually, and, of course, McDonaldization. George Ritzer, author of a popular book titled *The McDonaldization of Society* . . . treats McDonald's as the "paradigm case" of social regimentation and argues that "McDonaldization has shown every sign of being an inexorable process as it sweeps through seemingly impervious institutions and parts of the world."

Is McDonald's in fact the revolutionary, disruptive institution that theorists of cultural imperialism deem it to be? Evidence . . . could be marshaled in support of such a view but only at the risk of ignoring historical process. There is indeed an initial, "intrusive" encounter when McDonald's enters a new market—especially in an environment where American-style fast food is largely unknown to the ordinary consumer. In five cases, . . . McDonald's was treated as an exotic import—a taste of Americana—during its first few years of operation. Indeed, the company drew on this association to establish itself in foreign markets. But this initial euphoria cannot sustain a mature business.

Unlike Coca-Cola and Spam, for instance, McDonald's standard fare (the burger-and-fries combo) could not be absorbed into the preexisting cuisines of East Asia. . . . Spam quickly became an integral feature of Korean cooking in the aftermath of the Korean War; it was a recognizable form of meat that required no special preparation. Coca-Cola, too, was a relatively neutral import when first introduced to Chinese consumers. During the 1960s, villagers in rural Hong Kong treated Coke as a special beverage, reserved primarily for medicinal use. It was served most frequently as *bo ho la,* Cantonese for "boiled Cola," a tangy blend of fresh ginger and herbs served in piping hot Coke—an excellent remedy for colds. Only later was the beverage consumed by itself, first at banquets (mixed with brandy) and later for special events such as a visit by relatives. There was nothing particularly revolutionary about Coca-Cola or Spam; both products were quickly adapted to suit local needs and did not require any radical adjustments on the part of consumers.

McDonald's is something altogether different. Eating at the Golden Arches is a total experience, one that takes people out of their ordinary routines. One "goes to" a McDonald's; it does not come to the consumer, nor is it taken home . . .

From this vantage point it would appear that McDonald's may indeed have been an intrusive force, undermining the integrity of East Asian cuisines. On closer inspection, however, it is clear that consumers are not the automatons many analysts would have us believe they are. The initial encounter soon begins to fade as McDonald's loses its exotic appeal and gradually gains acceptance (or rejection) as ordinary food for busy consumers. The hamburger-fries combo becomes simply another alternative among many types of ready-made food.

The process of localization is a two-way street: It implies changes in the local culture as well as modifications in the company's standard operating procedures. Key elements of McDonald's industrialized system—queuing, self-provisioning, self-seating—have been accepted by consumers throughout East Asia. Other aspects of the industrial model have been rejected, notably those relating to time and space. In many parts of East Asia, consumers have turned their local McDonald's into leisure centers and after school clubs. The meaning of "fast" has been subverted in these settings: It refers to the *delivery* of food, not to its consumption. Resident managers have had little choice but to embrace these consumer trends and make virtues of them: "Students create a good atmosphere which is good for our business," one Hong Kong manager told me as he surveyed a sea of young people chatting, studying, and snacking in his restaurant.

The process of localization correlates closely with the maturation of a generation of local people who grew up eating at the Golden Arches. By the time the children of these original consumers enter the scene, McDonald's is no longer perceived as a foreign enterprise. Parents see it as a haven of cleanliness and predictability. For children, McDonald's represents fun, familiarity, and a place where they can choose their own food—something that may not be permitted at home.

. . . Localization is not a unilinear process that ends the same everywhere. McDonald's has become a routine, unremarkable feature of the urban landscape in Japan and Hong Kong. It is so local that many younger consumers do not know of the company's foreign origins. The process of localization has hardly begun in China, where McDonald's outlets are still treated as exotic outposts, selling a cultural experience rather than food. At this writing, it is unclear what will happen to expansion efforts in Korea; the political environment there is such that many citizens will continue to treat the Golden Arches as a symbol of American imperialism. In Taiwan, the confused, and exhilarating, pace of identity politics may well rebound on American corporations in ways as yet unseen. Irrespective of these imponderables, McDonald's is no longer dependent on the United States market for its future development. . . .

As McDonald's enters the 21st century, its multilocal strategy, like its famous double-arches logo, is being pirated by a vast array of corporations eager to emulate its success. In the end, however, McDonald's is likely to prove difficult to clone.

Thinking Critically

1. In what ways can locals transform McDonald's into local institutions?

2. In what ways is McDonaldization unaffected by local actions?

3. In what ways can localization be worrisome to those who fear McDonaldization?

4. Have you or anyone you know eaten in McDonald's in East Asia (or anywhere else in the world)? If so, in what ways was it and was it not different from eating in McDonald's in the United States?

Bryan Turner surveys the ways in which McDonald's has modified itself in order to fit into various regions of the world—Russia, Australia, Asia, and the Middle East. He demonstrates the global power and reach of McDonald's and McDonaldization. He focuses on the food and concludes that McDonald's has made major modifications in its menu in many locales. He sees this as compromising the basic McDonald's model—burgers and fries—at least as far as food is concerned. Turner's limited perspective is shaped by his view that: "At the end of the day, McDonald's simply is a burger joint." If this book has demonstrated anything, it is that McDonald's, and the process of McDonaldization that it played a key role in spawning, is far more than a burger joint. Rather, it is a structure that has served as a model for the restructuring of a wide range of social structures and social institutions in the United States and throughout the world.

33

The McDonald's Mosaic

Glocalization and Diversity

Bryan S. Turner

There is considerable ethnographic evidence that McDonald's outlets have adjusted to local circumstances by incorporating local cuisines and values into their customer services. The success of global McDonald's has been to organize and present itself as a local company, where it specifically aims to incorporate local taste and local dishes—the curry potato pie from Hong Kong, the Singapore Loveburger (grilled chicken, honey, and mustard sauce), and the Teriyaki burger (sausage patty) and the Tukbul burger with cheese for the Korean market. Let us take the Russian example. The Russian experience of Western culture in the last decade has been intensely ambiguous. The obvious seduction of Western consumerism that had begun in the 1970s continued into the early 1990s, and young people in particular rushed to embrace the latest Western consumer goods and habits. Yet unsurprisingly, the promise of a widespread democratic consumer culture has not been fulfilled. Among older Russians, there has been a growing

Editor's Note: From Turner, B., "The McDonaldization Mosaic: Globalization and Diversity," in *American Behavioral Scientist,* 47(2), copyright © 2003, reprinted with permission of Sage Publications, Inc.

nostalgia for a putative Russian "way of doing things" and a concomitant suspicion of Western cultural institutions.

In this context of disappointed ambitions and expectations, one would expect McDonald's to be an obvious target of Russian hostility. Even in Western countries themselves, McDonald's is often seen as representative of the detrimental, exploitative, and pervasive reach of global capitalism. For many critics, McDonald's exploits and poisons workers. Its culture of fast and unimaginative food is symbolic of the worst aspects of consumerism. From a Russian perspective, the characteristics of McDonald's, including its style—such as its particular forms of graphic design and its presentation of food—its emphasis on customer service and training, and its standardized global presence are decidedly Western. Russia is a society in which, as a result of its communist legacy, personal service, friendliness, and helpfulness are still corrupt bourgeois customs.

Of interest, however, Russians have a decidedly ambivalent view of McDonald's, in part because they are pragmatic in their responses to Western influences. Seventy years of Soviet rule has taught them to be judicious in their use of principle because they have learned to live with inconsistency and contradiction. McDonald's offers a surfeit of cultural contradiction because, notwithstanding the overtly Western style of McDonald's, there are also numerous forms of convergence with Russian habits and values.

First, there is the compatibility of the Fordist labor process, food process, and purchasing protocols in McDonald's with those that were developed during the Soviet period in Russia and that have continued under postcommunism. These processes and protocols, although often different in content, are consistently Fordist in form and structure. In both a McDonald's and postcommunist setting, there are clear expectations of standardized and predictable products, delivery of products, staff and their uniform dress, and consumer protocols. In both settings, production and social interaction are rule driven and steered through authoritarian decision-making processes.

Second, the formal standardized structure and method of operation of a McDonald's restaurant is underpinned by an egalitarian ethos. In particular, the egalitarian ethos in Russia has been manifested in disdain for the external trappings of a service culture (as a sign of inequality) and is currently manifested in popular contempt for the ostentatious consumption of "the new Russians." McDonald's presents its food as sustenance for the "common people." In addition, the way of eating the food, using hands rather than knives and forks, appeals to ordinary people in a country where haute cuisine has been seen as, and continues to be defined as, a form of cultural pretension. The service culture of McDonald's is based on a commitment to a formal equality between customer and service assistant.

Finally, the actual content of McDonald's food has a definite appeal to Russian taste. For example, McDonald's food, such as the buns, sauces, and even the meat, tends to be sweeter than the average European or Asian cuisine. Desserts are generally based on dairy produce and include exceedingly sweet sauces. Potato chips and fried chicken appeal to the Russian preference for food fried in saturated fat rather than food that is grilled or uncooked. Thus, although McDonald's might be seen as a harbinger of the worst of Western cultural imperialism, the pragmatic Russian will usually be prepared to frequent McDonald's restaurants because of the quality and compatibility of the food with Russian taste and the familiarity of the setting and delivery process. However, the cost of McDonald's food in Russia is prohibitive and for many is a luxury item for which the average family must save.

In Australia, by contrast, McDonald's culture is highly compatible with a society that has embraced egalitarianism to such an extent that cultural distinction is explicitly rejected in such popular expressions such as "to cut down tall poppies" and by the emphasis on mateship. Historically, the Australian food consumption has contained a high level of meat, especially lamb and beef. Dietary innovations such as replacing lard by canola resulted in a 50% cut in sales in Sydney stores. McDonald's has been particularly successful down under, where it is claimed by the *Weekend Australian* that a million Australians consume more than $4.8 million worth of burgers, fries, and drinks at the 683 McDonald's stores each day. McDonald's arrived in Australia in 1971, opening 118 stores in its first year. The company had an important impact on services in Australia, where it led the way in modernizing work practices, corporate culture, and philanthropy. Their business strategy involved the development of community and educational links through Rotary clubs and churches. McDonald's successfully survived much local criticism against American cultural imperialism and developed educational programs that have been addressed to kindergartens and schools. McDonald's built playgrounds and distributed toys. Through the development of McHappy Day, it donates generously to hospitals and charities. It also developed Ronald McDonald House Charities that in 2001 raised $2.4 million for charity. Ray Kroc's four commandments—quality, service, cleanliness, and value—have been adopted as core elements in a two-unit educational diploma that can be taken in certain Australian high schools as components of their educational experience.

Although it has been a significant commercial success and now controls 42% of the fast-food market, the high-water mark was achieved in the mid-1990s when 145 stores were opened in the space of 2 years. Sales figures have become static, customer satisfaction is declining, and McDonald's has been the subject of public criticism. McDonald's suffered economically when the Liberal Government of John Howard introduced the GST (General Sales Tax) and McDonald's hamburgers were not exempt. The result was 10% decline in sales, and they failed to achieve their target of 900 stores by the year 2000. McDonald's has responded to this decline in several ways, including the diversification of their products into McCafes and by moving up-market into Mexican-style restaurants and sandwich bars.

In Asia, McDonald's outlets have been successful in penetrating local markets. In the process, however, McDonald's products have been changing. The doctrine that societies that are connected by trade do not go to war is being tested in the case of China and Taiwan. For example, Taiwan has 341 and the People's Republic of China has 326 McDonald's restaurants. The new Chinese elite in its drive to industrialize and modernize society has accepted McDonald's outlets because McDonald's is seen to epitomize healthy food based on nutritious ingredients and scientific cooking. Although the Party is still in control and formally promotes communist ideals of loyalty and dedication, young people have adopted the Ronald McDonald backpack as a sign of modernist consumerism. McDonald's entered Taiwan in 1984, where it now sells 92 million hamburgers and 60 million McNuggets to a population of 22.2 million. McDonald's has become ubiquitous partly by adding corn soup to its regular menu once it was realized that no meal is complete without soup. McDonald's in Taiwan also abandoned its antiloitering policy once it accepted the fact that students saw the air-conditioned McDonald's as an attractive and cool venue for study. Other changes in this densely populated society followed, such as building three-storey outlets that can seat more than 250 people at a time.

South Korea is another society that enthusiastically embraced McDonald's. The first outlet was opened in Apkujong-dong in Seoul during the 1988 Olympic Games and expanded rapidly to become the second largest fast-food service retailer after Lotteria. The World Cup provided important marketing opportunities for McDonald's, and the company sought to increase its outlets, adding another 100 restaurants. The company initiated a "Player Escort" scheme to select Korean children to participate by escorting soccer players to the football dome. The current McDonald's president Kim Hyung-soo has adopted the sociological expression "glocalization" to describe the customization of McDonald's menus to satisfy the demands of local customers by developing Korean-style burgers such as Bulgogi Burger and Kimchi Burger. Another promotional strategy has been to make Internet available in its restaurants located in famous hang-out places for Korean youth, such as the ASEM mall and Shinohon.

The market in Asia is also diversifying as further Westernized commodities and lifestyles are imported. . . . The growing demand for coffee in

Asia, where it is now beginning to challenge the cultural hegemony of tea. . . . in the last 5 years, Starbucks has become as widespread as McDonald's. . . .

McDonald's has responded by creating McSnack. . . . It offers chicken and beef curry rice, bagels and English muffin sandwiches, and waffles. It also offers nine different hot and cold coffee drinks. The important feature of the coffee craze is that Korean customers expect to loiter in the outlets, which are used as meeting places and spaces for study. McDonald's staff tolerate customers who sit for hours inside the restaurant or on chairs outside hardly buying anything. During their university examinations period, students are packed into McSnack and so actual customers often find it difficult to secure a seat. Customers also bring food into McSnack from other restaurants to eat at the nice, clean, air-conditioned outlets.

These national case studies show us how McDonald's fast-food outlets interact with local cultures. Perhaps the best illustration of these local tensions is in the Middle East, where 300 McDonald's have opened, mainly following the Gulf War. McDonald's has been successful in Saudi Arabia, where McDonald's has spread rapidly, despite periodic fundamentalist boycotts, and where its stores are closed five times a day for prayers. The company now intends to open McDonald's in Afghanistan. In Turkey, McDonald's started to open branches in the 1980s in Istanbul and Ankara. Although McDonald's has expanded to around 100 outlets, almost half of these are in Istanbul. There is a McDonald's in Kayseri, the center of the Islamist vote in Istanbul. The only remarkable protest against McDonald's was held at the Middle East Technical University when it tried to open a branch there in the 1990s, but this protest came from socialists not Islamic students. Ironically, Muslim couples often use McDonald's as a place to meet because they know that their traditionalist parents would not dine there. McDonald's in Turkey also has been sensitive to Islamic norms and it offers *iftar,* an evening meal served during the Ramadan. In Egypt, McDonald's has also become popular and serves sandwiches, Egyptian boulettes, and other local items. Although Egyptian intellectuals condemn Kentucky Fried Chicken and McDonald's as examples of Western corruption of local taste and cuisine, McDonald's now exists without conflict alongside street vendors and local cafes.

McDonald's outlets have paradoxically been popular in many Muslim societies, despite strong anti-American sentiments, because parents recognize them as places where alcohol will not be served. In addition, the mildly exotic Western taste of a burger and fries is an alternative to local fare. Indonesian youth use McDonald's in the same way that Western youth gravitate toward shopping malls. With temperatures consistently in the

30°C range (90°F) and humidity often more than 80%, McDonald's is simply a convenient, clean, and cool place to be. The company has once more adapted to local taste by introducing sweet iced tea, spicy burgers, and rice. The economic crisis in early 1998 forced McDonald's to experiment with a cheaper menu as the price of burgers exploded. McDonald's customers remained with the company to consume McTime, PaNas, and Paket Nasi. For many years, McDonald's has advertised its products as *halal,* reassuring its Muslim customers that its products are religiously clean. Similar to Egyptian McDonald's, in Indonesia, a postsunset meal is offered as a "special" during Ramadan. To avoid any criticism of Americanization, McDonald's is a local business that is owned by a Muslim, whose advertising banners proclaim in Arabic that McDonald's Indonesia is fully owned by an indigenous Muslim. Proprietors also will proudly boast their Muslim status by the use of post-pilgrimage titles such as *Haji.*

Conclusions: Cultural Liquidity

These local case studies show how the rational model of McDonald's adjusts to local cultural preferences, but the result is a diminution of the original McDonald's product (the burger and fries). In fact, the more the company adjusts to local conditions, the more the appeal of the specifically American product may be lost. At the end of the day, McDonald's simply is a burger joint. Therefore, . . . we need to distinguish between specific studies of McDonald's and macro-studies of McDonaldization as rationalization. . . . The global reach of McDonald's is hardly at issue, and I have attempted to illustrate some of the complexity of that reach through several vignettes of McDonald's in Russia, Australia, the Middle East, and Asia. The spread of McDonald's clearly illustrates the fact that McDonaldization has been a powerful force behind the administrative rationalism of modern societies. With globalization, rationalization has become a global dimension of the basic social processes of any modern society. In this sense, the McDonaldization thesis is also a potent defense of the continuing relevance of Weber's general sociology of modernity.

More fundamentally, the diversification of McDonald's through its interaction with local cultures has produced new management strategies, consumer cultures, and product range that depart radically from the Fordist linearity of the original model. McDonald's is slowly disappearing under the weight of its fragmentation, differentiation, and adaptation. . . . The unstoppable march of McDonald's through urban society has come to an end.

Thinking Critically

1. Is McDonald's simply a "burger joint"?

2. Does the nature of the food served matter much from the point of view of McDonaldization?

3. What stresses and strains does McDonald's face in other national settings?

4. How do you account for the fact that McDonald's now appears to be more successful outside the U.S. than inside the U.S.?

5. Is McDonald's disappearing as a result of local adaptations?

Melissa Caldwell offers a detailed anthropological study of the ways in which McDonald's and its food have become part of local culture in Russia. On one level, Russians personalize McDonaldized public spaces (e.g., holding birthday parties in McDonald's). On another level, they bring aspects of McDonald's into their intimate, everyday lives; they "domesticate" them. Thus, they prepare foods at home that are modeled after those served in McDonald's. Caldwell sees this as evidence that Russia is not McDonaldized, but rather transforms what McDonald's brings to Russia into genuinely local products. This is localization in her view, not McDonaldization. In Pieterse terms, it is closer to cultural hybridization than cultural convergence. However, like Turner, Caldwell focuses largely on the food and not on the basic principles that lie at the base of McDonaldization.

34

Domesticating
the French Fry

McDonald's and
Consumerism in Moscow

Melissa L. Caldwell

During my yearly research trips to Moscow, I periodically visited my friend Veronika who lives in a small town several hours outside the city. Concerned that Moscow's metropolitan setting was sapping my energy and giving me an atypical view of Russian life, Veronika insisted that these visits and her home-cooked meals would both rejuvenate me and provide a more 'authentic' Russian experience. Shortly after I had arrived at Veronika's apartment in summer 2000, my hostess arranged a large bowl, electric mixer, fresh strawberries from her garden, and vanilla ice cream on her kitchen table. She explained that an acquaintance had told her about the latest craze in Moscow: the 'milk cocktail' (*molochnyi kokteil*). More commonly known as 'milkshakes' to American consumers, these milk cocktails

Editor's Note: From Caldwell, M., "Domesticating the French Fry: McDonald's and Consumerism in Moscow," in *Journal of Consumer Culture*, 4(1), 5–26, copyright © Sage Publications, Ltd. 2004. Reprinted with permission.

were introduced to Russia by McDonald's in the early 1990s. Given that I am an American and presumably experienced in such matters, Veronika asked me to do the honors. When I was done mixing, my friend called her 85-year-old father, a decorated Second World War veteran, into the kitchen to have a sample. The older man skeptically took his glass and left the room. Within minutes, he returned with an empty glass and asked for a refill.

Today, with more than 75 outlets throughout Russia, McDonald's is a prominent feature in the local landscape. In Moscow, where the majority of restaurants are located, the physical topography of city streets and pedestrian walkways is shaped by large red signs with recognizable golden arches and arrows directing pedestrians and motorists to the nearest restaurant, and local residents use McDonald's restaurants as reference points when giving directions to friends from out of town. Political demonstrators use McDonald's restaurants as landmarks for staging and dispersal areas such as during an anti-government and anti-American demonstration in early October 1998, when marchers first assembled at the McDonald's store at Dobryninskaia metro station and were then joined by additional supporters when the procession went past the outlet at Tretiakovskaia station. Muscovite acquaintances who participated in the demonstration ate lunch beforehand at the McDonald's at Dobryninskaia metro station. Whereas school groups formerly took cultural excursions to sites such as Lenin's tomb, museums and factories, today these same groups take educational tours through McDonald's restaurants and the McComplex production facilities.

Muscovites' experiences of McDonald's offer an instructive intervention into theories about the nature of globalization and the local/global tensions that social scientists have ascribed to transnational movements. Specifically, Muscovites' efforts to incorporate McDonald's into their daily lives complicate the arguments proposed by Giddens, Ritzer, Tomlinson and others that the homogenizing effects of global movements such as McDonaldization elide meaning from daily life. Instead, Muscovites have publicly affirmed and embraced McDonald's and its products as significant and meaningful elements in their social worlds. More importantly, however, Muscovites have incorporated McDonald's into the more intimate and sentimental spaces of their personal lives: family celebrations, cuisine and discourses about what it means to be Russian today. In so doing, Muscovites have drawn McDonald's into the very processes by which local cultural forms are generated, authenticated and made meaningful. It is by passing through this process of domestication that McDonald's has become localized.

In this article, I am concerned with the ways in which Russian consumers' experiences with McDonald's depart from local/global paradigms that juxtapose 'the global' with an authentic and unquestionably indigenous 'local.'

As I will describe, Russian consumers are blurring the boundaries between the global and the local, the new and the original, through a set of domesticating tactics grounded in flexible ideologies of trust, comfort and intimacy. Through the application of these principles, Russian consumers render McDonald's restaurants and food as locally constituted (and, more importantly, as locally meaningful) phenomena and not simply as transnational entities with local features or as local entities enmeshed in transnational forces. Ultimately, my task in this analysis is to explore how the 'local' itself is reinvented through processes of domestication.

This motif of 'domestication' calls attention to Russian practices of consumption that link ideas about home and intimacy with ideas about the nation. In Russia, after an initial period in the early and mid-1990s when foreign goods were valued precisely for their *foreignness*, Russian consumers have refocussed their attentions on the merits of domestically produced goods. When making selections in the marketplace, Russian shoppers consider such qualities as the cultural heritage and ethnic background of producers and their products. The appeal of the inherent *localness* of goods has only been heightened in the wake of Russia's August 1998 financial crisis, when the mass departure of transnational firms from the country not only created opportunities for domestic companies to meet market demands, but also prompted customers to support local industries for both patriotic and economic reasons. A nationwide 'Buy Russia' campaign that explicitly invoked the rhetorics of nationalism and insiderness associated with the segmentary system of *Nash* ('ours') appealed to Russian consumers to give priority to domestically produced goods.

Because the flexible discourse of Nash invokes claims of intimacy and familiarity, it incorporates both the imagined space of the nation, occasionally rendered as *otechesvennyi* (which means 'fatherland' and 'domestic industry,' also 'patriotic'), and the physical space of the home, usually rendered as *domashnii* (which means 'of the home'), or even more simply as *bytovoi* ('of daily life'). An approach that employs this dual sense of 'home' is critical for understanding the larger significance of McDonald's induction into Russian social life. At the same time that McDonald's and Muscovites' home lives intersect in intriguing and powerful ways, so that consumers are both taking McDonald's home with them and bringing their home lives to McDonald's, Russians' encounters with McDonald's also reflect their interest in nationally constituted local cultures.

More important, however, while the process of Nash typically evokes a sense of nationalist qualities, Russian consumers also use it more simply to demarcate feelings of intimacy that are not exclusively national. Specifically, the emphasis on sentimental familiarity, trust and comfort that is embodied in the Nash ideology transcends absolute distinctions between local and foreign and instead creates more abstract categories of insider and outsider. As I describe later in this article, the flexible and inclusive nature of Nash emerges clearly when Russians apply it to indicate that their relationships with foreign persons and products are intimate, ordinary and meaningful. In this sense, a consideration of domestication as a form of Nashification approximates the process by which goods and values acquire a state whereby they seem natural and ordinary. . . .

To pursue this theme of domestication, I consider . . . the specific case of McDonald's and an examination of the processes by which the company and its products have been incorporated into Muscovites' daily lives. This discussion resonates with other accounts of how transnational food corporations have entered foreign markets by simultaneously responding to local practices and cultivating new local interests oriented to the company's goals. From this discussion, I address the processes by which Muscovite consumers have encouraged and shaped the company's efforts to 'go native' and what these efforts reveal about Russian social practice. . . .

Locality, Home and Meaning in Globalization Theories

[In] the complexities of the local/global experience in Russia . . . the origins of specific goods and behaviors are often less important than the values that Russians attach to them. Even as local and foreign observers depict McDonald's as the ultimate symbol of cultural imperialism, many Russian consumers who support local businesses and commodities have transferred that support to McDonald's. As McDonald's has lost its strangeness and become familiar and comfortable, it has become, in very tangible ways, domesticated. Thus, an approach that focusses on the processes by which the local is invented and rendered familiar is more productive for understanding the case of McDonald's in Moscow. As Appadurai notes, the production of the local is a continuous process of creativity and adjustment. What this means is that although the social processes of localization may be culturally specific, the content of local culture is continually invented.

In the rest of this article, I explore the processes by which Muscovites and McDonald's have collaborated to achieve this domestication. This process of domestication is twofold and reflects the cooperative efforts of McDonald's and Russian consumers. The first section presents a more familiar narrative of how McDonald's interprets local interests and carefully responds to—or exploits—them. The second section, however, presents an alternative vision of the domestication of McDonald's in Russia. Specifically, by illustrating how Russian customers actively rework McDonald's to fit their own needs and values, this section emphasizes the agency and autonomy of Russian social actors as they engage with global processes.

From the Exotic to the Mundane: Cultivating Friendship, Intimacy, and Trust

Within consumption studies of postsocialist societies, McDonald's has emerged as a prime symbol of the processes and stakes at work in negotiations among local, regional, national and global forces. For the specific case of Russia, the foreign/local tension is particularly significant in light of McDonald's role among Russian institutions and its place within Russian culinary traditions. Throughout Russia's history, food has been both a celebrated aspect of Russian cultural, social and political life and an evocative symbol of national tastes and practices. This importance was heightened during the Soviet period when, as in other socialist states, control of the food services sector provided a key venue for articulating and implementing political philosophies and social control.

Soviet leaders linked their visions of an egalitarian communist society with the goals of producing and distributing sufficient food supplies for the population. To accomplish these tasks, authorities put the entire sphere of food services under state control; the culinary arts were standardized through the professionalization of food workers and the regulation of cuisine. Food production shifted from home kitchens and private restaurants to communal kitchens, state-owned cafeterias and food shops, workplace canteens and cafeterias run by consumers' societies. It was within this modernist vision of industrialized food services that privately owned transnational food corporations such as McDonald's first emerged.

After 14 years of negotiations with Soviet authorities, George Cohon, president of McDonald's Canada and *not* McDonald's USA—a distinction that Soviet leaders requested because of political tensions between the Soviet Union and the USA—opened Russia's first outlet in 1990. To attract new customers, the company quickly immersed itself in Russian daily life by highlighting not its novelty and foreignness, but its very ordinariness. Specifically, the company crafted itself as a place where ordinary people work and visit. . . .

More revealing, however, are McDonald's explicit efforts to position itself vis-à-vis Russians' cherished principle of Nash as a marker of trust, intimacy and sociality. First, McDonald's acknowledged the value that

Russian consumers have historically placed on social networks and concepts of collective responsibility by situating itself as a responsive member of the local community. In addition to such activities as sponsoring athletic events and donating profits to a children's oncology program, the company has collaborated with local officials to develop fire safety programs in the city and established a Russian branch of the Ronald McDonald Children's Charity Fund. On a more individual level, McDonald's directly facilitates connections among consumers. In summer 2000, displays in several restaurants invited children to join a collectors' group to exchange toys and meet new people. Children treat the statue of Ronald McDonald that is invariably to be found in each restaurant as a friend with whom they sit and visit.

McDonald's officials next responded to local ideas about health and nutrition as essential qualities of Nash products. Russian consumers articulate food preferences through evaluations of the purity and healthiness of particular foods. Many Russians initially found the anonymity and technological regulation of McDonald's austere and sterile kitchen facilities, as well as the mass manufacture of foodstuffs, unnatural and disquieting. . . .

In contrast, Russians determine the healthiness and authenticity of foods according to where they are produced and by whom. More specifically, consumers privilege fruits and vegetables that are grown on farms in the Russian countryside or in gardens at private summer cottages (*dachas*) and then collected or prepared by friends or relatives. . . .

In their responses to these local preferences, McDonald's executives have joined other Russian companies in promoting the local origins of their produce. Using billboards, signs on the sides of freight trucks and tray liners, McDonald's advertises its contract with a Russian agricultural corporation whose name explicitly invokes the symbolic power of the Russian countryside and personal gardening, *Belaia dacha* ('white cottage'). McDonald's thus reassures customers not only that its produce is Russian-grown, but also that it meets 'the standards accepted by the Russian Federation' and that it uses 'only the highest quality meat without additives and fillers.' . . .

McDonald's efforts to cultivate a sense of trust among Moscow consumers emerged most visibly when the company explicitly appropriated the rhetoric of Nash. . . .

McDonald's had begun invoking the rhetoric of Nash in posters that reminded consumers that the company was 'Our McDonald's' (*Nash Makdonalds*). This move enabled McDonald's to position itself within the parameters of the imagined—and, more importantly, *trusted*—collectivity to which its Muscovite customers belonged. Moreover, McDonald's claimed status as a local entity by cultivating . . . the essential features of local culture. . . .

. . . Russians are autonomous social actors who themselves encourage, accept, shape and discipline this sense of familiarity and intimacy. . . . As the Russian McDonald's case illustrates, this process is one that Russian consumers are actively producing and fashioning. In the next section, I turn to a discussion of how Muscovites express their autonomy by creatively incorporating McDonald's into their most intimate and personal activities: their home lives.

Feeling at Home: McDonald's as Comfort Food

Initially, Muscovites' relationship with McDonald's was framed through themes of novelty and exoticness. . . .

. . . For many Muscovites, McDonald's has become so ordinary that it is no longer culturally marked. This shift to invisibility emerged vividly in conversations with schoolchildren and college students about what constituted Russian foods. Intriguingly, in their responses, students often included transnational foods such as McDonald's and Coca-Cola. When asked why they had included these items as 'Russian,' students typically replied that they simply took them for granted and did not contemplate their origins.

Another example that illustrates this process of domestication is the extent to which Russian consumers have accepted, and even facilitated, the inclusion of McDonald's foods in Russian cuisine. . . . Despite a long culinary history, however, Muscovites' food practices are changing as imported foods become more available. As one young woman observed: 'In Moscow it is impossible to distinguish between Russian and foreign foods because they are so mixed.' A specific example of these changes is evident in the 'milkshake craze' that my friend Veronika described when we prepared milkshakes at her home. By the end of the 1990s, milkshakes were available in both fast-food and high-end restaurants throughout Moscow as well as at temporary sidewalk food stalls. Even vendors in the lobbies of Moscow's finest theaters and opera houses had added fresh milkshakes to their more typical intermission offerings of elegant chocolates, open-faced sandwiches topped with smoked fish and caviar, and champagne. Russian restaurant owners now provide French fries with their main courses, and vendors at walk-up sidewalk stands include, among the usual assortment of candy bars, chips and nuts, Russian-made knock-offs named *Big mak* and *gamburgr roial* (as Quarterpounders are called in Russia).

Nevertheless, these examples point only to the spread of foods inspired by McDonald's throughout the commercial sphere. What is more intriguing is the extent to which Muscovites have incorporated McDonald's into their 'home cooking' (*domashchnaia pishcha*), a domain that Muscovites consider uniquely Russian. . . .

What was particularly instructive about . . . insistence that foods prepared at home are authentically Russian was that their repertoires of Russian cuisine included imitations of McDonald's foods. Like several middle-aged mothers I interviewed, my landlady Anya periodically attempts to make hamburgers at home to please her children and grandchildren, who want to eat at McDonald's, but are unable, owing to cost or time constraints, to do so. In some cases, cooks have resorted to highly creative culinary reinventions such as the meal described by one of my students. When the student's sister studied in Moscow, her host family offered to make McDonald's hamburgers at home. The promised meal turned out to be fried cabbage between two pieces of bread.

More revealing, however, were the responses I received from schoolchildren . . . four out of nine children independently depicted Russian-style fried potatoes (*zharennye kartoshki*), a staple in most families' meals, in recognizable McDonald's French fry boxes. In a similarly illuminating incident at a birthday party I attended, the guest of honor, a friend's four-year-old daughter who loved French fries, could barely contain her excitement at the news that we would have fried potatoes for dinner. When she was presented with the homemade French fries, however, she took one look at them and shrieked in horror: 'But they're not McDonald's!'

Collectively, these transformations in local food habits reveal that Muscovites have effectively turned the tables on McDonald's and transformed it not simply into something that is familiar and ordinary, but into something that is authentically indigenous as well as desirable and personally meaningful. More significantly, as the comments and actions of the schoolchildren whom I interviewed illustrate, McDonald's has become the local standard against which Russians' own food practices are measured. In this respect, as McDonald's has been more fully domesticated, it has lost its distinctiveness as something alien and visible and has instead become part of everyday life.

The routinization and habituation of McDonald's into the most ordinary and intimate aspects of Muscovites' daily lives are most vivid within the context of negotiations over the parameters of both domestic and domesticated space. As illustrated in the previous section, Muscovites are taking aspects of McDonald's into their homes. Yet, more and more, they are also taking their home lives into McDonald's, a practice that Muscovite employees facilitate by rarely limiting the amount of time that customers spend in the restaurants. For individuals without accommodation, such as visitors to the city and homeless persons, McDonald's serves as a surrogate home. I have frequently observed visitors using the bathrooms to bathe themselves and to wash out their clothes and dishes. Street children also find the restaurants to be safe havens. The store managers of a central Moscow McDonald's allow these children to sit at the tables and eat food that has been left on diners' trays. On one occasion, I watched as the store manager engaged several homeless children in friendly conversation and offered to help them with their problems. Even Muscovites who have apartments and jobs nearby elect to go to McDonald's to sit and enjoy their homemade lunches (and sometimes even a bottle of beer or two) that they have brought with them into the restaurant.

Other Muscovites have transferred their social lives to McDonald's. Instead of gathering for meals at someone's home, as was a more usual practice during Soviet days when meals in private kitchens were more cost-effective and safe from the prying eyes of others, friends, relatives and colleagues now meet at McDonald's to socialize or conduct business. . . . During interviews that I conducted with a group of schoolchildren who lived several hours away from Moscow (and the nearest McDonald's), the students excitedly described how frequently they traveled to the city with their friends simply to have dinner at McDonald's. Similarly, several college students confessed that before they had come to Moscow to study, they were unfamiliar with McDonald's. After spending a few months in the city, however, they had quickly begun congregating at McDonald's with their friends for late night meals and conversations.

Birthday parties, which Muscovites generally observe at home or at the family cottage, now represent the most obvious example of these efforts to refashion McDonald's as a domestic and socially significant space. Brightly colored posters and flyers invite children to celebrate their birthdays with a formal party organized and hosted by McDonald's staff. Such events occur regularly throughout the city and, on weekends, the restaurants are often busy with multiple parties taking place simultaneously. . . . Muscovites with more limited resources organize their own birthday parties at McDonald's. I sat near one such party and watched as a group of children chatted and played together at a table that their parents had decorated themselves. The parents first delivered their food orders from the counter and later divided a cake and other sweets that they had brought with them from home. . . .

As a place invested with meaning, value, delight and, more importantly, heightened sociality, McDonald's is an intrinsically and authentically local space.

The Domestic Other: Creating the New Local

In many ways, Muscovites' experiences with McDonald's appear to resonate with the premises underlying the McDonaldization thesis: that the routinizing nature of McDonald's facilitates its insinuation into the organization and regulation of daily life and that McDonald's inherent rationality replaces indigenous, and hence more authentic, meaning with its own set of values and practices. At this point in time, however, it is impossible to predict whether complete McDonaldization will eventually be achieved in Russia. Yet preliminary comparison of McDonald's with other food transnationals in Moscow suggests that, as of now, McDonald's has not yet achieved the same degrees of rationality in Muscovites' everyday lives.

Specifically, we can look to the spread of coffee shops and sushi bars (sometimes coexisting in the same café) across Moscow during the past three years. There is an obvious sameness particularly among Russian coffee shops, as managers educate their clientele as to proper (i.e., American-style) coffee etiquette and tastes. The manager of one coffee shop boasted that his goal was to turn his Russian patrons into American coffee connoisseurs. Muscovite consumers have visibly adapted themselves to these changes by substituting cappuccinos and espressos for their more usual afternoon teas or instant coffees and by learning to debate the subtleties of muffins, bagels and other American pastries. Most noticeable is the change in social relations that has accompanied these shifts: previously, afternoon tea was a social occasion when co-workers would stop working for a few moments to sit and socialize with each other. In Moscow's coffee shops, however, it is common to see individuals sitting alone and working on school or work projects while drinking a cup of coffee. In contrast, even as Muscovites treat coffee shops as impersonal and generic settings, they continue to approach McDonald's as a trusted social space where they gather with friends and relax. More importantly, Muscovites are actively manipulating McDonald's by refashioning the eating experience to reflect their own ideas of what constitutes private space and personally meaningful activities. Hence, at this stage, McDonald's has not yet reached the same degree of homogeneity as that pursued and promoted by its competitors.

I have grounded my analysis in an ethnographic perspective, that proposes that Muscovites are autonomous social agents—even when their choices are constrained by external forces. Thus, by focussing on Muscovite consumers as individuals who actively engage with the institutions and forces with which they coexist, I have drawn attention to the ways in which Muscovites produce and enact the domesticating process of Nash. Although Muscovites may in some ways be complicit partners with McDonald's in this process, it is ultimately these consumers who set the indigenous standards that McDonald's must exploit and satisfy. Finally, because my intent in this article was to highlight the ways in which Muscovites are finding and making meanings within new cultural systems, a focus on the domesticating process of Nash as a particular form of localization calls attention to the ways in which Muscovites do not simply appropriate and refashion foreign elements as familiar and special, as happens in processes of glocalization, but rather reorient their attitudes, feelings and affections in order to experience and know the foreign as something mundane and, hence, part of the local landscape. Despite the power of McDonald's to position itself as local, Muscovites are the final arbiters of this distinction.

In this article, I have suggested that the uniqueness of the McDonald's experience in Russia is evident in the ways that consumers affirm its place in local culture not simply by embracing it as just another part of the ordinary routines of daily life, but more accurately by taking it for granted. For many Muscovites, McDonald's has become . . . 'invisible.' Furthermore, at the same time as Muscovite consumers have accepted McDonald's as a local and personally meaningful experience, they have privileged it over other, more visibly foreign and uncomfortable, experiences. This quality of domestication emerged clearly when two Muscovite friends, a young middle-class married couple, recounted their driving vacation across the USA. Vera commented that because she and her husband were comfortable with the service and food at the McDonald's near their home in Moscow, they stopped at a McDonald's restaurant along an American interstate, but were surprised to find dirty facilities. They were even more astonished, she added, to discover that the food in the American McDonald's was not as tasty as that in Russia. Ultimately, Vera and her husband decided not to visit another McDonald's while they were on vacation, but to wait until they returned to Russia. As Vera noted, the McDonald's restaurants in Moscow were familiar and trustworthy and thus distinct from their North American prototypes.

By extending values of trust and intimacy to McDonald's, not only are Russian consumers reworking local understandings of such fundamental concepts as the private and the public, the domestic and the foreign, the personal and the popular, but they are also setting the standards that McDonald's must meet in order to flourish. McDonald's is more than a localized or a glocalized entity in Russia. By undergoing a specifically Russian process of localization—Nashification—it has become a locally meaningful, and hence domesticated, entity.

Thinking Critically

1. From the point of view of McDonaldization, how do you interpret the tendency for Russians to have children's birthday parties at McDonald's?

2. From the point of view of McDonaldization, how do you interpret the tendency for Russians to prepare food (e.g., milkshakes) at home modeled after that at McDonald's?

3. Is all of this evidence of localization? Or a deeper level of McDonaldization?

4. How did fast food become "comfort food" for Russians?

5. Should critics of McDonaldization rejoice or be more fearful because of the fact that it has become "invisible" in Russia?

Uri Ram offers an interesting case study of McDonald's in Israel. Although McDonald's has been successful, it has not destroyed the local falafel industry. Rather, part of that business has McDonaldized, while another has been "gourmetized." Depicted is a complex mix of the global and the local rather than one winning over the other. Ram puts this in the context of the debate between one-way (e.g., McDonaldization, although now that process is multidirectional and not just running from the United States to the rest of the world) and two-way (Appadurai's landscapes) models of globalization. Ram responds creatively that both approaches are correct but on different levels. Structurally (and this resembles Bryman's view on systems), he sees a one-way model predominate, but, symbolically, it is a two-way street. So, much of the falafel industry in Israel has been transformed structurally into an industrial-standardized system—a McDonaldized system. Symbolically, a two-way system is operant with the falafel and the McDonald's hamburger coexisting and mutually affecting one another. Thus, although Israel is characterized by a structural uniformity, symbolically, Israel remains different from other societies, including the United States. However, Ram seems to betray this perspective by arguing that Israeli differences have only "managed to linger on." Such phrasing seems to indicate that even to Ram, symbolic differences, like structural differences, are likely to disappear leading to increasing McDonaldization in both realms.

35

Glocommodification

How the Global Consumes the Local—McDonald's in Israel

Uri Ram

O ne of the more controversial aspects of globalization is its cultural
implications: does globalization lead to universal cultural uniformity,
or does it leave room for particularism and cultural diversity? The global-
local encounter has spawned a complex polemic between 'homogenizers'
and 'heterogenizers.' This article proposes to shift the ground of the debate
from the homogeneous-heterogeneous dichotomy to a structural-symbolic
construct. It is argued here that while both homogenization and heteroge-
nizations are dimensions of globalization, they take place at different societal levels: homogenization occurs at the structural-institutional level;
heterogenization, at the expressive-symbolic. The proposed structural-
symbolic model facilitates a realistic assessment of global-local relations. In
this view, while global technological, organizational and commercial flows

Editor's Note: From Ram, U., "Glocommodification: How the Global Consumes
the Local McDonald's in Israel," in *Current Sociology*, 52(1), 11–31, Sage
Publications, 2004, © International Sociological Association/ISA. Reprinted with
permission.

need not destroy local habits and customs, but, indeed, may preserve or even revive them, the global does tend to subsume and appropriate the local, or to consume it, so to say, sometimes to the extent that the seemingly local, symbolically, becomes a specimen of the global, structurally.

The starting point for this analysis is the McDonaldization of Israeli culture. McDonald's opened its first outlet in Israel in 1993. Since then, it has been involved in a variety of symbolic encounters . . . the encounter between McDonald's, as the epitome of global fast food, and the local version of fast food, namely the falafel . . . local idioms have thrived, though only symbolically. On the structural level, they have been subsumed and appropriated by global social relationships.

Global Commerce Encounters the Local Eating Habitus: McDonald's and the Falafel

The industrialized hamburger first arrived on Israel's shores back in the late 1960s, although the chains involved at the time did not make much of an impression. In 1972, Burger Ranch (BR) opened a local hamburger joint that expanded into a chain only in the 1980s. It took the advent of McDonald's, however, for the 'great gluttony' of the fast hamburger to begin. McDonald's opened its first branch in October 1993. It was followed by Burger King (BK), the world's second largest hamburger chain, which opened its first branch in Israel in early 1994. Between McDonald's arrival and the year 2000, sales in the hamburger industry soared by 600 percent. By 2000, annual revenues from fast-food chains in Israel reached NIS 1 billion (about US$200 million according to the 2002 exchange rate). McDonald's is the leading chain in the industry, with 50 percent of the sales, followed by BR with 32 percent, and BK with 18 percent. In 2002 the three chains had a total of 250 branches in place: McDonald's, 100; BR, 94; and BK, 56.

McDonald's, like Coca-Cola—both flagship American brands— conquered front-line positions in the war over the Israeli consumer. The same is true of many other American styles and brands, such as jeans, T-shirts, Nike and Reebok footwear, as well as mega-stores, such as Home Center, Office Depot, Super-Pharm, etc. . . . As for eating habits, apart from the spread of fast-food chains, other Americanisms have found a growing niche in the Israeli market: frozen 'TV dinners,' whether in family or individual packs, and an upsurge in fast-food deliveries. These developments stem from the transformation of the familial lifestyle as an increasing number of women are no longer (or not only) housewives, the growth of singles households, and the rise in family incomes. All this, along with accelerated economic activity, has raised the demand for fast or easy-to-prepare foods. As has happened elsewhere, technological advancements and business interests have set the stage for changes in Israeli eating habits. Another typical development has been the mirror process that accompanies the expansion of standardized fast foods, namely, the proliferation of particularist cuisines and ethnic foods as evinced by the sprouting of restaurants that cater to the culinary curiosity and open purses of a new Yuppie class in Tel Aviv, Herzliya and elsewhere.

As in other countries, the 'arrival' of McDonald's in Israel raised questions and even concern about the survival of the local national culture. A common complaint against McDonald's is that it impinges on local cultures, as manifested primarily in the local eating habitus both actual and symbolic. If Israel ever had a distinct national equivalent to fast food, it was unquestionably the falafel—fried chick-pea balls served in a 'pocket' of pita bread with vegetable salad and tahini (sesame) sauce. The falafel, a Mediterranean delicacy of Egyptian origin, was adopted in Israel as its 'national food.' Although in the 1930s and 1940s the falafel was primarily eaten by the young and impecunious, in the 1950s and 1960s a family visit to the falafel stand for a fast, hot bite became common practice, much like the visit paid nowadays to McDonald's. The falafel even became an Israeli tourist symbol, served as a national dish at formal receptions of the Ministry of Foreign Affairs. Indeed, one kiosk in Tel Aviv advertises itself as a "'mighty' falafel for a mighty people."

Despite the falafel's fall from glory in the 1970s and 1980s vis-à-vis other fast foods, such as *shawarma* (lamb or turkey pieces on a spit), pizza and the early hamburger stands, and notwithstanding the unwholesome reputation it developed, an estimated 1200 falafel eateries currently operate in Israel. Altogether, they dish up about 200,000 portions a day to the 62 percent of Israelis who are self-confessed falafel eaters. The annual industry turnover is some NIS 600 million—not that far short of the hamburger industry. Thus, surprisingly enough, in the late 1990s, McDonald's presence, or rather the general McDonaldization of Israeli food habits, led to the falafel's renaissance, rather than to its demise.

The falafel's comeback, vintage 2000, is available in two forms: gourmet and fast-food. The clean, refined, gourmet Tel-Avivian specimen targets mainly yuppies and was launched in 1999—five years after McDonald's landed in the country—in a prestigious restaurant owned by two women, famed as Orna and Ella. Located in the financial district, which is swiftly being gentrified, it is known as 'The Falafel Queens'—a hip, ironic feminist version of the well-known 'Falafel King'—one of the most popular designations for Israeli falafel joints, which always take the masculine form. The new, 'improved' gourmet model comes in a variety of flavors. Apart from the traditional 'brown' variety, the Queens offer an original 'red' falafel, based on roasted peppers, as well as 'green' falafel, based on olive paste. Beverages are a mixed bag, including orange-Campari and grapefruit-arrack ice. Owner Ella Shein rightly notes that the falafel's revival reflects a composite global-local trend:

> We have opened up to the world culinarily speaking, we have been exposed to new raw materials, new techniques, a process that occurs simultaneously with a kind of return to one's origins, to one's roots.

Apart from its 'gourmetization,' the falafel has simultaneously undergone 'McDonaldized' standardization. The Israeli franchise of Domino's Pizza inaugurated a new falafel chain, setting itself a nationwide target of 60 branches. Furthermore, its reported intention is to 'take the tidings of Israeli fast-food abroad.' The falafel has thus been rescued from parochialism and upgraded to a world standard-bearer of 'Israeli fast food,' or, as one observer put it, it has been transformed from 'grub' into 'brand.' In fact, the Ma'oz chain already operates 12 falafel eateries in Amsterdam, Paris and Barcelona and, lately, also in Israel. The new chains have developed a 'concept' of 'clean, fresh, and healthy,' with global implications, because: 'if you are handed an inferior product at "Ma'oz" in Amsterdam, you won't set foot in the Paris branch' either. In contrast to the traditional falafel stand, which stands in the street and absorbs street fumes and filth, the new falafel is served indoors, at spruce, air-conditioned outlets, where portions are wrapped in designer bags and sauces flow out of stylized fountains. At Falafels, the balls are not moulded manually, but dispensed by a mechanical implement at the rate of 80 balls/minute. There are two kinds—the Syrian Zafur and the Turkish Baladi. And as befits an industrial commodity, the new falafel is 'engineered' by food technicians and subjected to tastings by focus groups.

Like any self-respecting post-Fordist commodity, the falafel of the new chains is not only a matter of matter but, as stated above, of concept or, more precisely, of fantasy, rendering the past as nostalgia or retro. Branches are designed in a nostalgic style—in order to evoke yearning within the primary target sector—and they carry, in the name of 'retro,' old-fashioned soda pops. This is the local Israeli habitus dusted off, 'branded' and 'designed' so as to be marketed as a mass standardized commodity. Another trendy aspect of the new falafel is its linkage to the new discourses on the environment or nutrition. The proprietor of Ma'oz notes that 'salads, tehini, and falafel are healthy foods, and we have taken the health issue further by offering also whole-wheat pita bread. The health issue is becoming so central that we are now considering establishing a falafel branch that would serve only organic vegetables.' To sum up, the distinction between the old falafel and the new, post-McDonald's falafel, is identified in a local newspaper report as follows:

> If in the past every Falafel King took pride in the unique taste [of his own product, the secret of] which was sometimes passed down from father to son, and which acquired a reputation that attracted customers from far and wide, in the [new] chains, the taste would always be the same. Uniqueness and authenticity would be lost for the sake of quality and free market rules.

One major change is Israel's culinary habitus as a result of its McDonaldization, therefore, is the demise of the old 'authentic' falafel and the appearance of the new commodified 'falafel 2000.'

But McDonald's had to surmount another—no less challenging—culinary hurdle: the Israeli carnivorous palate. . . . Given this hankering for meat, especially of the grilled variety, the McDonald's hamburger appeared rather puny, and the Israeli consumer tended to favour the Burger King broiled product. In 1998, McDonald's bowed to the Israeli appetite, changing both the preparation and size of its hamburger. It shifted to a combined technique of fire and charcoal, and increased portion size by 25 percent. The Israeli customer now has the distinction of being served the largest hamburger (120 grams) marketed by McDonald's worldwide. But the most striking fast-food modification to the Israeli habitus is the 'Combina' (the Hebrew equivalent of 'combo'), launched in 2001 by Burger Ranch—a packaged meal for four eaters that taps into the local custom of 'sharing' and, to quote the marketing blurb, allows for 'a group experience while retaining individual dining expression.'

It may thus be concluded that the interrelations of McDonald's and the falafel are not simply a contrast between local decline and global rise. Rather, they are a complex mix, though certainly under the banner of the global. Indeed, the global (McDonald's) contributed somewhat to the revival of the local (the falafel). In the process, however, the global also transformed the nature and meaning of the local. The local, in turn, caused a slight modification in the taste and size of the global, while leaving its basic institutional patterns and organizational practices intact. The 'new falafel' is a component of both a mass-standardized consumer market, on the one hand, and a post-modern consumer market niche, on the other. This sort of relationship between McDonald's and the falafel, in which the global does not eliminate the local symbolically but rather restructures or appropriates it structurally, is typical of the global-local interrelations epitomized by McDonald's.

Discussion I: 'One-Way' or 'Two-Way'?

Based on this case analysis, how, then, are we to conceive the relations between global commerce and local idioms?

The literature on relations between the global and the local presents a myriad of cases. Heuristically, the lessons from these may be condensed into two competing—contrasting, almost—approaches: the one gives more weight to globalization, which it regards as fostering cultural uniformity (or homogeneity); the other gives more weight to localization, which it regards as preserving cultural plurality, or cultural 'differences' (or heterogeneity) . . . the former is known also as cultural imperialism and McDonaldization, . . . The latter is known also as hybridization. . . . For the sake of simplicity we shall call the former the 'one-way' approach, i.e., seeing the effect as emanating from the global to the local; and the latter, as the 'two-way' approach, i.e., seeing the effect as an interchange between the global and the local.

The most prominent exponent of the one-way approach is George Ritzer, in his book *The McDonaldization of Society*. Ritzer, more than anyone else, is responsible for the term that describes the social process of McDonaldization. . . .

Contrary to this one-way approach . . . the literature offers another view, which we call here the two-way approach. This view considers globalization only a single vector in two-way traffic, the other vector being localization. The latter suspends, refines, or diffuses the intakes from the former, so that traditional and local cultures do not dissolve; they rather ingest global flows and reshape them in the digestion.

Arjun Appadurai, for one, asserts that it is impossible to think of the processes of cultural globalization in terms of mechanical flow from center to periphery. Their complexity and disjunctures allow for a chaotic contest between the global and the local that is never resolved. . . .

One typical significant omission of the two-way perspective is its disregard for imbalances of power. . . . Positing 'localization' as a counterbalance to globalization, rather than as an offshoot, some of the cultural studies literature is indeed rich in texture and subtlety when depicting the encounters of global commerce with local popular cultures and everyday life. This literature is at its best when acknowledging that its task is to 'twist the stick in the other direction,' from the top-down political-economic perspective to a bottom-up cultural perspective. It falters, however, when it attempts to replace, wholesale, the top-down approach with a bottom-up one, without weighting the relative power of the top and the bottom.

The latter move is evident in an ethnographic study of McDonaldization conducted in Southeast Asia by a team of anthropologists [Chapter 32].

They argue overall that even though McDonald's transformed local customs, customers were nonetheless able to transform McDonald's in their areas into local establishments; this led them to conclude that McDonald's does not always call the shots. They claim that, in the realm of popular culture, it is no longer possible to distinguish between the 'local' and the 'external.' Who, they protest, is to say whether or not Mickey Mouse is Japanese, or Ronald McDonald, Chinese; perhaps, this attests to a 'third culture' that belongs neither to one nationality nor the other, but constitutes rather a transnational culture.

This ethnographic discussion stresses the variety of supplemental dishes McDonald's has included on its menu in order to accommodate various local cultures. Applying this approach to our case study, the new falafel, for instance, can be considered a manifestation of . . . hybridization of McDonald's. The new falafel assimilated some of McDonald's practices, but accommodated them to local traditions and tastes.

The two-way approach to the global-local encounter is usually portrayed as critical and espoused by radical social scientists, because it 'empowers' the sustainability of local cultures and fosters local identities. . . .

Discussion II: 'Both Ways'

. . . To the question of homogenization vs heterogenization in global-local relationships, we suggest here the following resolution: (1) both perspectives are valid; (2) yet they apply to discrete societal levels; and (3) the one-way approach is restricted to one level of social reality, the structural-institutional level, i.e., patterns and practices which are inscribed into institutions and organizations; the two-way approach is restricted to the symbolic-expressive level of social reality, i.e., the level of explicit symbolization. Finally, (4) we suggest a global-local structural-symbolic model, in which the one-way structural homogenization process and the two-way symbolic heterogenization process are combined. Thus, heuristically speaking, our theoretical resolution is predicated on the distinction between two different levels, the structural-institutional level and the expressive-symbolic level.

While each of the rival perspectives on the global-local encounter is attuned to only one of these levels, we propose that globalization be seen as a process that is simultaneously one-sided and two-sided but in two distinct societal levels. In other words, on the structural level, globalization is a one-way street; but on the symbolic level, it is a two-way street. In Israel's case, for instance, this would mean that, symbolically, the falafel and McDonald's coexist side by side; structurally, however, the falafel is produced and consumed as if it were an industrialized-standardized (McDonaldized) hamburger, or as its artisan-made 'gourmet' counterpart. . . .

The two-way approach to globalization, which highlights the persistence of cultural 'difference,' contains more than a grain of empirical truth. On the symbolic level, it accounts for the diversity that does not succumb to homogeneity—in our case, the falafel once again steams from the pita; the Israeli hamburger is larger than other national McDonald's specimens (and kosher for Passover . . .). On the symbolic level, the 'difference' that renders the local distinctive has managed to linger on. At the same time, on the structural level, that great leveller of 'sameness' at all locales prevails: the falafel has become McDonaldized. . . .

A strong structuralist argument sees symbolic 'differences' not merely as tolerated but indeed as functional to structural 'sameness,' in that they are purported to conceal the structure's underlying uniformity and to promote niches of consumer identity. In other words, the variety of local cultural identities 'licensed' under global capitalist commercial expansion disguises the unified formula of capital, thereby fostering legitimacy and even sales.

. . . A variety of observers—all with the intention of 'giving voice' to the 'other' and the 'subaltern'—may unwittingly be achieving an opposite effect. . . . Exclusive attention to explicit symbolism may divert attention from implicit structures.

Transnational corporations are quick to take advantage of multiculturalism, postcolonialism and ethnography, and exploit genuine cultural concerns to their benefit. It is worth quoting at some length a former Coca-Cola marketing executive:

> We don't change the concept. What we do is maybe change the music, maybe change the execution, certainly change the casting, but in terms of what it sounds like and what it looks like and what it is selling, at a particular point in time, we have kept it more or less patterned. . . . [our activity] has been all keyed on a local basis, overlaid with an umbrella of the global strategy. We have been dealing with various ethnic demographic groups with an overall concept. Very recently . . . the company has moved to a more fragmented approach, based on the assumption that the media today is fragmented and that each of these groups that are targeted by that media core should be communicated to in their own way with their own message, with their own sound, with their own visualization. . . .

The case study presented here has shown a number of instances of the process whereby global commodities appropriate local traditions. To recap with the example of the 'new falafel,' McDonaldization did not bring about its demise, but, indeed, contributed to its revival, vindicating, as it were, the two-way perspective. The falafel's new lease on life, however, is modelled after McDonald's, that is, a standardized, mechanical, mass-commodified product, on the one hand; or responds to it in a commercial 'gourmetized' and 'ethnicitized' product, on the other hand. In both cases, global McDonaldization prevails structurally, while it may give a symbolic leeway to the local. . . . Indeed, from the end-user's or individual consumer's perspective, the particular explicit symbolic 'difference' may be a source of great emotional gratification; but from the perspective of the social structure, the system of production and consumption, what matters is the exact opposite—namely, the implicit structural homogenization.

Thus, the question of global homogenization vs. local heterogenization cannot be exhausted by invoking symbolic differences, as is attempted by the two-way approach. 'McDonaldization' is not merely or mainly about the manufactured objects—the hamburgers—but first and foremost about the deep-seated social relationships involved in their production and consumption—i.e., it is about commodification and instrumentalization. In its broadest sense here, McDonaldization represents a robust commodification and instrumentalization of social relations, production and consumption, and therefore an appropriation of local cultures by global flows. This study . . . proposes looking at the relations between the global and the local as a composite of the structural and symbolic levels, a composite in which the structural inherently appropriates the symbolic but without explicitly suppressing it. . . .

This is what is meant by glocommodification—global commodification combining structural uniformity with symbolic diversity.

Thinking Critically

1. In terms of fast food, in what ways has Israel grown more like the United States?

2. In terms of fast food, in what ways has Israel grown less like the United States?

3. Are whatever differences that remain in Israel, and elsewhere, merely "hanging on"?

4. Is McDonaldization a one-way or a two-way process?

5. Would a critic of McDonaldization be optimistic based on this analysis of the Israeli fast-food industry?

In this chapter, I address the relationship between McDonaldization and the ideas developed in a more recent book of mine, The Globalization of Nothing (2004, 2007). In that work, I develop a theoretical model to help us grapple with the issues raised throughout this section. Many of the perspectives discussed earlier (e.g., hybridity) relate to the idea of glocalization, but I create the term "grobalization" to deal with the imposition of cultural forms on other societies (cultural convergence). From my point of view, McDonaldization is best thought of as a specific type of grobalization.

In addition, I create the terms "nothing" (social forms that are centrally conceived, controlled, and lacking in distinctive content) and "something" (social forms that are locally conceived, controlled, and rich in distinctive content). Clearly, McDonald's, its products, and its systems are paradigmatic forms of nothing. (An example of something would be a local farmer's or craft market.) Although I discuss various permutations and combinations, it is clear that McDonaldization fits best under the heading of the grobalization of nothing. Further, it is so powerful that it threatens the other major forms of globalization, especially the glocalization of something.

36

Globalization and McDonaldization

Does It All Amount to . . . Nothing?

George Ritzer

Globalization

[G]lobalization can be defined as "the worldwide diffusion of practices, expansion of relations across continents, organization of social life on a global scale, and growth of a shared global consciousness." It is clear that the world has been affected increasingly by globalization in general, as well as by the subdimensions of that process enumerated in this definition.

McDonaldization can be seen, at least in part, as one of a number of globalization processes. While it is important to remember that McDonaldization is *not* only a globalization process (for example, it is also revolutionizing life *within* the United States), it is clear that in at least some of its aspects, it can be considered under that heading. Let us look at the relationship between

Editor's Note: From Ritzer, G., *McDonaldization of Society, Revised New Century Edition*, copyright © 2008, reprinted with permission of Sage Publications, Inc.

McDonaldization and each of the four aspects of globalization that make up the definition of that term as it was employed above.

First, the *practices* (for example, putting customers to work, routinely eating meals quickly and on the run, using drive-through windows) developed by McDonald's (and other leaders of the fast-food industry) in the United States have been diffused to fast-food restaurants in many other countries around the world. More generally, a wide range of practices that define many different McDonaldized settings (for example, education, law enforcement) have similarly been disseminated globally. Thus, for example, universities in many parts of the world have been drawn toward the increasing use of large lecture-style classes, and police forces in many countries employ many of the efficient techniques for law enforcement and crowd control pioneered in the United States.

Second, many intercontinental *relationships* that did not exist before came into being as a result of the proliferation of McDonaldized systems. That is, the deep linkages among and between McDonaldized systems have necessitated a large number of such global relationships. For example, there are strong ties among the various restaurants around the world that are part of Yum! Brands, Inc. (for example, Kentucky Fried Chicken outlets in various geographic locales). Less formal, but no less important, are the relationships between law enforcement agencies or universities as they share knowledge of, and experiences with, the latest advances in the McDonaldization of their respective domains.

Third, the ensemble of these relationships has led to *new ways of organizing social life* throughout the world and across the globe. To put it most generally, the ways in which the social world is organized, even across great distances, have been McDonaldized. Thus, not only has the way people eat been restructured (for example, less in the home and more in fast-food restaurants) but so has the way higher education (fewer personal tutorials, more large lectures) and law enforcement (the increased use of "assembly line" justice) are structured. In innumerable ways, the organization of everyday life has been altered, sometimes dramatically, by the spread of McDonaldization across the globe.

Finally, McDonald's, to say nothing of the many other McDonaldized systems, has led to a new *global consciousness*. There are those who are well aware that they are part of an increasingly McDonaldized world and who revel in that knowledge. Thus, some people are more willing to travel to far-off locales because they know that their ability to adjust to those settings will be made easier by the existence of familiar McDonaldized settings. However, there are others with a similar (if not greater) level of awareness who abhor the process and what it is doing to their lives and the lives of many throughout the world. Such people may be disinclined to travel to at least some places because they know they have become so highly McDonaldized. Most generally, McDonald's and other McDonaldized businesses are such active and aggressive marketers that people can hardly avoid being conscious of them and the way they are changing their lives and the lives of many others throughout the world.

Globalization: Glocalization and Grobalization

. . . *Glocalization* can be defined as *the interpenetration of the global and the local, resulting in unique outcomes in different geographic areas.* That is, global forces, often associated with a tendency toward homogenization, run headlong into the local in any geographic location. Rather than either one overwhelming the other, the global and the local interpenetrate, producing unique outcomes in each location.

This emphasis on glocalization has a variety of implications for thinking about globalization in general. First, it leads to the view that the world is growing increasingly pluralistic. Glocalization theory is exceptionally sensitive to differences within and between areas of the world. Thus, the glocal realities in one part of the world are likely to be quite different from such realities in other parts of the world. Such a view of the world leads one to downplay many of the fears associated with globalization in general (and McDonaldization more specifically), especially the fear of increasing homogeneity throughout the world.

This absence of fear of the negative aspects of globalization is associated with a tendency on the part of those who emphasize glocalization to argue that individuals and local groups have great power to adapt, innovate, and maneuver within a glocalized world. Glocalization theory sees individuals and groups as important and creative agents. Thus, while they may be subject to globalizing processes, these powerful individuals and groups are not likely to be overwhelmed by, and subjugated to, them. Rather, they are likely to modify and adapt them to their own needs and interests. In other words, they are able to glocalize them.

Thus, social processes, especially those that relate to globalization, are seen as relational and contingent. That is, forces pushing globalization emanate from many sources, but they generally face counterforces in any given area of the world. Consequently, what develops in any area is a result of the relationship between these forces and counterforces. This also means that whether or not the forces of globalization overwhelm the local is contingent on the specific relationship between the forces and counterforces in any given locale. Where the counterforces are weak, globalizing forces may successfully impose themselves, but where they are strong (and to glocalization theorists, they appear strong in most areas), a glocal form is likely to emerge that uniquely integrates the global and the local. Thus, to fully understand globalization, we must deal with the specific and contingent relationships that exist in any given locale.

From the point of view of glocalization, the forces impelling globalization are *not* seen as (totally) coercive but, rather, as providing material to be used, in concert with the local, in individual and group creation of distinctive glocal realities. Thus, for example, the global mass media (say, CNN or Al-Jazeera) are not seen as defining and controlling what people think and believe in a given locale but, rather, as providing them with additional inputs that are integrated with many other media inputs (especially those that are local) to create unique sets of ideas and viewpoints.

There is no question that glocalization is an important part of globalization, but it is far from the entire story. Furthermore, while, as we will see, some degree of glocalization occurs under the heading of McDonaldization, another side of globalization relates better to McDonaldization. That aspect of globalization is well described by the concept of grobalization, coined in my book *The Globalization of Nothing*, for the first time as a much-needed companion to the notion of glocalization. *Grobalization focuses on the imperialistic ambitions of nations, corporations, organizations, and the like and their desire, indeed need, to impose themselves on various geographic areas.* Their main interest is in seeing their power, influence, and in some cases profits *grow* (hence the term *grobalization*) throughout the world. Grobalization involves a variety of subprocesses, three of which—capitalism, Americanization, and McDonaldization—are not only central driving forces in grobalization but also of particular interest to the author. While all three were dealt with in *The Globalization of Nothing*, the focus below will naturally be on McDonaldization. That is, McDonaldization is both a major example of, and a key driving force in, grobalization.

Grobalization leads to a variety of ideas that are largely antithetical to the basic ideas associated with glocalization. Rather than emphasizing the great diversity among various glocalized locales, grobalization leads to the view that the world is growing increasingly similar. While it is recognized that there are differences within and between areas of the world, what is emphasized is their increasing similarity. Thus, grobalization theory is especially sensitive to the increasing number of similarities that characterize many areas of the world. This, of course, tends to heighten the fears of those who are concerned about the increasing homogenization associated with globalization.

In contrast to the view associated with glocalization, individuals and groups throughout the world are seen as having relatively little ability to adapt, innovate, and maneuver within a grobalized world. Grobalization theory sees larger structures and forces tending to overwhelm the ability of individuals and groups to create themselves and their worlds.

In yet another stark contrast, grobalization tends to see social processes as largely unidirectional and deterministic. That is, the forces flow from the global to the local, and there is little or no possibility of the local having any significant impact on the global. As a result, the global is generally seen as largely determining what transpires at the local level; the impact of the global is not seen as contingent on what transpires at the local level or on how the local reacts to the global. Thus, grobalization tends to overpower the local. It also limits the ability of the local to act and react, let alone to act back on the grobal.

Thus, from the perspective of grobalization, global forces *are* seen as largely determining what individual(s) and groups think and do throughout the world. For example, this view accords far more power to grobal media powers such as CNN and Al-Jazeera to influence people in any given geographic area than does the viewpoint that emphasizes glocalization.

McDonaldization and Grobalization

In terms of globalization, the McDonaldization thesis contends that highly McDonaldized systems—and more important, the principles that lie at their base—have been exported from the United States to much of the rest of the world. Many nations throughout the world, and innumerable subsystems within each, are undergoing the process of McDonaldization. To put it another way, the influence of McDonaldization has been *growing* throughout much of the world, and this clearly places it under the heading of *grobalization*. The major driving force is economics—the ability of McDonaldized systems to increase profits continually is based on the need to steadily expand markets throughout the world. However, other factors help account for the growing global presence of McDonaldization, including a deep belief in the system by those who push it and a strong desire on the part of those who do not have it to obtain it.

McDonaldization is obviously a global perspective, especially a grobal one, but it is both less and more than a theory of globalization. On the one hand, McDonaldization does not involve anything approaching the full range of global processes. . . . On the other hand, McDonaldization involves much more than an analysis of its global impact. For example, much of it involves the manifold transformations taking place *within* the United States, the source and still the center of this process. . . . Thus, McDonaldization is not coterminous with globalization, nor is it solely a global process. Nonetheless, McDonaldization has global implications and can thus be a useful lens through which to examine changes taking place around the globe.

What is clear is that McDonaldization deserves a place in any thoroughgoing account of globalization, especially grobalization. There can be little doubt that the logic of McDonaldization generates a set of values and practices that have a competitive advantage over other models. It not only promises many specific advantages, it also reproduces itself more easily than other models of consumption (and in many other areas of society, as well). The success of McDonaldization in the United States over the past half century, coupled with the international ambitions of McDonald's and its ilk, as well as those of indigenous clones throughout the world, strongly suggests that McDonaldization will continue to make inroads into the global marketplace, not only through the efforts of existing corporations but also via the diffusion of the paradigm.

It should be noted, however, that the continued advance of McDonaldization, at least in its present form, is far from assured. In fact, there are even signs in the United States, as well as in other parts of the world, of what I have previously called *de-McDonaldization*. . . . Nonetheless, at the moment and for the foreseeable future, McDonaldization will continue to be an important force, and it is clearly and unequivocally not only a grobal process but also one that contributes mightily to the spread of "nothingness."

Nothing-Something and McDonaldization

I have now discussed the ideas of glocalization-grobalization as they relate to McDonaldization, but a second set of ideas—nothing-something, also derived from *The Globalization of Nothing*—needs to be discussed here. As we will see, these ideas relate not only directly to McDonaldization but also to its relationship to globalization in general and grobalization-glocalization in particular.

Nothing can be defined as a *"social form that is generally centrally conceived, controlled and comparatively devoid of distinctive substantive content."* It should be abundantly clear that any McDonaldized system, with the fast-food restaurant being a prime example, would be a major form of nothing. However, it is important to point out that there are many other examples of nothing that have little or no direct relationship to McDonaldization.

Let us look at the example of a chain of fast-food restaurants from the point of view of the basic components of our definition of nothing. First, as parts of chains, fast-food restaurants are, virtually by definition, centrally conceived. That is, those who created the chain and are associated with its central offices conceived of the chain originally and are continually involved in its reconceptualization. For their part, owners and managers of local chain restaurants do little or no conceptualizing on their own. Indeed, they have bought the rights to the franchise, and continue to pay a percentage of their profits for it, because they want those with the demonstrated knowledge and expertise to do the conceptualizing. This relative absence of independent conceptualization at the level of the local franchise is one of the reasons we can think of the franchise as nothing.

We are led to a similar view when we turn to the second aspect of our definition of nothing—control. Just as those in the central office do the conceptualization for the local franchises, they also exert great control over them. Indeed, to some degree, such control is derived from the fact that conceptualization is in the hands of the central office; the act of conceptualizing and reconceptualizing the franchise yields a significant amount of control. However, control is exercised by the central office over the franchises in more direct ways as well. For example, it may get a percentage of a local franchise's profits, and if its cut is down because profits are down, the central office may put pressure on the local franchise to alter its procedures to increase profitability. The central office may also deploy inspectors to make periodic and unannounced visits to local franchises. Those franchises found not to be operating the way they are supposed to will come under pressure to bring their operations in line with company standards. Those that do not are likely to suffer adverse consequences, including the ultimate punishment of the loss of the franchise. Thus, local franchises can also be seen as nothing because they do not control their own destinies.

The third aspect of our definition of nothing is that it involves social forms largely lacking in distinctive content. This is essentially true by definition of chains of franchised fast-food restaurants. That is, the whole idea is to turn out restaurants that are virtual clones of one another. To put it another way, the goal is to produce restaurants that are as alike one another as possible—they generally look much the same from outside, they are structured similarly within, the same foods are served, workers act and interact in much the same way, and so on. There is little that distinguishes one outlet of a chain of fast-food restaurants from all the others.

Thus, there is a near perfect fit between the definition of nothing offered above and a chain of fast-food restaurants. However, this is a rather extreme view since, in a sense, "nothing is nothing." In other words, all social forms (including fast-food restaurants) have characteristics that deviate from the extreme form of nothing. That is, they involve some local conceptualization and control, and each one has at least some distinctive elements. To put this another way, all social forms have some elements of somethingness. Consequently, we need to think not only in terms of nothing but also in terms of something as well as a something-nothing continuum.

This leads us to a definition of something as *"a social form that is generally indigenously conceived, controlled, and comparatively rich in distinctive substantive content."* This makes it clear that neither nothing nor something exists independently of the other; *each makes sense only when paired with, and contrasted to, the other.*

If a fast-food restaurant is an example of nothing, then a meal cooked at home from scratch would be an example of something. The meal is conceived by the individual cook and not by a central office. Control rests in the hands of that cook. Finally, that which the cook prepares is rich in distinctive content and different from that prepared by other cooks, even those who prepare the same meals.

While nothing and something are presented as if they were a dichotomy, we really need to think in terms of a *continuum* from something to nothing, and that is precisely the way the concepts will be employed here—as the two poles of that continuum. Thus, while a fast-food restaurant falls toward the nothing end of the continuum, every fast-food restaurant has at least some elements that are different from all others; each has some elements of somethingness associated with it. Conversely, while every home-cooked meal is distinctive, they are likely to have at least some elements in common (for example, they may rely on a common cookbook or recipe) and therefore have some elements of nothingness. Therefore, no social form exists at the extreme nothing or something pole of the continuum; they *all* fall somewhere between the two. However, it remains the case that some lie closer to the nothing end of the continuum, whereas others lie more toward the something end. In terms of our interests here, fast-food restaurants, and more generally all McDonaldized systems, fall toward the nothing end of the something-nothing continuum.

Nothing-Something and Grobalization-Glocalization

I turn now to a discussion of the relationship between grobalization- glocalization and something-nothing and its implications for our understanding of McDonaldization. Figure 36.1 offers the four basic possibilities that emerge when we crosscut the grobalization-glocalization and something-nothing continua. It should be noted that while this yields four "ideal types," there are no hard-and-fast lines between them. This is reflected in the use of both dotted lines and multidirectional arrows in Figure 36.1.

Quadrants 1 and 4 in Figure 36.1 are of greatest importance, at least for the purposes of this analysis. They represent a key point of tension and conflict in the world today. Clearly, there is great pressure to grobalize nothing (Quadrant 4) and often all that stands in its way in terms of achieving global hegemony is the glocalization of something (Quadrant 1). . . .

While the other two quadrants (2 and 3) are clearly residual in nature and of secondary importance, it is necessary to recognize that there is, at least to some degree, a glocalization of nothing (quadrant 2) and a grobalization of something (quadrant 3). However, whatever tensions may exist between them are of far less significance than those between the grobalization of nothing and the glocalization of something. A discussion of the glocalization of nothing and the grobalization of something makes it clear that grobalization is not an unmitigated source of nothing (it can involve something) and glocalization is not to be seen solely as a source of something (it can involve nothing). . . .

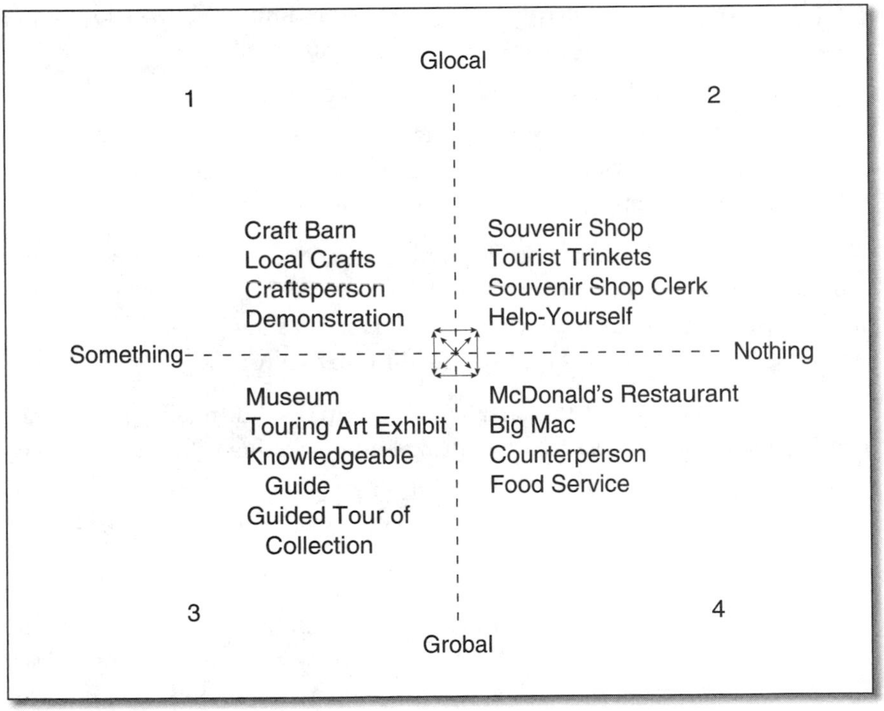

Glocal

1   2

Craft Barn   Souvenir Shop
Local Crafts   Tourist Trinkets
Craftsperson   Souvenir Shop Clerk
Demonstration   Help-Yourself

Something- - - - - - - - - - - - - - ⊠- - - - - - - - - - - - - - Nothing

Museum   McDonald's Restaurant
Touring Art Exhibit Big Mac
Knowledgeable   Counterperson
  Guide   Food Service
Guided Tour of
  Collection

3   4

Grobal

Figure 36.1   The Relationship Between Glocal-Grobal and Something-Nothing With Examples

SOURCE: Adapted from George Ritzer. *The Globalization of Nothing 2.* Thousand Oaks, CA: Pine Forge Press, 2007, p. 120.

The Grobalization of Nothing

The example of the grobalization of nothing in Figure 36.1 is a meal at McDonald's. There is little or nothing distinctive about any given McDonald's restaurant, the food served there, the people who work in these settings, and the "services" they offer. And, of course, there has been a very aggressive effort to expand the presence of McDonald's throughout much of the world. Thus, the global expansion of McDonald's (and other fast-food chains) is a near-perfect example of the grobalization of nothing.

The main reasons for the strong affinity between grobalization and nothing are basically the inverse of the reasons for the lack of such affinity between grobalization and something. For example:

1. Above all, there is a far greater demand throughout the world for nothing than something. This is the case because nothing tends (although not always) to be less expensive than something, with the result that more people can afford the former than the latter (as we know, McDonald's places great emphasis on its low prices and "value meals").

2. Large numbers of people are also far more likely to want the various forms of nothing because their comparative simplicity and lack of distinctiveness appeals to a wider range of tastes (the food at McDonald's is famous for its simple and familiar—salty and sweet—taste).

3. In addition . . . that which is nothing, largely devoid of distinctive content, is far less likely to bother or offend those in other cultures (although it has aroused outrage in some cultures, McDonald's simple and basic foods have shown the ability to fit into many different cultures).

4. Finally, because of the far greater potential sales, much more money can be, and is, devoted to the advertising and marketing of nothing, thereby creating a still greater demand for it than for something (McDonald's spends huge sums on advertising and has been very successful at generating great demand for its fare).

Given the great demand, it is far easier to mass-produce and -distribute the empty forms of nothing than the substantively rich forms of something. Indeed, many forms of something lend themselves best to limited, if not one-of-a-kind, production. A skilled potter may produce a few dozen pieces of pottery and an artist a painting or two in, perhaps, a week, a month, or even a year(s). While these craft and art works may, over time, move from owner to owner in various parts of the world, this traffic barely registers in the total of all global trade and commerce. Of course, there are the rare masterpieces that may bring millions of dollars, but in the main, these one-of-a-kind works are small-ticket items. In contrast, thousands, even many millions, and sometimes billions of varieties of nothing are mass-produced and sold throughout the globe. Thus, the global sale of fast food like Big Macs, Whoppers, Kentucky Fried Chicken, as well as the myriad other forms of nothing, is a far greater factor in grobalization than the international sale of pieces of high art (for example, the art of Van Gogh) or of tickets to the Rolling Stones' most recent world tour.

Furthermore, the economics of the marketplace demands that the massive amount of nothing that is produced be marketed and sold on a grobal basis. For one thing, the economics of scale mean that the more that is produced and sold, the lower the price. This means that, almost inevitably, American producers of nothing (and they are, by far, the world leaders in this) must become dissatisfied with the American market, no matter how vast it is, and aggressively pursue a world market for their products. The greater the grobal market, the lower the price that can be charged (McDonald's can buy hamburger meat on the global market at rock-bottom prices because of the huge number of burgers it sells), and this, in turn, means that even greater numbers of nothing can be sold to far reaches of the globe in less-developed countries.

Another economic factor stems from the demand of the stock market that corporations that produce and sell nothing (indeed, all corporations) increase sales and profits from one year to the next. The stocks of those corporations (and McDonald's has recently been one of them) that simply meet the previous year's profitability, or experience a decline, are likely to be punished in the stock market and see their stock prices fall, sometimes precipitously. To increase profits continually, the corporation is forced, as Karl Marx understood long ago, to continue to search out new markets. One way of doing that is to constantly expand globally. In contrast, since something is less likely to be produced by corporations, certainly the large corporations listed in the stock market, there is far less pressure to expand the market for it. In any case, given the limited number of these things that can be produced by artisans, skilled chefs, artists, and so on, there are profound limits on such expansion. This, in turn, brings us back to the pricing issue and relates to the price advantage that nothing ordinarily has over something. As a general rule, the various types of nothing cost far less than something. The result, obviously, is that nothing can be marketed globally far more aggressively than something.

Also, nothing has an advantage in terms of transportation around the world. These are things that generally can be easily and efficiently packaged and moved, often over vast areas. The frozen hamburgers and french fries that are the basis of McDonald's business are prime examples of this. Clearly, it would be much harder to package and move fresh hamburgers and freshly sliced potatoes, especially over large distances. Furthermore, because the unit cost of such items is low, it is of comparatively little consequence if they go awry, are lost, or are stolen. In contrast, it is more difficult and expensive to package something—say, a piece of handmade pottery or an antique vase— and losing such things, having them stolen, or their being broken is a disaster. As a result, it is far more expensive to insure something than nothing, and this difference is another reason for the cost advantage that nothing has over something. These sorts of things serve to greatly limit the global trade in items that can be included under the heading of something.

. . .

The Case for McDonaldization as an Example of the Grobalization of Nothing

. . . McDonaldized systems must be standardized. Thus, they cannot help but impose themselves (and their standardized products and systems), at least to some degree, on local markets throughout the world. Although McDonald's may adapt to local realities in various ways, its basic menu and the fundamental operating procedures remain essentially the same everywhere in the world. In this sense, McDonald's can be seen as the epitome of the grobalization of nothing. Thus, the "nothingness" of its standard fare and its basic operating principles tend to threaten, and in many cases replace, local fare and principles of operation.

The enormous expansion in the international arena of the giant fast-food chains that originated in the United States is one manifestation of the grobalization of nothing. In many ways, however, the mere existence of standard American chains in other countries is *not* the most important indicator of the grobalization of nothing in the form of the spread of McDonaldization; rather, it is the existence of indigenous clones of those McDonaldized enterprises in an increasing number of countries throughout the world. After all, the presence of American imports could simply be a manifestation of an invasion of isolated and superficial elements that represent no fundamental threat to, or change in, a local culture. But the emergence of native versions does reflect an underlying change in those societies, a genuine McDonaldization, and powerful evidence of the grobalization of nothing.

The following examples reflect the power of McDonald's to transform local restaurants. They are also manifestations of nothing in the sense that they are largely lacking in distinctive content and aping many standards developed by McDonald's and others of its ilk.

- The success of the many McDonald's in Russia led to the development of indigenous enterprises such as Russkoye Bistro. Said Russkoye Bistro's deputy director, "If McDonald's had not come to our country, then we probably wouldn't be here." Furthermore, "We need to create fast food here that fits our lifestyle and traditions. . . . We see McDonald's like an older brother . . . We have a lot to learn from them."

- In China, Ronghua Chicken and Xiangfei Roast Chicken emulate Kentucky Fried Chicken. The Beijing Fast Food Company has almost a thousand local restaurants and street stalls that sell local fare. Several of the company's executives are former employees of KFC or McDonald's, where they learned basic management techniques. Even "the most famous restaurant in Beijing—Quanjude Roast Duck Restaurant—sent its management staff to McDonald's in 1993 and then introduced its own 'roast duck fast food' in early 1994."

- In Japan, the strongest competitor to McDonald's is Mos Burger (with over 1,500 outlets), which serves "a sloppy-joe-style concoction of meat and chile sauce on a bun." The corporate parent also operates chains under other names such as Chirimentei, a chain of 161 Chinese noodle shops in Japan (and 2 more in the People's Republic of China), Nakau (rice and Japanese noodles) with 82 outlets, and Mikoshi, 4 Japanese noodle houses in California.

- In Seoul, competitors to McDonald's include Uncle Joe's Hamburger (the inventor of the *kimchi* burger, featuring an important local condiment made from spicy pickled cabbage) and Americana.

Beyond providing a model for local restaurants (and many other local institutions), McDonaldization poses a threat to the customs of society as a whole. This involves the grobalization of nothing to the degree that distinctive local customs are dropped and replaced by those that have their origins elsewhere and are lacking in distinction. For example,

- While their parents still call them "chips," British children now routinely ask for "french fries."

- In Korea (and Japan), the individualism of eating a meal at McDonald's threatens the commensality of eating rice, which is cooked in a common pot, and of sharing side dishes.

- As in the United States, McDonald's has helped to transform children into customers in Hong Kong (and in many other places).

• Immigrants to Hong Kong are given a tour that ends at McDonald's. If all cities did this, there would, at least in this case, be nothing to distinguish one city from another.

• In Japan, McDonald's is described as a new "local" phenomenon. A Japanese Boy Scout was surprised to find a McDonald's in Chicago; he thought it was a Japanese firm.

As local residents come to see McDonald's and McDonaldized systems as their own, the process of McDonaldization, and more generally the grobalization of nothing, will surely embed itself ever more deeply into the realities of cultures throughout the world. For example, the traditional and quite distinctive Japanese taboo against eating while standing has been undermined by the fast-food restaurant. Also subverted to some degree is the cultural sanction against drinking directly from a can or bottle. The norm against eating with one's hands is holding up better (the Japanese typically eat their burgers in the wrappers so that their hands do not touch the food directly). Nevertheless, the fact that deeply held norms are being transformed by McDonald's is evidence of the profound impact of McDonaldization. It reflects the grobalization of nothing in the sense that norms common in the United States and elsewhere (for example, eating while standing and drinking from a can) are now replacing norms distinctive to Japan (and many other nations).

McDonaldization and the globalization of nothing are powerful global realities, but they do not affect all nations, nor do they affect nations to the same degree. For example, Korea, unlike other East Asian locales, has a long history of anti-Americanism (coexisting with pro-American feelings) and of fearing that Americanism will destroy Korean self-identity. Thus, one would anticipate more opposition there to McDonaldization than in most other nations.

Despite the negative effects of McDonaldization on local customs, we must not forget that McDonaldized systems bring with them many advances. For example, in Hong Kong (and in Taipei), McDonald's served as a catalyst for improving sanitary conditions at many other restaurants in the city.

In addition, McDonaldization has at times helped resuscitate local traditions. For example, although fast-food restaurants have boomed in Taipei, they have encouraged a revival of indigenous food traditions, such as the eating of betel nuts. More generally, Benjamin Barber (Chapter 25) argues that the spread of "McWorld" brings with it the development of local fundamentalist movements ("Jihads") deeply opposed to McDonaldization.

However, in the end, Barber concludes that McWorld will win out over Jihad. To succeed on a large scale, he says fundamentalist movements must begin to use McDonaldized systems (such as e-mail, the Internet, television).

Thinking Critically

1. Does McDonaldization in the end amount to nothing (as that term is defined here)?

2. Does globalization in the end amount to nothing (as that term is defined here)?

3. Make a case for the glocalization of something as the hope against McDonaldization and the spread of nothing.

4. Make a case for the grobalization of something as the hope against McDonaldization and the spread of nothing.

5. Which is the stronger hope, the glocalization or the grobalization of something? Why?

This chapter—an excerpt from Globaloney *by Michael Veseth—critically analyzes McDonaldization, the globalization of nothing, and their relationship to one another. Veseth sees rationalization, or McDonaldization, as the "ugly side" of globalization. But, he also wonders whether we really learn much about globalization through an analysis of the fast-food restaurant. However, in analyzing McDonaldization I am interested, as Veseth himself states, in much more than the fast-food restaurant, and there is little doubt that McDonaldization is at least one important global process. Given the rise of indigenous McDonaldized restaurants, as well as other organizations in other societies and their exportation to the United States, I also have my doubts about the association Veseth makes between Americanization and McDonaldization (although the latter certainly had its roots in the former).*

Veseth creates the interesting idea of "McNothing" to combine my ideas on McDonaldization and nothing. He clearly likes much about the idea of the globalization of nothing, but he also offers several critiques of it. However, most of the criticism results from a failure to understand and follow through on what I mean by nothing and something. In fact, he does understand my definitions but leaves them behind when it comes to critique. Most of his criticisms stem from a tendency, shared by many, to slide into thinking of nothing as relating to meaning rather than to structures that are centrally conceived, controlled, and lacking in distinctive content. Thus, to respond to his criticisms: Movies are meaningful to me, but they are still nothing from the point of view of this definition; McDonald's customers do manufacture meaning, but it is still within the context of nothing (the structure of the McDonald's restaurant and its menu); gourmet chefs do try to prepare dishes exactly the same way, but what they do is not centrally conceived, controlled, and lacking in distinctive content—it is something not nothing.

Veseth makes much of Starbucks and what he claims is my changed views on it. I did think in 1998, and still do, that Starbucks serves high-quality coffee. However, in now using it as an example of nothing, I am not contradicting the idea that the coffee is of high quality. As I take pains to point out in The Globalization of Nothing, *although nothing is usually associated with mediocre products, this need not necessarily be the case (and, conversely, something is not necessarily high in quality). Thus Starbucks coffee is both high in quality and nothing (centrally conceived, controlled, and lacking in distinctive content).*

37

Globaloney

Michael Veseth

Rationalization: The Ugly Globalization

Capitalism's tendency to reward and therefore promote efficiency is well known. It is the secret behind Adam Smith's pin factory and invisible hand. For Marx and Engels, it is the force that enables global capitalism to transform foreign countries, not simply penetrate them. Capitalism's drive for greater and greater efficiency causes it to do for society in general what it did for Adam Smith's pin factory in particular: break it down into basic components and reassemble it in the most starkly efficient fashion. There is not much harm done (and much benefit produced) when the division of labor is applied to the manufacture of pins. The stakes are higher when whole societies are involved, as some have suggested. This, not the superficial influence of advertising and electronic media, is the truly ugly side of globalization.

Efficiency, and the process of rational calculation that is necessary to achieve it, reaches its zenith inside a McDonald's restaurant. The American sociologist George Ritzer observed this fact in his 1993 book, *The McDonaldization of Society: An Investigation into the Changing Character*

Editor's Note: From Veseth, M., "Rationalization: The Ugly Globalization," in *Globaloney*, copyright © 2005 Rowman & Littlefield Publishers, Inc. Reprinted with permission.

of Social Life. If you make even a casual study of a McDonald's restaurant you will see Ritzer's point. McDonald's makes efficiency the top-most goal and consciously organizes its assembly line accordingly. This is not news, of course, since the McDonald brothers began doing this way back in the 1950s, even before they sold their name and business to Ray Kroc. What is interesting, however, is how McDonald's has managed to rationalize both sides of the counter. This is where Ritzer comes in.

It is easy to see the production side of McDonald's efficiency. Specialized technology and a highly organized division of labor produce standardized menu items quickly and efficiently. Service may not be quite as fast as in the San Bernardino store, where orders were filled in 30 seconds, but the menu is much larger and competitive factors have forced McDonald's to permit customers to make some special orders. All in all, it is a highly structured, very efficient production line for food of reliably consistent quality and relatively low price.

What may be more significant, however, is how McDonald's has transformed the way that its customers behave. In traditional restaurants, customers are relatively passive participants in the food service operation. They arrive, are seated, and given menus. Wait staff deliver water and other beverages, take the order and deliver it, assuring that everything is exactly as requested. Staff typically check on the customers at several points during the meal, which may be multicourse and require changes in cutlery, glassware, and so forth. Finally, the bill is delivered and paid, change given, and table cleared and reset before it can be turned over to the next group of customers.

Compare this to a typical fast-food experience. Customers arrive and queue to give their orders at the counter, choosing from the standard items listed on the backlit overhead display. The order is given, payment made, and the customer waits for the food to arrive at the counter. (In fast food, customers, not staff, do the waiting.) The customer gets her own condiments and eating utensils, fills her own cup, finds her own table, and then clears it when finished. Customers do much of the work of running the restaurant, work that would otherwise be performed by paid staff. (Over at the drive-through window, customers are actually making their own home and office deliveries!) And they do this work rapidly, efficiently, and without apparent displeasure. Actually, customers don't seem to be aware that they are doing McDonald's work; they just go through the paces automatically. The miracle of the modern McDonald's is that its customers work for the firm but draw no wages. The experience of cooking a meal and eating it is thus transformed from an art to a highly engineered, precisely coordinated production process.

McDonald's is an excellent example of the process that the great German sociologist Max Weber (1864–1920) called "formal rationalization."

According to Weber, Ritzer explains, "*formal rationality* means that the search by people for the optimum means to a given end is shaped by rules, regulations, and larger social structures. Individuals are not left to their own devices in searching for the best possible means of attaining a given objective. Weber identified this type of rationality is a major development in the history of the world." Weber's analysis of formal rationalization focused on bureaucracy as an institution that organized a certain segment of society to achieve certain goals quickly and efficiently. A successful bureaucracy is able to process large numbers of people relatively quickly and in a highly predictable manner. Individual variations are tightly controlled, with rules and regulations generally relied upon rather than variable (and therefore unreliable) human judgment within a tightly defined division of labor. There are few "surprises," especially unpleasant ones.

A successful visit to a modern health maintenance organization clinic illustrates a bureaucracy at work. The division of labor, both within offices and among specialties, is obvious. The steps of making appointments, gathering information, making diagnoses, planning treatment, performing tests, filling prescriptions, etc., are all discrete and handled by specialists. Information technology is used to share information and coordinate the stages. The patient (you) moves efficiently through the production line, through various locations, until you are discharged, instructions in hand, into the parking garage. The term *patient* is well chosen because, as in the fast-food restaurant, the customer does all of the waiting, while the assembly-line workers are kept in constant, efficient motion. Other public and private bureaucracies, including income taxation and pension and insurance systems, work much the same way.

George Ritzer gave the name *McDonaldization* to the way that formal rationalization organizes contemporary society, especially in the United States, I think. McDonaldization is characterized by efficiency, calculability, predictability, and the use of technology to control human behavior. McDonaldization is not about McDonald's, Ritzer says, it is about the transforming force of rationalization. Rationalization has many advantages, Ritzer notes. More goods and services can be made available to a larger segment of the population with greater convenience with respect to time and place. Lower cost increases affordability. Workers and customers alike confront a standardized process that is therefore stable and familiar. Uniform treatment means that discrimination due to gender, race, age, or ethnicity is reduced. Standardization means that many products are safer. A high degree of coordination means that technology is rapidly diffused.

McDonald's is a good example of each of these characteristics. When you go to McDonald's you know that there is little chance that you will have an unexpectedly good meal. The sandwiches, fries, and drinks will be just what you expect and no better. But no worse, either. The flip side of standardization is that bad surprises are systematically reduced (although the certainty of occasional human and equipment failures mean they can never fully be eliminated). If you've ever had an expensive meal with poorly prepared or unsafe food served (slowly) by a surly waiter, you know what I am talking about. There are few high points in a Big Mac value meal, but few lows, either.

I think this is why McDonald's is so popular in formerly Communist countries, despite prices that are high relative to weekly income. Under communism, people could be pretty sure of poor food and worse service in most cases, but sometimes they were pleasantly surprised. McDonald's is the other way around. The food is consistently decent. You provide most of the service yourself, so you are not dependent on the whims of a surly waiter. Not a bad deal, compared to the alternative.

If formal rationalization and McDonaldization were limited to McDonald's I don't think we would have very much to complain about. Ritzer's concern, which is shared by many others, however, is that what is true about McDonald's may also be true more generally. It's not about the burgers. It's about the lives behind the burgers and the limited and automatic roles we play as efficient producing and consuming agents. What is the final consequence as formal rationalism spreads from McRestaurant to McMall to McCinema to McHospital to McUniversity to . . . to what? To McChurch?

This is what seems to worry Benjamin Barber. Barber sees the rationalization process (and writes about it in *Jihad vs. McWorld*), but he is apparently more concerned with who has the power in the system (hence his misplaced concern with the infotainment telesector), not realizing that the power is the system. The power lies in the rationalization process itself. This is true even in the most unlikely places, such as the infotainment telesector.

Many people see increasing concentration in the print and electronic media and worry about the potential for abuse of influence. This is a legitimate concern, but it assumes that these firms want power, that they want to control what we believe, whereas I think they really want our money. What I see is increasingly fierce competition among the media giants, which drives them to ever bolder acts of rationalization. On television, for example, the reality show essentially gets audiences to produce their own shows just as McDonald's gets customers to fill their own drink cups. A true monopolist could become lazy and just show reruns or cheap game shows. It is competition and the quest for efficiency that drives them to extremes. It's not the manipulative power of the media giants that I fear, it is the possible effects of their drive to rationalize.

Thomas Friedman both recognizes the rationalization process inherent in globalization and, I think, embraces it. This accounts for Friedman's sunny but realistic attitude toward globalization. As a political reporter covering the Middle East and other troubled regions, Friedman has seen more than his share of irrational acts. I think he'd take economic rationalism over political or social irrationalism any day. He is hopeful that global capitalism will help people learn how to coordinate their actions and behave rationally—which means that they would try not to go to war, for example—even when they are not in a McDonald's. I sure hope he's right, but it is a long shot. Many people have argued that war is irrational because it is too expensive, but this doesn't seem to have stopped war. Perhaps McDonaldization—a deeper cultural process that starts with production and consumption and then eventually is absorbed into a society's DNA—will work where mere hunger for money has failed.

The Threat of McNothing

If globalization is McDonaldization, where does that leave us? As you might expect, opinions differ. George Ritzer used to hold out hope for McDonaldization, not Thomas Friedman's hope that a rationalized world will be a rational one, but hope that standardization and rationalization could produce some good things along with mountains of mediocre mass-market stuff. He seemed to be taken with his experiences at Starbucks, for example.

At Starbucks, Ritzer noted in 1998, standardization and technology do more than just reduce cost and control human behavior, they also produce consistently high-quality products for which customers were willing to pay a premium. "Thus, Starbucks indicates that it is possible to McDonaldize quality . . . when there are technologies that ensure high and consistent quality, and when enough patrons are willing to pay large amounts of money for the product." Ritzer seemed to think that Starbucks and Ruth's Chris Steak House and a few other high-quality chains were the start of something important.

But now he's changed his mind. Ritzer's 2004 book *The Globalization of Nothing* looks at the proliferation of Starbucks in London and sees nothing to love. "Such a uniform chain is one of the prime examples of nothing and its proliferation in the most visited areas of the city tend to give it the feeling of nothingness." Ritzer has decided that meaningful content is difficult to globalize because it is too tied to time and place, too human, too special. To be successful, globalization has to bleach the authentic content out of products and services, make them standard, uniform, and meaningless. This, presumably, is why Nike's swoosh logo is so successful—it doesn't mean a thing.

What makes *something* different from *nothing?* You might think it is just a matter of taste—or lack of it—and I think there is something to this, but Ritzer proposes a sort of matrix of meaning to help separate content from void. Somethingness and nothingness form a continuum. Products or experiences closer to the something end of the spectrum are associated with these characteristics: unique, specific to time and place, humanized, and enchanted (capable of surprise). Nothingness, on the other hand, is characterized by its generic, timeless, placeless qualities and the tendency to be impersonal and disenchanted (rationally predictable). Dinner at a friend's apartment lies toward the something end of the continuum, even if you just order in Chinese food. Dinner at the local Ruth's Chris Steak House, on the other hand, is sort of nothing, even if it is delicious. Going trout fishing is something; going shopping at the mall is nothing.

This taxonomy helps us understand how Ritzer's reaction to Starbucks might have changed, although this is only speculation. Perhaps Ritzer was taken when the first Starbucks opened in his neighborhood, and he learned to order his special type of coffee drink ("I'll have a tall skinny vanilla latte, extra foam") and became a "regular," known by the staff and recognized by other customers. Perhaps this enchantment faded away as he saw his own special experience replicated almost endlessly by other "regulars" wherever he went. Or maybe it was that seeing Starbucks in London made him associate it with Americanization, and this offended him. Or maybe he just got tired of standing in line and switched to Diet Coke; I don't really know. In any case, the coffee drinks that were so "something" in 1998 have become "nothing" today.

The Globalization of Nothing is a very interesting book because, like the best globalization stories and metaphors, it appears at a time of social upheaval and uncertainty and tells us why we are so anxious and what will come to pass in the future. We are anxious, clearly, because globalization is stripping our lives of meaning as products and relationships are rationalized down to nothing. The more globalization proceeds, the more we have and the less it means to us. Existential questions inevitably arise.

But, while I share his anxiety, I am not convinced Ritzer is right. His Starbucks turnaround bothers me a bit as does the fact that he seems to find a lot of meaning in motion pictures, which seem to me to be the ultimate embodiment of nothingness, for the most part: mass-produced, centrally controlled, identical entertainment experiences supplied indiscriminately to millions at low cost in highly controlled artificial environments by cynical media oligopolists. It's just everything that Ritzer finds empty in other circumstances. But then I'm also a bit suspicious of Ritzer's tendency to find "something" in things that he personally likes (such as chrome and glass roadside diners) while he sees only "nothing" in things that he doesn't like, such as McDonald's. I worry that Ritzer has fallen into a sort of cultural elitism, which is hard to avoid when you are evaluating the content of culture.

A more serious criticism is that Ritzer distinguishes between something and nothing based upon the conditions of production. A McDonald's meal is nothing, for example, in part because it is standardized—they are all the same. But he thinks that a fine gourmet meal is something (and would be impossible to globalize) in part because of its variability—it is different each time the skilled chef makes it. But I find both sides of this division problematic.

I suspect that the customers at McDonald's are at least sometimes able to manufacture their own meaning, regardless of the rationalized environment. Standard-issue french fries can take on a life of their own when shared with grandchildren at Sunday lunch. If consumers are to be classified as part of the rationalized production process, then we must consider that they are full participants in the meaning creation business, too, and can sometimes make something out of nothing.

As for gourmet meals, I have eaten my share of them at wonderful restaurants. These meals were far from mass produced, but it would be a mistake to think that their pleasure comes from daily variation and inspiration. In my experience, great chefs work hard to find just the right recipe and then work even harder to see that it is prepared *exactly* the same way each time.

I am suspicious of the idea that globalization is the end of culture and meaning and hopeful, even confident, that authentic content can be preserved. To his credit, George Ritzer is hopeful, too. He ends *The Globalization of Nothing* with a brief discussion of a movement that tries to use globalization against itself, to preserve the local and the authentic. This is the Slow Food movement, which is the subject of a chapter of this book.

But I do take seriously the rationalizing force of capitalism and globalization that is driven by capitalism, so there are limits to my optimism. I am especially mindful of the argument made many years ago by the Austrian American economist Joseph Schumpeter in his book *Capitalism, Socialism, and Democracy*. Like Benjamin Barber, Schumpeter feared that capitalism would destroy democracy, but he was not worried about Jihad, McWorld, or the infotainment telesector. Rather, Schumpeter was worried about the effect of rationalization on society.

Schumpeter, you see, believed that society advanced due to the efforts of bold, heroic figures. This was especially true in business, where the figures are called entrepreneurs, but the idea also holds in politics, science, and the arts. Most of us take small risks with life and mainly play it safe. But a few people take bigger risks, and some of them achieve breakthroughs that really make a difference. These risk takers, even when they fail, are the real sources of social drive and change—he called it "creative destruction"—in Schumpeter's view. Without them, the world is a pretty stagnant, uninteresting place.

The problem, Schumpeter believed, is that capitalism's drive to rationalize is really quite intense, and he thought it would eventually destroy the culture that produces entrepreneurs. Capitalism, as a dynamic force, will slowly fade into stagnant socialism, Schumpeter thought, as rational calculation replaced entrepreneurial risk taking. Thus, he said socialism will overcome capitalism, just as Karl Marx predicted, but not through a worker revolt. Nope, the culture of calculation will swallow up capitalism from the inside out.

Schumpeter's view of politics is less well known, but he tended to see it in the same way he viewed the economy. He saw democracy as a competitive political marketplace. Like the economy, progress came through the actions of bold political entrepreneurs who took the risk of providing real leadership. And he thought that democracy, like capitalism, would be destroyed as a dynamic social force as bold political entrepreneurs were replaced by vote-calculating political managers, content to follow voters rather than leading them. Thus does democracy die, in Schumpeter's world, the victim of rationalism, not Jihad or McWorld.

* * *

Where does our study of globalization and McDonald's leave us? I don't know about you, but I feel like I have learned a great deal about McDonald's but not very much about globalization. This is the problem with using McDonald's or any single product or industry as a metaphor or image for something as complex as globalization. We quickly become caught up in the particular case and risk making false generalizations. Meanwhile, the true general globalization case, if it exists, remains unstudied for the most part.

McDonald's may in fact be an especially poor example to use in studying globalization. McDonald's seems to have a special meaning to Americans that it may or may not have to others. You can almost tell how an American feels about her country by what she has to say about McDonald's. We end up, as I have argued here, with an American view of America, not an objective analysis of globalization.

That said, studying McWorld is not entirely a waste of time. Ritzer's analysis of McDonaldization usefully highlights the rationalizing force of markets and makes us aware of the potential of cold calculation to benefit and to harm. What we need to do is to find a way to think about this process that isn't bound up in a particularly American set of values. That's what

I try to do . . . by looking at globalization from a different angle—through the bottom of a glass of wine.

Thinking Critically

1. Is it fair to describe rationalization/McDonaldization as "ugly"?

2. If so, is there not also a "pretty" side to rationalization/McDonaldization?

3. Which is more important, the ugly or the pretty side? Why?

4. What does Veseth mean by "McNothing"? Is it appropriate to fuse McDonaldization and Nothing in this way?

5. Did Ritzer really change his mind on Starbucks? Is it possible to both praise the quality of Starbucks' coffee and see it as "nothing"?

PART IV

Pedagogical Questions

1. How are cultural differentialism, cultural convergence, and cultural hybridization defined? Which one of these theories applies best to the current cultural conditions in the United States?

2. Samuel Huntington argues that the fundamental source of conflict in this new world will not be primarily ideological or economic but cultural. In that sense, does the economic cooperation between the United States and Saudi Arabia conflict with this theory? Discuss the authority of cultural norms and values in terms of global economy.

3. Does localization provide an antithesis to McDonaldization? If so, in what ways?

4. Does global culture promote convergence or divergence? Are local cultures the world over in decline? Are we witnessing the birth of a single global culture?

5. One of the causes of cultural change is diffusion, which is the spread of cultural traits from one society to another. Is cultural change a one-way process? Can you identify any elements of your way of life that are derived from other cultures?

6. How does globalization contribute to the transformation of the local?

7. How does McDonaldization operate on the structural-institutional level and on the symbolic-institutional level? Which one is more effective on the transformation of local cultures?

8. Do you think McDonaldization promotes uniformity or hybridity?

9. Are global homogenization and local heterogenization exclusive processes? Is there a third alternative?

10. Does McDonaldization necessarily relate to the proliferation of "nothing"? How does glocalization operate within the "something-nothing" continuum?

11. Although "nothing" tends to be less expensive than "something" for the individual in the short run, it proves to be more costly on social, environmental, political and economic levels. Cite examples of the tension

between "nothing" and "something" beyond those discussed in this part of the book.

12. Is it possible for "something" to be economically successful on a global scale?

13. Define grobalization and glocalization. Which one do you think is more influential on the creation and distribution of cultural products such as art and music?

14. Why is grobalization a more detrimental factor for local cultures than glocalization? Could glocalization be construed as an end product of grobalization or is it a different process?

15. What is glocommodification? Do you think it's "globaloney"?

PART V

Conclusion

In this concluding essay, Izberk-Bilgin and Ahuvia issue a strong challenge to the McDonaldization thesis. They argue that while McDonaldization might have been an apt term to capture the reality of a Fordist world of consumption that existed a quarter of century ago when the term was first created, it does not well-describe contemporary realities. Among the changes are global protests against McDonald's and McDonaldization, post-Fordist production techniques, more fragmented consumers and consumer tastes, and a desire for more individualized products and services. Of great importance is the rise of the Internet (see also, Chapter 15 and Jurgenson's discussion of the de-McDonaldization of the Internet), especially Web 2.0, which requires more flexible and open systems. In this essay ebayization is proposed as a paradigm for this new world, especially as it relates to consumption. eBayization is seen as having three basic dimensions: variety (as opposed to the limited offerings at fast food restaurants), unpredictability (as opposed to the predictability of McDonaldized systems), and market-mediated control (rather than the control of a McDonaldized system like McDonald's). eBayization is a very attractive idea, at least as it applies to the Internet. It may replace McDonaldization or it may come to co-exist with McDonaldization, which may continue to be preeminent in more material worlds like the fast food restaurant.

38

eBayization

Elif Izberk-Bilgin and Aaron Ahuvia

S ince the publication of *McDonaldization of Society* in 1983, the use of McDonald's as a metonym[1] for Weberian modernization has become so commonplace that a Google search for "McDonaldization" finds more than 92,000 references. Continuing his work on this topic twenty five years after he introduced the term, Ritzer continues to develop his argument that McDonald's, with its uniformity, efficiency, calculability, and control, remains a telling metonym for the forces of late modern capitalist globalization.

McDonaldization is a product of historical conditions, such as industrialization and modernization, that characterized early modern capitalism. Within this historical context, McDonald's emerged as a potent symbol of democratized consumption, uniting people of all economic strata to enjoy the quintessential American food under its roof. Fast-food restaurants quickly became the epitome of the post-war American cultural landscape. Conformist consumption in this period served as a passport to middle-class status for millions of Americans recovering from the Great Depression and WWII. It is within this socio-historical conjuncture that we should understand the appeal of predictable products, standard service, and affordable goods that the process of McDonaldization, in Ritzer's term, came to provide.

---

[1] A metonym is a particular type of metaphor in which a part of a larger entity represents the whole: e.g., a "headcount" for a count of people.

Editor's Note: Written especially for this volume and used by permission of the authors.

However, as early as the 1970's we saw the emergence of trends that would many years later begin to render McDonaldization less culturally relevant, even as the McDonald's franchises continued to multiply. The anti-corporate counterculture of the late 1960's that began as a loose student movement was fueled by a mounting number of mainstream consumers fed up with what they saw as a homogenous marketplace and authoritarian marketers engaged in what some saw as cultural engineering. Rejecting conformity, these consumers gradually sought more authenticity and social distinction through customized products that reflected their identities and unique lifestyles. Hence, an increasingly fragmented consumer society in terms of tastes, lifestyles, preferences, and a growing demand for differentiated market offerings, marked this emerging postmodern consumer culture.

On the economic front, the increasing saturation of consumer markets by the early 1970's reduced the profitability of 'high output-low unit cost' mass production, as unsold inventories had to be liquefied at ever lower margins. Moreover, the growing demand for customized products and rapidly changing cultural trends no longer seemed to justify manufacturers' expensive capital investments. Facing a darkening economic outlook, industry leaders and businessmen began to realize the need for a new approach in manufacturing: flexible specialization. This new regime of flexible production, also known as post-Fordism, is characterized by novel technologies of production and information flow. Innovative techniques like just-in-time management and electronic data interchange were developed during this period to support this new mode of accumulation. Initially gaining impressive momentum in business circles, the flexibility credo soon extended well beyond the firm to the political landscape as neo-liberal politics became popular; flexible manufacturing required de-regulation and de-centralization not just within the confines of the factory but also in the social and legal organization of the market society.

Challenging the merits of rationalization and globalization, consumers react by mobilizing street demonstrations, organizing anti-market fests, forming consumer-advocacy group, fashioning alternative communities, creating virtual awareness platforms (e.g., www.cleanclothes.org; www.organicconsumers.org), or simply altering consumption habits to reflect fundamentalist ideological stances. This counter-consumer culture has two strands: while voluntary simplicity advocates may reduce their overall level of consumerism, the other strand of counter-consumer culture simply shifts consumption away from McDonaldized brands towards customized offerings that allow for more individual expression, products from smaller producers with a homespun image and an anti-McDonaldization ethos, or even corporate brands like Apple that strike a rebellious anti-corporate pose.

Hence, this counter-consumer culture can be just as consumerist as the McDonaldized cultural segments it disdains, and the move away from McDonaldization should not be equated with waning consumerism in general, but rather a shift towards a different style of consumerism.

In addition to this ideological confrontation, the emergence of virtual marketplaces, novel forms of exchange (e.g., file sharing), web 2.0 and cyber communities, when coupled with the shift towards experiential economies in the West, industrialization in the East, and the weakening of the nation state, require ever more flexible, openly accessible, mobile, and diverse forms of social and economic organization. Such new forms of organizations not only challenge our extant notions of competition, productivity, and social responsibility, but also outline a new logic of post-industrial market society where the rationalization symbolized by McDonald's is no longer the assured formula for financial performance or cultural relevance. Accordingly, we suggest that eBayization, as a postmodern form of economic and social organization powered by information technology, better represents the deregulated, differentiated, and liquid nature of contemporary society as well as the organizing principles of postindustrial enterprises.

eBayization

eBayization diverges from previous modern forms of economic and social organization like McDonaldization in three key aspects: variety, unpredictability, and market-mediated control. eBayization, as we define it, occurs when businesses and other institutions attempt to thrive through embracing these three features. These three features of eBayization do not always parallel Ritzer's McDonaldization features of efficiency, calculability, predictability, control, and irrationality of rationality. Broadly conceived, efficiency and calculability will be aspects of any successful large scale business and are a heritage of modernization that remains prevalent in eBayization. However, as we will discuss in a later section in more detail, McDonaldization implies a particular style of efficiency and calculability reminiscent of McDonald's resulting in narrow product lines and moderate quality offerings, neither of which is inherent to the processes eBay uses to achieve efficiency and calculability. Ritzer's notions of predictability and centralized control are directly contradicted by eBayization's embrace of variety and market mediated control. Finally, Ritzer's notion of the irrationality of rationality is not a designed in feature of McDonaldization so much as an unintended consequence. eBayization too has its share of unintended consequences, and we address some of these in our conclusion.

428   PART V   Conclusion

Variety

While McDonald's sells essentially one product line through over 31,000 different brick-and-mortar locations, eBay offers over 2,500,000 different product lines from one virtual location. An eclectic hodge-podge of consumers seems to provide a market for even the most peculiar things. Indeed, eBay's first auction is renowned for fetching $14.83 for a broken laser pointer, sold to a collector of broken laser pointers. Today, the variety of products eBay offers can boggle even a jaded mind; recent items on sale have ranged from a charming historic Texas town complete with its high-school and library to anatomical parts. Such variety is typical of the internet, and makes eBay a prominent example of what is being called a 'long tail' business. The long tail has been described as "the end of the 80/20 rule" because in contrast to most conventional businesses where a few hit products provide most of the profits, a long tail business has a vast array of infrequently purchased products that cumulatively become the mainstay of the enterprise. A former Amazon employee describes the long tail as, "We sold more books today that didn't sell at all yesterday than we sold today of all the books that did sell yesterday."

Unpredictability

The key to McDonald's success is predictability, which ensures that there are no surprises and no risk in either the environment or food and that only a little decision-making is required. Taming reality by achieving predictability and control was always a component of the modernist project. While the scientific and technological developments of the modern period largely achieved this goal in certain technical domains, the events of 9/11 fully brought home the fact that the world at large is not a predictable place. Any pertinent metonym for the dominant American zeitgeist needs to capture the uncertainty and ambivalence of contemporary American society.

Part of the pleasure eBay provides is the excitement of exploration; consumers never know what unexpected product will pop up on the computer screen or what the final price will be. On a less positive note, consumers are also never sure what the quality, condition, or even authenticity of the product will be when it arrives. For example, studies show that upwards of 90% of 'Louis Vuitton' and 95% of the 'Tiffany' items on eBay were counterfeit. Yet, this element of surprise and serendipity, for better and worse, fits well with a post-industrial zeitgeist concerned with uncertainty and risk.

In a sense, eBay thrives on providing mediating platforms among spontaneous acquaintances exchanging unpredictability. Indeed, the gifts—both material and virtual—and product commentary serendipitously exchanged among complete strangers serve as social glue in the open-access and anonymous platforms of eBay, Facebook, MySpace, and a myriad of other web 2.0 contexts where consumers construct virtual social solidarity. While such solidarity is far removed from richer forms of face-to-face relationships, virtual and temporal relationships are nevertheless typical of the kind of sociability that a American society—with its continuously negotiated, fluctuating, and loose conceptions of identity and community responsibilities—often engenders.

Whether it is the surprise of what is in the box, the strange forms of commodity one comes across (e.g., 'foreheads for sale for advertisement purposes,' '25,000 friends delivered to your MySpace account in 2 days for a starting bid of $36' are among the recent auctions), or the possibility of mediatization (e.g., 'Virgin Mary in Grilled Cheese' and 'Tawny Peaks Breast Implants' auctions), eBay provides surprise, delight, disappointment, and occasional offense to consumers—and becomes successful in the process.

Market-Mediated Control

McDonald's is founded on the principle of controlling every part of the production process, right down to zealous efforts to grow standard size potatoes. eBay also includes mechanisms of control, but limits them to a very restricted set of key areas such as the sale of illegal or highly regulated products, and of course, rules to ensure that eBay gets its share of the proceeds. But whereas control is a central strategy for McDonald's, eBay's primary strategy is to harness and ride the cacophony of billions of buyers and sellers by shifting direct control from a centralized bureaucracy to the market. Indeed, eBay is so adamant on maintaining low levels of direct control over user posting that when luxury goods producers tried to force eBay to take action against people selling counterfeit goods through its website, eBay fought them in court to protect its policy of very loose control over what its users say and sell. In this sense, eBay very much reflects the deregulation trend of post-Fordist years and the period of intensified globalization that follows. The new global economic order and the deregulation of markets ensure that power and control are used to maintain a smooth functioning system and to increase the profitability of the enterprise, but not to influence the individual consequences for each party involved, placing the responsibility of each action squarely on the individual's shoulders. As such, eBayization is a fitting metonym for this dominant zeitgeist which is suspicious of large rationalized systems.

The fluidity arising from market mediated control allows people to shift back and forth easily between the roles of buyer and seller. This dual role and the consumer empowerment it brings along is quite different than what Ritzer calls McDonald's modern quest to create passive and lifelong consumers, particularly out of children. Criticizing McDonald's marketing to children, Ritzer writes that " . . . McDonald's has historically been defined by its efforts to cater to children with a clown (Ronald McDonald) as its dominant symbol, its playgrounds, its carnival-like atmosphere, its child-oriented foods, and its promotional tie-ins with many movies and toys . . . In these and other ways, McDonald's has sought to make children lifelong consumers of its products." In contrast, eBayized enterprises do not try to create passive consumers. Rather these institutions depend on interactive and creative consumers capable of performing as producers devising captivating narratives, inventing products (e.g. evil Kermit), and providing authentic offerings. Even children become producers in these platforms, writing the adverts of the toys they sell on eBay or creating their profiles on social networking websites.

Economic organizations such as eBay excel in the global marketplace by facilitating commerce and information exchange. eBay provides consumers mechanisms through which they can control their transactions. For example, PayPal provides reasonable financial security of online payments, Skype allows buyers and sellers to communicate for free, and eBay's feedback tools allow consumers to rate the seller's performance while enabling vendors to build online reputations. In addition, eBay community blogs help disgrace unethical buyers, warn community members about scams, and relieve the frustration of cheated users. While these tools and mechanisms facilitate consumers' transactions and somewhat reduce the criminal risk involved, consistent with a market-driven society, eBay clearly leaves individuals with the ultimate responsibility to conduct their own research about the authenticity of the items for sale and sellers' backgrounds, declining to actively participate in the resolution of buyer-seller conflicts. This 'buyer (and seller) beware' principle causes pervasive problems as evidenced by the fact that online auctions are the single largest source of consumer fraud complaints reported to the Federal Trade Commission and that sellers are finding ways to game the online reputational systems. Perhaps more surprisingly, sellers are also frequent victims of scams where payment is cancelled or reversed after the product is received.

From a macro-perspective, the societal and global consequences of market-mediated control are potentially quite serious. The policy preference for market mediated control rests in free market economic theory, which rests in turn on the assumption that consumers can accurately assess the risks and rewards of their purchases. This assumption has long been disputed with regards to typical consumers. However, the 2008 collapse of global financial markets made clear that this assumption does not always hold even for the most sophisticated professional investors backed by the world's largest financial firms. The deregulation of financial markets in general, and mortgage markets in particular, led to eBayization of these markets. In this process, these markets become less homogenized, less predictable, and more market-mediated. The flourishing of new and innovative financial products caused a temporary boom in profits. However, it turned out that even the sophisticated professional investors who were purchasing these instruments were unable to accurately assess the risk associated with them. When the speculative bubble in US housing prices burst and home values fell, the losses to investors were far greater than they had anticipated and the derivatives that these investors had purchased as a form of insurance turned out not be solvent. In other words, the overreliance on financial markets' self-regulating capacity quickly brought about a stagnation of the global financial system, triggering a global recession.

While eBayization tends to flourish in the context of deregulation, eBayization is not synonymous with low levels of government activity. Just as businesses can create eBayized systems to help them reach their profit objectives, governments can create eBayized systems to help them reach their policy objectives. eBayized government policies are likely to operate through the use of government imposed incentives to influence behavior within a market without directly limiting choice.

Global warming provides an example of how eBayization is both part of the problem but potentially also part of the solution. It is easy to see how eBayization is part of the problem of global warming. High levels of consumption are largely to blame for global warming, and since both McDonaldization and eBayization are processes that facilitate massive levels of consumption, both are implicated in rising world temperatures. At the same time, carbon cap-and-trade systems provide an example of how eBayization may be part of the solution. Rather than a McDonaldized policy of centralized control producing a standardized solution, the eBayized carbon cap-and-trade policies are designed to maximize efficiency through the consciously crafted application of market forces. Through carbon-trading, business are encouraged to limit carbon emissions because these emission 'savings' can be sold for profit, just like stocks and futures, at Carbon Exchanges throughout the world. Advocates of cap-and-trade systems hope that once businesses have the financial incentive to reduce pollution, entrepreneurs will develop a plethora of innovative pollution reduction technologies. Cap-and-trade advocates also assume that businesses will choose wisely between these technologies so as to maximize pollution reduction and hence their profit. However, whether this system will provide the efficient solutions it promises, or another collapse like the mortgage meltdown, remains to be seen.

In sum then, eBayization offers consumers of risk society market-mediated experiences with all the risks and rewards that it entails, both empowering and disempowering consumers in the process.

Concluding Remarks

For many people beyond our shores, McDonald's remains the quintessential symbol of American-style modernity, at least for the time being. Yet, as industrialization moves from the US and Europe to become more strongly associated with the developing world, a Fordist-style business like McDonald's may no longer seem to capture the specifically American ethos, much less the dominant zeitgeist of contemporary Western society. As American culture shops around for a new iconic institution to serve as a metonym for the dominant zeitgeist, we suggest we look where everything else can be found: eBay.

Thinking Critically

1. How well does eBayization apply to the physical world, including at McDonald's itself?

2. In what ways does McDonaldization persist online, including on eBay?

3. Is the eBay consumer creative and empowered or passive and controlled?

4. What groups of people are most likely to experience an eBayized versus McDonaldized world?

5. Should eBayization replace McDonaldization as the process that best captures today's world?

PART V

Pedagogical Questions

1. Do you think eBayization will replace McDonaldization as a metonym for the contemporary world?

2. What is it about the Internet in general, and eBay in particular, that makes it more amenable to eBayization than McDonaldization?

3. How do the ideas about McDonaldization raised throughout this volume relate to your own life?

4. How do the specific ideas discussed in Chapter 38 relate to your life?

5. Would you like to live in a more or less McDonaldized world? Why?

6. What would a less McDonaldized world look like? What would life in it be like?

7. What would a non-McDonaldized world look like? Is such a world possible given the complexities of contemporary society?

Index

About the Editor

George Ritzer is Distinguished University Professor at the University of Maryland, where he has also been a Distinguished Scholar-Teacher and won a Teaching Excellence Award. He was also awarded the 2000 Distinguished Contributions to Teaching Award by the American Sociological Association, and in 2004, he was awarded an honorary doctorate by LaTrobe University, Melbourne, Australia. He is perhaps best known for *The McDonaldization of Society* (translated into over a dozen languages and now in its 5th edition) and several related books, including *Expressing America: A Critique of the Global Credit Card Society* and *Enchanting a Disenchanted World: Revolutionizing the Means of Consumption*. His latest effort in this domain is *The Globalization of Nothing 2* (2007). He edited *The Encyclopedia of Social Theory* (2005) and the 11-volume *Encyclopedia of Sociology* (2007), and he is the founding editor of the *Journal of Consumer Culture*.

About the Contributors

Aaron Ahuvia is a Professor of Marketing at the University of Michigan-Dearborn's School of Management.

Benjamin R. Barber is Distinguished Senior Fellow at *Demos*.

Barbara G. Brents is a member of the Department of Sociology, University of Nevada, Las Vegas.

Alan Bryman is a member of the Department of Social Sciences, Loughborough University, UK.

Melissa L. Caldwell teaches in the Department of Anthropology, University of California, Santa Cruz.

John Drane has taught in the universities of Stirling and Aberdeen in Scotland, and is an adjunct professor at Fuller Seminary, Pasadena, California.

Jos Gamble teaches at the School of Management, University of London, UK.

Kathryn Hausbeck teaches in the Department of Sociology, University of Nevada, Las Vegas.

Ian Heywood is on the faculty of the Department of Environmental and Geographical Sciences, The Manchester Metropolitan University, UK.

P. D. Holley is a member of the Department of Social Sciences, Southwestern Oklahoma State University.

Elif Izberk-Bilgin is an Assistant Professor of Marketing at the University of Michigan-Dearborn's School of Management.

Kristine Peta Jerome is affiliated with Queensland University of Technology, Australia.

Nathan Jurgenson is a PhD candidate in the Department of Sociology, University of Maryland.

Andrew J. Knight is a member of the Department of Criminology, Sociology, and Geography, Arkansas State University.

Lee F. Monaghan is a member of the Department of Sociology, University of Limerick, Ireland.

Carol Morris is a member of the Department of Geography at the University of Nottingham, Nottingham, UK.

Joel I. Nelson is on the faculty of the Department of Sociology, University of Minnesota.

Wayne Northcutt is a member of the Department of History at Niagara University.

Jan Nederveen Pieterse teaches in the Department of Global Studies, University of California, Santa Barbara.

Sara Raley teaches at McDaniel College.

Uri Ram teaches in the Department of Behavioral Sciences, Ben Gurion University, Israel.

Matt Reed is a Research Fellow in the ESRC Centre for the Study of Genomics in Society (EGENIS), University of Exeter, UK.

Matthew B. Robinson is affiliated with the Departments of Political Science and Criminal Justice, Appalachian State University.

Bryan S. Turner is Professor in the Department of Sociology, Wellesley University.

Hielke S. Van Der Meulen is a member of the Rural Sociology Group, Wageningen University, and Ark of Taste & Presidia, Slow Food, The Netherlands.

Michael Veseth is Professor of Political Economy at the University of Puget Sound.

Malcolm Waters is on the faculty of Hobart University, Tasmania, Australia.

James L. Watson is a member of the Department of Anthropology at Harvard University.

Adam Weaver is a member of the Department of Tourism Management at Victoria University of Wellington, New Zealand.

Gary Wilkinson teaches at the Scarborough School of Education, University of Hull, UK.

D. E. Wright, Jr. is a member of the Department of Social Sciences, Southwestern Oklahoma State University.